God, Man, and Devil

Judaic Traditions in Literature, Music, and Art

Ken Frieden and Harold Bloom, *Series Editors*

God, Man, and Devil
Yiddish Plays in Translation

Translated and Edited by
NAHMA SANDROW

Syracuse University Press

The paper used in this publication meets the minimum
requirements of American National Standard for Information
Sciences—Permanence of Paper for Printed Library Materials,
ANSI Z39.48-1984. ∞

LIBRARY OF CONGRESS CATALOGING-IN-PUBLICATION DATA

God, man, and devil : Yiddish plays in translation / translated and edited
by Nahma Sandrow.
   p.   cm. — (Judaic traditions in literature, music, and art)
   Includes bibliographical references.
   1. Yiddish drama—Translations into English.   1. Sandrow, Nahma.
II. Series.
PJ5191.E5G55   1998
839´.12308—dc21 98-29003
ISBN 0-8156-2786-6 (cloth : alk. paper).
ISBN 0-8156-2787-4 (pbk. : alk. paper)

Manufactured in the United States of America

In memory of my grandmother Ella (Yelye) Gurevitsh Slavin, who loved theatre and romantic stories; of my grandfather Jacob (Yashe) Slavin, who sang me "Rozhinkes mit mandlen" ("Raisins and Almonds"); and of their daughter Miriam, who was my dear mother.

NAHMA SANDROW is the author of *Vagabond Stars: A World History of Yiddish Theater* and *Surrealism: Theater, Arts, Ideas*. She has also written about a variety of ethnic theaters and other subjects. She wrote the books for two award-winning musicals, *Vagabond Stars* and *Kuni-Leml*, both based on Yiddish theater material. A graduate of Bryn Mawr College and Yale University School of Drama, she is a professor at Bronx Community College CUNY. Nahma Sandrow lives in New York City with her husband William Meyers and their son Isaac and daughter Hannah.

Contents

❧

Acknowledgments

◦᪢᪤◦

My teachers David Roskies and Mordkhe Schaechter.

My friendly consultants Rabbi Gershon Freidlin (for Yiddish theater material), Norman Kotker (for verse), Yochanan Muffs (for jesting), Joachim Neugroschel (for insights into translating), Cynthia Ozick (for insights into the languages of the Jews), Isaiah Sheffer (for insights into Yiddish and English on the stage), and Michael Steinlauf (for insights into *shund*).

At the YIVO Institute for Jewish Research: Dina Abramovicz, Zachary Baker, Stanley Bergman, Richard Carlow, Leo Greenbaum, Herbert Lazarus, Fruma Mohrer, and Marek Web.

Richard Siegel and the National Foundation for Jewish Culture for support of an early version of *Bronx Express*.

The Plays-in-Translation Repertory Company, in alphabetical order: Ira Berger, Faina Burko, Richard Carlow, Edward Cramer, Marsha Cummins, Richard Engquist, David Fishman, Rhea Gaisner, Jules Harlow, Sara Jacobs, Johanna Kaplan, Todd Kirchmar, Seymour Lesser, Herbert Liebowitz, Cynthia Mann, Isaac Meyers, William Meyers, Mori Mickelson, Yocheved Muffs, Allen Nadler, Nathan Perl, David Roskies, Bevya Rosten, Naomi Schrag, Isaiah Sheffer, Richard Siegel, Edward Silberfarb, Joseph Silberfarb, Charles Simon, David Szonyi, Yael Ukeles, Joshua Waxman, Maron Waxman, Nachum Waxman, and Robert Youdelman.

For friendship and professional advice: Ed Cramer, Dr. Joseph C. Landis, Susan Yankowitz, and Robert Youdelman.

For help with word processing: Isaac Meyers and William Meyers.

For being my family: Hannah, Isaac, and William Meyers.

Note on Transliteration

❧

The YIVO Institute for Jewish Research has devised a clear, simple system for transliterating Yiddish phonetically into Roman characters:

ey = as in the English h*ey*
ay = as in the English sk*y*
i   = as in the English sk*i*
e   = as in the English h*e*n
u   = as in the English w*oo*d
tsh = as in the English ma*tch*
kh = gutteral h, more often rendered in English as the German *ch*,
       as in Sholom Alei*ch*em or "le*ch*aim"

This system renders all other sounds just as in English. There are no silent letters in this sytem, so that the names Tsine and Stere, for example, have two syllables, and Yosele and Motele have three. Stress is rarely on the last syllable. When diminutives such as "-l," "-ele," "-ke," or "-enyu" are added on to the end of a name, they are never stressed.

I followed the YIVO system for most names and titles. But sometimes I overruled it in favor of the spelling the person himself seems to have favored. Hirschbein, for example, would be Hirshbayn according to the YIVO system, Peretz would be Perets, and Sholom Aleichem would be Sholem Aleykhem.

When characters use Hebrew, I transliterated it the way Yiddish-speakers would pronounce it. This is the Ashkenazik way, which can still be heard in many ultra-Orthodox or Hasidic communities today. It is quite different from the Sephardic pronunciation of modern Israeli Hebrew. The Hebrew words and phrases used in these plays are for the most part so common that mispronunciation in performance could be conspicuous and distracting. I strongly suggest, for *God, Man, and Devil* especially, that anyone who intends to speak the lines aloud but is unacquainted with the Ashkenazik pronunciation should make an effort to find a person or a recording to listen to.

Nahma Sandrow
New York, New York
November 1997

God, Man, and Devil

Introduction
Yiddish Drama in the Yiddish World

୶ഀൟ

I picked these plays because I like them. They do not add up to a full representation of the scope of serious Yiddish drama. Too many styles are missing: no
mystical symbolism, for example; no heroic history; no slice of grim life; no
love story interspersed with romantic and comical duets. (The two additional
scenes in the appendix are there primarily to show off the raucous quality occasionally characteristic of Yiddish theater, especially in popular performance.)
Nevertheless, an examination of these five plays and playwrights can show a
great deal about Yiddish drama.

The five playwrights had much in common. All were born in the nineteenth
century and lived into the twentieth. All began writing in Eastern Europe and
moved to New York. (Pinski eventually moved to Israel.) All used several languages comfortably, as did most of their audiences, and were aware of theater
being made by their contemporaries in other languages. All wrote in other
forms as well as drama and in more than one style. All these writers were aware
of political movements of their time, and most of them personally participated
in various politically left-wing efforts to make the world better.

All the plays in this volume consider some version of the question: What
makes life morally good and worth living? They do so in a variety of modes,
sometimes aiming for tears, sometimes for belly laughs. But all, even the comedies, are typical of the literary Yiddish repertory in their essentially serious approach to human behavior.

My intention is to convey a sense of the complexity and creativity of Yiddish drama in the short span of less than seventy years when serious professional dramatists were writing for the serious professional stage. It seems
artificial to organize an overview of this repertory chronologically or themati-
cally, since the authors were contemporaries and all shared worlds, concerns,

aesthetics. Therefore, this preface begins with a brief historical background and then moves on to five sections, each focusing on a particular play. The sections overlap; each section contains critical and historical material which is directly relevant to the other plays as well. For example, allegorical drama is discussed apropos of *Shop* and religious ritual on stage is discussed apropos of *Bronx Express,* even though allegorical abstractions and religion figure, one way or another, in most of the plays in the collection. So as I discuss the plays themselves, one by one, I will also be filling in the larger picture.

Specifics of how I translated and edited each play, as well as textual notes and production histories, will appear separately at the beginning of each play. This arrangement is for the convenience of people planning to perform the plays as well as for readers. Further information about plays, personalities, the theater, and its historical background is available in my book *Vagabond Stars: A World History of Yiddish Theater,* published by Syracuse University Press in 1996.

Yiddish professional secular theater has a short history. It did not begin until Avrom Goldfadn's performance at Shimen Marks's Pomul Verde (Green Tree) wine garden in Jassy, Rumania, in 1876. However some nonprofessional religious drama in the Yiddish language did exist long before then.

The development and fortunes of the drama paralleled the development and fortunes of the language. The Yiddish language developed in the late Middle Ages in the Rhineland, out of German, Hebraic, and Romance elements. Over the next centuries, as the population that spoke it moved gradually eastward, it integrated a strong Slavic component as well. The earliest kind of Yiddish play, the amateur folk play called the Purim *shpil,* seems to have existed as long as the language.

Plays were generally presented at the holiday of Purim. In the European calendar, the end of winter is the season of release and revelry—from Aristophanes to Mardi Gras—and Purim plays were part of this atavistic tradition. Indeed, theater itself was (and still remains) forbidden to Jews for the rest of the year; rabbinic tradition disapproves of theater, which is alluded to in the very first psalm as *moshav letsim,* the "seat of scoffers." Purim, commemorating Queen Esther's heroic rescue of Persian Jews from destruction, is the one time of year when Jewish law permits impiety, drunkenness, and cross-dressing in a Mardi Gras-like spirit which also sanctions theater. (Similar plays were occasionally presented at the winter holiday of Hanuka and to celebrate weddings.)

Purim plays most often tell biblical stories. The most common is the story of Queen Esther and King Ahashuerus of Persia, which is the story read from the *megile* (scroll) in synagogue on Purim. The next most common story is of Joseph and his brothers. But many others appear, and occasionally other kinds of plots. All these are presented in doggerel verse, either handed down or newly composed, enlivened by irreverent and anachronistic jokes. Typically, Purim plays were presented by amateur groups going house to house for no reward beyond brandy and cake and donations to charity, though occasionally they were presented in larger venues. Purim plays are presented to this day in many places, though more often nowadays in languages other than Yiddish.

The Yiddish world also had professional performers performing their own material within ritual settings. The best known, the *badkhen* (wedding bard or jester), still exists in some traditional communities. His rhymes, which he creates at least in part spontaneously for the occasion, draw on Talmudic learning, sad wisdom, and sheer foolery.

At the start of the nineteenth century, the Yiddish language was still primarily a vernacular for common conversation. Hebrew was the honored language, the language of prayer and scholarship, and was also to become the vehicle of the Zionist movement. All men (though not necessarily women) knew some Hebrew and some Talmudic Aramaic; men who were respected read and wrote Hebrew well. Most people also knew the language of their surroundings, such as Russian or Polish.

In the middle of the nineteenth century, the circumstances of eastern European Jews changed enormously. To describe the changes in very broad strokes, industrialization in the region and the growth of an urban middle class encouraged commerce, freedom of movement, and freedom from constraints of religious law and community pressure. Crucial to this development were new political developments in the region, most notably under the liberal Czar Alexander II: legalization of secular printing in Yiddish, which resulted in the widespread existence of presses and publishing houses; Jewish access to university education; and a relative relaxation of censorship for Jews and non-Jews alike.

Underlying these events was a deeper change in thinking. The Enlightenment (in Yiddish, *haskole*), a broad movement in eighteenth- and nineteenth-century European cultural history, had involved a shift from religious belief to rationality. For the Jews of western and central Europe, the form it had taken was rejection of religious tradition in favor of participation in the larger life of modern Western culture. This movement, centered in Germany, was associated with German language and culture. As it moved eastward in the second half of the nineteenth century, the Enlightenment became associated with such romantic attitudes as focus on the individual human will rather than on divinity or on tradition, and nationalism as expression of the national soul. Among eastern European Jews, the Enlightenment allied itself with the development of Yiddish as a secular modern language.

Enlightened eastern European Jews knew Yiddish, Hebrew, and a local language. They had some knowledge of the higher literature in Polish or Russian, and probably in German as well. Urban middle-class girls might even be taught some French. Acquaintance with secular literature in other languages created readers and writers for such a literature in Yiddish. The first substantial Yiddish newspaper appeared in 1862, and the first major dictionary (Russian-Yiddish) in 1869. There was an explosion of popular novels and journalism. Serious writers published works in Yiddish, under pseudonyms at first because writing in Yiddish still commanded so little respect. By the end of the century, Yiddish had risen to become not only a medium for fine literature but a passion in itself.

Sophisticated Yiddish-speaking intellectuals, familiar with theater in other languages, now began to write domestic comedies to be read aloud for private pleasure. The best-known plays of the Enlightenment were Shloyme Etinger's *Serkele* (1830), Avrom Ber Gotlober's *Der dektukh (The Bridal Canopy; or, Two Weddings in One Night)* (1838), and Yisroel Aksenfeld's *Der ershter yidisher rekrut (The First Jewish Recruit)* (1861). Mendele Moykher Sforim, "the grandfather of Yiddish literature," wrote *Di takse (The Meat Tax)* in 1869. Since the heroes of these plays were enlightened, they spoke a fancy, heavily Germanic form of Yiddish called Daytshmersh.

In the second half of the nineteenth century, a new form of Yiddish performance appeared, bridging the traditional and the new. Broder singers were a totally secular combination of jester and preacher and cafe entertainer. They performed their own songs and monologues, funny but also serious, in urban cafes and wine gardens. Berl Broder (1815–1886), nicknamed for his Galician home town Brody, was the first; the genre became known by his name. He, Velvl Zbarzher (1826–1883), and Eliakum Zunser (1836–1913), the three most famous, were simultaneously successful as wedding jesters, as Broder singers, and as literary figures whose lyrics were published and widely read.

Avrom Goldfadn (1840–1908), the father of Yiddish theater, was heir to both the Yiddish tradition and the Enlightenment. He was fond of folk tradition, especially folk songs and *badkhen* performances. He also studied with Gotlober, traveled European capitals, and attended theater. Around 1876, when commerce stimulated by the Russo-Turkish War brought to cities like Jassy a potential Yiddish-speaking theater-going public, Goldfadn appeared in the Green Tree wine garden. The first evening he presented a program of recitations like a Broder singer's, but for his second appearance he put together a rudimentary play. It was an instant success, the first of many shows he wrote, produced, and directed.

Goldfadn's plays were basically operettas for the Yiddish masses who had never seen a play before: "a jig, a song, a quarrel, a kiss." Simple and solid, theatrical and fun, they might rest on a domestic plot, a romance, or a historical or biblical pageant. They were almost always didactic. Many of his stories demonstrate the evils of such old ways as superstition, in *Koldunye; oder, Di makhsheyfe (Koldunye; or, The Witch)* (1879), and forced marriages, in *Der fanatik; oder Tsvey Kuni-Lemls (The Fanatic; or, The Two Kuni-Lemls)* (1880). Others preach the glories of Jewish history *(Shulamis; or, The Daughter of Jerusalem)* (1883) and the dreams of the new Zionist movement *(Ben-Ami; or, Son of My People)* (1907). His characters Kuni-Leml and Shmendrik and his songs "Raisins and Almonds" and "For Your Birthday" took on the status of folk art. In 1933, when Mikhl Weichert wrote his sad comedy *Di familye Tanentsap (The Tanentsap Family)*, he used Goldfadn's *Kuni-Leml* as his play within a play. Goldfadn's theater material, variously adapted, continues to appear to this day.

Within months of Goldfadn's debut there were more companies, and more writers turning out plays for them to perform. The most prolific were Schomer (Nokhem Meyer Shaikevitch [1849–1905], Joseph Lateiner (1853–1935), and "Professor" Moyshe Ha-Levi Ish Hurwitz (d. 1910). They provided rousing entertainment, mixing plain Yiddish with Daytshmersh, partly to make the more heroic characters sound lofty, and partly to fool censors in the many shifting periods and places when Yiddish was illegal. From this period on, the demand for popular entertainment was so pressing that writers often used plays from other languages, either classics or current hits, cannibalizing and superimposing Jewish names and settings, or sometimes simply plagiarizing. In addition, at all periods there were straightforward translations and serious adaptations of contemporaneous popular hits as well as of dramas from the world repertory by such authors as Molière, Shakespeare, Ibsen, and Sudermann. From the beginning, the Yiddish community's appetite for theater was remarkable. Some of the many competent professional playwrights who turned out scripts well into the twentieth century were Mark Arnshtayn, Gershom Bader, Yoel Entin, Max Gabel, Khone Gottesfeld, N. Kalmanovitsh, Z. Kornblit, Zalmen Libin, Isidore Lilien, Nakhum Rakov, Moyshe Richter, William Segal, Anshl Shor, Moyshe Zeifert, and Isidore Zolatarevsky. Vigorous popular theater remained a bulwark of traditional culture, so that traditional cultural values remained associated with dramaturgical and theatrical conventions from the past.

By the turn of the century, playwrights with more intellectual ambitions were writing more sophisticated plays in a range of genres. By 1950, in less than one century, Yiddish drama had managed to telescope and recapitulate much of the development of Western drama. Folk play with ritual function, costume operetta, melodrama, well-made domestic problem play, naturalism, symbolism, expressionism—all these overlapped and coexisted. While the popular repertory, with its yearning for bygone days, continued to treat parochial concerns and universal comforts, resisting all change except superficial novelties, more literary playwrights pulled forward toward the dramaturgical avant-garde. Meanwhile plays returned as revivals and adaptations. Sometimes directors staged old favorites in radically new styles—most often expressionism at the service of politics. For example, the Moscow Yiddish Art Theatre (GOSET) in 1926 adapted Goldfadn's biblical *Tsente gebot (The Tenth Commandment,* also called *Thou Shalt Not Covet)* as a comedic attack on capitalism.

Plays were often published, not only in book form but also in the many newspapers and journals. These ranged from sketches in the daily press to serious short and long plays that could simply be read, but were also available for private or amateur production. Amateur groups were active in small towns as well as large cities. Members were often extremely dedicated, whether a group's goals were art for its own sake, art for the furthering of Yiddish culture, propaganda for a specific political position, fundraising for a cause, or simple fun. Because they did not have to please a ticket-buying public, amateur groups were a home for much of the literary repertory that otherwise might not have gotten done at all, or been revived.

The press gave much space to drama: reviews, reflective pieces, memoirs, comments in letters to the editor, even whole journals devoted to theater. In addition, the press responded to the popular interest in theater as show business, providing such material as gossip about the stars. Drama was a frequent topic for lectures and debates. Yiddish communities in western and eastern Europe, North and South America, South Africa and Australia—for a while even in the Far East—had amateur and professional theater, either locally based or touring; and they had related books and journals, either locally published or imported. Drama was integrated into energetic intellectual life and explicitly considered an expression of Yiddish (secular) cultural aspirations and identity.

God, Man, and Devil (Got, mentsh, un tayvl) (1900)

The first passion of Jacob Gordin (1853–1909) was an ideology of Tolstoyan spirituality through working the land. He organized disciples into an agricultural Brotherhood and wrote for the Russian press, emigrating in 1891 just in time to escape the czarist police. In New York he wrote for the Yiddish press but remained part of a circle of Russian (Jewish) intelligentsia, none of whom attended Yiddish theater because compared to the Russian it was on such a low level. When that same year he wrote his first play, *Siberia,* he approached it as he approached everything else, as a reformer with a mission—in his own words, "as a scribe sits down to write a Torah." He wrote constantly, under a variety of pseudonyms, in an effort to support his large family, and many of his plays are not memorable. But some of his plays won immediate respect and have kept it forever after. They became the first serious repertory in the Yiddish language. In fact, Gordin was the first to suggest that such a thing could exist. The period of about 1891 to 1905 is still often referred to as the Gordin era. In those years Gordin dominated his world, dedicating his personal charisma to the propagation of his ideals.

Gordin's primary theatrical mission concerned dramaturgy. He insisted on fidelity to text, with no ad-libbing. Before, actors had always had the right to pad their parts at will, speaking or singing, but Gordin intimidated them, going so far as to stop the show to scold them for stepping out of character. He denounced Daytshmersh as a crippling affectation and insisted on honest Yiddish. He permitted no music unless it was somehow integrated believably into the action.

He aimed for verisimilitude: an on-stage logic permitting spectators to believe that the characters were behaving as real people would in those circumstances. He also aimed for verity in a deeper sense. At the turn of the century, Hutchins Hapgood noted that the highest praise Lower East Side Yiddish theatergoers could give was "how true." A letter from a reader to the editor of the Jewish daily *Forward* said, "*God, Man, and Devil*, where Hershele Dubrovner follows the devil and his money destroys him, started up a struggle in my heart which was telegraphed by a sigh to my most idealistic and holiest emotions. I saw living people, real people whom I know and understand: not stage coincidences, but life circumstances, which affect people and drive them to the saddest of dramas."

Yiddish actors, famous for temperament and energy, strove for truth through intense emotion. Their audiences responded wholeheartedly, sometimes even with tears. In the nineteenth century, when an audience wept, it was the tribute that sensitive people paid to the truth. Two generations after strong men had wept at Dickens' readings of the death of Little Nell, Yiddish theater remained perhaps the last Western theater where deep, sincere weeping was still appropriate.

The dramatic form most associated with tears—and the structure closest to Gordin's plays—is melodrama. At the heart of melodrama is the struggle of good and evil, with good always victorious in the end. Despite this strict schema, melodrama in the hands of a playwright like Gordin is not simpleminded. Thus in *God, Man, and Devil*, Hershele falls victim to the sport of God and Satan, but it is really his own weakness that destroys him, as foreshadowed in the hint of hubris with which he "oversalts" his piety. And in a final ambiguity, though by the final curtain the devil concludes that virtue has triumphed, Hershele is punished all the same.

God, Man, and Devil, like all Gordin's best-known plays, has typical melodramatic elements. For example, the minor characters have "humors"—Pese's toothaches, Dobe's charms, Leyzer's rhymes and secrets—which produce an instant comic effect. Gordin alternates this low comedy with high seriousness, playing the two extremes off against each other. Thus the superstitions are meant to be laughable, yet to intensify the threatening atmosphere. Also, Gordin adroitly manipulates dramatic symbols so that they make his ideas clear while at the same time adding emotional resonance to the characters' actions. Prayer shawls, carrying a wealth of sacred yet homely associations, work this way on several levels, and when in act 4 Khatskl throws down the bloody shawl, the gesture creates a thrilling theatrical moment. (Ibsen, whose work

Gordin certainly knew, had used the wild duck in a similar fashion only sixteen years earlier.)

Music is another standard component of melodrama, and music, especially a setting of the Twenty-Third Psalm, is woven into the action of *God, Man, and Devil.* Also, as in many other Yiddish plays, such aural elements as bits of prayer, the tune of Torah cantillation, and the very sound of Hebrew invoke tradition and lend texture and emotional resonance. Generally Yiddish drama tends to be aural rather than visual, perhaps in keeping with the traditional prohibition against graven images, and the encouragement of musicians rather than visual artists. *God, Man, and Devil* is only one of many Yiddish plays that have violinists and pianists as protagonists. Such characters are often romantic symbols of soulfulness, spiritual yet free of rabbinic fetters; moreover, they provide opportunities for weaving in music.

Melodrama derives dramatic power from moral instruction. This made the form particularly congenial to Yiddish theater. Perhaps partly in response to the rabbinic distrust of theater, the didactic impulse, in one form or another, remained prominent in much Yiddish drama. Thus the most conspicuous forms on the serious Yiddish stage are melodrama and expressionism, in which characters can be seen as personified abstractions, and the domestic problem play, in which characters act out solutions to difficult situations.

Gordin always defined himself as a teacher, offstage (by writing books and articles and lecturing) as well as through theater. He taught moral lessons, which for him included politics: in his *Lear,* the bad son-in-law is hypocritically pious while the good one, who behaves decently to the old man, is a rationalist adherent of the Enlightenment. His primary political messages were socialism, which led him to denounce both capitalism and trade unionism, and women's rights. He also taught his public about Western culture. In *God, Man, and Devil,* for example, he introduced them to the Faust story; in *Sappho* (1990), to the Greek god Apollo; and in his *Jewish King Lear* (1892) and *Mirele Efros; or, The Jewish Queen Lear* (1893), to Shakespeare's *Lear.* In the theater, melodrama's structure and symbols were his principle teaching methods, but not the only ones. *God, Man, and Devil* has a folky frame in heaven, very much like the medieval Christian *Everyman,* explicitly laying out the moral lessons. In *God, Man, and Devil,* Gordin also uses a specific teaching device that was his trademark: the quotable philosophical epigram, as when Freydenyu sighs, "What is every pleasure? A short preface to a long, long pain."

Gordin's actors revered him both because he dignified their profession and because he gave them wonderful roles. Sometimes he wrote for specific actors. He wrote *Sappho* and *The Kreutzer Sonata* (1902), both about strong women who suffer bravely for love, specifically for the beautiful Bertha Kalish. For Sara Adler, he wrote *On a heym (Homeless)* (1907), about a simple country woman who immigrates to join her husband but cannot adjust to modern New York. Jacob Adler played his Jewish King Lear. Both the American Keni Liptzin and the Polish Ester Rokhl Kaminska played the title role in his *Mirele Efros; or, the Jewish Queen Lear* and were considered to be dueling for primacy in the role. David Kessler, who had great dramatic power and a fine singing voice, played Hershele Dubrovner in *God, Man, and Devil,* but Gordin made sure that when Hershele dies, each character gets his own curtain line. Even after Gordin's death, when the masses were tired of his style and the intelligentsia had moved on to fresher reforms, it was not uncommon for actors to choose a Gordin vehicle for their own personal benefit nights. Yiddish theater was famous for fans' passionate adoration of actors, another way in which it was typical of nineteenth-century Western theater.

One of the most famous lines in Yiddish drama comes near the conclusion of *God, Man, and Devil* when Khatskl says, "Reb Hershele Dubrovner, you play-acted a comedy with God." Such pairing of life and theater entered deeply in the Yiddish imagination. In fact, Gordin's own deathbed line was "finita la commedia." A popular Yiddish corollary to the notion of life as theater was the notion of theatergoing as an intensification of life, a moment when the spectator is most truly himself. And this makes sense as a metaphor for the culture's religious source. Clear distinctions within a profoundly interconnected universe are at the essence of Jewish religious practice; the sense of proscenium as clear distinction allows for a passionate bond between audience and stage.

Gordin was a major figure in drawing the battle line between high art and low *(shund)*. In all cultures both extremes exist. But in Yiddish theater—and Yiddish literary culture as a whole—the distinction is emotionally freighted and the subject of ferocious debate. Gordin declared Yiddish theater a serious institution, representing the language and its speakers at their best and linked with the culture's finest aspirations. This attitude transforms the issue of high art or low into something more than an aesthetic question. In the nineteenth century, the emerging Polish national culture, which is to say the intellectual environment of many Yiddish-speaking intellectuals, similarly integrated dramatic literature and language with national identity. The criteria of *shund* are always subjective, though, and always shifting. Ironically, the great Isaac Leyb Peretz, scorning old-fashioned melodrama in favor of avant-garde symbolism and naturalism, called Gordin's plays *shund*.

Although Gordin began as a Russian writer, once he arrived in America he wrote only in the Yiddish language, so that the majority of his work, including all his plays, were written in Yiddish. Nevertheless, he was part of a generation of Russian Jewish intellectuals whose cultural affinities were Russian at least as much as they were Jewish. Gordin's plays have a particularly Russian quality much like Tolstoy's *The Power of Darkness* (1886) and *Redemption (The Living Corpse)* (1900), as well as the high-strung pitch and the pessimism of Ostrovsky's *The Storm* (1859). *God, Man, and Devil* even resembles the *Power of Darkness* in some specific dramaturgical elements, and further echoes of Tolstoy are perhaps audible in the angels' philosophizing in *God, Man, and Devil*'s prologue.

This Russian quality is the most conspicuous connection between Gordin's works and those of his younger contemporary Leon Kobrin. Kobrin wrote in Russian first; in fact, it was Gordin's influence that turned him to Yiddish. Kobrin began in 1898 with a melodrama on which Gordin collaborated: *Mina; or, The Ruined Family from Downtown.* He wrote plays for almost half a century; as late as 1931 he had a success with the domestic drama *Riverside Drive,* in which Yiddish-speaking greenhorn grandparents and English-speaking grandchildren struggle, but fail, to communicate. However *Yankl Boyle,* which he dramatized in 1913 from his own novel as a starring vehicle for David Kessler, most resembles Gordin in tone and atmosphere, characterizations, and sheer weight.

The protagonist of *Yankl Boyle,* Yankl himself, is a young man whose father, an innkeeper, has let him grow up quite ignorant of Jewish learning and practice. They live among the local fishermen and wagoners, both Jews and non-Jews. Yankl is wild, simple, and practically illiterate. He is a perfect match for Natasha, the non-Jewish serving maid at the inn, and they are in fact in love. But his father is dying. In a powerfully atmospheric deathbed scene, to the sound of peasants carousing in the next room, the father makes Yankl swear to marry the Jewish girl to whom he has been betrothed. Yankl is in agony, burdened on the one hand by his vow to his father (and superstitious fear that his father's ghost will avenge disobedience) and on the other by his love for Natasha, who is pregnant. In the end, he kills himself.

Green Fields *(Grine felder)* (1916)

The career of Peretz Hirshbein (1880–1948) as a Yiddish writer began when he moved to Warsaw and entered the orbit of Yitskhok Leyb Peretz (1852–1915), the mentor of many Yiddish writers. Peretz's apartment was the center for ideas animating the Yiddish literary universe. His was a primary force behind the explosion of Yiddish novels, poetry, journalism, and belles lettres. In 1910 he organized a mass meeting in Warsaw for the uplifting of Yiddish theater; thousands attended despite fear of a pogrom. Peretz's personal relationship with many writers influenced their lives—most conspicuously, in the way he proselytized them into devoting their talents to Yiddish. As the first generation of serious secular Yiddish writers developed, they were also developing Yiddish as a modern literary language.

Peretz himself wrote some twenty dramatic works—most of them never performed—in several distinct genres. His earliest plays, depicting the miserable lives of Jews in urban poverty, were influenced by the naturalism of Emile Zola's *Therese Raquin* (1873), Gerhart Hauptmann's *The Weavers* (1892), and Maxim Gorki's *Lower Depths* (1902). His one-act *Sisters* (1906) shows three desperate women, impoverished, struggling to survive and protect each other in the Jewish slums of Warsaw. The oldest is a widow with a sick child. The second is already a fallen woman. The play is really hers, and the role was played by Ester Rokhl Kaminska and other stars. She seduces the youngest sister's boyfriend, sacrificing herself because she knows he is no good and she wants to protect the girl—for a little while, at least—from ruin and the streets.

Peretz's best-known plays, however, are not naturalist but symbolist. Intensely in touch with Polish currents of art and thought, Peretz was sympathetic to the romantic Young Poland movement, and he greatly admired the symbolist works of the Polish writer Stanislaw Wyspianski. This was also the period of William Butler Yeats, Hugo von Hofmannsthal, August Strindberg, and Maurice Maeterlinck. Serious Yiddish theater artists gave particular attention to Peretz's *Baynakht oyfn altn mark (Night in the Old Marketplace)*, a dramatic poem that he subtitled "Dream of a Fever Night." He wrote at least three versions of this between 1907 and 1928. *Baynakht oyfn altn mark* takes place at midnight in a town of Jews living in medieval tradition and poverty. The ghostly personae flicker in and out till at dawn all return to their graves. Connections are made more by sound and image than by character relationships; atmosphere, not plot, is what the play is "about," though the attitude toward the painful physical and emotional poverty of the community informs the piece and is available as political statement. In the later versions, a *badkhen* provides some continuity of action. When Granovsky staged it at the Moscow Yiddish Art Theatre (GOSET), he called it a "tragic carnival."

Two of Peretz's less famous symbolist plays are *Di Goldene keyt (The Golden Chain)* (1907) and *In polish oyf der keyt (Chained in the Synagogue Anteroom)* (1908). *Di Goldene keyt,* which Peretz once named as his own favorite, portrays a family of several generations. The action is orchestrated as much as it is dramatized, using nonrealistic forms of dialogue such as choral speaking and devices such as alliteration. What sets it in motion is the effort by the family patriarch, a hasidic rabbi, to bring on the Messiah by refusing to let Sabbath end. The "golden chain" remains a familiar image for the continuity of Jewish—or, specifically, Yiddish—culture. In *In polish oyf der keyt,* a rebellious young man is chained near the synagogue. A wedding is being planned for a young woman with whom he has a relationship, then it is called off, then preparations begin again, and finally the young woman kills herself.

Like his mentor Peretz, Hirschbein's own first plays were "slices of life." He began in Hebrew with *Miriam,* the tragic story of a poor girl who is seduced and ends up on the streets. When he switched to Yiddish, his early plays earned him the nickname of "cellar poet," because they were about impoverished Jews starving in cellar apartments. Next, still following Peretz, he experimented with symbolism in several short plays such as *Oyf yener zayt taykh (Beyond the River)* (1908), this time earning the nickname "the Jewish Maeterlinck." Thus by 1908, Hirschbein and others were writing, in Yiddish, plays in tune with the avant-garde of other European cultures.

Unlike playwrights in other languages, however, Hirshbein had virtually no adventurous actors to perform his work. So he himself organized the first experimental Yiddish theatre troupe. His intention was to present his own plays and other modern plays, both original Yiddish plays and translations from other languages. He modeled his company on Stanislavski's Moscow Art Theatre as well as on the small groups in other European cities, trying to incorporate the most forward-thinking principles of staging: primacy of the director's vision; ensemble work rather than (in the Yiddish term) *starizm;* serious technical training and sense of mission; and focus on the play as a whole. Active in his new young company was Jacob Ben-Ami, an actor who had trained in Russian theater. The group, based in Odessa, lasted two years. Its best-known successors were the Vilna Troupe, the Warsaw Yiddish Art Theater (VYKT), the Yiddish Art Theatre, and the Irving Place Theatre in New York, and the Moscow Yiddish Art Theatre (GOSET).

The life of a wandering player suited Hirschbein. As a yeshiva boy he had roamed the countryside from one village to the next, like his character Levi-Yitskhok in *Green Fields*. Hirschbein joined the immigration to America and then continued to travel widely all his life. His travel books of impressions of Jewish communities of Palestine, South Africa, and India (where he met Ghandi) are full of appreciation of the world's diverse charms. What interested him most was life outside the familiar ghettos. Hirschbein himself was a miller's son from a small Polish village, and *Green Fields* was part of a notable stream of Yiddish literature with settings in the rural countryside. In the Soviet Union, plays and novels portraying Jews as stalwart farmers suited the ideological agenda. In the United States, too, nature poetry and the stories of farmers and ranchers were not unknown. In 1926, for example, Hirshbein directed a dramatization of Isaac Raboy's novel *The Jewish Cowboy*.

Green Fields was one of a group of four pastorales, most of which Hirschbein wrote in America. The first to be produced was *A Farvorfn Vinkl*, (generally known as *A Secluded Nook*) (1913). Jacob Ben-Ami chose it to inaugurate a literary series at the Irving Place Theatre, where it was an enormous success. The others were *Der Shmids Tekhter (The Blacksmith's Daughters)* (1915) and *Di Puste Kretshme* (most often translated as *The Idle Inn* but also known as *The Empty, Abandoned, Vacant,* or *Haunted Inn*) (1911).

The Idle Inn was such a success that, in 1921, Ben-Ami went on to star in a Broadway production. It shares with *Green Fields* a light touch (not typical of the more literary Yiddish theater): a way of saying much less than could be said, and saying it obliquely. But the tone is much darker. A horse dealer named Bendet lives in the country with his wife, his old father, and his daughter Mayte. Bendet wants to marry his daughter Mayte off to Leybish, the neighbor's son, and plans to set the young couple up in an inn that currently stands abandoned in the fields. This inn is widely believed to be haunted. Mayte is in love with her strapping cousin Itsik, but Bendet believes that Itsik has stolen his horse, and Mayte submits without argument to her father's will. Act 2 shows Mayte's wedding to Leybish. Guests keep crowding into the little house. People dance to klezmer music. The excitement crescendoes as merchants on their way to a fair appear mysteriously and present gifts to the bride. At the height of the celebration, Mayte and Itsik slip out. The curtain falls as Bendet discovers their disappearance. In the next act, in the middle of the same night, the runaways have built a little campfire in sight of the ruined inn. A search party appears and instead of hiding, Mayte calls to them and is taken home to her father's house. But at the final curtain, the couple are reunited when Itsik picks her up and carries her off.

Although Mayte tries at one point to explain why she acts as she does, her motivations don't make sense as she switches from spitfire to milquetoast, and that flaw makes the play feel unsatisfying. Nevertheless, it has many fine elements: the mysterious presence of the inn, a wonderfully theatrical middle, and some fierce encounters between the young lovers.

Green Fields was popular with audiences from the start. It was also popular in the sense that its subject is typical of low rather than of literary Yiddish drama. Nothing is really at stake except young love, and young love triumphs as it is bound to do. Where *The Idle Inn* is erotic, *Green Fields* is romantic. Its values are decent behavior, health, and fresh air—above all, harmony with nature. This harmony involves not only apples, calves, and haying but also peace between old friends and, above all, happy new marriages. That these seem more important than rituals or learning was a welcome message for rapidly assimilating audiences. Levi-Yitskhok glimpses this himself; it is clear that it is precisely his learning, piety, and refinement that allow him to feel that ethical values and nature itself supersede ritual. He liberates himself from the old system of matchmaking in order to become part of the natural order by claiming his mate.

No worries from outside intrude here. There is no hint of the political upheavals that accompanied World War I—the poverty, urbanization, disorientation, and assimilation that were making Dovid-Noyekh's world seem a faraway paradise to émigrés and even to people who stayed home. There is no anti-Semitism. The subtext is nostalgia for a lost homeland and lost innocence.

The characters are presented as realistic, though of little depth. Tsine is a charming hoyden, Rokhl a mamma—both stock Yiddish drama types. Levi-Yitskhok is a touching innocent, and something more than that. Tsine and Levi-Yitskhok both learn something, Hirsh-Ber expands under the pressure of love, and Elkone actually comes to see the error of his ways. Most of the characters are not articulate, and the images they use are farm images: Hirsh-Ber's head is described as full of horses, women as quarreling like geese. Levi-

Yitskhok becomes eloquent when he describes piety, and Dovid-Noyekh and Elkone achieve flashes of simple eloquence when they struggle to express longings for spiritual beauty.

Shop (Shap) (1926)

H. Leivick (1888–1962) was a dramatic hero in his own life, and his own experiences inform his plays. Born Leivick Halpern (he took the pen name years later to avoid confusion with another writer), he was the ninth child of an impoverished family living near Minsk. Sent off to yeshiva at the age of ten, he suffered hunger and privation. By the Revolution of 1905, when he was seventeen, he was already committed to political action as a member of the Yidish socialist organization, the Bund. In 1906 he was arrested twice, the second time spending a long period in chains, flogged, in solitary confinement awaiting trial. But he kept up resistance, once pursuing a hunger strike, and at the trial spurned a chance to plead his youth, apologize, and get a reduced sentence. Instead, he repeated his intention to struggle against tyranny and was sentenced to four years of hard labor followed by exile for life in Siberia. In 1912 he arrived in chains at a village in eastern Siberia on the banks of the Lena River. But soon afterwards he managed to escape, with the help of money raised for him by people in America who had read poems he had been having smuggled out of prison. He fled on foot and by horse-drawn sledge across the tundra and over the frozen Lena. In 1913 he arrived in New York. There he preferred on principle to earn his living as a physical laborer rather than as a writer, so he worked as a paperhanger for most of the rest of his life. By the time that he died in 1962, after a long illness, he was perhaps the best known and best loved Yiddish poet in America.

Leivick remained true to the political convictions articulated in *Shop* by the character Mina while suffering the scruples voiced by the character Lipman. Almost all his best-known works derive one way or another from his musings on politics; the course of the Revolution and of Communism itself are the text or sometimes the subtext of his work. His most obviously committed revolutionary play was *Hirsh Lekert,* the true story of a shoemaker who was hanged in 1902 for trying to assassinate the governor of Vilna. Lekert was a popular hero; there was even a folk ballad about him. This play was performed very often in the Soviet and elsewhere, and when Leivick visited the Soviet Union in 1925, he was welcomed in triumph. However, the injustices and suffering that came with the Revolution concerned him. Finally in 1929, when the Communists justified the pogrom and massacre by Arabs of Jewish settlers in Hebron, Leivick turned away from them, and was vilified by them from then on.

The Yiddish literary world was intensely attuned to distinctions in political loyalties. Virtually all secular writers considered themselves somewhere on the left. But along that left there were very many distinct positions. The intense intellectual life was virtually inextricable from political opinions and commitments. Many publications were aligned with political organizations. Which productions got reviewed, and where, and how favorably were all overtly influenced by politics. The satirist and playwright Isaac Moyshe Nadir (Isaac Reiss), who remained Communist right up until the Soviet alliance with Hitler, was only one of the more savage attackers of Leivick and other backsliders. In this world, when it came to politics, there was no such thing as a private matter of conscience.

It is as a poet rather than a playwright, however, that Leivick is best known. In fact, he actually called several of his plays, including *The Golem,* which is the most famous, not plays but "Dramatic poems."

Leivick began in a sense to write *The Golem* when he wrote his first play, *Di keytn fun meshiakh (The Chains of the Messiah),* in solitary confinement in 1908 in his late teens. Perceptible in it are the preoccupations, the themes that were to concern him for the rest of his life, as well as many of the symbols and images that he continued to use. It derives from a traditional tale that God commanded the angels to keep the Messiah chained up until the world was ready for him, but that one angel refused to cooperate. In the play, that rebellious angel, together with the prophet Elijah, wander the world trying to help humanity become better people so that the Messiah will be liberated to come and alleviate their suffering. *Di keytn fun meshiakh* explores the suffering, as well as the means of deliverance, which were to remain Leivick's great themes.

The Golem, a "dramatic poem in eight scenes," reworks another old legend. A *golem* is a kind of robot created to rescue the Jews. The notion of a *golem* already existed in the Talmud, but the story that provides the plot has long been attached to sixteenth-century Prague. In Leivick's version, the rabbi of Prague forms and animates a huge clay figure to fight for the Jewish community, which has been threatened by blood libel. The *golem* once alive becomes all too human: frustrated and sad, also brutal and violent. This disappointing reality seems to reflect Leivick's disappointment in the outcome of the Revolution. Two beggars appear. The older is Elijah, the younger is the true Messiah, but the rabbi tells them that the world is not yet ready, so they must continue wandering as people continue suffering.

Written in 1920 and soon widely read, *The Golem* was not produced until 1925, in Hebrew translation, by the Habima theater ensemble in Moscow. The first performance of the Yiddish original was by Moscow amateurs in 1927. The second professional production was in Polish translation in Lublin in 1928. The first professional Yiddish production was by the Vilna Troupe in Cracow in 1929. Although *The Golem* has rarely been performed in its original form, there have been many adaptations in English and other languages—most recently, at the 1998 International Festival of Puppet Theater in New York, by the Czechoslavak-American Marionette Theater.

In 1932, Leivick was back in solitary confinement, this time spending four years in a Denver sanitarium recovering from tuberculosis. There he composed *Geule Komedye (Salvation Comedy)*, which explores the dreams dreamed by the golem while the clay figure lay waiting to be animated.

Meanwhile, Leivick also wrote a very different kind of play: one belonging to the genre called *tsaytbilder* (literally: pictures, or scenes, of the times), which were realistic depictions of conditions in Lower East Side tenements and sweatshops. His play *Shmates (Rags)*, was first produced at New York's Yiddish Art Theatre in 1921. Moyshe Maze, the protagonist, is an elderly man, who was respected as a scholar in the Old Country but is now reduced to sorting rags in a sweatshop. When his co-workers, pathetic old men, decide to strike, Maze refuses because he is outraged by the notion that a penny or two more an hour will compensate for their lost dignity and meaningless days. Meanwhile one of Maze's daughters has just married the boss's son. Maze disapproves, however, and is enraged by people's assumptions that this connection is the reason he won't strike. The play is about his individual rage; it is not couched in political terms, except for the pathetic strikers, and Maze is so unremittingly bitter that his family seem victimized by him rather than by any political system. Nevertheless, the situation and many of the scenes are strong, and the role of Moyshe Maze proved a good vehicle for Maurice Schwartz in New York and Avrom Morevsky in Vilna.

Leivick seems to have considered *Shop,* too, a realistic *tsaytbild.* It portrays a plausible range of people who happen to have washed up in same shop. There are the two silly shop girls; the goons; Shloyme-Khayim with his old-fashioned stories; and Ber, the former wagoner who is on his way up within the union. Details like the shop's social hierarchy, designer on top, are observed from life.

It is even realistic that many of these characters have two identities: who they used to be in the Old Country and who they are now. In fact, it was not uncommon for a Jewish revolutionary to have more than two identities because he began by jettisoning the family and identity of his youth. The struggle to reconcile layered identities was a fact of life in the Jewish immigrant community. At the same time, it is an intrinsically dramatic situation. It is the conscious subject of many works, such as Abraham Cahan's novel *The Rise of David Levinsky,* and the subtext of many, many others. Beyond verisimilitude, the negotiating of multiple identities resonates with metaphysical implications.

Similarly, characters in *Shop,* as in many other Yiddish plays, shift languages in faithful representation of how those people spoke. To begin with, the Yiddish language developed from several different sources. The Hebrew component is associated with religion, and because religion is inextricable from the culture as a whole, normal Yiddish-speaking life uses many words of Hebrew origin. German, Romance, and Slavic components are likewise deeply integrated. A person speaking Yiddish is not normally thinking about such distinctions, though on occasion they may surface into his consciousness. (The only obvious indication is in the writing, which preserves Hebrew spelling for many words of Hebrew origin.) In addition, there are the borrowings from other languages. In plays set in the United States, borrowings from English are the most conspicuous, such as *shop* (for which there is no exact Yiddish equivalent), and *pikl* (pickle) (for which there is). In *Shop* the Operator swears in Russian, the girls sing in English, and Leyzer uses Hebrew to refer to religion. This is realistic. It is also dramatic. Yiddish playwrights often played with misunderstandings, puns, and other hazards of bilingualism, especially for comic effect. Finally, Yiddish-speakers typically spoke Yiddish to each other and another language or two to non-Yiddish speakers. And if they changed their lives, they may well have changed the languages they lived them in. Their personal histories were in layers of experience, each accessible by a different language.

Although *Shop* is a realistic play, it is definitely a poet's rendering of a slice of life. The play is constructed on several planes simultaneously. A plot is imposed: before, during, and after the strike. Three separate love stories thread from act 1 to resolution in act 4: Gertie and Leybl, Mina and her two suitors, and Raya and Barkon. Forebodings of Raya's end provide suspense even after the strike is settled, and her death gives punch to the final curtain. The arc of overall construction resembles four musical movements, with variations in emotional color and a flowing orchestration of scenes. Machine sounds create atmosphere. Snatches of music—old-country folk melodies, Russian revolutionary songs, American popular tunes, and jazz—drift in and out, making dramatic points. The wedding song and the wedding dance with its mechanized choreography intensify the action from realism to expressionism. In fact, the characters themselves are used like musical motifs.

Furthermore, rather than psychological depth, the characters may be said to carry metaphorical or allegorical functions. True, they are more than just abstractions—more subtle, more human, and more searching. Still, Mina is obviously the ideologue for whom the ends justify the means, and Wolf the lapsed revolutionary. The play is sad. Less than ten years after the Revolution, Leivick was exploring the degradation of ideals and the possibility that ends do not always justify means. Gertie and Leybl seem the hope of the future, but they are young and untested, allowed the benefit of the doubt. The humanist Lipman (possibly representing Leivick himself) is passive and weak. It is the tormented traitor Wolf who gets the big curtain scene, and his is the star role.

Although most of his work was thoughtful and lyrical verse, Leivick did write several more plays after *Shop. Keytn (Chains)* (1930), produced by Maurice Schwartz, seems to be a response to the Communist condoning of the Hebron massacre. Leivick responded to World War II, most famously with the volume of poems *In Treblinke bin ikh nit geven (I Was Not in Treblinka)*, but also in dramas. After visiting camps for displaced persons, he wrote *A khasene in Fernvald (A Wedding in Fernvald)* (1949) about the first wedding between survivors in a camp, and *In di teg fun Iov (In the Days of Job)* (1953).

The Treasure (Der Oytser) (1906)

David Pinski (1872–1959) came from an unusually cosmopolitan and worldly background. His family were among the few Jews privileged to live in Moscow, outside the Pale, by virtue of his father's position as supplier to the czar's army. His father loved music and theater and took the boy to the best the city had to offer. By 1890, when the Jews were expelled from Moscow, Pinski was already a modern intellectual. Beginning in his teens, he lived for periods in Switzerland, Vienna, and Berlin, studying, writing, and editing various left-wing and literary journals. (He eventually studied toward a doctorate in German literature at Columbia University.) In 1892, about to enter medical school in Berlin, he met Peretz in Warsaw, showed Peretz his writing, and was persuaded by Peretz to become not a doctor but a Yiddish writer.

An indication of his commitment to Yiddish literature, as well as of his academic bent, is that in 1909 he wrote a history of Yiddish drama, which he divided into three "acts": first Goldfadn, Hurwitz, and Lateiner; then Gordin; and finally the era of modern, serious drama, which was then only just beginning.

Pinski's best-known works are personal rather than sociological, political, or philosophical. They explore the psyches of mature, intelligent people who still seem contemporary to us, even when the setting is not. In *Yeder mit zayn got (To Each His Own God)* (1912) a middle-aged man and his no-longer-young niece struggle to make decent, honorable lives for themselves in America. She, who in the Old Country was an intellectual and revolutionary, is driven by loneliness to the humiliation of advertising in the newspaper classifieds for a husband. He is driven to desperate measures by his predatory young wife because he can't make a lot of money. (Both David Kessler and Maurice Schwartz played the role in New York. Paul Baratoff played it in London.)

Pinski was interested in psychological abnormality. His first notable play was *Isaac Sheftl* (1899), the tragedy of an inventor, a natural genius, unwordly and inarticulate, whose ruin is inevitable because of his social situation. *Profesor Brener* (1911) depicts a man who realizes that he is too old for the young woman he loves and, in despair, considers suicide. The title character of *Di muter (The Mother)* (1901), played by several famous actresses, dies brokenhearted from cruel rejection by her adult children. The most violent of Pinski's plays is *Beser nisht geboyrn vern (Better Never to Have Been Born)* (1914), in which a young Coney Island man rapes and kills his upstairs neighbor. (This play appears in Pinki's collected works, but there is no record that is was ever performed.) Pinki also applied his psychological explorations to historical figures such as Alexander the Great and Diogenes.

Sex plays a powerful role in many of Pinski's plays. *Gavri un di froyen (Gavri and the Women)* (1908) portrays a passionate triangle, with both women glorying in their submission to their man as virile life force. *Dovid Hamelekh un zayne vayber (King David and His Wives)* (1915) devotes scenes to Mikhal, Bathsheba, and the other women of the biblical account. The best known of Pinski's plays about passion between men and women is *Yankl der shmid (Yankl the Blacksmith)* (1906), in which the hero struggles desperately against the temptation to betray his wife with a seductive other woman. Although it was not the norm for serious Yiddish dramatists to explore sexual relationships, I included one scene from *Yankle der shmid* in the appendix of this volume.

However, Pinski did not write the only erotic dramas of literary value in Yiddish. The best-known such work is *Got fun nekome (God of Vengeance)* by Sholom Asch, a play that scandalized Yiddish audiences in 1907 (and—in translation—Broadway audiences in 1922). The protagonist of *God of Vengeance* is the owner of a whorehouse. He lives in the same house upstairs, deluding himself into thinking that he is keeping his daughter totally innocent. As the play begins, he has bought himself holiness in two forms: a Torah scroll to keep upstairs and a pious bridegroom for his daughter. But he discovers that the girl has been sneaking downstairs, drawn by an erotic relationship with one of the whores, and she runs away to become a prostitute herself, shattering his crazy dream.

Fishl Bimko was best known for his plays about the underworld, especially *Ganovim (Thieves)* (1919), which was published with a glossary of Yiddish underworld slang spoken by the characters. His *Amerike ganef* (the title a humorous expression meaning "American thievery" or "that thief, America"), which traces a group's journey from home all the way to Ellis Island, also features pimps and whores.

In a very different tone, elevated and poetical rather than gamey, Alter Kacyzne, Aron Zeitlin, and others wrote dramas about people in high places—romantic combinations of love, royalty, and consideration of the position of the Jews. The diction tends to be lofty, and a recurrent theme involves the love between a Christian aristocrat and a Jewish girl. Kacyzne's best-known play is *Der dukus (The Duke)* (1925); he also wrote plays about Prometheus (1920) and King Herod (1926). Zeitlin's best-known work of this type is *Esterke;* he also wrote *Yankev Frank* (1929), a play about the false messiah Shabtai Zvi and the Baal Shem Tov, the founder of Hasidism. In S. Ansky's *The Dybbuk* (1920), probably the most successful and widely produced drama ever written in Yiddish, mystical religiosity intensifies a drama of erotic attraction between two young souls.

Pinski also wrote a number of plays focusing primarily on ideas, especially in relation to the Jews. The notion that plays ought to teach a lesson is particularly intense in Yiddish culture, though of course not unique to it. Interpretation of any ambitious literature leads thoughtful critics to find the author's deeper meanings. But in Yiddish drama the process often seems rather naked. Characters stand for ideas, and they act as they do so that audiences can consider what is the right way to act. It is not uncommon for serious Yiddish plays to seem as if they are only part of an entire evening designed to culminate in discussion. This effect was often accomplished by production techniques, especially expressionist staging, which added intellectual dimension and comment by such means as costuming characters to represent all capitalists, labeling elements of the sets, and having actors move mechanically—like parts of a system rather than individual human beings. But a number of serious Yiddish plays were actually written in order to dramatize abstractions, and even employed characters named simply Man, or Jester, or Marketwoman, or Beggar.

A common form for Yiddish allegories is the family drama. Pinski's *Der letster yid,* also performed as *Di familye Zvi (The Last Jew,* or *The Zvi Family)* (1905)—one of many such plays written after the Kishinev pogrom of 1903— shows a family's reactions to a pogrom. One son copes by fighting for Zion, one by fighting for the Revolution. When their old grandfather goes to die to protect the Torah, the third brother, a weak and assimilated intellectual, goes to certain death simply to defend the old man he loves. Jewishness is the ultimate loyalty. *The Last Jew* was produced in New York in 1905. Two years later it was smuggled into Russia sewn into a coat lining, but censors prevented Stanislavski from staging it at the Moscow Art Theater. Similarly, Sholom Aleichem's *Tsezeyt un tseshpreyt (Scattered to the Winds,* or *Scattered and Dispersed)* (1903) depicts a family whose adult children, responding to a moment of danger, choose political positions, including assimilation, and discuss their positions. This play too had a number of productions, though Sholom Aleichem himself criticized it as "not a drama but a feuilleton." Debate itself is the real action of such plays; ongoing history in the world outside supplies the suspense.

Another genre of allegory depicts a group of Jews in some unspecified historical time and place, in an attempt to suggest the painful situation of the Jews through the ages. Pinski's play *Der shtumer meshiakh (The Mute Messiah)* (1911), for example, follows a Jewish community as they are exiled from their homes in a kingdom called Illyria, though Pinski actually based the circumstances on Jews in fourteenth-century Germany. Their rabbi has been tortured by the cruel prince and his tongue cut out, so his daughter dedicates herself to speak his thoughts, rallying the exiles as they make their painful way toward Palestine. When the prince dies and the Jews are invited to turn back, they are only too glad to do so. Because she cannot speak well enough to persuade them to continue on to Zion, guilt and misery lead her to suicide. Many Yiddish authors, including Dymov and Hirschbein, tried this kind of play, often in a kind of blank verse or a poeticized, elevated, declamatory rhetoric. Leonid Andreyev's *The Life of Man* (1906) was one of the contemporary non-Yiddish dramas, admired by Yiddish intellectuals, that tried to dramatize deep issues in similar fashion.

Pinski's *The Treasure* has quite a different sort of plot. The spine is simply Tilye's determination to find a husband. What gives it texture is the way it builds in momentum and size. The first act is the family's race to find gold. The second act adds the rest of those few characters who have individual faces, and ratchets up the time pressure. The third act raises the stakes still higher with the imminent arrival of the suitor, the loss of Khonye's job, and the world filtering into the hovel. The last act has exploded out of the family's hovel to fill the universe which is the village, not only its living inhabitants but also its dead. Death—present all along in the gravestones, the wails of mourners, and the shed where Khonye washes corpses—increases its threat and takes over the stage. The tone also changes from a comic take on naturalism to an expressionist spookiness and desperation.

Much of the fourth act is a prolonged, orchestrated crowd scene. Crowd scenes crop up relatively often in serious Yiddish dramas and comedies, for both aesthetic and political reasons. In the 1880s, the duke of Saxe-Meiningen had won fame for his own company by directing, or choreographing, crowd scenes so that the masses represented masses yet at the same time behaved onstage like collections of distinct individuals. In the period when Pinski wrote *The Treasure,* expressionist staging used crowds as major presences, moving and speaking as inhuman embodiments of abstractions. Just as such plays portrayed characters less as individual human beings than as machine parts in a mechanized world, crowd scenes were a means of transforming play texts about individuals into plays about political forces and group will. In this way, successful Soviet revivals of well-known plays by Goldfadn and Sholom Aleichem purported to transform them from humorous portrayals of old-fashioned Jewish life to satires exposing the evils of pre-Revolutionary Jewish capitalists.

Bronx Express (Bronks ekspres) (1919)

Osip Dymov (last name also spelled Dimow, though his real name was Yosef Perlman: 1878–1959) came from such an assimilated background that until 1907 he wrote all his plays and other works in Russian, with others translating them into Yiddish for production. After that year Yiddish became the primary language for some of his work, though he may have continued to write first drafts in Russian and then translate them himself. (In the last decade of his life, he wrote an original play in English as well, which was performed in New York and London.) He wrote symbolist plays, plays addressing the problem of Jewish wanderings and sufferings through the ages, and plays of romance and comic observation.

Dymov's biggest success was the lovely *Yoshke muzikant (Yoshke the Musician)* (1914), also known as *Der zinger fun zayn troyer (The Singer of His Sorrow)* or *Der gedungene khosn (The Hired Bridegroom).* Yoshke loves a servant girl who loves the son of the house. When he wins the lottery, he gives her all the prize money so that she can marry the man she loves. This bittersweet love story was reworked in 1925 by Yankev Shternberg and the actor Joseph Buloff. Buloff played Yoshke in the Vilna Troupe production, which was such an enormous hit that the troup even presented a command performance for the queen of Rumania. The play has had many productions, in Hebrew, Polish, and German translations as well as in Yiddish. Buloff himself directed and starred in it at the Folksbiene in 197.

Like Levick's *Shop,* Gordin's *Homeless,* Pinski's *To Each His Own God,* and many other Yiddish plays written in the United States, *Bronx Express* deals explicitly with the immigrant experience. The protagonist asks whether what he has gained in America is worth what he has lost. Many plays produced by American immigrant communities have tackled this subject in a wide variety of tones, attitudes, and languages. *La Careta* by Rene Marques *(The Oxcart)* (1951), for example, ends with a family's decision to return home to Puerto Rico. Similarly, Kobrin's *Riversayd drayv (Riverside Drive)* (1931) ends when characters go back to the Old Country. But in real life, Jews rarely did that, and it is clear that the Hungerproud family have no intention of leaving.

In *Bronx Express* religion has nothing to do with the mystical or divine. Its representative, the old teacher, is a comic figure living in the past, when he had some authority. Yom Kippur, the Day of Atonement, is still a potent concept here, but only as a metaphor for decent, ethical behavior, family life, honest labor, self-respect, and national identity—all precious to the individual and to the community as a whole. Similarly, in Leivick's *The Golem,* the Jews are threatened by Gentiles, but religion itself is a spiritual experience equally accessible through Christianity. In Pinski's *To Each His Own God,* when the protagonist refuses at great cost to work on Sabbath, this is not piety but an effort to preserve his personal dignity. In many popular melodramas, such as Lateiner's *Dos yidishe harts (The Jewish Heart)* (1908), and Zeifert's (plays written with Boris Thomashefsky, *Dos pintele yid (The Little Spark of Jewishness)* (1909), as well as Dymov's own *Der eybiger vanderer (The Eternal Wanderer)* (1907), Jewishness meant pride and honor. The hero or heroine makes a grand speech affirming Jewishness in the teeth of oppression, at the cost of love or even life. In the theater, as opposed to the synagogue, when religion keeps lovers apart, it may be nothing more than a plot device.

Ritual as stage moment establishes settings and adds a resonance that may be intensified by the spectator's own nostalgia or guilt. Lighting Sabbath candles or performing marriages under a canopy happens in many plays and even in vaudeville numbers. Cantorial renditions of liturgical music are also common. The *badkhen* appears as a character in a number of twentieth-century Yiddish plays, often representing Jewish tradition in general or specifically Old-Country Yiddish culture. Purim plays in modern guise also recur occasionally in one way or another in Yiddish theater; *The Megile of Itsik Manger* is a charming reenactment of the story of Esther as if presented by Purim players in an Old World village. Of course, Yiddish theater is secular by definition. The ultra-orthodox never have attended secular professional theater though groups may mount ambitious amateur productions to raise funds for charity at Purim time.

The characters in *Bronx Express* talk about Sholom Aleichem (Sholem Rabinowitz, 1859–1916), the classic novelist and journalist and one of the creators of modern Yiddish literature. In fact, *Bronx Express* alludes to Sholom Aleichem's comedies and has some affinities with them in tone, attitude, and energy.

Sholom Aleichem's best-known comedy is the playful *200,000* (also known as *Der groyser gevins,* or *The Big Win*), in which a tailor wins the lottery. Sudden wealth complicates life for him and his family, especially his pretty daughter, and they all are on the whole relieved when he loses it and becomes a simple working man again. Hirschbein's company scored their first success with two short Sholom Aleichem comedies with bite: *Mazl Tov* (1899) and *Mentshn* (1908—translated as *People* or *Servants,* and in a later version called *Ristokratn),* about the difficult lives of the domestic servants in a bourgeois Jewish household. Sholom Aleichem's *Shver tsu zayn a yid (Hard to Be a Jew)* (1914), dramatized from his novel *Der blutiger shpas (The Bloody Jest),* also had a number of productions, most recently at the Folksbiene in a musical adaptation by Bryna Turetsky, entitled *Double Identity.* The plot takes place in czarist St. Petersburg, when it was almost impossible for a Jew to get permission to live there. A young Jewish man who wants to study there trades identities with his buddy, a Gentile aristocrat. Inevitably, both fall in love with the same girl. Then anti-Semitism and other dangers threaten. In the end, their lark has serious consequences. Apart from his plays, Sholom Aleichem often worked in the conversational form, in the dialogues or first-person narratives particularly congenial to early modern Yiddish literature. His series of monologues in the voice of a dairyman named Tevye was dramatized in several versions, including the English *Fiddler on the Roof.*

Sholom Aleichem is beloved especially for his evocation of authentic folk types speaking juicy Yiddish with energy and relish. His plays, like Goldfadn's, have continued to appear and reappear; he survives not only as a writer but as an icon. Several famous productions in the USSR under Stalin used his texts as statements of anticapitalism. But even these productions seem to have owed their wild popularity to their subversively affectionate portrayal of the Yiddish "national" culture, which was already disappearing. There is a parallel with *Bronx Express,* which looks like an indictment of soulless America but feels like homage to the varied joys of life here. Not only the domestic, virtuous characters but also the jazzy and flamboyant—Dymov seems fond of them all.

Yiddish plays were written for about a century. This was the century when all modern secular Yiddish culture evolved with intensity and complexity. Yiddish theater was part of that culture. As the Yiddish-speaking community lived out the dramas that were their complicated destinies, Yiddish playwrights shared their experiences and made them art.

God, Man, and Devil (Got, Mentsh, un Tayvl)
(1900)

JACOB GORDIN

໑ֈ๖

This translation of *God, Man, and Devil* is based primarily on the text published in New York in 1903 by the *Internasyonale Bibliotek Kompanye* and reissued in 1911 by the *Farlag fun dem Soyrkl fun Yankev Gordins fraynd* (The Circle of Friends of Jacob Gordin). There are other less reliable printed texts. But because the play was performed many times, all over the world, by professionals and amateurs, there were many variations, and it is impossible to know exactly what was performed.

This translation is shorter than the original because I edited out many repetitions. Repetitiveness was more acceptable to audiences of Gordin's period than now. Some of the repetitiveness of the text seems to be simply recorded from performance variations. In particular, Dobe's charms and Leyzer's rhymes and secrets were designed to give actors infinitely elastic opportunities for comic bits, and I removed a number of such moments. The exclamations *oy; vey iz mir* ("woe is me"); and (in act 1) "my teeth" occurred particularly often. I saved an occasional "oy" for the older characters, who are supposed to be old-fashioned, and sometimes substituted "ah" or "oh." But mostly I just omitted it. Similarly, I translated *vey iz mir* as "oh my God," "Father in Heaven," or some similar interjection, but mostly I just omitted it.

In the text, characters are identified sometimes by one version of their names and sometimes by another. The suffixes *-enyu, -ke, -l,* and *-ele* are affectionate diminutives. Thus Freyde becomes Freydenyu, Pese becomes Pesenyu, and Tsipe becomes Tsipenyu or Tsipke; Hershl and Hershele are versions of Hersh. The characters address each other in various ways. However, I regularized the character identifications to the forms that appear in the list of characters at the beginning of the play.

The syllables of the names are stressed as follows:

HER-she-le du-BROV-ner
UR-i-el
PES-en-yu or PE-se
TSIP-en-yu or TSI-pe
FREYD-en-yu
LEY-zer
KHATS-kl DRAKH-me
DO-be
MO-te-le or MO-tl
BER-l LAP-tyukh
e-FROY-im

See the Note on Transliteration.

Reb simply means *Mr.* It is not a way of addressing a rabbi.

Hebrew words are in italic. It was common to quote a passage of religious significance in the Hebrew original and follow it with the colloquial vernacular translation. In Yiddish, this was part of the normal sound of conversation between pious men. Such regular shifts back and forth can still be heard today, generally between Hebrew and Yiddish (though sometimes an analogous process now occurs between Hebrew and English). However, as play dialogue for actors in English it would mean saying the same thing twice. So I preserved some of the original Hebrew for the sake of the sound, trusting that it is clear that what follows is the character's own translation into the vernacular.

A related complication is that it is normal for Jews, whatever language they speak, to refer to ritual practice by Hebrew words. I have never heard anyone who actually puts on a prayer shawl every Sabbath call it a prayer shawl rather than a *talis.* Such Jews say not ram's horn but *shofar,* not wedding canopy but *khupe* (pronounced *KHU-pe*) or *khupa,* even in the midst of a conversation conducted entirely in English or some other language. For such Jews, translation may actually sound jarring and unnatural. Here I used the English "prayer shawl" most of the time, to make sure the reader would understand. However for performance, a director can judge his audience and use either all English or all Yiddish (*TAL-is,* plural *ta-LES-im*).

God, Man, and Devil takes place in a religious household in a religious community in a town in nineteenth-century Russia. There, religious concepts and religious practice entirely structured and suffused people's lives. Furthermore, the characters in this play are thinking about religious matters constantly. Indeed, religion dominates the setting, the plot, and the essential metaphor of the play. The dialogue refers constantly to religious matters. It does so on a conscious level, as when Khatskl describes the ambiguous state of the engagement by saying that it's neither dairy nor meat, meaning neither of the two distinct categories of kosher food.

Deeper than this is the level at which religion is built into the Yiddish language. For example, the word "kosher" recurs constantly in this play. Sometimes it means ritually pure (a kosher prayer shawl). But often, by extension, it means decent, honest, righteous, good (a kosher wife, a kosher child, in act 3 even kosher wealth). Even when used in this metaphoric sense, as an ordinary Yiddish adjective, it is spelled not according to Yiddish orthography but in the original Hebrew. Religious terminology is so organic to the Yiddish language that many words are spelled this way, even though they are pronounced as Yiddish and used without an obtrusive consciousness of their linguistic source.

Obviously much of this cannot be conveyed in a translation which is to be read and possibly performed. For the drama to be effective, clarity and smoothness are necessary. Thus I used various synonyms for "kosher," which meant that the meaning was clear though the metaphoric force was lost. Similarly, when in act 2 Khatskl calls himself a "plain third meal," referring to the weekly supper which ends the Sabbath, I settled for "a plain plate of kasha." The greetings *sholem aleykhem* ("peace upon you") and *got hilf* (roughly: "god's help") became just "hello" and similar ordinary phrases.

In the following paragraphs I will explain some of the references which remain in the dialogue and some which have been lost in translation. It is important to remember that Gordin's audiences got them all. Some in his audience no longer observed any rituals at all. Most still followed some elements of the Jewish calendar and observed some laws. But all of them got all the references, which were part of the culture and embedded in the language.

Torah scrolls are still copied by hand on parchment using a quill pen, and the profession of scribe is sacerdotal and thus highly honored. When a scribe finishes a scroll, he recites a phrase to the effect that the Torah strengthens us. In act 1, the other men join in a musical setting of the phrase. In the synagogue, the phrase is also repeated whenever the congregation finishes reading a book of the Pentateuch. The scribe immerses himself; ritual immersion in running water remains a ceremony of purification on a number of prescribed occasions for men and women both.

Hanuka is celebrated for eight days by lighting a candelabra, one more candle each night; by eating pancakes and other fried foods; and by spinning a top *(dreydl)*. The four sides of the top are inscribed with four Hebrew letters. These are the letters which begin the words of a Hebrew sentence: "A great miracle happened here." This refers to the event in 70 B.C., when the Jews drove the Syrians out of Palestine and relit the lamp in the Temple in Jerusalem, keeping it burning even without enough oil. Traditionally children spin the top to win pennies or nuts.

Modesty between the sexes is still strictly observed in orthodox communities. In the first act, Freydenyu is reluctant to sing because men are not supposed to hear women's voices singing. Unrelated men and women are technically forbidden to stay alone together; Dobe mentions this in the third act and Pese in the fourth. Betrothal is a ceremony, with a celebration, in itself. At the wedding, bride and groom stand together under a canopy. Leyzer uses *khupe vekidushin* (KHU-pe ve-ki-DU-shin), meaning "canopy and consecration" (act 2), and *simn tov un mazl tov* (SIMn tov un MAZl tov), meaning "a good omen and good fortune"—both common phrases associated with weddings. Childlessness is grounds for divorce, and it is true that there is legal precedent for ending a childless marriage, though many husbands did not do so.

As a wedding jester *(badkhen)*, Leyzer draws on traditional material and technique. Gordin's audiences would almost all have heard a jester, though possibly long ago back home at a country cousin's wedding. (There are still some jesters performing today.) Jesters performed in rhyme and were expected to be able to make up both serious and humorous rhymes spontaneously. At weddings, before the ceremony, the jester formally seated the bride. After the groom veiled her, the jester, often standing on a chair, addressed her and her female guests with philosophical reflections designed to evoke tears. A really fine jester was considered a kind of artist. The jester was also expected to be learned enough to quote from the Talmud and the Bible and to play with *gematria* (numerology—numerical values of Hebrew and Aramaic words). Leyzer's demonstration in act three is adept. He uses standard favorite devices, such as the number of organs, rather than recondite allusions. I changed some of the Hebrew so as to create phrases whose first letters are easier sounds for an audience to keep track of. I also adjusted the insults derived from the name Mischief, so that instead of going into first Russian and then Yiddish, they operate directly in the vernacular. Of course, Mischief is an English word and works only in English; my intention was to give audiences the illusion that they are following complicated wordplay between languages.

There are many other references to ritual in the play. The Evil Impulse and Good Impulse, mentioned in act 1, are common concepts. Also in act 1, Hershele quotes the liturgy, "Who is like you?" and Dobe refers to the autumn holiday Sukkos. In act 2 Khatskl quotes in Hebrew from a special prayer recited each month at the new moon; Leyzer picks it up and gabbles a lot of it because the Hebrew is a string of alliterative words. I tried to convey the same effect by quoting Psalm 148, still ending up with the new moon. Acts 3 and 4 mention the Passover ceremony, the *seder.* Leyzer's question "Why is this day different?" is a playful quotation from a series of four questions asked during the *seder.* The *seder* also mentions the "bread of affliction" eaten by the Israelites as slaves in Egypt, symbolized by unleavened bread. Mourners rip their lapels in formal token of mourning. Leyzer mentions this at the end of the play. Tsipenyu mentions it in act 3, but there it seemed to require too much explanation, so I rendered it as "We grieve. We mourn." When Hershele says, "Blessed is the righteous judge," he is simply reciting the appropriate formulaic response for when one hears of a death.

Yom Kippur, the Day of Atonement, follows the lunar New Year celebration Rosh Ha-shono and completes the season known as the High Holy Days, which falls in September or October. Scenes 2 and 3 of act 4 allude to familiar passages from the liturgy for the Day of Atonement. The imagery of judgment and final reckoning, the comparisons of human beings to dust and shadows, even turns of phrase—all come from the Yom Kippur liturgy. So does Hershele's last line (which does not appear in every version of the text) about how God waits for repentance. Also, it is only in the High Holy Day season that the ram's horn *(shofar)* is blown.

All of the above-mentioned religious practices are part of mainstream Ashkenazik Judaism. Dobe's superstitions, on the other hand, were typical of ignorant Eastern European Jews of the lower classes. For example, many believed that mentioning evil allows evil to enter, as does sneezing, and also that spitting keeps bad things away. "No evil eye," "God forbid," and "in a lucky hour" were frequent, often even perfunctory, charms to keep evil away, and can still be heard. Such superstitions in many cultures are especially active defending against the special dangers related to childbirth, death, and the nighttime. The baying of dogs was associated with evil. In the original play, the devil is named Mazik, a common word for mischievous devil as well as a humorous and affectionate term for an obstreperous child.

Jewish law requires men and married women to cover their heads, and custom leads many orthodox men to wear full beards. In the first and second acts, the devil, being dressed not as a pious Russian Jew but simply as a European, is probably the only clean-shaven man on the stage; however, in that setting, even he would not be totally bare-headed. By act 3 or 4, Hershele may also have shaved.

Readers familiar with colloquial Yiddish sayings may spot some editorial changes. The proverb that Tsipenyu quotes at the start of act 1 is "If God wills, even a broom can shoot." I adjusted it to fit her action with her shoe. Also, at the end of act 3, Hershele actually tells Mischief that he doesn't believe everything he says is "Torah noodles," which is appropriately vulgar and vivid but too startling for audiences, so I took out the "noodles." Here I will also mention that in act 3 Dobe actually reports squeezing her granddaughter's boils, which I changed to dosing her for worms.

The Angels' choruses in the Prologue are translated very closely, even to the rhyme schemes (or their absence). The lofty diction, elevated to the edge of absurdity—or so it seems to modern sensibilities—is heavily Germanic: Daytshmersh. At the opposite extreme is the Slavic-flavored speech of the coarser characters.

Jacob Gordin considered it his mission to educate the Jewish masses. *God, Man, and Devil* teaches some of the lessons he considered most important. The evils of capitalism, industrialism, and empty religiosity are clearly depicted. Furthermore the play instructs Jewish audiences about the larger European culture by referring to "the German doctor," who is of course Faust.

At the first production of *God, Man, and Devil,* at the Thalia Theatre in New York on September 21, 1900, David Kessler played Hershele, S. Tornberg played Leyzer, Morris Moshkovitsh played Uriel Mazik, Leon Blank played Khatskl Drakhme, Jacob Cohn played Motele, Mary Wilensky played Pesenyu, Sonya Nadolski played Dobe, Bertha Kalish played Freydenyu, and Dina Stettin Feinman played Tsipenyu. Kessler, Moshkovitsh, Blank, and Kalish were major stars, and the others were also established actors. In 1906, the play was published and performed in German under the title *Gelt (Money).* By 1908 there were several productions in several different Russian translations, and one in Hebrew. Two years later there followed a Polish language production and a Ukrainian. Maurice Schwartz's Yiddish Art Theatre produced a new version in

1928 with sets by Mordechai Gorelick and costumes by the inventive pup-
peteers and graphic artists Mod and Kotler. Schwartz revived it yet again in
1953, alternating performances in Yiddish and English. The WPA's Yiddish
affiliate, the Yiddish Theatre Project, included *God, Man, and Devil* in its repertory. The play was considered a classic and staged most recently by New York's
Folksbiene in 1975 with David Ellin as Hershele, Leon Liebgold as Mazik,
Moishe Rosenfeld as Motele, and Zypora Spaisman as Dobe. In 1950 a film
version appeared, in which the play is much cut and the acting is old-fashioned, making the film a period piece even when it was new.

Jacob Gordin (1853–1909) was born in Russia and died in New York City.
He was an extremely influential figure in Yiddish culture, as journalist, lecturer,
and dramatist. More than any other single person, he was responsible for making drama a major part of Yiddish intellectual life. Among his best-known
plays are *The Jewish King Lear, The Kreutzer Sonata,* and *Mirele Efros.* (The intro-
ductory essay to this book tells more about Gordin and about *God, Man, and
Devil.*)

Characters

HERSHELE DUBROVNER, a scribe, about forty-five years old
PESENYU, his wife
LEYZER, his father, a former wedding jester
FREYDENYU, eighteen years old, his niece
TSIPENYU, sixteen years old, his niece

KHATSKL DRAKHME, his friend, a weaver
DOBE, his wife
MOTELE, his son, a weaver

URIEL MISCHIEF (SATAN)
GOD
AN OLD ANGEL

CHORUS OF YOUNG ANGELS
CHORUS OF OLD ANGELS

WORKERS
SERVANT

NONSPEAKING ROLES:

BERL LAPTYUKH, a worker

DOCTOR

WORKERS

NEIGHBORS

Scene

After a prologue in heaven, the play takes place in Dubrovne, Russia.
Prologue. Heaven.
Act I. Hershele Dubrovner's impoverished house.
Act II. Comfortable drawing room of Hershele's new home.
Act III. Same, but furnished much more luxuriously.
Act IV. Scene 1. Khatskl Drakhme's impoverished house.
Scene 2. Courtyard of Hershele's factory.
Scene 3. Hershele's office.

Time

The end of the nineteenth century.
Prologue. Just before the start of the action.
Act I: A winter evening.
Act II: Almost a year later.
Act III: Three years later.
Act IV: About a year later.

Prologue

In heaven. The throne of honor above. Below: heavens, clouds, many stars. Many cherubs float in the air. Older angels at the steps of the throne. SATAN *stands alone at a distance.*

CHORUS OF YOUNG ANGELS.
Death comes to everything. All that lives, dies.
Life itself is undying.

All that wills and that strives must die.

Willing and striving alone are undying.

CHORUS OF OLD ANGELS.

Truth is eternal, eternally one.

Goodness and beauty in truth become one.

CHORUS OF YOUNG ANGELS.

Forms die, but matter lives.

The idea of form is undying.

Idea and matter are spirit and nature

And, once interwoven, the two are undying.

CHORUS OF OLD ANGELS.

Truth is eternal, eternally one.

Goodness and beauty in truth become one.

CHORUS OF YOUNG ANGELS.

A world of pure matter—no idea, no form—

What's that but a void and a chaos?

Intellect has power to animate matter,

Creating and shaping a world out of chaos.

CHORUS OF OLD ANGELS.

Truth is eternal, eternally one.

Goodness and beauty in truth become one.

CHORUS OF YOUNG ANGELS.

Up the natural ladder of life

Forms keep striving to rise higher still.

Which of these forces develops the striving:

Intellect, is it, or spirit, or will?

CHORUS OF OLD ANGELS.

Truth is eternal, eternally one.

Goodness and beauty in truth become one.

(*A mighty blast of the ram's horn is heard. Movement.*)

AN OLD ANGEL. He is coming! He is coming! The creative spirit of eternity, the undying spirit of truth! (*All kneel except* SATAN.)

GOD. (*Invisible. His voice is heard from the throne of honor.*) Eternity and harmony in the heavens and in all worlds, in inconceivable space and in infinite time.

ALL ANGELS. He was, he is, and he will be.

GOD. What's the news? Is Satan here among god's children?

SATAN. (*Approaches, bows.*) Here I am, reverend lord. (*Apart.*) It's so boring and monotonous here in heaven. Time seems to stretch on forever. All that livens them up a little is the news I bring from the world of humans. Those stupid mortals envy the gods. The fools! Where there's no misfortune, there is no good fortune. There's no joy where there are no tears, no pleasure where there's no desire, no emotions where there exists no suffering, no happiness where there's no struggle, no novelty where there is no distress! They don't realize down there that one instant in the life of one weak little man is more interesting than a mighty god's whole eternity. And so—ha-ha!—the gods could be humans and don't want to, the people want to be gods and can't.

GOD. Where have you been now, Satan?

SATAN. Walking up and down upon the earth.

GOD. What's the news among Adam's children, whom we created in our own divine image?

SATAN. No news at all. They keep doing the same stupid things over and over.

GOD. What? Nothing new among those creatures who strive ever higher and further, who do not rest for even the blink of an eye, who care only for new discoveries, new developments—progress?

SATAN. Their spirit strives upward, but they are sunk very deep in the filth and dirt of their material life. They have established very many new things, but they still blunder about in their old, decayed, moldy injustices. On the outside, they have greatly improved and beautified themselves, but on the inside they are even more corrupt and deformed than before.

GOD. Satan, you are the spirit of denial; therefore you deny humanity's good creations. You are dark and see everything around you as darkness. How can it be? Thousands of years have passed since Adam ate from the Tree of Knowledge and I drove him from the Garden of Eden. For thousands of years, ever since then, he has been moving steadily forward, and you find him still in the same spot? Nonsense!

SATAN. It's true, Old Lord, that man has gone very far from the gates of the Garden of Eden. If he were still in his old spot, he would certainly have turned back inside. Because what he was looking for he hasn't found, while your guards, the two cherubs, have become old and weak, and the sharp swords which you gave them have become rusty and blunt. No, man really did march far away from the gates of Eden. But what was the use of that if he carried his primitive nature along with him? He drags his old packs from one place to another. He has amassed great fortunes, but he remains a robber and a beggar. He has invented brilliant devices to make his life easier, but all he thinks about is how to make other people's lives harder. He has powerful machines to annihilate the obstacles set for him by nature, and he uses these machines primarily to annihilate his fellowmen. Old Lord, Adam's children are still divided into Cains and Abels: the Abels always get murdered, the Cains remain murderers forever. Inside the enlightened up-to-date human being sits the same old Adam.

GOD. I see that the enlightened up-to-date human being does not please you. To tell the truth, I too found the old-fashioned human being much more sympathetic. Tell me this: have you heard, or perhaps you yourself have met, there on earth, my true beloved servant Hershele Dubrovner? Such a servant and worshiper is a joy even for the greatest god of gods.

SATAN. Hershele the scribe? Hershele Dubrovner? I know him. A Jew—a child of your old beloved people. He copies your holy commandments on calfskin and earns his few groshen in your holy name.

GOD. He is remarkably pious, isn't he?

satan. Yes, he's pious. He doesn't know any better.

GOD. He is an extraordinarily generous man, isn't he?

SATAN. Yes, he's generous. Every pauper would like to give charity—if he could.

GOD. Have you ever seen anyone as pure in his family life?

SATAN. The way he lives protects him from temptations.

GOD. Isn't he a true, sincere, devoted friend?

SATAN. That's because he has nothing to share.

GOD. Satan, be quiet. He is a righteous man.

SATAN. People are righteous when the righteousness doesn't cost them much, or when the righteousness brings them some profit. Let me put him to the test and you'll see for yourself how much you can depend on even the finest and best of them.

GOD. I will see it.

SATAN. Done. This job won't be hard for me.

GOD. What do you think you will use on him?

SATAN. You permitted me to test your loyal servant Job by means of sorrows. Nowadays a Jew is used to sorrows. The learned Dr. Faust sold me his soul for an instant of pleasure. But such deals work only with Gentiles; no Jew would pay a high price for pleasure. Almighty Lord, permit me to try him with money, yes, with money, with coins.

GOD. You believe that with this good, pious, serious Jew, all his thoughts deep in my Torah—that such a trivial thing as money will have any effect on him?

SATAN. People who have freedom, fame, power, land—they give it all up for money. How much more so a Jew, for whom money is his only protection. Oh, just let me at him with a little bag of gold, and you'll see what becomes of his piety, goodness, righteousness, family life, friendship, and all the other virtues you brag about.

GOD. Go make your try.

SATAN. Out of many, you had one left, Old Lord, and now you have lost that one too. I know that you can't make a bargain off a Jew, so this game will cost me a lot. (*Counts on his fingers.*) Piety? That's an old deeply-rooted habit, I'll have to pay well for that. Goodness? Only fools are good. As soon as a man gets smart, good-bye goodness. Family life? That's only a lie, under the veil of piety—a legal form of slavery, debauchery wearing the mask of righteousness. I won't have to pay a groschen for family life. I'll just ask my niece, the Evil Impulse, to help me out a little. Righteousness? Well, if righteousness is how he makes his living, I will have to pay him his price for it. We're going to have sport, Old Lord. I know that the sport of the gods is very hard on men, poor things, but that's their own fault. If man insists on being oppressed (*winks at the throne*), then let him keep right on suffering and moaning. (*Ram's horn blast.*)

GOD. Unity and harmony in the heavens, in all the worlds, in ineffable space, in all eternity. (*Disappears.*)

ALL ANGELS. He was, he is, he will be.

CHORUS OF YOUNG ANGELS.
> Death comes to everything. All that lives dies.
> Life itself is undying.
> All that wills and that strives must die.
> Willing and striving alone are undying.

CHORUS OF OLD ANGELS.
> The truth is eternal, eternally one.
> Goodness and beauty alone are undying.

Curtain

Act I

A big, impoverished room. The two windows onto the street are frosted over, and one pane is broken and stuffed with a rag. Upstage is a big white table on which lie a few sheets of parchment and a Pentateuch, covered by an old ark cover. A lamp burns on the table. A big inkwell with a few quill pens. On the side, another table, covered with a white table-cloth. Near the door, an oven. Against the wall near the door, five candles are burning in a nine-branched Hanuka candelabra. A bed hung with a red curtain stands between the oven and the wall. On the wall hangs a violin in a black bag.

PESENYU, *one cheek wadded and wrapped with bandages, peels potatoes at the oven where a fire is burning. She wears an old warm bathrobe.* LEYZER *and* FREYDENYU *sit near the Hanuka lights. He is pulling feathers from a big goose wing, and she is trimming them and cutting points with shears.* TSIPENYU, *one foot up on a little stool, is binding up the sole of her shoe with a little strip of rag.*

PESENYU. Tsipenyu, may you be healthy, what are you sewing?

TSIPENYU. Almost done, Aunt Pese. I'm tying on the sole of my shoe with a little piece of rag. When I walk, the snow keeps slipping in and shooting back out. You know what they say: if God wills, even a boot can shoot. Now, what should I tell them?

PESENYU. Say Reb Khatskl, Dobe, and Motele should all come right over, we're having a party. Oy, my teeth!

TSIPENYU. I'll say we're giving a grand ball.

LEYZER. She laughs! One cheerful pauper is better than two gloomy rich men.

PESENYU. Let it be a ball. Say first of all today is the fifth candle of Hanu-ka. This is the day fine people eat potato pancakes. Of course we don't have any goose fat and no fine flour. So we'll make our own kind of feast: chopped herring and . . . oy, my teeth.

TSIPENYU. I can make rhymes like grandfather: A holiday feast / For King David, at least. / Salty fish / Potatoes in a dish. (*Ties up her head in an old warm shawl.*)

LEYZER. Toothache / And honey cake. / Oy, Tsipi mine, / You ruin my rhyme. Sh. Come here, I have to tell you a secret. (*Speaks into her ear.*) Tell them . . . sh! . . . There's a whole bottle of raisin wine.

TSIPENYU. (*Winks at him and laughs.*) Ah! "Drank his liquor / Quicker and quicker"?

PESENYU. And besides, today—in a lucky hour—your uncle is finishing the Torah scroll he's been copying for the last six months. Tell them Uncle said that they should come celebrate for the Torah's sake. (*Takes off her bathrobe and throws it over* TSIPENYU.)

TSIPENYU. A perfect fit. I'm on my way. (*Off.*)

PESENYU. My teeth! I feel like clawing at the walls. Freydenyu, what are you doing over there? Don't you know that it's forbidden to work by the light of Hanuka candles? Father-in-law dear, it's a great sin.

LEYZER. (*In Talmud-study tune.*) Don't be afraid, it's no sin, it's feathers for quills for copying a Torah.

FREYDENYU. Yes, Aunt Pese, it's holy work. You ask Uncle. It's a good deed, really. God's Torah and God's work are one and the same.

PESENYU. Such bitter cold. Tsipenyu could catch cold, God forbid. I know I caught cold in my teeth because the draft blows in the window there. God in Heaven, let him get a commission for copying. We need money so badly. Tsipenyu is altogether ragged. Neither of you has anything to wear. You're a young woman already, no evil eye. We ought to be making you a new dress and . . . and . . . I don't know, maybe soon—in a lucky hour—you'll be a bride.

LEYZER. (*Says into her ear.*) That rascal Motele has outgrown his baby clothes.

FREYDENYU. I won't pretend. I understand. Reb Khatskl wants a match between me and his son Motele. I would rather not take such a heavy yoke on my shoulders. But if Uncle says I should marry, of course I will obey. Only, clothing is silly. I mean, it's a very great sin for Jewish girls to get so many dresses when they marry. Expensive beautiful clothes are unnecessary. You need warm clothes because of the cold, but if you're ugly, pretty clothes won't help.

PESENYU. You're right. It was the Evil Impulse who created pretty clothes.

LEYZER. They say that the first elegant tailor was the Evil One himself.

PESENYU. Father-in-law dear, why do you need to mention him in the house, and at night besides? Help, my teeth! An old man who doesn't know any remedy for toothache! Maybe you don't care.

FREYDENYU. Auntie, rhymes can't magic away a toothache. Quite the opposite, I think: rhymes can give you a toothache. And grandfather's rhymes in particular!

LEYZER. Sh! A secret. I do have a good remedy. You say I don't care. Now you'll see. (*Goes to the corner and takes the broom.*) You, dear daughter, take the broom. Lay it with one end on the threshold. Put your left hand in front of the swollen cheek. What are you looking at? Do what I tell you. (*She does everything he says.*) Now step over the broom three times back and forth, and every time spit and say, "Tfoo, I don't care. Tfoo, I don't care. Tfoo, I don't care."

PESENYU. (*Jumps over the broom.*) Tfoo, I don't care. Tfoo, I don't care. Tfoo, I don't care.

LEYZER. Well, if you don't care, silly, why should I?

FREYDENYU. Once a wedding jester, always a wedding jester, perhaps, Grandfather.

LEYZER. Yes, Freydenyu, a jester is always a clown, / A beggar always goes round the town, / And even when she's dead, a girl likes a pretty new gown. (*A noise.* FREYDENYU *leaves the shears lying open in a conspicuous spot on the table.*)

PESENYU. Sh! Who's there?

TSIPENYU. (*Runs in, frozen.*) They're on their way. (*She dances with cold.*) So cold! Grandpa, I told them your secret: "Rhyme, shmyme, / Just have a good time." Ooh, the frost has pinched my ears and my nose. (PESENYU *helps her take her things off.*) Oh, what I heard at Reb Khatskl's! Aunt Pese, is it really true? Dobe told me that maybe today Freydenyu and Motele may . . . Oh, oh, naughty girl! Bad girl! (*She throws herself onto* FREYDENYU *with kisses.*)—may celebrate? (*Kisses.*) An engagement party? An engagement party?

FREYDENYU. Oh, let go of me. Anyway, what's this celebration to you?

TSIPENYU. I'm going to be an in-law. I'll dance, I'll eat honey cake, I'll show off the way in-laws do.

LEYZER. With, it may be, / Some rhyming from me. (*Traditional tune.*) Weep, lovely bride, cry all you women—(*A noise.*) Somebody is coming. (*He gets scared, sits down, and stays quiet.*)

PESENYU. It's our people. (*She opens the door.*) Come in, come in. Guests! Welcome! (*Enter* KHATSKL, DOBE, *and* MOTELE, *all dressed warmly.*)

ALL. Good evening, good evening. (*They undress.*)

DOBE. (*She looks around intently.*) How are you, Freydenyu? (*She kisses her.*) No evil eye, no evil eye (*spits three times*), you shine like a wholesome loaf just out of the oven. (*Looks.*) God be with you, who left the shears open? You don't dare leave shears open, God forbid. (*She closes the shears.*)

PESENYU. Sit, sit, Reb Khatskl, sit. Dobe's waiting to be asked. (*All sit down.*)

TSIPENYU. *Sit, Motele. (She gives him a chair.)* He's embarrassed, the rascal. *(He sits.)*

MOTELE. If you say I'm embarrassed, I'll get even more embarrassed. Better be quiet.

KHATSKL. How are you, Reb Leyzer? How is business? Your merchant ships at sea haven't sunk? Your warehouses haven't burned down? Your affairs aren't ruined?

LEYZER. *(Quietly.)* God forbid, Reb Khatskl, nothing of mine has sunk and nothing is destroyed.

KHATSKL. And where is our Reb Hershele Dubrovner, our fine piece of piety, our great scholar, our silken Jew? *(He looks around.)* As long as he's not here, I'll smoke a pipe. *(Smokes.)* Doesn't smoke, doesn't eat well, doesn't drink—not flesh and blood, almost. Well, where is he?

LEYZER. You know yourself that every time a Torah scribe comes to the name of God, he goes first to the ritual bath. *(He lifts the ark cover off the table.)* You see, he's on the last verse. He is about to write the last "God," so he has gone to immerse himself.

KHATSKL. Immerse himself in cold like this! That must be refreshing. Reb Leyzer, I believe there are not many pious Jews like your Hershele around nowadays. *(They talk quietly.* DOBE *and* PESENYU *chat quietly.)*

TSIPENYU. Motele, why are you quiet? Say something.

MOTELE. I don't know what to say. I'm not a good talker.

FREYDENYU. Why do you think it's necessary to talk? Sometimes it's a lot easier when people are quiet. I think that people often tell lies and say silly things because they want to talk when they haven't got anything to say.

TSIPENYU. Oh, do you mean me?

FREYDENYU. When a person has something to say, he should say it, and if not he should keep quiet.

TSIPENYU. With me, he did have something to say, but he's afraid of you.

MOTELE. Why am I afraid? Freyde isn't a bear, and I'm not a coward.

DOBE. *(To* PESE.*)* You've got a toothache again. *(Holds her own mouth, recites magic charm.)* Good stay, evil away! Do exactly what I tell you: take a piece of paper, very thin; take a fork; prick out a star with six points, and—

KHATSKL. *(He looks at the wall.)* And that's our Hershele's fiddle? Does he still play once in a while?

FREYDENYU. Ah, very seldom, Reb Khatskl. Sometimes at night after Sabbath or on a holiday.

TSIPENYU. Ah, you reminded her! When Uncle plays, she quivers.

FREYDENYU. Yes, when Uncle plays, it seems to me it lights up the house. Everything changes when the violin speaks and weeps. It seems to me the violin is telling the story of what the Jews have suffered in exile, and how life will be someday, someday, when the Messiah comes.

PESENYU. She dies over the violin. She won't eat, won't drink, won't sleep, just play for her.

TSIPENYU. You know, she sings Uncle's Psalm of David just exactly the way the fiddle plays it.

KHATSKL. Yes, God blessed him with all the gifts. We grew up together, we were friends as schoolboys—and here I ended up nothing more than a workingman, a weaver, and he is a scholar, a refined person. You'd have expected the opposite. My father was the best Talmud teacher in Dubrovne, and his father—

LEYZER. His father was and still is Leyzer the Jester. Yes, well, I wanted to make a musician out of him, but he ended up copying Torah scrolls, of all things. It happens. Sit and patch a shoe / Is the best the old man can do, / But the sons—What a shock! — / They seem to come from finer stock.

PESENYU. Father-in-law dear.

LEYZER. Eh, I ... I ... Reb Khatskl, sh! (*Speaks into* KHATSKL'*s ear.*) She ... she sings the Psalm of David exactly the way he plays it.

KHATSKL. Maybe, Freydenyu, before Uncle comes, you would sing to us a little? Today is Hanuka, why shouldn't we enjoy ourselves? What do you say, Motl the Bandit?

MOTELE. I say that anybody can play. You take and you play. (*He sneezes.*)

DOBE. For a good year! Motele, pull your ear.

FREYDENU. No, Reb Khatskl, I can't. Uncle says that a woman mustn't sing when there are men in the house.

KHATSKL. A woman? You are a woman? Do I know? A girl, a child, a— Never mind, you can sing, that's how I interpret the law.

PESENYU. Sing, why not? Hershele won't be home for a while yet.

MOTELE. I wouldn't ever wait to be begged.

ALL. Sing. Sing.

KHATSKL. I am a plain man. But according to my common sense, singing is never a sin. Let her sing. Well, Freydenyu, let's hear. (*He sings to get her started.*) *Mizmor le-Dovid,* the Psalm of David, "The Lord is my shepherd."

FREYDENU. (*Begins bashfully.*) *Mizmor le-Dovid* ... I can't.

TSIPENYU. Just look how she holds back.

ALL. Come on, sing. Sing.

FREYDENYU. (*She sings.*) *Mizmor le-Dovid: Adoshem ro-i, lo ekhsor . . .* (*All listen attentively. At the end, the men join in.*)

TSIPENYU. Help! Here comes Uncle! (*All move.* HERSHELE *comes in wearing an old fur coat.* KHATSKL *goes to him.* HERSHELE *gestures with head and hands for no one to speak to him. He washes his hands, sits down at the table, kisses the Torah and writes.*)

PESENYU. Sh! The last verse. (*All remain silent.* HERSHELE *writes.*)

LEYZER. (*In* KHATSKL*'s ear.*) You know? Sh. He's writing the last verse.

HERSHELE. (*He pulls himself together joyfully.*) Praise God, great and mighty! *Khazak!*

HATSKL and LEYZER. (*Sing.*) *Khazak, khazak, veniskhazek!* (*All hum along.*)

HERSHELE. Good evening, all. Reb Khatskl, how are you? (*He gives a hand to him and to* MOTL.) When we all see each other in good health, we ought to thank and praise God, bless his name. Children, I want to give you your Hanuka coins. We have no smaller children, so they are our little ones. For you, Freydenyu, five kopecks, and for you, Tsipenyu, three kopecks. And Motele, don't worry, for you (*searches his pockets*)—on my word, I don't have one groschen more.

PESENYU. Hershenyu, dear, you just had a gilder.

HERSHELE. Coming from the bathhouse I met . . . poor thing, let's not discuss it . . . I don't have a penny left. Motele will forgive me.

KHATSKL. Do you think, Reb Hershele, that Motele considers a kopeck a coin? He weaves a prayer shawl like nobody's business. He already earns from eight to twelve rubles a month.

DOBE. No evil eye. Good stay, evil away. (*She spits three times.*)

MOTELE. I knew that here you think of the girls as little children, so I brought a Hanuka top. You see, a whole machine. (*He shows a big top.*)

TSIPENYU. Ooh, let's really play. Trr! (*She spins the top.*) *Nun, giml, hey, shin.* I know all the Hebrew words. *Nun* for *nes, giml* for *godol, hey* for *hoyo, shin* for *shom*—that makes *Nes godol hoyo shom,* "A great miracle happened there." *Nun* doesn't win, *shin* doesn't win, *hey* wins, *giml* wins. Well, don't I remember?

HERSHELE. Yes, children, a great miracle happened there. And it is only through miracles and wonders that we live in the world. Praised is God and praised is his name.

DOBE. They say that when Hanuka lights are burning in Jewish houses, all the evil spirits hide in Gentile houses.

TSIPENYU. Freydenyu, sit closer. Reb Motl, got any kopecks? We're going to play.

MOTELE. I've got big money on me: two five-kopeck pieces and a ten.

FREYDENYU. I'm not going to play. I like to listen to Uncle talk.

HERSHELE. Play, children, be happy. Today is a holiday for us all, but for you children, today may be, God willing, a holiday of holidays.

KHATSKL. That rascal Motl pretends not to hear.

HERSHELE. I only regret that Pesenyu can't celebrate together with the rest of us. Poor thing, she has a toothache. Maybe you should ask an expert?

DOBE. Yoshe Moyshe the teacher is a very great expert. For two kopecks he writes "toothache" on an egg and "fever" on three almonds.

HERSHELE. Excuse me, Pesenyu, you take care of the guests, while I talk things over with Reb Khatskl. (*They go to the side and talk.*) Father, forgive me, would you be so kind as to come over here. Reb Khatskl, I think it is disrespectful for us to be telling secrets here without him. It's just not proper when an older man is in the house. (LEYZER *goes to them.*)

KHATSKL. "Honor your father" is very important, of course. But I'm a plain plate of kasha, and according to my common sense, a good deed is good when you don't oversalt it.

TSIPENYU. Freydenyu, you know what they're talking about? You bad girl! Even my pulse is knocking. Motl, put a kopeck in the can. (*They play.*)

MOTELE. I'm going to win it all from you.

FREYDENYU. Yes, I never win. I always lose. (PESENYU *puts a decanter of wine and glasses on the table.*)

PESENYU. Would the men like to make a blessing in the meantime?

DOBE. (*She looks at the glasses.*) God help you, how can you have put out a chipped glass on the table? If you drink from a glass with a chip, God forbid, the evil spirit—not to be thought of, not to be thought of in any Jewish house—can take control.

PESENYU. What are you saying? And I didn't know! (*She takes the glass off.*) Well, everybody? Hershele, maybe for Hanuka?

HERSHELE. Yes, yes, they will take a little bit of wine. To Father's health, and yours, Reb Khatskl. Don't worry about me. I am strict with myself. It is not, God forbid, that I want to seem finer than other people. It is just that I believe that so long as a Jew is in exile, he should drink only to welcome the Sabbath and when Sabbath ends. What do you say, Reb Khatskl, maybe I am oversalting a little, but that's not such a bad fault. Excuse me, Father. (*He leads him to the table.*)

KHATSKL. I'm a plain man, but to my way of thinking, when a Jew finally manages some kind of celebration, why shouldn't he take a swallow and forget the sorrows of exile for a while? Why should the Gentile have everything his own way? A Jew shouldn't get drunk, God forbid. But once in a while to take a little and cheer the pauper up—why not?

LEYZER. (*He pours himself a glass of wine, becomes lively.*) "And off he toddled / With his bottle. / Drank his liquor / Quicker and quicker." (*Looks at his son and gets scared.*) I mean, to life! God should send us good luck. (*He makes the blessing and drinks thirstily.*)

KHATSKL. (*He takes a glass.*) We've been together since childhood, my dear friend, and now with God's help, maybe we'll be family too. To life. (*He drinks.*) What do you say, Reb Hershele, will you have a drink?

HERSHELE. Me? Today Freydenyu may perhaps, with God's help, become a- an in-law. For her sake- I mean, for the sake of all of you, I will play a little bit. (*He goes to take the fiddle.*)

FREYDENYU. (*She runs to the violin.*) Oh, Uncle is going to play! Uncle is going to play! (*She takes the violin from the wall.*) Uncle is so kind. My hands are actually trembling. Aunt Pese, haven't I gotten positively red? (*She takes the violin out of the sack delicately.*) Usually, everything here is plain, not like Sabbath, just weekday, but when Uncle plays, it's exactly as if something comes from another world. I'm afraid that Uncle will laugh at me, but I believe that the way that the first violin came to mankind was that an angel lost it and it fell down from heaven. (*She gives* HERSHELE *the violin.*)

HERSHELE. Yes, Freydenyu, everything comes from heaven. God gives a person sorrows and gives him a way to comfort himself. He gives us a voice for praising our Lord and for singing about happiness. He allows musicians to praise the creator of the universe and to have pleasure themselves. (LEYZER *finds a time when his son isn't looking and drinks another glass.* HERSHELE *tunes the violin, rosins the bow, speaking reflectively.*) A pretty prayer, the Psalm of David. *Adoshem ro-i. Mo ekhsor?* "Since God is my shepherd, what more do I need? On green grass, by quiet waters, he will let me rest, he will lead me along the paths of righteousness, refreshing my soul." *Gam ki eylekh be-gey tsalmoves,*

"Even walking into Satan's valley of death, I am not afraid."

DOBE. Not to be thought of, not to be mentioned in the nighttime.

HERSHELE. (*Reflective.*) I am not afraid, because he, my God, is with me. Yes, he, my God, is with me. (*Plays. All listen attentively, especially* FREYDENYU. *Somebody knocks on the window.*)

PESENYU. Sh! I think someone's knocking. (*All listen. A voice is heard.*)

DOBE. Oy, I think I hear a dog howling. We should have turned over the sole of a shoe.

TSIPENYU. The sole of my shoe is tied on with a rag. (*She runs to door.*) Who's there? (MISCHIEF *enters, wearing a handsome fur coat and European clothes.*)

MISCHIEF. Excuse me. Is this a Jewish home?

TSIPENYU. You can see for yourself we aren't Turks. Come in and shut the door, if you don't mind.

MISCHIEF. (*He stumbles on threshold.*) The black year! I almost fell.

DOBE. Ay, not to be thought of! Not to be thought of in anyone's home!

PESENYU. Sir, in our home we do not mention such things. We don't hear any curses here—no cursing, God forbid.

MISCHIEF. Excuse me. Good evening. First of all I'm going to tell you without preface who I am and what I'm doing here. I come from Warsaw. I deal in lottery tickets.

ALL. What's that?

MISCHIEF. Prize tickets. You pick a number and you win money. With a ticket like this it's very easy to get rich. It's Hanuka time now, so I've come for a few days to you Jews in Dubrovne. I know that every night there are people sitting together in every Jewish home, so I come in and show my tickets. I have tickets from Brunschweig, Leipzig, Warsaw. (*He takes tickets out of his pocket.*) You understand? You can win fifty thousand at one time, and all of a sudden you become a rich man.

PESENYU. How much? Oh, my teeth!

MISCHIEF. Fifty thousand rubles.

PESENYU. You hear, Hershele?

DOBE. You hear, Khatskl?

HERSHELE. I am very sorry that you took the trouble for nothing. But since you are already here, warm yourself. We don't drive anyone from the house, God forbid. (*He gives his hand.*) Sit down. What's your name?

MISCHIEF. My name is Uriel Mischief.

DOBE. Mischief, no less? Not to be thought of.

TSIPENYU. (*Quietly.*) Motl, have you ever heard such a name? (*She pinches him.*) Mischief! (*They play and laugh.*)

KHATSKL. Trading in what might happen some day. To my way of thinking, if you're selling something, show me the plain merchandise on the shelf.

MISCHIEF. (*He shows a lottery ticket.*) Here is the merchandise. It's a little piece of paper? Paper money is no merchandise either. But it's riches all the same. In the biggest banking businesses, on the exchanges, there's no merchandise to see there either, but millions pass from one hand to the other only by means of little pieces of paper. True, this ticket isn't money, but imagine: for a few rubles you buy the possibility of winning the big prize and thousands of possibilities of at least winning back the amount it cost you to play. I leave you a ticket like this, and I don't take a single groschen now. You hear? For no money at all you get in your pocket the hope of becoming a rich man, soon. Instead of living in a narrow, dark, cold house with broken windows and broken chairs, you'd live in a beautiful, warm, light apartment with big rooms, with beautiful furniture, with shelves full of fancy foods. Just the hope of that is worth something. You know that without such a ticket, you have no hope at all of escaping a pauper's life.

HERSHELE. Dear friend, I draw all my hope from my Father in Heaven, and what I win from him, that is my prize. What he gives me, that is what I am happy with. Why base hopes on a paper ticket, when I have a good, all-powerful Father in Heaven?

MISCHIEF. What do you mean, "he gives you"? Try it. Do nothing and count on his throwing you food down from heaven. Won't you die from hunger? (LEYZER *drinks furtively.*) Don't you see that in this world, he who waits to be given doesn't get? Only the one who has sense and takes for himself? Our good, all-powerful Father in Heaven gives you sense so you can live like a human being, but if you insist on living like an animal, be my guest. What do you mean, you draw all your hope from him? What do you think, a miracle will happen for your sake? Take a look, the young people are playing. (*He takes the top.*) *Nun, giml, hey, shin:* "A great miracle happened there." The *nun,* which means the *nes,* the miracle, doesn't win. The *shin,* which means *shom,* there, doesn't win either. What does win? *Giml* for *godol:* great, clever, talented. What else wins? The *hey.* That means *hoyo:* what took place, the fact, the truth. A miracle doesn't win, no. What's over there, I don't know where, what nobody sees and nobody grasps, that doesn't win. Ah, you're no Jew.

HERSHELE. God help you! What do you mean, I'm no Jew, God forbid?

MISCHIEF. A figure of speech. I mean, don't be stubborn. Take the ticket. I guarantee you, you'll win fifty thousand. You hear? Without labor, without suffering, without any bother at all—fifty thousand rubles!

HERSHELE. Let me alone, I beg you. What do you mean, I will win fifty thousand? Who will I win it from? Who will give me fifty thousand for free? If I am lucky and win, then there will have to be unlucky ones who will lose this fifty thousand, God forbid. I won't do it. (*He remains thoughtful.*)

LEYZER. Whenever a beggar knocks, / The rich man drops coins in his box. / For charity a tenner, / And then he eats his dinner. (*He gets scared.*) I . . . I want to say, Hershele, that the money you win is paid by the treasury. What do you care? Let them pay. (*He goes to* MISCHIEF.) Sh! Excuse me, I wanted to ask you (*in his ear*), what time is it? (*He sits down.*)

HERSHELE. And besides everything else, what do I need such a fortune for? I don't even want to know what one would do with it.

KHATSKL. Now, Reb Hershele, forgive me, you're talking like too much of an innocent. When you have gotten the prize, you'll know what to do with it. Take me: I am a weaver, my Motl is a weaver, we weave kosher prayer shawls, and it earns us a kick in the pants. Who profits? Not the weaver. With our callused hands, we pull the hot knishes from the oven, and who swallows them? A parasite. Why? Because we are too poor.

DOBE. Khatskl, don't talk like that. (*Reciting charm.*) Good stay, evil away.

KHATSKL. But if you had money, Hershele, we would have our own looms in the house and we wouldn't have to work for the-black-year-knows-who.

DOBE. Not to be thought of, not to be thought of in any Jewish home

PESENYU. Hershele, a person with money can take care of himself. Is poverty with toothache really so sweet?

TSIPENYU. You could start by buying us warm clothes. My shoes wouldn't be tied together with a rag, and you could give Freydenu a dowry and make her nice wedding clothes.

MOTELE. If the Jew would give me fifty thousand, I would take it right away without questions.

DOBE. Reb Hershele, maybe the Jew has a light hand? Luck comes only through a light hand.

FREYDENYU. I don't need any pretty clothes. Uncle and all of us have always been happy without money, and lucky too.

MISCHIEF. He was not lucky and not happy, he just didn't know any better. None of the unlucky people who live in poverty would be such terrible paupers if they knew what they lacked. If they demanded better, they would have it better. Admit it: why should you suffer hunger, cold, want? Why should your children go barefoot and naked when you can win fifty thousand and live well? What am I talking about, fifty thousand? You must understand, money runs to money. Once you have fifty thousand, the thousands grow and grow. Reb Hershele, if you don't want anything good for yourself, have pity on the children. They are just beginning to live in the world.

PESENYU. Isn't he right, after all?

MISCHIEF. You have only daughters?

DOBE. No children at all, not to be thought of for any Jewish woman.

PESENYU. (*Friendly.*) It was not God's will to give us any children. These are nieces. My sister died when Tsipenyu was born. Freydenyu was two years old. She was just a little bit of a thing like that. So I raised them.

MISCHIEF. Take, take a ticket. I'm not asking a single groschen for it now. You are not doing anyone any harm. Searching for ways to get free of poverty is no sin. (*He gives* HERSHELE *the ticket forcibly.*) You won't find fifty thousand just lying in the street. Fifty thousand!

PESENYU. How will we know if we won the fifty thousand?

MISCHIEF. Don't worry, I'll be sure to let you know. I keep watch. I get a percent of it.

PESENYU. So you take some? In other words, there's already not a whole fifty thousand left for us.

MISCHIEF. No, God forbid, I don't take from your share. You get fifty thousand to the last groschen.

HERSHELE. Excuse me, Sir, you have totally confused me. What does this mean? Oh, God and Father, what should I do? (*He holds the ticket and doesn't know what to do.*)

KHATSKL. Reb Hershele, excuse me, I'm a plain man, but I must say, the man is right. What does it mean, you ask God what you should do? Do you believe he really cares whether you take a ticket or not? To my way of thinking, God is God—with God's help—and a man must be a man. If you want to take a ticket, you take it. No? You don't take it. But you don't need to mix him in such things.

HERSHELE. I tell you what. If I do win, God forbid, I will know that God in heaven has paid me in advance for all the Torahs I will copy till I die. I will be able to sit peacefully all my days and copy Torahs for poor communities, for soldiers' prayer groups, for schools and little synagogues.

MISCHIEF. Time enough for that once you've won the prize.

HERSHELE. (*He considers the ticket.*) Who could believe it that a man can become rich through a little piece of paper? Ah! Ah! "Dear Father in Heaven, how great are your wonders." *Mi-khomoykho bo-eylim, hashem?* "Who is like you?" *Mi-khomoykho nedor ba-koydesh, noyro tehiloys, oyse feleh?*

PESENYU. Hershele, if we had enough money, maybe I could travel to a good doctor, and maybe still, please God, be blessed with a son.

DOBE. Pese, may you be healthy, I just heard a way to children. (*Quietly.* MISCHIEF *hears.*) You take a dry old willow twig left in synagogue from last Sukkos, you steep it like tea, and you drink it nine times.

LEYZER. (*He looks around and drinks.*) You drink nine times, remember that.

MISCHIEF. (*He opens his wallet, and a golden imperial falls out. He goes aside and writes something. Meanwhile he speaks.*) Reb Hershele, there is a better way to get children.

TSIPENYU. Uncle dear, show me the pretty ticket. (*She shows* MOTELE.) See, Motele.

FREYDENYU. What is there to see? (TSIPENYU *pulls the ticket away from* MOTELE *and tears it.*)

HERSHELE. (*Beside himself.*) You tore it? The devil should . . . Oh, my God, don't punish me for those words. Look what I almost said.

MISCHIEF. No harm done, it's all right if it's a little bit torn. I was saying, Reb Hersh, there is a better way to children. A righteous Jew should not live more than ten years with a barren woman as his wife. Divorce your old woman and take your pretty young niece. (*He indicates* FREYDENYU.)

FREYDENYU. Oh, God help you, what are you talking about? Oh, no, what are you saying? (*She covers her face with her hands.*)

PESENYU. What? (HERSHELE *takes a look at her and turns away.* PESENYU *wants to say something angry, but notices the imperial and steps on it with her foot and remains standing there, confused.*)

MISCHIEF. I'm joking. A good night. It's only a joke. (*He puts on his fur coat.*)

DOBE. Khatskl, he's leaving. Maybe you should take a ticket too? Why do they deserve fifty thousand and not us? Ah. You see, something itches my right eye, a sure sign we'll have troubles. (*She scratches her left eye.*)

KHATSKL. Dobe, you don't begrudge it to him? Let him win. What's his, what's mine, it's all the same. You won't have any troubles. It's your left eye that itches you.

DOBE. It's the left? But that's a certain sign of a celebration.

LEYZER. (*Drunk.*) "So off he toddled / With his bottle. / Drank his liquor / Quicker and quicker." Freydenyu, he says you're the better way. You see, Hershele, you've won something already. "So off he toddled / With his bottle . . ."

HERSHELE. Father dear, would you be so kind as to go aside by yourself, I beg you.

LEYZER. No! No! (*Sings.*) "So off he toddled / With his . . ."

HERSHELE. Excuse me, Father, I don't want to dishonor you, God forbid. The opposite: you shouldn't suffer any shame, God forbid. (*He picks him up and carries him off.*)

LEYZER. (*He kicks with his feet and yells.*) No! No! Let go of me. "So off he toddled / With his-"

MISCHIEF. I sold them a lottery ticket faster than I expected. It's a serious business to win a big prize and get rich just like that. Good night, all. (*Exit.*)

Curtain

৵ৠৣ

Act II

HERSHELE*'s rich new living room.* LEYZER *sits and makes a little mouse by folding his big red hanky.* TSIPENYU *stands at the mirror braiding her hair.* HERSHELE*'s violin lies in its case on a table.*

LEYZER. (*He steals over to her.*) Peep! Did the mousie scare you? When you marry Motele, I'll make little mice for your little kitty-cats.

TSIPENYU. What do you mean, when I marry my sister's bridegroom?

LEYZER. Sh! (*He looks around, frightened.*) Nothing said, nothing heard. (*He sits in corner.*)

TSIPENYU. Grandpa, tell the truth. Are you glad that we're so fancy now? I feel just as if I was wearing Uncle's silk coat. It doesn't fit somehow. Honestly, when my shoes were tied up with rags, they squeaked better.

LEYZER. Kitten, it's only till you get used to it. Me, I feel fine here already because I was born to be a rich man. Silly child, is it so bad to eat pot roast with white bread and be able to take a little drop every so often? (*Sings.*) "So off he toddled / With his bottle—"

TSIPENYU. (*Joins in*) "Drank his liquor / Quicker and quicker." You know, people laugh at us. They call us the fresh-from-the-oven rich folks.

LEYZER. What do you think, stale rich folks taste better? I'll tell you the truth, I would be totally happy if . . . if . . . Come here, I'll tell you a secret. (*Speaks in her ear.*) Tsipenyu, it's different with me. Among nice people, a son has respect for his father, but I'm scared of Hershenyu.

TSIPENYU. What are you scared of, that he'll hit you?

LEYZER. I'm just scared, pure and simple. I gather up my courage like a hero, but I am afraid of him. In my mouth, I'm still a jester, but the truth is I'm a little man, and he crushes me with his learning, and his piety, and his goodness. When he's around, Leyzer the Jester becomes two feet smaller, Tsipenyu. And now since he has become rich, when he gives me a look, a tickle starts up in the back of my neck. It seems like money chills a person's eyes. I am a little man, child, but I can't find a place for myself here.

TSIPENYU. You're a little man and you love a little drop.

LEYZER. Yes, I am a little man now. But there was a time, once upon a time, long ago, when I was great and famous in my profession. When I arrived at a wedding, people used to point me out with a finger. All the women used to whisper, all the girls used to shriek with joy, "That's him! That's him!" And when I settled down to jesting, it used to get quiet like in synagogue during the silent prayer. My eyes used to spark up with fire, my heart began to fan and flutter, all the musicians were inspired, and the fiddle used to cry and speak at my command. The women used to cry like on the Day of Atonement. The bride poured bitter tears. Drunkards became holy. It was a good, sweet, lovely time.

TSIPENYU. Grandpa dear, why are you upset? If you want, let's make a wedding right here. Imagine that I'm a bride. Here, I'll seat the bride and veil her without a groom. (*She sits and covers her own head with a shawl.*) I like this game.

LEYZER. You want to hear? Well, then. The fiddle goes Te De De Dum. (*He sings the tune for veiling the bride and then stands on a chair. He uses the special sing-song tune for jesters' couplets addressing a bride.*) Ah, weep, little bride, pour out your tears. / Now bid farewell to all your happy childhood years.

TSIPENYU. Oy, oy, oy! (*She pretends to sob and wipe tears.*)

LEYZER. Your days of freedom are no more. / Already you swim towards an alien shore. No longer will you laugh and sing all day. / The chains of womanhood—how heavily they weigh. / (TSIPENYU *listens in earnest.*) Your lovely youth is coming to an end, / No Mama with you now, no Papa, and no friend. / Your heart, dear bride, will fill with bitter sorrow. / Come, weep a tear today for every sad tomorrow. / (TSIPENYU *is really weeping now.*) They pluck you from your childhood like a flower. / Oy, your life will fade and wither in an hour.

TSIPENYU. Honestly, it really does make a person gloomy. (*She weeps.*)

LEYZER. With aching heart you set out on the road of life. / You'll bear the burdens soon of mother and of wife. / (PESENYU *enters, richly dressed.*) And when, dear bride, you weep your bitter tears . . .

PESENYU. Ah, Father-in-law dear, the things you think of! (LEYZER *gets scared and sits in a corner.*) Look at that, Father-in-law makes jokes, and she cries. (*She dries* TSIPENYU*'s tears.*) Silly child. We have nothing else to do: either we sleep or we cry. The truth is, since we won the big prize, I don't know what to do with myself. And Hershele has become like a stranger, too, somehow. Always preoccupied, worried. Somehow, in poverty people are closer to each other.

TSIPENYU. Are you sorry Aunt Pese?

PESENYU. Sorry? God forbid. Thank God, every day we put on the samovar, it's warm in here, we have something to wear. But I thought it would be better.

TSIPENYU. Maybe it's not that winning the prize was bad, but that together with the prize we won Mischief. That ruins the whole stew.

PESENYU. Silly, he is a partner, after all. Hershele in business by himself is like a blind man.

LEYZER. If Hershele could make mischief without Mischief, we could mischief Mischief out of here. (*Noise offstage.*) Sh! They're coming. (*He gets frightened and sits.*) Leyzer, hide the jester.

HERSHELE. (*Wearing beautiful silk coat. Deep in conversation with* MISCHIEF.) Where did you learn all these things?

MISCHIEF. I have read all the philosophy books that there are in Hebrew.

HERSHELE. What does it mean that there is no *oynesh,* no punishment? Should everyone do as he pleases? People would sin like wild beasts. They would tear and trample each other underfoot. Man without limits is a creature of thievery and murder.

MISCHIEF. Well, I think that it would be better for us to say to God: I don't want your *oynesh,* and I don't need your reward. Don't punish me and don't reward me, and let's be quits.

HERSHELE. If there is no reward and no punishment, what does man have to live for? Our joy is struggling against what we must not do, and our happiness is doing what is good and holy. Without that, a man is no man.

LEYZER. (*Unexpectedly.*) Reb Uriel, excuse me. (*He calls* MISCHIEF *over to him.*) Sh! I wanted to ask you what time it is.

MISCHIEF. Reb Hershele Dubrovner's father shouldn't act so foolish.

HERSHELE. Father, don't be offended. Why not sit by yourself? You have your own room now. (LEYZER *gives a look as if he wants to say something, becomes frightened and goes out noisily.*) Yes, our Blessed God created evil so that man could do good.

MISCHIEF. If it wasn't man that created evil, why should man be punished for it? (*He takes out cigars, smokes.*) Smoke a cigar, Reb Hersh. These are very good cigars.

HERSHELE. A cigar is only smoke. Reb Uriel, God created good and evil and gave man free will. Man's will is absolutely free. (MISCHIEF *looks at him a long time.*)

TSIPENYU. Do you understand what they're talking about? It sounds like magic spells to me. Let's go to grandpa instead. He crept away looking beaten, poor thing. (*Exit.*)

MISCHIEF. You say that a man has free will? Try the cigar, I'm telling you it's a remarkable cigar.

HERSHELE. Well, all right, I'll try. (*Smokes.*)

MISCHIEF. Free will, you say? How free can it be if the will is blocked? When what you want you must deny yourself; what pleases you is not allowed; what you long for is forbidden by laws, quotations, customs, false opinions, foolish habits? No. As soon as it's a matter of "one should" or "one shouldn't," the will is crippled. However, we are getting too deeply into philosophy. We need to talk business.

HERSHELE. Pesi, forgive me, we have to talk. (*He gestures that she should leave.*)

PESENYU. Once upon a time, when you used to copy Torahs, I used to be able to sit and darn a sock, and watch you and enjoy you. But nowadays? Well, that's how it is. (*Off.*)

HERSHELE. Oh, she reminded me. I keep meaning to begin to copy a Torah scroll that I promised to donate, but I can never find the time.

MISCHIEF. You'll find time later, probably. Reb Hersh, I want to talk to you about a very important matter. I have a plan.

HERSHELE. Oh, business plans. I'm afraid of those. Not for nothing did the wise men say that commerce is robbery. (*He coughs from the cigar and throws it away.*) Feh!

MISCHIEF. Once upon a time maybe commerce was robbery. Today it is free competition. You're not taking anything away from anyone by violence. You want to risk your money and undertake something? Do it. Someone else wants to do the same thing? No one prevents him. If you're smart, you'll earn. If you're not smart, you'll break your head. Listen, I think we should stop loaning money for interest. First of all, it's against Jewish law. True, with the money we always give a receipt that says that the percentage that we take isn't really exactly interest. But why bother fooling God with legal fictions? Not that I mind that so much: if God lets himself be fooled, then the more fool God.

HERSHELE. Ah, Reb Uriel, be careful, God will pay you back with interest and without a receipt.

MISCHIEF. Second of all, in such a small town, our loans will never expand into a big banking operation. There are plenty of paupers who need loans. But paupers are better suited for use as labor.

HERSHELE. Reb Uriel, I know only one thing: whatever we do with the money, it is not like copying Torahs. When I copied a Torah, I knew it wouldn't make me a rich man, but I felt happy because I had done a holy work, godly labor, *melekhes elokim*. It seems that happiness lies not only in the thing we do but also in the purpose for which we do it. What is the purpose of wealth?

MISCHIEF. Oh, stop being a dreamer. Be a practical person with practical goals.

HERSHELE. But I don't know the purpose.

MISCHIEF. My dear friend, just tell me you'd like to be a pauper again, in a dark cold little house, barefoot and naked and eating bread and chickpeas.

HERSHELE. To tell the truth, no. But now that I am fed and clothed, why look for more? Can I eat five suppers and wear seven overcoats?

MISCHIEF. The richer you are, the freer and stronger and smarter you'll be. You'll have more honor, more pleasure. You'll be able to make yourself happy and your children after you. Yes. Yes. You can still have children; you're a young man, full of life and power.

HERSHELE. Children? Ah, don't talk about that, I beg you. That calls up frightening, sinful thoughts.

MISCHIEF. The man who has power isn't afraid of it. He achieves whatever he strives for. A weak man sins constantly in his thoughts. But the strong man gets it all over with at once. If it's a sin, he sinned one time. Is it better to sin a thousand times in thought or once in deed? Oh, don't be a hypocrite.

HERSHELE. That is true. After all, God already knows that I want to sin and that I sin in my thoughts. We are false and hidden only because we are afraid of people.

MISCHIEF. Reb Hershele, listen to my plan. It also has to do with a holy labor, a *melekhes elokim.* Millions of Jews need prayer shawls, *talesim.* Here in this town, the *talesim* are manufactured by small entrepreneurs or by the workers, the weavers, themselves. We'll open a *talis* factory right here with machines, steam, and everything. The small entrepreneurs will have to get out of our way, and the workers will be grateful to come work for us. Just count up what you accomplish: you're busy making godly merchandise, you give work to hundreds of poor people, you fill the entire town with commerce and livelihood. The righteous Jews will have your godly merchandise, cheap, and we'll make a profit.

HERSHELE. I like that. That is a good plan. Good and useful for everybody. Reb Uriel, you have a good head, and I think that God could not have sent me a better advisor. Yes, I like the plan. (*He sighs.*)

MISCHIEF. The plan pleases you; the advisor, thank God, pleases you too; and yet you are somehow so sad. Reb Hershele, you have sorrows. I feel you are carrying a hidden pain in your heart. (*Suddenly offstage the voice of* FREY-DENYU *singing the setting of the Psalm of David that* HERSHELE *played on the violin in Act I. They listen.*)

HERSHELE. Reb Uriel, you are an intelligent man. You are certainly not my enemy. For a long time I have wanted to get your advice. I am afraid to trust myself in such a serious matter. And . . . and . . . I will tell you the truth: if I often sin in my thoughts, if I carry a pain in my heart, it is your fault, too, a little bit.

MISCHIEF. Mine? God forbid!

HERSHELE. For a long time . . . The first evening that you were with us, on Hanuka . . . you said that . . . that Freydenyu . . . my wife's niece . . . that . . .

MISCHIEF. What could I have said about Freydenyu, God forbid? Did I say that she is as pretty as a rose in the month of May, radiant as the sun, that her two eyes are like luminous stars, her voice like the music of angels, her teeth mother-of-pearl, her lips like two red rubies, her throat carved from marble? Or what did I say?

HERSHELE. Both girls grew up in my home, but she was always dearer to me. With one word you uncovered a thought which was buried deep, which I had never been bold enough to think until then. Now I want to bury the thought again, but it stays so strong in my mind. I drive it away, but it won't let go. God in Heaven, I don't know what I should do.

MISCHIEF. God created much happiness and good fortune in human life. All man has to do is live. One lives in the world only once. Reb Hershenyu, time doesn't stand still. The years fly, joy passes.

HERSHELE. What are you saying? That is not Jewish talk, not Jewish thoughts. Let me go. (MISCHIEF *holds him.*) Let me go. You want to poison me with your sinful thoughts. You want to destroy my last spark of Jewishness. Let go!

MISCHIEF. Sh! What are you making such a fuss for? Do what you think best. I'm only saying that there are feelings which speak to Jews the same as to everyone else. In any case, if you're such a pious Jew, how can you live with a barren woman more than ten years? You know that that is considered the sin of Onan ben Yehuda, which may even deserve the death penalty. Besides, what is a person's life in this world without children? Why are you robbing yourself of the greatest happiness, the greatest consolation? Now you have the means to provide for your wife till death. She will be able to live better than she ever dreamed. You want my advice? Don't think, don't hang back: over and done with! Such things happen every day among us Jews. Gray old men divorce their old wives and take young girls. You are still a young man. Ah, you think too long about every foolish thing, that's why you have no will left for doing anything. (FREYDE'S *voice sings.*) Here she comes. Well, what do you know, I seem to have forgotten to lock the strongbox. (*He sings along.*) "Yea, though I walk through the valley of the shadow of death, I will fear no evil," (*ironically, to heaven*) . . . *ki oto imodi,* "for you are with me." (*Off.*)

HERSHELE. Wait, Reb Uriel. Stay here. To be alone with her right after that conversation, when my whole body is burning, and my head is mixed up . . . The way he talks, it seems like the right thing to do. According to law, also, I am right. Nevertheless, all the same, I still can't feel that it is decent and good.

Don't think so long, he says: over and done with. (*He sits down at the table where the fiddle lies.*) God in Heaven, I am afraid, I am afraid, I am afraid. (*He strikes his hands together and trembles so that the table trembles too.* FREYDE *enters.*)

FREYDENYU. Uncle, what is the matter? (*He covers his face.*) Do you feel sick, God forbid? (*She wants to take his hand, but he won't let her.*) What is it? Are you angry at me?

HERSHELE. Yes, I am angry, but not at you, God forbid. I am angry at myself. I am angry because lately I have gradually been changing into a different man. Freydenyu, I am afraid that I am no longer Hershele Dubrovner.

FREYDENYU. I see, I feel and understand that the man who is speaking to me now is Reb Hershele Dubrovner and no one else.

HERSHELE. Freydenyu, you are a clever girl, you're a good, pious child, and I know I can tell you the whole truth. Listen. I've been living with your aunt some twenty years and we have no children. We have no children. I have nothing against her, God forbid. She is a fine wife and has never, God forbid, caused me any heartache. But . . . you understand, a righteous Jew should not live with a wife who is barren. A Jew should marry just in order to have children. You're not supposed to marry except to have children. And besides, I want to have a child. One child at least. If I could have one son! Freydenyu, it seems that I will have to divorce Aunt Pese.

FREYDENYU. Poor Aunt Pese, it will break her heart.

HERSHELE. It is very hard on her, poor thing. It is. But she is a pious woman and will certainly accept what Jewish law commands. Listen, Freydenyu, I wanted to ask you . . . Ah . . . imagine that I have already divorced her and . . . and . . .

FREYDENYU. You don't have to say any more. I would be false if I pretended I didn't understand and didn't know what to say. I won't tell a lie, Uncle. There was a reason why it struck me like a thunderclap overhead when . . . that time, Hanuka, at the fifth candle . . . You remember, when Reb Uriel said . . . ? There is a reason why I tremble every time you look at me. But she is my second mother. May God punish me if I do anything bad to her, God forbid.

HERSHELE. Child, who would have the heart to do anything bad to her? If she won't accept a divorce of her own free will, I will not force her, God forbid. But . . . if yes . . . and . . . and . . . if she herself agrees that it shouldn't be someone else, not a stranger, to take her place here, will you . . . (*His whole body trembles.*) Will . . . Do you think . . . that . . . Ah, Freydenyu, how hard it is to talk about such things. (*Both are silent a long time.*) You don't speak?

FREYDENYU. Uncle, you know my answer.

HERSHELE. Freydenyu, don't forget, you are a young girl and I am forty two years old.

FREYDENYU. Next to you, a young man looks like a foolish child, a nothing. When you say something, it's exactly as if a prophet speaks, and whatever you do, it's what a great man does. Ah, Uncle, when you take your violin, and your eyes become inspired and a heavenly light lights up your face, exactly as if the heavenly presence rests on you, then . . . then . . . I believe that my heart, my soul, my life, none of it belongs any more to me, and I think how happy I would be if I could stay till I die in a house where you are. If I could stay at your feet. (*She sinks to his feet.* HERSHELE *looks at her, takes the violin and plays the Psalm of David. She looks at him and whispers the words. When she says, "Through the Valley of the Shadows of Death,"* MISCHIEF *enters silently and stands unnoticed. After playing, long pause.*) Uncle, I believe that I love you.

HERSHELE. But . . . if . . . God forbid . . . we're not, Freydenyu . . . are we sinning against God, blessed be he?

FREYDENYU. I don't know. Maybe. But I believe that I love you very much.

HERSHELE. Child, Freydenyu, maybe we should give up thinking about it . . . Maybe it is a misfortune?

FREYDENYU. I don't know. Uncle, all I can say is the truth: I love you.

HERSHELE. (*Beside himself.*) Help me, Lord of the world. If it is only a temptation from Satan, God forbid, help me. Don't abandon me, God. I have never in all my life felt the way I feel now. I am losing my mind, God forbid. I am forgetting . . . may it not happen! . . . I am forgetting that I am a Jew, that I am a human being, that there is a holy law, that there is a god over all.

MISCHIEF. Reb Hershele, I wanted to ask you . . . (FREYDENYU *awakes as if from sleep, stands up, and exits slowly.*)

HERSHELE. Yes, Reb Uriel, you are right. If a person wants to do something, he shouldn't think it over too much because the longer he thinks it over, the more he sins. (TSIPENYU *runs in and opens the middle door.*)

TSIPENYU. Only the musicians are missing, otherwise the whole wedding party is here. All the in-laws. Let's have a proper welcome for the groom's side! (PESE *appears.*)

PESENYU. (In doorway.) Come inside. Come in. Hershele is here.

KHATSKL, MOTELE, DOBE. Hello. Hello. (MISCHIEF *takes paper, sits to write.*)

PESENYU. Sit down. Sit down. It's such an occasion nowadays to see somebody in the house. Just a minute, I'll bring compote and honey cake and snacks right away. (*Off.*)

TSIPENYU. Look, Motele's got such a nice new silk coat. (*Whistles.*)

DOBE. You mustn't whistle in the house, you bad girl. Whistling calls the don't-even-think-about-its.

MOTELE. She's a don't-even-think-about-it herself.

KHATSKL. How are you, Reb Hershele? You look, God forbid, as if there's something you need.

MISCHIEF. (*He sits at the table and writes.*) Every man feels there's something he needs. Anyone who doesn't is not a man.

KHATSKL. Excuse me, maybe you have no time right now? I have come to you to talk about two things. Reb Hershele, we are two old good friends, and since God helped you and you have risen—

DOBE. No evil eye, no evil eye, and spite the no-good one. (*She spits.*)

KHATSKL. I've always figured that if you've got, it's exactly the same as if I've got. But since I didn't need, I haven't asked.

HERSHELE. You are right, Khatskl. Don't forget, though, that I have a partner. He has an opinion too. (MISCHIEF *goes to get more paper.* LEYZER *comes in silently, frightened, and looks around.*)

KHATSKL. I'm a plain plate of kasha, and I'll tell you: to my way of thinking, having Mischief as a partner with an opinion is not very "Halleluya praise the Lord."

LEYZER. What it is, is (*begins reciting psalm*) "Halleluya from the skies. Halleluya sun and moon, Halleluya shining stars, Halleluya heavens beyond heavens . . ." (*He glances at his son and gets scared.*) Reb Khatskl, a second. (KHATSKL *goes to him.*) Sh! I wanted to ask you: Is it a new moon this Sabbath? (*He sits in a corner.*)

KHATSKL. Oh, don't bother me now with the new moon. (HERSHELE *goes over to his father and quietly says something angry to him.*)

DOBE. Something itches in my nose. That's a sign that, god forbid, there's going to be a fight. (MISCHIEF *goes to* MOTELE.)

MISCHIEF. Motele, what is this? You're wearing an earring like an old lady?

MOTELE. Yes, I'm wearing an earring, but not like an old lady, like a young man. (TSIPENYU *laughs.*)

DOBE. Oy, long life to you, do you know what kind of an earring that is? Seven pieces of silver collected from seven couples who have seven fathers-in-law and seven mothers-in-law and seven parents. As long as he is wearing it, the Don't-think-about-it can't stand within four lengths of him.

MISCHIEF. (*He goes close and examines the earring.*) Remarkable. (*He sits back down in his place.*)

HERSHELE. Well, Khatskl, let's hear, what did you want to say?

KHATSKL. I'll tell you without a song and dance. We're making prayer shawls now, my Motele and me. We are good weavers and when we do a job of work, we do it.

DOBE. Oy, is he a worker, no evil eye! (*Quietly.*) He doesn't know that the water I give him to drink early every morning, I boil it first with parsnip heads with garlic skins. It's very good for the health.

KHATSKL. The bosses we work for are murderers and robbers. They say that only decent, pious Jews should weave *talesim,* and they themselves are liars and pickpockets. The boss is a thief, but he wants the worker to be a saint. So we held a meeting, some weavers and me and Motele, and we want to set up our own cooperative. Berl Laptyukh is with us too. He knows a kind of starch to make a plain *talis* look like silk, antique changeable silk. In strips, sort of. So I came for you to give us money. We'll call it a loan.

HERSHELE. Yes, why not? (*He looks at* MISCHIEF *and gets scared like* LEYZ-ER.) I would give it to you, of course, only, you see, now you don't need it. Soon, God willing, we will be opening a big *talis* factory here, and you will all be taken care of, God willing—all of you.

KHATSKL. Really? Then you know what? Let's all be partners. Study Torah together.

HERSHELE. You will see, the whole town will be almost like partners. No one will starve, God forbid.

KHATSKL. Really? So we don't have to dance with the bear. Well, what do you know? Now to the other business. I would like to ask you, Reb Hershele, what's going on with our match. Freydenyu is somehow yes a bride and not a bride. The match is somehow not dairy and not meat. I don't understand why we have to stretch it out and put it off. Both Motele and Freydenyu are already of an age to stand under the canopy.

DOBE. No evil eye.

LEYZER. Wedding canopy, *khupe vikidushin,* wedding canopy, *khupe vikidushin,* wedding canopy, *khupe ve—*

HERSHELE. (*Angry.*) Father! (LEYZER *gets scared and hides himself in his corner.*)

MISCHIEF. (*He goes over to* HERSHELE.) You see, the account is correct. (*Quietly.*) Reb Hershele, now that you have started, don't stop in the middle. Remember my advice: over and done with. (*He sits back down.*)

HERSHELE. Yes, Reb Khatskl, you are right. (*Trembles.*) It is indeed time to talk about that. But first I want us to . . . first we should hear what she . . . what Freydenyu herself has to say. (PESENYU *comes with a tray full of snacks and napkins.*)

PESENYU. You see? Nothing to complain about . . . (*Takes napkin.*) Only, these things, I don't know, do you use it before you eat or after you eat? (*She puts it on table.*)

TSIPENYU. I'm going to call Freydenyu right now. Get it over with. When the older sister is off the market, the younger one can have a hope too. Grandpa, when I become a bride, you will be my jester. (*Off right.* HERSHELE *trembles.*)

PESENYU. What is it, Hershele? Look how his hands tremble, just as if he wanted to rob somebody, God forbid. Dobe, eat, this was baked with pure egg whites.

DOBE. They came out good, no evil eye. There now, we are about to become true family. (*She kisses her. Enter* FREYDENYU *and* TSIPENYU.)

HERSHELE. Freydenyu, I would like to ask you. That is, not I. Reb Khatskl is asking. He wants to know what is happening about the engagement.

KHATSKL. I'll tell you, like a plain man. You are somehow too wishy-washy. I don't know, maybe now you are not pleased with our whole arrangement. You're an aristocrat now, and Motl is still the son of Khatskl Drakhme.

FREYDENYU. The engagement? Reb Khatskl, I will tell you the truth. We were never formally engaged, after all. If I was silent before, it's not because I liked Motl. I only believed that it had to be like that. But now . . . Don't be angry at me. I can't.

DOBE. Motl wasn't swooning over you, either. Khatskl, you see? I told you, I saw a black cat in a dream, so there you have it.

PESENYU. Freydenyu, you don't want the match? What is it? Why not?

LEYZER. (*From his corner.*) She'd rather stay home with her family.

HERSHELE. (*Angry.*) Father, if you want to sit decently, sit there, and if not, I'll ask you to excuse yourself.

TSIPENYU. Really? It's beneath your dignity now that you're a princess? Admit it, Auntie, isn't it hard on Motele?

MOTELE. Don't think I'll take it so hard. Who wants a wife who makes you feel uncomfortable?

TSIPENYU. Of course, we feel uncomfortable around her. She doesn't belong to our family.

FREYDENYU. Don't torture me—I'm asking you. Please.

TSIPENYU. I believe that you can have a rich uncle, and even so it's no disgrace to be Reb Khatskl Drakhme's daughter-in-law.

PESENYU. Freydenyu, if it is because God, blessed be his name, has helped Uncle and you consider yourself too fine, that is a very big sin.

DOBE. Remember, Motele, as we were coming here, we met a peasant woman with an empty bucket? You see? She doesn't want a match like us.

KHATSKL. I don't consider my Motl damaged goods, God forbid. Not at all. If she isn't willing, she probably has her own reasons.

HERSHELE. I will explain her reasons to you. Listen, there is no one here but ourselves, almost one family. If Freydenyu does not want the match, maybe the match pleases Tsipenyu. You may trust me, she will certainly receive dowry and wedding presents like the child of a respectable family. But now I want to talk to you about a different thing altogether. Not about the children. I want to talk about myself. That is, about Pesenyu and me. At the new moon of Elul it was twenty-two years since our wedding, and as you know, God has not blessed our marriage with children. What does a person live for if not for the sake of children?

PESENYU. (*Sadly.*) Yes, that's how it is. The women often used to wonder how a pious Jew like Hershele could live so many years with a barren woman. But I always told them: my Hershele is another kind of man altogether, and the two orphans who live in our home are our children. (FREYDENYU *weeps.*) Yes, Hershele is right, Freydenyu. What does a man live for if not for the sake of children? You two are our children, and we live only for your sakes. (*She kisses* FREYDENYU.)

HERSHELE. You misunderstood me, Pesenyu. That is not what I meant. I mean . . . I want to have children of my own.

KHATSKL. (*Quietly.*) He wants to have children of his own. To my way of thinking, that means he wants a different wife.

ALL. What?

LEYZER. The jester's eye saw it long ago.

HERSHELE. Yes, Pesenyu, if I deserve anything from you, don't be angry at me. I want a divorce.

PESENYU. Divorce? What do you mean, Hershele? You never said a word about it.

HERSHELE. I never said, but I have been thinking about it a long time.

PESENYU. Divorce? Oh, God in Heaven, my God in Heaven. (*She weeps. All the women wipe their tears.*)

HERSHELE. That is to say, if you don't want to, I wouldn't force you, God forbid. You'll stay here in the house the way you were, and no one will dare to dishonor you. And I will bear it with love.

PESENYU. No, Hershele, I know, you are a pious Jew, a fine man. If you believe we have to get a divorce, then it can't be helped. Probably it's a decree from heaven. We'll get a divorce. Father in Heaven. (*She weeps.*)

KHATSKL. (*Quietly.*) Why didn't the decree from heaven come before the money?

DOBE. Oh, Pese dear, I told you, when you bless the new moon, always say the Lamentations of Mother Rachel. She was barren too, poor thing.

PESENYU. What good is talking now? Probably Hershele knows what he's doing. Oh, Father in Heaven, I did not expect such a blow. But if there is no choice, it can't be helped.

FREYDENYU. (*She falls on* PESE*'s neck.*) No, Aunt Pese, there is a choice. I'll get married. I'll marry Motl right away. I . . . (*She can't talk for weeping.*)

MOTELE. I don't want to be tossed around. Yes or no. To tell the truth, you're too fancy for me. You're not my taste. Tsipenyu is something else.

HERSHELE. Pesenyu, why are you crying so?

PESENYU. Only a little . . . God won't punish me for tears.

FREYDENYU. Aunt Pese, dear Aunt Pese, it's not my fault. (*She weeps.*)

PESENYU. Silly child, how can it be your fault? My child, if it is fated from God that we should divorce, no force can keep us together. (*She takes a look at* FREYDENYU.) What? You? Ah, that's what you mean? You mean, you . . . I, old fool, I didn't understand. Well, Freydenyu, better you taking my place than a stranger, after all. Better you whom I considered almost my own child. God give you happiness. Husbands like Reb Hershele aren't easy to find. Twenty-two years living together, and I didn't hear one bad word from him, God forbid. Don't cry, silly. I will be with Tsipenyu, but I won't forget you either. And

. . . Freydenyu, when God blesses you with little children, I will nurse them like my own, like my grandchildren. If I can't be a mother, at least I will be a grandmother. (*They weep in each other's arms.*)

HERSHELE. How can a man go his own way if he must trample someone else at every step? How can one get a little bit of happiness for himself if he must rip it out with flesh and blood? No. His whole philosophy is a lie. I will never be happy. (*He weeps bitterly.*) Pesenyu, don't be angry at me. I don't deserve your pious tears. I am a lot worse than you considered me. I know, I feel, how hard it is for you now. Oh, Pesenyu, Pesenyu. (*All weep.* MISCHIEF *contemplates* HERSHELE *ironically.*)

Curtain

❧

Act III

Three and a half years later. Drawing room in HERSHELE*'s home, much more richly furnished than in Act II. Flowers, drapes. It's night; lamps burn on the tables. In a corner among flowers a big iron strongbox where* MISCHIEF *sits counting big packets of money.* LEYZER *walks restlessly around the room.*

LEYZER. Remarkable. You can tear yourself in pieces, it isn't there. Again: akhme, bakhme, gakhme, dakhme, hakhme. (*Yells at the door.*) Hurry up. Did you hear Reb Uriel? (*A Jewish servant brings in a bottle of wine with two glasses.*) Where was I? Hakhme, vakhme, zakhme.

MISCHIEF. (*Goes to the wine and pours.*) Will you take a little? I love you when you're drunk.

LEYZER. I'm afraid that my poor brain / Can't even remember how to bless a glass of wain . . . wine. (*He drinks a whole glass.*) Reb Uriel, I've been torturing myself for two whole days to find a rhyme for the name Khatskl Drakhme, and I'm tearing myself into pieces. I go along the alphabet: *Alef:* akhme, *bes:* bakhme, *giml:* gakhme, *daled:* dakhme, *hey:* hakhme. It's not there. (*Toasts.*) Life! (*Drinks more.*)

MISCHIEF. Yes. Khatskl Drakhme doesn't go in much for rhyming. Sit down, Reb Leyzer, we'll have a drink and a chat. (*They sit.* MISCHIEF *sips slowly.*) How old are you?

LEYZER. (*Drinks.*) The seventies have rolled over me. Reb Uriel, I wanted to ask you: when is Hershele supposed to come home?

MISCHIEF. Maybe today, maybe a few days more. You miss him, and he probably misses his nice little wife.

LEYZER. God should burn me up alive / If I miss my son the scribe. I feel at home here only when he's not at home. (*Toasts.*) Life! (*Drinks.*) A remarkable thing, I have groped my way through the whole alphabet. *Fey:* fakhme, *kuf:* kakhme, *resh:* rakhme.

MISCHIEF. (*Sips thoughtfully.*) Here you have a man, created in the form of God. He has lived out more than seventy years, and what is he? What has he lived for? What has he accomplished? What does he understand better than a cow does? Goes and breaks his head over a rhyme for akhme, bakhme, gakhme. All their lives, people break their heads looking for the rhyme. Suddenly comes the angel of death and says, "Pious jester, an end to rhyming." Drink, Reb Leyzer. "So off he toddled / With his bottle."

LEYZER. Reb Ley-ZAHR / Drinks like the czar, / and Reb Zar-KING / Drinks like a king. (*Drinks.*) You laugh at my rhyming, eh? Give me your ear over here, and I'll tell you a secret! Sh! You—I beg your pardon—are a fool. When a child's belly hurts, we give him a toy. What do you think—the stomachache goes away because of a toy? Not at all. The child tricks himself with the little toy and forgets for a while that his belly hurts. My dear friend Reb Uriel, everybody's belly hurts. You are a clever man, you distract yourself with one kind of toy. Another man plays with something else. I play with rhymes. But it's only because my belly hurts. (*Sings.*) "So off he toddled / With his bottle. / Drank his liquor / Quicker and quicker." (*Drinks.*)

MISCHIEF. Your belly hurts? That's not bad.

LEYZER. You ask how is Leyzer the Jester better than a cow. Hah. Leyzer Jester may be a cow but a cow can't be a jester. You have to know how to do it. You want to hear what I can do? For example. They call my son Zvi Hersh. Hersh is spelled *hey, ayin, resh, shin. Hey, resh, shin* starts the Hebrew words *Hatsadik rosho shel or,* which in plain Yiddish means "The head of the righteous shines." If you want the letters backwards, they stand for "Shall not the righteous hear?" And in case you're interested, my son's name Zvi Hersh clearly shows that God created ten measures of speech. Because a measure is in Hebrew a *kav,* spelled *kuf, vov,* and the numerical value of the letters *kuf, vov* is a hundred and two, same as the letters in Zvi. And Hersh, when you turn the letters around, adds up to ten, which is to say, ten *kav,* ten measures. Aha! Or let's say, your name is Uriel, spelled *alef, vov, resh, yod, alef, lamed. Alef,* one; *vov,* six; *resh,* two hundred; *yod,* ten; *alef,* one; *lamed,* thirty. Together that makes two hundred and forty-eight, which we call in Hebrew *ramakh,* the number of a man's outer organs. And if you like, *ramakh* reversed is *khamor,* a donkey. Or it's *mokhor,* tomorrow, when we'll eat cold noodle pudding. And if you like, it even makes *rekhem,* a womb. Without having to stop and think, I can scramble the letters of Uriel to make these words: *Eyli or,* "My God is light"; *Ya-or li,* "He will give me light"; *lo yiru,* "They will not see." And that's only the Hebrew. In Russian letters, Uriel makes *orilo,* which is Russian for a sock on the chin, isn't that right? And if you're still not satisfied, let me mention that the letters of Mischief spell Murderer, Stool Pigeon, Cheat, Fake. You ask what Leyzer the Jester is? He's a man with a soul like all men. He's a Jew, and a Jew has a good head and has sense. You think you're a wise man because you laugh when you feel like laughing and cry when you feel like crying? I am more skillful than you are. I laugh and jest when I feel like crying, when my heart is torn inside me and nobody knows why. Truly, what of my entire life is left for me, and what have I got here in this big rich house? Ah. "So off he toddled . . ." Sh! Bend down your ear. I'm going to go say that you ordered another bottle of wine. "So off he toddled / With his bottle. / Drank his liquor / Quicker and quicker. / Drank it in / And wet his chin." (*He exits with the empty bottle.*)

MISCHIEF. (*Thoughtful.*) There you have man: a vulgar fool who talks like a wise man. A thinker who's a clown. Makes faces like a monkey and feels like a god. Dreams like a king and lives like a slave. (*Noise.*) Ah, my partner's pretty little wife. (FREYDENYU *comes through the inner door. She is very richly dressed and bejeweled.*)

FREYDENYU. Are you here by yourself, Reb Uriel? There's no letter? (*She goes to the mirror.*)

MISCHIEF. No. Since Reb Hershele didn't write, I think he'll come today. Freydenyu, permit me to say you don't have to look in the mirror. Cold glass doesn't do your beauty justice.

FREYDENYU. Looking in the mirror has become a habit of mine lately. I have nothing else to do. I am totally occupied with myself. It is very sad and boring to live in this world, don't you agree, Reb Uriel?

MISCHIEF. Life is a beautiful garden full of fruit trees. Fruits of joy and pleasure grow over people's heads. But people don't want to reach up a little bit to get at these fruits. All they do is tear off the bitter green leaves, chew them, and complain that life is not delicious. To chew the leaves is permitted; to eat the fruit, forbidden. Except for once, when the woman dared to enjoy the forbidden fruit. She had the happiness of eating and of giving all mankind the fruits of the *ets hada-as,* the Tree of Knowledge. And sooner or later they would have tasted the *ets hakhayim,* the Tree of Life, as well.

FREYDENYU. I'm not educated and don't understand what you said about the Tree of Knowledge and Tree of Life, but I do know that after Mother Eve had pleasure from the forbidden fruits, then came death, pain, tears, and suffering. And what is every pleasure? A short preface to a long, long pain. I put on a new dress, decorate myself with jewelry; it gives me pleasure for a second; then it becomes ugly to me, and my heart hurts.

MISCHIEF. One must keep finding fresh pleasures.

FREYDENYU. No, pleasure can't make a person happy, and life gives no joy.

MISCHIEF. You can't have much joy here in Reb Hershele's house.

FREYDENYU. Here in this house I took the place of the fine woman who was my second mother. Reb Hershele's house has reminded me of that, with every passing second, for more than three years now.

MISCHIEF. You keep remembering because you were united with Reb Hershele not by a feeling of suffering but only by a feeling of divinity. Divinity is heavenly, but we live on earth. Our first response to a woman is divine. But a husband's duty is to bring this goddess down and make her into a wife. It is horrible, vulgar, unpoetic, but it is nature's will.

FREYDENYU. (*Not listening.*) Oh, if only I at least had a child.

MISCHIEF. You expect joy from children? Children steal women's charm, make women sick and old before their time, tear them away from the whole lively world. They rob women of youth, freedom, and beauty, and make them vulnerable to love and to suffering. Senseless. Rich, educated women do all they can to avoid having children. (*Noise.*) Who is it that's coming? (DOBE *enters.*)

DOBE. Come in, sister-in-law. Freydenyu, you're sitting alone with a man? (*Quietly.*) Tell him to go away. He has an evil eye. (FREYDENYU *gives him a look.*)

MISCHIEF. I understand. (*Leaving.*) Just watch out for the Evil One.

DOBE. (*She covers her ears.*) As I hear nothing, so may nothing harm me. Freydenyu, your aunt is here with me. Pesenyu, come in. (PESENYU *enters. She has aged greatly.*)

FREYDENYU. Oh, Aunt Pese, it's been so long since you were in our house.

Oh my, how old you've gotten. You're not angry at me?

PESENYU. No, child, why should I be angry at you? It's nothing. When I entered the house, a blow struck my heart. Just an old lady, that's all. (*She wipes away a tear.*) So, Freydenyu, how are you?

FREYDENYU. How I am? Me? I'm fine. I'm rich, and I have no mother. Oh, Aunt Pese. (*She falls on* PESENYU'S *neck, weeping.*)

DOBE. We know your husband isn't here—that's why we came. Tsipenyu was coming with us too, but she changed her mind. Besides, we met a priest on the way.

FREYDENYU. How is Tsipenyu? Is she healthy?

DOBE. No complaints. Two children like diamonds. Just yesterday I dosed the older one for worms.

PESENYU. We came to ask you a favor. Times are very bad for us now. Reb Khatskl and Motl are practically penniless, and we'll all have to beg from house to house, God forbid.

DOBE. Your factory has strangled us. It stands like a big not-to-be-thought-of in the village and strangles us all. Pese's money, Tsipenyu's dowry, our own little piece of poverty—bad luck has gotten it all. If you would only ask Reb Hershele. A young wife can manage anything. An old wife they can throw out, but for a young wife they'll do anything. (TSIPENYU *opens the door.*) You changed your mind again?

TSIPENYU. (*Enters. She is very poorly dressed and looks bad.*) I came. What can I do? If you can't get over, you have to go under. My, my, what clothes and jewelry on our rich lady. Do you remember, Aunt Pese, she used to keep on complaining that clothes and jewelry are rags? (*She looks around.*) Your house looks nice, big sister.

FREYDENYU. Do you envy me? Tsipenyu, all this doesn't make a person happy.

TSIPENYU. Whoever envies you, may her eyes fall out.

DOBE. Oy, Tsipke, you're absolutely determined to fight? Take a look, you've probably put a stocking on inside out again.

PESENYU. No fighting, God forbid. We've come to ask Freydenyu to help us.

FREYDENYU. Oh, Sister, how bad you look, you poor thing. You're a ruin.

TSIPENYU. Not from dancing, believe me.

FREYDENYU. The children have made you old and sick. You're so young.

Just three years since your wedding and you have two children already.

TSIPENYU. Children are our only comfort, our joy, our contentment. There is no greater happiness than children—according to us paupers. What rich people believe, I wouldn't know. My older daughter climbs all over the whole house. When she walks, she waddles like a little duck, may she be healthy. Her little voice rings in every corner.

DOBE. No evil eye. Tfoo. (*She spits.*)

TSIPENYU. And the baby hums in her little cradle like a pigeon. Now that is wealth. That is holy wealth. It can't be robbed or stolen away. You get it from God, and you give it back to God's world. Yes, children, that is a true fortune.

DOBE. God's greatest blessing is children. I am already, no evil eye, forty-five years old, and you see I wear an amulet so I shouldn't . . . you know . . . miscarry, God forbid.

FREYDENYU. All the same, when you were a girl, you made jokes and laughed, and now, Tsipenyu, you're like an old woman.

TSIPENYU. A person can't make jokes her whole life. And if I don't laugh, that's because there are some people making us cry.

FREYDENYU. Tsipenyu, you speak to me as if you hate me. We are strangers now.

TSIPENYU. Yes, we are strangers. We are enemies. We work, we slave, we grieve, we mourn. And you, you rich people, you grab the last bite of food from our mouths. You're drowning us.

FREYDENYU. We are not your enemy. It's your own fault, Uncle says. He gave Aunt Pese five thousand rubles, and gave you a dowry, and Reb Khatskl took the money in order to compete with our factory. You made your own misfortune.

PESENYU. Reb Khatskl asked me for a few rubles once, then another few rubles. So I gave. Until there was no more money and no more business.

DOBE. Any evil we wish you, may that evil come upon us, God our Father and all Israel, amen.

FREYDENYU. What do I know? Uncle says.

TSIPENYU. You only know what Uncle says. You yourself are not a person? You don't know that once you had good friends, and now you are cut off from them? You had one sister, we were orphans, we grew up together, and now we are enemies, strangers. And you don't know that at all? You don't know that you took the woman who raised you like flesh and blood, and you drove her out of her own house and took her place? You don't feel that her heart is broken and her life is ruined forever? (*Weeps.*)

PESENYU. What are you talking about, God forbid? Just let Freydenyu be happy, and I . . . I . . . (*Weeps.*)

FREYDENYU. I didn't cut myself off from anyone. You cut me off. You see my wealth, my pretty clothes, but the wounded heart, nobody sees that. Aunt Pese, your misfortune did not make me fortunate, your broken heart did not fill my heart with joy. We both believed that that was the way things had to be. Aunt Pese, I wander here in a dark wood, all alone and . . . If you are not too angry at me, have pity on me. (*All the women weep.* LEYZER *enters, drunk, with a full bottle of wine which he puts on the table.*)

LEYZER. What is this? A whole ladies' choir. Four Jewish women, four noses full of tears. (*Sings in the sing-song in which jesters address brides.*) Oy, weep, women, weep, pour tear upon tear. / Perhaps God up in heaven will hear.

TSIPENYU. (*Wipes tears.*) Grandfather Leyzer laughs at our noses, but he himself drinks liquor quicker and quicker. How is my good old friend anyway?

LEYZER. Tsipenyu, my business affairs are going excellently. My factory has already provided me with a prayer shawl for a shroud. (*Sings.*) "So off he toddled—" (*Enter* MISCHIEF.)

MISCHIEF. Reb Hershele has arrived. (*All the women get frightened and don't know where to go. They run around like scared sheep.*)

FREYDENYU. Come, I'll let you out through my room. (*All the women leave in great disorder.*)

LEYZER. (*He drives the women with his hanky.*) Women, silence. Reb Leyzer, hide the jester. (*He sits in his corner.*)

MISCHIEF. You're drunk. Behave yourself. (*The servant opens the door.* REB HERSHELE *in traveling clothes follows him in, weary and carrying a suitcase.*)

HERSHELE. Good evening, Reb Uriel. What's been going on here?

LEYZER. Good evening, good fortune, good omen. Good omen and good fortune, good omen and good fortune. *Simn tov un mazl tov un mazl tov un simn tov—*

HERSHELE. You're so drunk that one can't even greet you properly. Maybe you should go to sleep. How is Freydenyu? (*He goes to her door.*) Freydenyu, I brought you red and green and yellow silks for dresses, and diamond earrings. (*Quietly.*) Later I'll give you a kiss, when I have time and no one is here.

LEYZER. I was a real pauper, just a jester, but when I came home from a journey, my old woman and I used to melt like sugar.

HERSHELE. Well, what's going on here at home? I followed your instructions and took as much on credit as possible. They don't ask questions. They just give.

MISCHIEF. I knew that if you traveled alone you would make a good impression. Yes, we have to pack away all we can now.

HERSHELE. "Pack it away," you say? (*He sees the bottle.*) What is this—wine? I wouldn't mind a glass right now. Will you smoke a cigar? (*He takes out a big cigar case and smokes.*)

MISCHIEF. I will drink some wine too, but not smoke. I have given up smoking. You see this type of corkscrew? It's English. (*He takes from his pocket a big knife with a corkscrew, opens the bottle, pours into the glasses, leaves the corkscrew lying on the table.*)

HERSHELE. Given up smoking? What kind of foolishness is that? This is a marvelous cigar. (*He drinks.*) This must be one of our cheaper wines. No bouquet. I don't understand what you mean: "pack it away." (*He smokes the cigar.*)

LEYZER. Give me the glass. I'll show you what "pack it away" means.

HERSHELE. Excuse me, get out of here, get out right now.

LEYZER. (*Scared.*) I'm going. (*Going.*) Reb Uriel, I wanted to ask you . . . Sh! Tell me, I beg you, is this a leap year? (*He looks at his son.*) I'm leading the jester out. (*Off.*)

MISCHIEF. The plan is very simple. (*Both drink.*) We have borrowed a great deal by now, and recently I stopped all payments out. Reb Hershele, we now have seventy-five thousand rubles cash in our strongbox. Here you have the strongbox key. (*Gives it to him.*)

HERSHELE. Seventy-five thousand? A nice sum, no evil eye. But then, it isn't ours, after all. We have to pay it back.

MISCHIEF. Pay it back? You calf! Reb Hershele Dubrovner, now is the time to go bankrupt.

HERSHELE. What do you mean? Go bankrupt when business is doing well and the strongbox is so full of cash? (*He pours himself more wine.*) You'll have a drink? (*He pours him more also.*) Bankrupt?

MISCHIEF. When business is bad, it's already late to go bankrupt. The time is now. My friend, this is even better than winning the lottery. In one stroke we become three times richer.

HERSHELE. (*He jumps up*.) We do? (*Thinks*.) But excuse me, Reb Uriel, God be with you, what do you mean? You know that what I want above all is to do business decently and remain a decent man and a righteous decent Jew.

MISCHIEF. Certainly. You are a decent man and a decent Jew. That's why it's so good for us to go bankrupt. From such a fine, decent man as Reb Hershele, the creditors will happily accept fifty kopecks on the ruble. In business, being decent means being smart, taking as much as possible in and giving as little as possible out. That's what all the big businessmen we owe money to do, and we'll do it too. But of course you'll remain a decent man and a good Jew, because what does this have to do with Jewishness? And the money will remain in the strongbox. Just count it yourself.

HERSHELE. Yes, let's count it right now and see how much the total comes to. (*They sit at table and count.*)

SERVANT. (*At the door.*) Sir, Reb Khatskl Drakhme wants to see you.

HERSHELE. Reb Khatskl? What can this be?

MISCHIEF. He is in very big trouble.

HERSHELE. Really? Well, let him in. (SERVANT *off.*) Reb Uriel, but how will we do it? Don't forget, going bankrupt is a serious matter.

MISCHIEF. Just leave it to me. (KHATSKL *and* MOTL *in. Both beaten down.*)

HERSHELE. Why so late? I just got home. I'm tired.

KHATSKL. I've got very little to say, Reb hershele.

HERSHELE. I heard you had a great deal to say about the synagogue elections. They shouldn't elect me head of the community? I give money to rent a synagogue, I build a ritual bath, and I haven't earned the honor? Well?

KHATSKL. Don't get mad, I didn't come to talk about honor. You're entitled to the honor, you are entitled to everything. Can't I see that with my own plain sense? Me, Motl, Berl Laptyukh, and our whole bunch, we work, we work ourselves out of our skins, and you get richer. We weave our own prayer shawls and run our business honestly. You, people trust; us, they don't. You, people pay; when we try to collect, they laugh at us. Yes, evidently you earned it, you're entitled to everything. You have the credit of the merits of the fathers.

MOTELE. (*Apart.*) You don't need the fathers when you've got Mischief on your side.

HERSHELE. You fool, you wanted to battle a factory with your bare hands. With your few groschen, you wanted to compete with capital? Whose fault is that?

KHATSKL. Berl Laptyukh knew the secret of how to use starch to make *talesim* like silk, and you stole the secret from us, plain and simple. It turns out you can get rich from thievery but not from work.

MOTELE. Sometimes I got so upset I actually thought of setting the factory on fire.

KHATSKL. Sh! Blockhead!

HERSHELE. (*Beside himself.*) You hear what nice talk? Set fire to my factory, my possessions, my fortune?

MISCHIEF. You mean our factory, our fortune.

HERSHELE. (*He doesn't hear.*) I would have had you rotting in jail. I would have had you sent off to Siberia. Nobody has any right to take what belongs to you away from you, and nobody has any right to take my own possessions away from me. (LEYZER *steals in.*)

KHATSKL. Why do you listen to him? Do I know what he's talking about? A boy. Nobody wants to take anything away from you, God forbid. We came to ask you to help us to rescue Pese's five thousand rubles, poor thing. After all we used to be true good friends.

HERSHELE. Friendship is friendship and business is business. Friendship is fine for you because you've got nothing to share.

KHATSKL. You used to be a generous man.

HERSHELE. When you have no sense, you're generous. How can I help you? Give you a little money, a charitable donation? It's only throwing away money. I know when and how to do someone a favor. Maybe I should give you so much that you'll become the big shot and I won't be able to compete with you? I don't believe you consider me that much of a fool.

MISCHIEF. (*Angry.*) You forget to mention that you still have a partner who can also have a little bit of a say.

LEYZER. You should listen to the partner with the little bit of a say the way I listen to my left earlock.

HERSHELE. You're here again? Didn't I tell you to go to sleep? (LEYZER *gets scared.*) Hey! Get him out of here. (SERVANT *comes and drags him out.*) We're going to have to pay to board him somewhere. It's an embarrassment to keep him in the house.

KHATSKL. So in other words, what can I take home with me?

HERSHELE. I'll go this far: I will see to it that Pese doesn't suffer because of you. I'll give orders to pay her twelve to fifteen rubles every month out of my account.

MISCHIEF. Our account, you mean.

HERSHELE. And you and your son can work for me in the factory.

MISCHIEF. For us, you mean.

HERSHELE. Yes, yes. You are pious Jews, and that's the right kind of work-ers to weave *talesim*. With me you'll make your living honorably and you'll live peacefully. How do you come to run a business? For that you need sense, mon-ey, know-how. Did you think you could run a business on miracles? You can't live on miracles in this world.

MISCHIEF. "A great miracle happened there."

HERSHELE. What can be more secure and peaceful? You work and you get paid.

MOTELE. Lying in the ground is even more secure and peaceful.

KHATSKL. I'm a plain man, Reb Hershele, and when you were still poor I could understand you—but now? I don't begin to understand. Friendship is nothing. You don't need a good heart to do a favor; you need to be smart. The man who is generous is a fool. It seems that hard work makes us stupider all the time, while you become greater scholars. Well, at any rate, thank you for giving us work. What good are complaints when you want to eat? Motl and I will start tomorrow. We're sorry we bothered you. Good evening. You're prob-ably right.

MOTELE. God will repay you the favor. (*They start out.*)

MISCHIEF. That's how it is. Whoever is stronger is right. Come, I'll give you a note for them to hire you tomorrow. (*Exeunt.*)

HERSHELE. (*He remains seated in thought.*) He thinks that I've changed. But I'm the same. And the proof is that he has lost Pesi's money, I'm not obligated to give her any more, but nevertheless I don't abandon her. As for him—it hurts me, my heart pains me, but he himself is to blame. Every man has what he earns. His own fault. It's what he says himself: I made the effort to learn and to understand life, and he remained the same plain Khatskl Drakhme. (*Stands up.*) A person ought to look inside a holy book once in a while. I haven't held a holy book in my hands since I myself don't remember when. (*He kneels by the suitcase and takes out a book.*) I took it along for nothing, I didn't even open it. (*Sits to study.*) Ah, Freydenyu's presents. I ought to go to her. I saw her only from a distance. (*Goes.*) Seventy-five thousand rubles. Better look over the books and count the money again. (*Goes to the strongbox, drags out big sacks of money, counts out thousands, and puts them in a sack.*) One thousand. (*Counts.*) Two thousand.

(*Counts.*) Three thousand—(FREYDENYU *enters in a white peignoir, her hair loose.*) What's the matter? God be with you. (*Closes the strongbox.*)

FREYDENYU. What was the shouting here? It seemed to me I heard Aunt Pese crying. I often think I hear—

HERSHELE. What do you think, child? What would your aunt be doing here?

FREYDENYU. I don't know—it often seems that way to me.

HERSHELE. Silly child, better to look at the earrings I bought you. (*Gives her a case.*)

FREYDENYU. (*Opens.*) Oh, how beautiful. (*Becomes excited.*) Like clear drops of water against the sun, that's how they shine. Ah, are they becoming? (*Puts them on.*) Are they pretty? (*Runs to the mirror.*) But what good does it do me? (*Becomes sad again.*) Nothing can make me happy while something like a serpent crushes my heart and sucks my blood.

HERSHELE. Freydenyu, I have a little work to do here. Go on, I'll come soon.

FREYDENYU. I know, you would rather stay here and count money.

HERSHELE. Listen, I talked with people. This summer, God willing, you and I will travel to Vienna to a specialist. God in Heaven, if you give me a son, I will ask nothing more of you.

FREYDENYU. No. I'm sick. I don't want to, I'm not meant to be a mother.

HERSHELE. If you are sick, God forbid! Of course not. Why do I need children? Your health is dearer to me than children. But what are you lacking, God forbid?

FREYDENYU. I lack nothing, and I have nothing. I am rich and I am much poorer than Tsipe. I took my mother's place and can find no place for myself. (*Weeps.*)

HERSHELE. I don't understand. What do you want?

FREYDENYU. I want to be happy. Give me happiness. Give me joy.

HERSHELE. Ah, Freyde, you yourself don't know what you desire.

FREYDENYU. I need nothing and I desire nothing. Only one thing. I want my sick heart to feel what I used to feel when you played the violin for me. Do you remember?

HERSHELE. You're a silly little thing. That was when we were first struggling for happiness. We can't feel like that any more, and we never will.

FREYDENYU. What? Did the violin lie to me then? No, no, that would be awful! Please, don't be cold to me, please.

HERSHELE. I'm not cold to you at all. (*Opens strongbox and takes a look.*) How much did I count up to? Three thousand, I think—right?

FREYDENYU. Come here. Take your violin. Play for me again. Just one more time. And I will sit here again at your feet.

HERSHELE. What are you saying, child? Play? It's been over two years since I even held the violin in my hand. I don't think I'll ever play again.

FREYDENYU. Never? Everything has died? It will never come back?

HERSHELE. Freydenyu, go in your room, calm down. I have to look over the accounts a little. Go on, child, have a good sleep. (*He gives her a cold kiss on the forehead.*)

FREYDENYU. (*Stands up, gives him a long look, and says quietly.*) Good night. (*Rushes off. We see how she stifles her tears. He doesn't notice.*)

HERSHELE. There really must be something the matter with her. Tomorrow we'll have to send for the doctor. (*Goes, empties an entire glass of wine, returns to the strongbox.*) This I counted already, three thousand. (*Lays the money he has already counted in a traveling bag.*) Four thousand. (*Counts.*) Five thousand. (*Counts.*) Six thousand. What is this? It seems to be nothing. Pieces of paper. And yet when you take a look in the strongbox and catch sight of so many little pieces of paper, your heart becomes full of joy, sleep disappears, you forget that you're tired, you're hungry. You forget everything. Every hundred note speaks to you like a living thing, every bond strokes you like a warm breeze. Ah, how much pleasure, joy, power, lie in these pretty little bits of paper. (*Enter MIS-CHIEF.*) Hooray. The thousands are growing like armies. Another army. Another thousand. Six. Seven. Eight.

MISCHIEF. What's this, Reb Hersh? You don't trust me? You're checking my accounts?

HERSHELE. (*Scared.*) It's you, Reb Uriel? I merely want to see, in case you made a mistake.

MISCHIEF. Yes, I see, I did make a little mistake. I trusted you too much, and I taught you too much about business. It bothered me, before, the way you said, "my money," "my factory," "my office," "I will give orders," "I will see." I'm afraid you're becoming too much of a boss for me.

HERSHELE. You can relax. You're as much a boss here as I am.

MISCHIEF. That's what you say. But what if you should go into competition with me? I never signed a contract because I took you for an innocent. I despise innocents, it's true, but I know they can be trusted. But now I'm afraid.

You're getting too smart, and there is too much cash in the strongbox.

HERSHELE. If you don't believe me, we can draw up a contract. I don't care. Tomorrow, even.

MISCHIEF. Tomorrow? Do your granny favors. I'm afraid right now. I won't be able to sleep all night. I saw you counting the money with too much pleasure. Exactly as if it were all yours.

HERSHELE. What do you want? I'd really like to know. Speak up: what do you want?

MISCHIEF. I simply want to take the seventy-five thousand rubles with me in the meantime. It's not so important—you've got me where you want me. (*He takes a few steps to the strongbox.*)

HERSHELE. (*He quickly throws all the packets of money into the sack and closes them up in the strongbox.*) What? I should just give you such a sum of money? What do you think, I've lost my mind?

MISCHIEF. Oh, now I see what you are. Why did I keep trusting you more and more?

HERSHELE. Fine, starting tomorrow you won't trust me any more.

MISCHIEF. Starting tomorrow? Oh, no. Tomorrow may already be too late. Don't think that you can take me in. You missed the target this time, my righteous Jew.

HERSHELE. And don't you think I'm always going to believe that everything you say is Torah. (*Trembles with distress.*)

MISCHIEF. Oh, I know you've become very wise; you learned it at my expense.

HERSHELE. You don't like me? Don't make me best man at your wedding. (*Locks the strongbox.*) Good night. I'm going to sleep.

MISCHIEF. You're mistaken. You're not going to sleep yet. (*Blocks his way.*) If you won't give me the money, give me a receipt that you took a hundred thousand to hold for me. Then if you should go bankrupt or I don't know what, I can at the very least put you in jail. I'll write it out right now and you sign.

HERSHELE. Oh, don't be a fool. I should sign papers for you? Which papers? What papers?

MISCHIEF. What? Not sign a receipt, either?

HERSHELE. No. You've trusted me this long, you'll trust me one night longer.

MISCHIEF. I won't trust you any longer. Give me a paper or the money.

HERSHELE. Damn you! You don't want to trust me? Don't. I'm going.

MISCHIEF. I don't trust you, and I won't let you go. I don't trust you. I don't trust you. (*He grabs the key from* HERSHELE *and runs to open the strongbox.* HERSHELE *won't let him.* MISCHIEF *throws* HERSHELE *off, grabs the pack with the whole sum of money and runs,* HERSHELE *after him.*)

HERSHELE. Thief! Murderer! Robber! Give me the money. (*Catches him.*) I won't let you out of here alive. Hand over the money. (*They struggle.* MISCHIEF *tears himself away, runs to the table and catches sight of the corkscrew.*)

MISCHIEF. Get away from me. You see the knife? I'm not responsible for myself now. (*While* MISCHIEF *speaks,* HERSHELE *keeps repeating: "My money, my money." His whole body trembles.*)

HERSHELE. Oh, you want to kill me? Grab my money? With a knife? A real murderer. Hand over the money. (*He drags the knife away from him. They struggle.* HERSHELE *stabs him in the throat with the corkscrew and yells.*) No! You'll croak first before you take away my money. It's my money. My money. (*A whole bag of money pours out over the floor.* FREYDENYU *and* LEYZER *run in frightened.*)

FREYDENYU. Father in Heaven, what happened?

HERSHELE. (*He gathers the money and throws it in the traveling bag like a madman.*) My money. My money. My money.

Curtain

~✻~

Act IV

SCENE I

A very poor room in KHATSKL'S *house. By the door a kneading trough with water. A table. A long wooden bench. Two chairs and a little stool. Against the wall a bed. A little cupboard.* KHATSKL *sits on the ground near the oven and with an ax splits big chunks of wood. At the table,* DOBE *knits a sock and counts stitches.*

DOBE. Twenty-one, twenty-two, twenty-three, twenty-four . . . Ah, I've lost a stitch already. (*She puts down the sock.*) Khatskl, don't chop wood on the threshold, you're going to chop the threshold, God forbid.

KHATSKL. Don't worry, Dobe, the threshold won't feel a thing. (*Chops.*)

DOBE. I don't care about the threshold. But if you chopped the threshold, God forbid, and Tsipe steps over the threshold, the child will be born with a split lip, God forbid.

KHATSKL. Dobe, is Tsipenyu . . . again? already . . . ?

DOBE. In a good, happy, lucky hour, thank God. And you don't even know that if you chop above the door, the child's top lip is split and if you chop at the threshold, it's the lower lip? You don't know anything—exactly as if you didn't grow up among decent people, God forbid.

KHATSKL. A plain plate of kasha like me can't understand how you can chop at somebody's lip when he isn't even there, when he isn't even born yet. But never mind—probably women know better about such things.

DOBE. You stop complaining and come here instead. Right here. Sit down on the little stool. Put out both hands. This way. (*Puts yarn on his hands and winds.*) Aha, Khatskl Jack of All Trades, you thought I'd let you sit without work? If you don't go work at the factory, you work for me at home. Carry water, chop wood. Hold the strip! I'm going to wind up a whole skein. (*She winds a long time. Both are silent. Then he begins to doze and slumps down with his head on her knee.*) He's asleep. I'm afraid to move. I don't want to wake him up suddenly. Let him sleep a little. (*She remains sitting quietly, altogether peaceful.*) I've heard that if you wake someone up suddenly, later he might, God forbid, become—(LEYZER *enters from street with a walking stick.*)

LEYZER. Hello, Reb Khatskl. Look, he's asleep. Reb Khatskl, are you still a thief?

DOBE. (*Embarrassed.*) Let him alone . . . He's just looking down.

KHATSKL. No, I really did doze off. (*He washes his hands in the trough.*) Hello, Reb Leyzer, how are you? Nowadays seeing you is a big treat.

LEYZER. Reb Khatskl, I have come to you without an invitation. I have to tell you something important. (*Takes him aside. Quietly.*) Sh! I have figured it out. I suffered a long time, but I found it. You know: in Egypt, *ho-lakhmo anyo*, "the bread of affliction"?

KHATSKL. Do I know? "The bread of affliction" means the bread of the poor man. That I know not only from the Passover service. I know it from life.

LEYZER. Sh! This is exactly that. You're staring at me? That is exactly this.

KHATSKL. What is this?

LEYZER. *Ho-lakhmo anyo*, if you turn it around, it becomes *ho-onyo lakhmo*, and it rhymes with Khatskl Drakhme. *Ho anyo lakhmo:* Khatskl Drakhme

KHATSKL. Oh, you old lunatic, sit down, be our guest.

LEYZER. (*Sits.*) And where are your whole crowd then, ha? (*With a tune.*) Why should a crowd be proud / Just because a crowd is loud? (*Quietly.*) Ho anyo *lakhmo:* Khatskl Drakhme.

DOBE. Tsipenyu went to the butcher shop. You know on weekdays we don't get any meat, so I told her to go in case she found something cheap, maybe a lung and liver or a calf's foot. And our in-law Pesi is at the rich man's house. They sent for her because Freyde is . . . again . . . Not to be thought of, not to be thought of, away from any Jewish home. Do you ever visit them there?

LEYZER. No. Why should I? I'm a foster child in the home of Efroyim the Fiddler now, and I feel as cozy as a blintz in sour cream. Why should I go there? They're ashamed of me, and I don't need the honor. But, just tell me, my dear friend Reb Khatskl, why is today different from all other days? Rascal, why in the world are you sitting home winding yarn? (DOBE *gets embarrassed again.*)

KHATSKL. Why am I sitting at home? Simple. Reb Hershele wanted to make me happy, so he promoted me to the rank of captain. That means I shouldn't work myself, only supervise and persecute the workers. So I thanked him. Not me, not Motl. We don't want any more of his favors. But if a man is a plain worker, shouldn't they give him enough work? Three days work and three days off. They let us earn just enough so we don't croak from hunger. Motele went alone to work in the factory and I—nothing else to do with my-self—I am Dobe's hired girl. This is Mischief's little game. Reb Hershele does-n't know; he doesn't give a thought to unimportant details like Khatskl Drakhme. And I will not go complain or beg help from him. (*Angrily chops a piece of wood.*) No. That my enemies won't live to see.

DOBE. Eh, that Mischief. He mischiefed us all. When he was sick, we be-lieved we would finally be rid of him. May I—I haven't washed my hands— not be punished for saying it. But he wiggled out of it. The good things God takes away, but misery he leaves on earth.

KHATSKL. He did go around bandaged for three months. They say they all but killed each other for money. And ever since that day, Hershele goes around all the time very preoccupied. Thank God I'm a pauper. At least no Mischief is going to bite me in the throat for money.

DOBE. Beryl Laptyukh says that it cost Reb Hershele millions and zillions of money to make up. Reb Leyzer, how much is a million zillion?

LEYZER. A lot.

KHATSKL. Yes, well, so long as it's quiet over there, billing and cooing. Now they're even better pals than ever, and Mischief is the whole cheese.

LEYZER. Oh, when I remember what went on that night. A scream: "Help! Guard!" My first-born with some bottle gadget. Mischief bloody as a pig. "Money!" "Money!" Blood. Both of them rolling on the ground, Freyde dead of fear, my soul on the point of my nose. Ah! Thank God now I live at Efroyim the Fiddler's. (*Goes to the cupboard.*) "So off he toddled / With his bottle. / Drank his liquor / Quicker and Quicker. / Took a drink / And gave a wink." (*Searches.* DOBE *laughs.*)

KHATSKL. Reb Leyzer, it's no use trying. You won't find even a lick. This Sabbath we even made the blessing for wine over dry challa.

LEYZER. Dry challa? Feh! And here is our Tsipenyu. (TSIPENYU *enters with a basket, a shawl on her shoulders. She is in a good mood.*)

TSIPENYU. A guest! Hello, Grandfather dear. Good that you came. I urgently need to ask you something. (*Leads* LEYZER *aside. He is very interested.*) Sh! Tell me, please. Ah, did it snow last winter? (*All laugh.*)

LEYZER. Oh, that's how it is, is it? Good. I have to admit it: good.

DOBE. Something is itching me somehow in my left ear. I'm afraid, I am afraid, we're going to get bad news, God forbid.

TSIPENYU. Mother-in-law dear, I did bring you bad news. No bargains. Twenty takers for every lung, and for every calf's foot, seventeen housewives. So I came home with no foot and no lung. Isn't that bad news? Are the children still asleep?

KHATSKL. Motele will come from work hungry, poor thing.

DOBE. All right, we'll cook him up fish-potatoes. He likes that and it will be good for his health, no evil eye.

TSIPENYU. Grandfather, potatoes with water, with a lot of pepper and without fish, is what we call fish-potatoes. Do you like that? Ko-tatoes? Ah, nothing seems to rhyme with potatoes.

LEYZER. For manna from heaven / No husband could wish, / If Tsipe will give him / Potatoes without—

TSIPENYU. (*Interrupts.*) "So off he toddled / With his bottle." Where is Aunt Pese?

DOBE. They called her to Freyde. Freyde is sick again, not to be thought of in our home. It happens to her every month. Have you ever heard of such a disease? Nothing hurts but you're sick; you're not crazy but you're not in your right mind. (TSIPENYU *remains sitting sadly.*)

KHATSKL. Melancholia. They say that all rich people catch that disease.

DOBE. It comes from women not having any children. What do you say about the way my left ear itches?

LEYZER. If I knew that our great rabbi Reb Hersh wasn't home, I would go over to see her. She may be a big rich lady, but I'm sorry for her all the same.

TSIPENYU. Yes, Reb Leyzer, go see her. You'll get credit for a good deed. She is very lonely. You should see her when it comes over her: quiet, like a dove, talks to herself, sings quietly, and so sad. (*All are silent. Pause. Sudden noise.* TSIPENYU *jumps up, frightened.*) Father in Heaven. What can that be? It tore my heart. (*A Jewish workingman runs in very frightened.*)

WORKER. God be with you. Please, don't be frightened. They're bringing your Motele home.

ALL. Oh, Father in Heaven, what is it, what's the matter?

DOBE. Something terrible has happened.

WORKER. His life is not in danger, God forbid. A wheel tore off his hand.

KHATSKL. The factory. The factory. Oh, the factory.

TSIPENYU. Where is he? Motele! Motele! (*Runs to door. Toward her come Jewish workers carrying* MOTELE. *He is smeared with blood, one hand wrapped in many white cloths through which blood can be seen. On top of all, a new white prayer shawl, also bloodied. She screams.*) God in Heaven! He's dead! He's dead!

DOBE. My child! My only child! My little Motele!

WORKERS. God be with you. He's only fainted. (*They lay him on the bed.*)

KHATSKL. God, now they weave your *talesim* on machines that rip our bodies. You see my son. My son. (*All by the bed.*)

TSIPENYU. Motele! Ay! I can't bear it. (*She and his mother scream next to him.*)

MOTELE. (*Regains consciousness. Tries to smile. With a very weak voice.*) Ah! Don't be scared. It's nothing. Just one hand. What's a hand to a worker? Mama, you know, he . . . Reb Hershele . . . he was standing right there by the window . . . not far from me . . . My blood spurted on him. Oh, Tsipenyu— (*Faints. Enter doctor and surgeon, hurrying.*)

KHATSKL. Motele, my child, be strong. Here comes the doctor. My son.

TSIPENYU. God in Heaven, Father in Heaven! What will become of us? What will become of us? (*Grieves.*)

DOBE. My child! My son! I've been struck down. My God! (*All weep. The workers wipe their tears. The doctor takes his instruments from his case. Many Jewish men and women look in, frightened, through the window and door.*)

SCENE 2

A courtyard near the factory. Noise of wheels and of machines banging. MISCHIEF *leads* HERSHELE *out.* HERSHELE *is pale.*

MISCHIEF. You still don't feel good? Come out here into the air a little. Who's there? Bring a chair over here. (*A worker brings out a chair.*) Just look how pale he turned.

HERSHELE. I saw red blood, so I turned white. (*Undoes the tie from his shirt.*)

MISCHIEF. What's the big fuss? That's life. This one tears off a hand, that one loses a foot, many are killed in war. Life doesn't stop for that, and the world isn't changed the slightest little bit. What does Motele signify in the great world factory called nature?

HERSHELE. Devil, you are right. Motele signifies nothing. Well, and Hershele signifies so much? Our poet says, "Man can be compared to a broken skull, to the shadow that slips away, to dust carried off by the wind, to a dream that disappears—"

MISCHIEF. Ah, that's the kind of old-fashioned little poem that the Jews always use to embitter their own lives and hurl themselves into fear and trembling. It's a long, long time since Job, our Jewish hero of misery, said the same wise thing: "Man is like grass that grows and is cut down, like a shadow that runs . . ." No. I much prefer what the learned German professor said: "I want pleasure. Let my eye enjoy everything, so that my soul will strive further."

HERSHELE. I am a Jew, and the old-fashioned little Jewish poems will live in me till I die. The man can be uprooted from me but not the Jew. No, the man who told you he would indulge with his eye and strive with his soul must certainly have been a Gentile. The Jew believes you cannot enjoy pleasure while the spirit is striving, and the spirit cannot strive while you are enjoying pleasure.

MISCHIEF. But one cannot be only a Jew. One must be a man.

HERSHELE. Yes, a man too. Once upon a time I used to imagine how awesomely the great ram's horn would sound as it announced Judgment Day and awakened the dead who lie in their graves, calling them to the throne of judgment. Mischief, when that fierce howl tore from Motl's breast today, it resounded more awesomely than the voice of the great ram's horn. The man screamed in him, Mischief, the true natural man. And no matter how deeply all human feelings were sleeping inside me, his howl awakened them. And when I saw the pale faces around him, their honest fright and pity, I understood that it is this howl that is the mighty ram's horn which calls us to Judgment Day, which breaks through our armor into our hearts, and awakens man from his grave. At that scream, Gentile and Jew, worker and boss, wise man and fool, all disappear. Only the man awakens. The man, the man.

MISCHIEF. Ah, I don't know what a Jew calls man. It certainly has nothing to do with strength, vigor, creativity, courage. No. Worrying like a weak woman, brooding, vacillating, drawing no pleasure from life, thinking a lot and doing very little—that is the Jewish man. Do you need that kind of man so urgently that you must call him out of the grave to come and poison your life? What are you looking at? Don't be afraid, there's no blood on you anymore. It's all washed off.

HERSHELE. Washed off or not, his blood doesn't frighten me. When I saw your blood on me that night, I felt frightened. I felt ugly, I felt bad. But his blood doesn't frighten me, it hurts me. I don't feel ugly. I feel a sharp pain.

MISCHIEF. Foolishness. Your nerves have had a little shock. It's your first time. Come, fresh air will make you healthy again. Berl Laptyukh, take the chair away. (*A Jewish worker takes the chair away.*) Foolishness. Once I saw, in a big factory, someone get caught on the big wheel. It lifted him very high up, still alive, and then it dragged him down and ground him to ash. (*Leads him.*)

HERSHELE. (*Thoughtfully.*) That's just how it is, evidently. The wheel of life lifts you high, all the way high, and then it throws you down and grinds you into ash, into ashes and dust.

MISCHIEF. A Jew without ashes and dust is like a Gentile without brandy and beer. Come, we'll take a little cognac ourselves. Just look how pale he is. You're still absolutely green. It's only a matter of getting used to it. In a big factory, feet get broken and hands get ripped every minute, and it's nothing. You just have to get used to it. Once upon a time, you could be sentimental, when a man worked with people. Now we work with machines, and you must be careful, strong, and cold as a machine. Do you see? Man has been caught up in it, so he has become man no longer. (*Both exit. Noise of machines and wheels.*)

SCENE 3

HERSHELE'S *office. A bookcase with Jewish religious books. His violin lies on top in a case. In the middle of the room, a writing table near which stands a tall iron strongbox and a few stools.* LEYZER *and* PESENYU *sit sadly.* FREYDENYU *walks around wringing her hand and singing the Psalm of David softly in a weeping voice. The light darkens gradually.*

PESENYU. Freydenyu, my child, what hurts you? Are you sick?

FREYDENYU. My heart hurts me, Aunt Pese. Something like a serpent sucks my blood. I can't find a place for myself. Nothing matters to me, and nothing makes me happy. I feel exactly as if I were swimming in a sea of misery and sadness. (*She goes to bookcase and takes violin and contemplates it.*)

LEYZER. But why is that? Why do you feel that way?

FREYDENYU. I don't know myself. All of a sudden such regret, such sadness, such heartache.

PESENYU. Father in Heaven. (*Quietly to* LEYZER.) I ought to run over there to see what is happening. But how can I leave her?

LEYZER. They're not letting anyone in, certainly not women. Women they drive out like geese. The doctor is operating now. (*Noise.*) Here comes the jester's boss, I'm afraid. (*Enter* HERSHELE *and* MISCHIEF. LEYZER *stands up.*)

HERSHELE. (*Very sad.*) Look—in my own office, such guests! Freydenyu, how are you? Did you come to see me?

FREYDENYU. I often come here and listen for the violin, but the violin is silent. She lies as quietly as a corpse. She used to speak. I wish I could hear her talking, once more. Did she lie to me? Didn't she tell me the truth?

HERSHELE. (*Puts the violin back.*) Calm yourself, Freydenyu, I beg you. Have pity on yourself, have pity on me.

FREYDENYU. (*Thoughtfully.*) The long gray days drag themselves out without light and without darkness, without cold and without warmth, without sorrows and without joy.

HERSHELE. No joy here and no joy at home. (*Sighs heavily.*)

FREYDENYU. Ah, I understand. Come, Aunt Pese. Uncle certainly wants to figure out his accounts and count his money over again. The money rings out, and the violin is silent. Reb Uriel, since you brought us the great prize, we have forfeited everything.

PESENYU. Yes, everyone has lost, and winning does no one any good.

MISCHIEF. Do you believe that? (*Opens the strongbox.*) Take a look, there is something worth figuring up and counting over. (*Both women off.*)

HERSHELE. (*Sits down.*) No. I have already counted over the money. I think, you see, that the time has come for a final accounting.

LEYZER. (*Has stood all this time frightened. He gestures with his hand and steals quickly to the door.*) Bye. (*Wants to run out.*)

HERSHELE. Forgive me, Father, I have been wanting to say something to you. Don't go away, please don't. Stay here. There is no living person in the house. I am here alone. I'm sorry, Father, that I let you be with strangers in your old age.

MISCHIEF. (*Aside.*) He is looking for man in the jester.

LEYZER. I'm not with strangers. At Efroyim the Musician's, we're like family. We understand each other. We have plenty to chat about, we reminisce about the old days. No, I'll tell you the truth, there with the strangers I am at home, and here at home I was among strangers. There, you understand, there is no melancholia. If there is something to eat, you dig in with an appetite. If there's no food, you tell jokes, you quarrel and make up, you laugh, you play checkers, you play a little music. There I let the jester out free in the air. I know that here he is an embarrassment to you, but there he fits in. Of course I can't make you pay Efroyim for such a good-for-nothing old father.

HERSHELE. No, Father, that's not what I meant. You misunderstood me.

LEYZER. I want to say, even if you didn't pay, Efroyim still wouldn't drive me out, God forbid. For paupers it's not so important. But here? What do I need here and what do I have here? Good day. No, it's getting dark: A good night / (*adds quietly*) And now turn out the light. (*Off.*)

MISCHIEF. So, do you have to be so afraid of man? Reb Hersh, in every man sits a jester.

HERSHELE. Yes. But in every jester sits man. You know, however great we may consider ourselves, however rich and strong we may be, we are afraid of man. When we build a synagogue, or a ritual bath, or when I wanted to build a hospital here, for example, or when I pay board for my father, that's only because I am afraid of man. Only because we want to pay off a small percentage, at least, of the great debt we owe him. Only because we believe we can cheat him, bribe him. Devil, nothing scares a man so badly as man himself. (*The room gradually becomes darker.*)

MISCHIEF. I don't understand. I know this one is afraid of God; others are afraid of Satan. You are afraid of man, of all things. Is man so very powerful?

HERSHELE. One can set things straight with God. And Satan counts for very little when one already considers himself skillful and wise. But man? Our rabbis say: The sins *beyn odom le-mokem,* "between man and God," are atoned for every year on the Day of Atonement. But *beyn odom l'odom,* "what one man sins against another"—to redeem that, tears don't help, or charity, or pleas and prayers and fasting. (*Noise.*) Sh. Who's there? (*A few Jewish workers lead in* DOBE *and* TSIPE. *They have been weeping a great deal.*)

WORKERS. Excuse us, Reb Hershele, the doctor said to lead them into the office. The operation can't go on because of them. We practically had to use violence to pull them away. (*Off.*)

HERSHELE. Come in here. Come, it's only us. (*Leads them.*)

DOBE. This is why I dreamed last Saturday night that I lost a tooth. It's not a tooth, it's an eye you've torn from me. You crippled my only child.

TSIPENYU. Mother-in-law, why do you have to talk? He is our boss, after all, and why should it matter to a boss? If Motl has no hands, someone else will work. (*Weeps.*)

HERSHELE. Tsipenyu, I am not only your boss, I am your uncle and your brother-in-law.

TSIPENYU. Since you divorced Aunt Pese, you are not my uncle. And because you have made my sister unhappy, you are no brother-in-law to me. (*Both exit through the inner door.*)

HERSHELE. Everyone is a stranger and an enemy to me. People look as if they feel like family with a rich man, as if they cherish his friendship dearly. But that's only the way it looks. When the time comes that they tell the truth about their feelings, then they are all his enemies, all strangers. It is only in dreams that he sees himself with other people; in reality, he is alone. Alone. Mischief, please, I want to be alone here now.

MISCHIEF. But I don't want to leave you alone now. I am afraid you are too upset. And . . . and a little too much worried about . . . man.

HERSHELE. How can you help me now? You were able to help me become rich, become great and famous. You brought me honors. But to make me happy, to calm me, gladden my spirit, make my sick soul healthy—that you cannot do. I beg you, leave me for now.

MISCHIEF. (*Sarcastically.*) Man wants to be alone?

HERSHELE. Yes, go. I want to be alone with myself. Don't you hear me? (*Angry.*) I'm telling you, get out of here!

MISCHIEF. (*Going.*) Bad to do business with a partner like that. All the elements which add up to happiness, and yet he cannot put them together and be happy. You want to help him? As soon as you leave him on his own a while, he starts to turn around, have regrets, repent. He remains deaf to what you say and listens to what man says. How can you do business with such creatures? (*Exit.*)

HERSHELE. I did not realize how very alone, how isolated I have become. Not one single friend, not one single person in the whole world to whom I can come now with my aching heart, weep out my sorrows, confess all my errors and expect one word of trust and hope. My own father feels uncomfortable in my home, the home of his only son. My Freydenyu? I don't understand her. I was busy with business and had no time to develop her friendship. She, the one I divorced, she was once my most faithful friend in the world, and now . . . now we are strangers. However bad I was, she would have forgiven me, because she . . . she was a true friend. True friendship doesn't keep account books. (PESENYU *enters.*) Oh—

PESENYU. There's no one here? I wanted to have brandy sent in. Freydenyu keeps getting attacks of weakness. (*Goes to the outer door.*)

HERSHELE. I am glad you've come. I wanted to speak with you.

PESENYU. With me? Not now. You are alone here, a man.

HERSHELE. It's not such a big sin.

PESENYU. No. But what can I talk with you about, or you with me? Since we are strangers now, after all. But why are you sitting in the dark? Shall I tell them to bring you in a lamp? (*In doorway.*) Bring a lamp.

HERSHELE. No, I want to sit in the dark. (*A servant brings a lamp. Exits.*)

PESENYU. Oy, when will they send somebody? (*Aside.*) Poor thing, poor thing, he has nobody to say a word to. (*Goes to door.* LEYZER *bursts in.*)

HERSHELE. What is it?

LEYZER. (*Frightened.*) Pese, forgive me, I have to tell you something. Sh!

PESENYU. Your secrets.

LEYZER. Pesenyu, for the first time in my life I have a secret that nobody will laugh at. (*Quietly.*) I just heard in the street that Motele did not survive the operation. Are they there? Nobody has the nerve to tell them.

PESENYU. Oh, how will Tsipenyu bear it? And the poor mother, poor thing. Father in Heaven! (*Both off.*)

HERSHELE. What is it now? Ah! What does it have to do with me, and how can it concern me? (*Walks about.*) What awaits me in the future? It is exactly as if I look into a dark emptiness, an abyss, a frightful nothingness. I am afraid. I am afraid to live. Living on like this terrifies me. But to transform my life is more than I can do. (*Suddenly clutches his head.*) A terrible idea comes to me. God, you know what I feel. You are good and will forgive me. I am afraid to live. I am afraid to live. (*He covers his face and does not notice that* KHATSKL *enters.* KHATSKL *looks beaten down and has been weeping. Pause.*)

KHATSKL. Excuse me, boss. (HERSHELE *is startled.*) Don't be startled. I have come to take home my heartbroken wife and my poor daughter-in-law, poor girl.

HERSHELE. So? They can go home already? The operation is finished?

KHATSKL. Yes, they can go home. Your doctor has finished what your factory began. Sh! I don't want them in there to know yet. (*Quietly.*) Reb Hershl, my son died under the knife.

HERSHELE. Oh, God in Heaven! Died? "Blessed is the righteous judge."

KHATSKL. Who says that there is a righteous judge? You? You believe that there is a righteous judge, and you must account for yourself in the end? Reb Hershele, that judge will not be satisfied with your final reckoning. Even I do not accept your final reckoning.

HERSHELE. Yes, Reb Khatskl, I . . . I do believe that sooner or later every man must submit his final accounts to God's judgment. But to you? Submit to your judgment?

KHATSKL. Yes, to me, your worker—to my judgment above all. Once we were brothers; now I am your laborer. Once I was your friend; now I am your servant. Once, before writing the name of God, you immersed yourself in water, and now you immerse yourself in our blood. In the blood of our innocent children.

HERSHELE. Khatskl, have mercy on me, I beg you.

KHATSKL. You had an old father whom you used to honor more than you had to, so it seemed to me, but did you have mercy on him? Did you have mercy on your wife, a decent pious woman who considered you an angel? Did you have mercy on your young wife who through you has become, poor thing, somehow confused in her mind?

HERSHELE. Through me?

KHATSKL. Yes, through you. Did you have mercy on your friend, your best comrade, and on his children? While you sit here and count money, a corpse lies in my house, a dead body, murdered by your money. You promised to make the whole town happy with your factory, but you robbed us all, you made us unhappy, corrupted us. Reb Hershele Dubrovner, you playacted a comedy with God. You wanted godly labor; you made prayer shawls for Jews. Look. See. (*He takes out of his bosom a bloodied prayer shawl.*) This is one of your prayer shawls. It is bloody. It is soaked in the blood of my child and in the tears of his poor little orphans. My dead son spoiled your shawl. Put it on my account. (*He rushes off into the inner room.*)

HERSHELE. (*He remains a long time without moving. Then he takes the prayer shawl and contemplates it.*) Soaked in his blood and in the tears of his orphans. Oh, mine is a big account, a heavy account. I have so much to pay, I feel I must go bankrupt. Bankrupt. Not the way I did with my partner Mischief. No. No, then I had something to pay my debts with and did not want to pay. This time I want to pay, but I have nothing to pay with. (*He opens the strongbox.*) Look at that. A strongbox full of money, yet it will not pay the smallest debt which one man can owe another. Oh, powerful rich man, how fearfully poor you are. (*He contemplates the prayer shawl and lays it on the strongbox.*) It takes too much talk to express all that I feel. Weeping out the pain would be easier, but I have no tears. (*He catches sight of the violin.*) Oh, I will play, play one more time. (*He takes the violin from the shelf, closes all the doors.*) Once such different feelings drew me to speak through you. Now you shall speak for me again, one more time. Freydenyu says you come from heaven. Carry my sighs and sobs back up there where you come from, together with your music. (*He plays the Psalm of David softly with feeling, then covers his face and remains still.*) Before, I had no tears, but now I feel that I will be able to weep. Yes. I weep. And a little piece of a poem comes back to mind, very well suited to a bankrupt who is closing out his business. (*He takes from the shelf a prayer book for the High Holy Days, stands at the strongbox as at a reading desk. Reads the Hebrew in the traditional chant.*) Ay. (*Long sigh.*) *Enosh mo yizkhe?* "What can a man deserve" and how can he be pure? *Tomey bivsoroy,* "he is impure in his flesh," unclean in his ways; his very death causes ritual impurity. *Kol yemey khayov toyhu . . .* (*Weeps.*) Yes, "all the days of his life are emptiness," his nights are a void, and his occupations are vanity. His life is like a dream. Fears pursue him constantly. By night he sleeps not, by day he rests not, *ad yirdom bakever,* "until he slumbers, until he slumbers in the grave." *Mo yesoynen odom khay?* "What can poor man complain of?" He was born to toil and suffer. If he gave charity, a funeral procession follows him to the cemetery. If he was wise, his wisdom goes down with him into the grave. "Yet till the day of his death, you await repentance."

(*He falls upon the bloodied prayer shawl and weeps. Then he comes to a decision and lifts his head decisively. He takes the shawl, fastens it to the handle of the strongbox, knots it around his throat, takes a long look around, sighs deeply, and sinks down. The strongbox hides his body. His shadow is visible. Pause. Then* FREYDENYU *appears.*)

FREYDENYU. The violin spoke again. She was telling the truth again. I listen and listen, but why did she fall silent? Oh, why don't you go on speaking? (*She sings softly.*) *Gam ki eylekh begey tsalmoves, lo iro ro, ki oto imodi.* Hershele, the violin is silent, and you are silent. Where are you? (*She suddenly notices him.*) Oh! Oh! (*She screams despairingly.* LEYZER, PESENYU, DOBE, TSIPENYU, KHATSKL *from inner door.* MISCHIEF *from outside. Servants bring lights.*) Oh, I'm afraid. I'm afraid to look at him.

ALL. (*Frightened.*) What is it? What has happened? (KHATSKL *notices him.*)

PESENYU. (*She helps take him down.*) I'm not afraid of him. My heart bleeds for him.

KHATSKL. Father in Heaven. (*He takes him down.*) He is dead. (*Weeps.*) "Blessed is the righteous judge." (*He and* LEYZER *lay him on the ground and cover him with the prayer shawl.*)

LEYZER. Not the jester now, just old Leyzer, mourning his son. (*He rips his own garment and weeps. All the women weep in despair.*)

MISCHIEF. (*Aside.*) So much money in the strongbox, and all the same he didn't want to live any more. What, then even the power of gold has its limits? How can that be? In other words, you can seduce a man with money, corrupt him, deform him, but you can never utterly destroy his soul? In that case, I seem to have lost my bet.

PESENYU. (*She falls on the body.*) Now, when he is dead, I am at least permitted to weep beside him. (*Weeps. All weep.*)

(*A ram's horn sounds in the distance.*)

CHORUS OF ALL ANGELS. (*Offstage, softly.*)
> Death comes to everything. All that lives dies.
> Life itself is undying.
> All that wills and that strives must die.
> Striving and willing alone are undying.

Curtain

Green Fields *(Grine Felder)*
(1916)

PERETZ HIRSCHBEIN

꙰

The texts published in *Grine Felder (Trilogye) Green Fields (Trilogy)* published by *Vilner Farlag fun B. Kletskin* (B. Kletskin, Vilna Publishers) (Vilnius, 1929) and by *Perets Hirshbayn-Bikher-Komitet* (Peretz Hirschbein Books Committee) (New York and Los Angeles, 1951) are virtually identical.

The syllables of characters' names are stressed as follows:

> DOvid-NOYekh (strongest stress on the NOY)
> ROKHl
> HERSH-BER (strongest stress on the BER)
> AVrom-YANkev (strongest stress on the YAN)
> elKONe
> GITl
> STEre
> LEvi-YITSkhok (strongest stress on the YITS)

(See the Note on Transliteration.) English speakers may not recognize the common English equivalents: David-Noah, Rachel, Abraham-Jacob, and Levi-Isaac.

Reb simply means "Mr." It is not a way of addressing a rabbi. Levi-Yitskhok is addressed as "Rebbe." A rebbe is a teacher and/or a spiritual guide rather than a congregational rabbi in the usual modern American sense. Levi-Yitskhok is also referred to by all the characters as "the rebbe," which I have translated as "teacher."

The dialogue contains religious references that may not be obvious. For example, it was common for young men to study for years in poverty, boarding or at least eating with benevolent families. It was (and in some communities still is) an honor to support a son-in-law who spent his whole life studying Jewish law. In act 1, when the girls are getting their first look at Levi-Yitskhok, Stere seems to be thinking of the legends about saintly men who wander the world unrecognized. When Levi-Yitskhok asks in act 2, "Why is this day different from all other days?" he is humorously quoting from the Passover *seder* ceremony. Later, he refers to the traditional notion that the world exists for the sake of the virtues (often expressed as: "on the credit" or "on the merits") of holy people living and dead. The good and evil impulses mentioned in act 3 are a common conception of the conscience's inner struggle for virtue. In describing Stere to Levi-Yitskhok, Elkone says she has a kosher heart, which is a common metaphor for being good, honest, or proper. Finally, when Levi-Yitskhok refers to the Talmud, the text actually specifies that book of the Talmud called the Mishne.

The characters often refer to the High Holy Days, which are Rosh Ha-Shono, the New Year's holiday, and Yom Kippur, the Day of Atonement. On these days, and in the ten days between, Jews are supposed to think about the year that has passed, assess their own behavior, and repent and rectify their sins. This involves paying back debts left unpaid, apologizing to people they have harmed or offended, and generally trying to right whatever wrongs they have committed. These days are very important in the Jewish calendar; in fact, when a Jew simply refers to *yontif* (holiday), or "the holidays," one assumes that the High Holy Day season is meant. Since *Green Fields* takes place in the spring and late summer and the High Holy Days generally fall in September or early October, the characters are particularly conscious of their approach.

I made one dramaturgical change. At the start of act 1, Dovid-Noyekh seems to understand perfectly well that there may be a match between Stere and Hersh-Ber. But a few minutes later, after the quarrel with Gitl and Elkone, when Rokhl says her son has a heart of gold, Dovid-Noyekh answers, "It would never have occurred to me. Elkone would have talked to me." That is so confusing that it seems to be a mistake, so I deleted "It would never have occurred to me."

Jacob Ben-Ami directed the first production of *Green Fields* at the Irving Place Theatre in New York on May 30, 1919. The years brought productions by many companies, including the famous Vilna Troupe. There were productions in Hebrew and English. The Yiddish Theatre Project of the WPA performed it, as well as Hirschbein's other three pastoral plays: *Di Puste Kretshme (The Idle Inn)* (1911); *A Farvorfn Vinkl (A Secluded Nook)* (1913); and *Der Shmids Tekhter (The Blacksmith's Daughters)* (1915).

Hirschbein eventually added two sequels to *Green Fields*. In *Tsvey shtet (Two Cities)*, Levi-Yitskhok and Tsine are already married with several children. They live in a town where he is a very respected rabbi. He has accepted a position in a larger city, and they move, but the old congregation resists his leaving. The old congregation so interferes with their new lives that finally it is necessary to strike a compromise: Khayim, the oldest son of Levi-Yitskhok and Tsine, who is already becoming a great scholar in his own right, takes over his father's old place. The third part of the trilogy, entitled *Levi-Yitskhok,* takes place back in the original country setting at Dovid-Noyekh's farm. Except for Rokhl, who has died, all the original characters from *Green Fields* are there. Levi-Yitskhok, Tsine, and their children are visiting. The plan is to marry Khayim to his cousin, Dvoyre, Avrom-Yankev's daughter. However, she is reluctant. When some of the older generation pressure her toward marriage, Levi-Yitskhok and Tsine defend her, and finally, after much soul-searching, she refuses the match. Levi-Yitskhok decides that he wants to spend the rest of his life studying quietly in the country.

The two sequels seem never to have been performed professionally. In 1974, however, David Licht created and directed a composite of all three plays for the Folksbiene ensemble in New York.

In its film form, *Green Fields* still remains one of the most populat of all Yiddish plays. Hirschbein wrote the screenplay with George Moskov, and Jacob Ben-Ami directed it in 1931. Filming took place in rural upstate New York. Because they could afford only one horse, Ben-Ami was careful to shoot Dovid-Noyekh's family showing only one end of the horse and Elkone's family showing the other. The film devotes much time to bucolic scenes of farm labor with choral singing and adds several passages of dialogue extolling the joy and nobility of working the land, ending with an emblematic shot of a plow—an unmistakable dose of agitprop, but charming all the same.

Peretz Hirschbein (1880–1948) was best known for *Green Fields* and his other plays about the lives and loves of rural Jews in the eastern European countryside. But he wrote plays in other styles as well. Beginning with the Hirschbein Troupe, which he organized in Odessa in 1908, he was associated with the Yiddish art theater movement. He was also a poet and journalist. (The introduction to this book tells more about Hirschbein and about *Green Fields.)*

❧

Characters

DOVID-NOYEKH, a farmer
ROKHL, his wife
HERSH-BER, their older son, in his twenties
TSINE, their daughter, in her late teens
AVROM-YANKEV, their younger son, in his teens
ELKONE, another farmer
GITL, his wife
STERE, their daughter, in her late teens
LEVI-YITSKHOK, a scholar, in his early twenties

Scene

Dovid-Noyekh's farm in the Russian countryside.
Act I. Outside the farmhouse.
Act II. Inside the farmhouse.
Act III. Outside the farmhouse.

Time

Around the turn of the century.
Act I. Afternoon in early spring.
Act II. Afternoon, early that summer.
Act III. Early evening, late that summer.

⁓✿⁓

Act I

DOVID-NOYEKH's *farm. Early spring, around midday. Right, a farmhouse. Left, a barn. Upstage, a garden. A few fruit trees. By the garden fence, a well.*

ROKHL. (*Sits in front of the house cutting up potatoes.* DOVID-NOYEKH *enters from garden.*) Finished all the planting so quick?
DOVID-NOYEKH. Stere came over. They're racing to see who finishes first.
ROKHL. Stere's always ready to go.

DOVID-NOYEKH. A terrific girl. Better worker than Tsine.

ROKHL. Remains to be seen who makes a better match.

DOVID-NOYEKH. Works like a mule. I couldn't carry a weight like that on my back.

ROKHL. Healthy as an apple, no evil eye. You know, really, a great help to Elkone.

DOVID-NOYEKH. That's just what I'm saying. And if she comes sneaking over here more often, it must mean something.

ROKHL. Elkone would like that.

DOVID-NOYEKH. You really think so?

ROKHL. You think Elkone would mind Hersh-Ber for a son-in-law? He would even scrape up some dowry from somewhere. And in fact, here they come.

ELKONE AND GITL. (*Entering.*) The cat comes, and here we are.

DOVID-NOYEKH. Where are you off to, Elkone.

ELKONE. How are you? I don't know, see what's going on in the world. I don't know, go around the villages a little.

ROKHL. How's the cow? Still limping?

GITL. If that was all, it wouldn't be so bad.

ROKHL. What now, God forbid?

GITL. No appetite.

DOVID-NOYEKH. That's not good.

GITL. Before Passover, even, I said we should sell her. I hate when you have to hand-feed a cow. Well, he didn't listen to me. So then she started limping. That's all we need.

ELKONE. You're not losing the family fortune on her.

GITL. What did my mother say: Just because God sits above, do I have to lie down on the ground?

ELKONE. When my old woman takes a dislike to something, there's no changing her mind.

ROKHL. I'm like that too. May God not punish me for saying so.

GITL. Why should I deny it?

ELKONE. She took a dislike to the teacher. I had to get rid of him. So now the children go around idle and empty-headed.

ROKHL. Did you see your Stere there?

ELKONE. What, she's over here?

GITL. She said she was going to help Tsine out a little with the potatoes so Hersh-Ber would help Elkone sometime maybe.

ROKHL. We were just talking about her, in fact.

GITL. You have no idea what a golden child she is. If Tsine doesn't ruin her.

ROKHL. What do you mean?

ELKONE. Tsine is full of mischief.

ROKHL. How can you say that?

DOVID-NOYEKH. I've said the same thing. You've spoiled her. An only daughter, after all. But so what? It hasn't ruined her.

ROKHL. Get out, you don't even know what you're talking about. Gitl dear, how can you think of saying such a thing?

GITL. I didn't mean it that way at all.

ROKHL. Remains to be seen which of them will make a nicer match.

ELKONE. Women. Quack like geese about their children: mine, yours, yours, mine.

DOVID-NOYEKH. Worth hearing, this time, what they're saying there.

GITL. Here Stere came to help her. Why pretend? Tsine wouldn't have done it.

DOVID-NOYEKH. Uh-oh! Now you see, Elkone, your old lady has started talking foolishness. Dovid-Noyekh's child is after all . . . Dovid-Noyekh's child.

ROKHL. That's why I really feel stabbed in the heart.

ELKONE. Come on, old lady. If you stay any longer, you'll say more foolishness. What next, Dovid-Noyekh?

GITL. I didn't mean anything by it, God forbid. Please God, all Jews should only have children like Tsine. Good-bye.

ELKONE. I should only have no more to worry about with my cow than you have with your Tsine. Eh, if I only had a big son. Come on, old lady, come on. Good-bye. (*Both exit.*)

DOVID-NOYEKH. You know, my wife, what I'm going to tell you? You've got a long tongue.

ROKHL. No, you look, if you don't mind. I'm the one with a long tongue?

DOVID-NOYEKH. All right, she has a long tongue. What do you care?

ROKHL. All I know is that it doesn't bother you if people talk about your own children.

DOVID-NOYEKH. I don't want to start up with him.

ROKHL. What gives her the right to say that Tsine ruins her Stere? We're supposed to feel honored that Tsine is friends with her daughter.

DOVID-NOYEKH. We would have gotten the potatoes planted without her, too, believe me.

ROKHL. I'm burning up. She better not say bad things about my daughter right to my face. She knows that Stere didn't come to help Tsine. She came for something else.

DOVID-NOYEKH. Now I don't know what you're talking about.

ROKHL. Stere came because Hersh-Ber is in the garden. Well, now do you understand?

DOVID-NOYEKH. Really, that's the true story?

ROKHL. What else?

DOVID-NOYEKH. She has her eye on Hersh-Ber?

ROKHL. Why not? Doesn't he have a heart of gold?

DOVID-NOYEKH. But Elkone would have talked to me.

ROKHL. He'll talk. Didn't you see how he kept quiet the whole time? Otherwise, do you think they would have let her come over here?

DOVID-NOYEKH. In that case it really is wrong for her to talk that way about Tsine.

ROKHL. So it remains to be seen. If it comes to anything . . . then I won't approve. You watch.

DOVID-NOYEKH. I had no idea that you could get so mad.

ROKHL. I have a good mind to ask her. Tsine! Tsine!

DOVID-NOYEKH. Don't bother her. Let her finish.

TSINE. (*Appears on the far side of the fence.*) You know, we're practically done already.

ROKHL. I'll be down right away too.

TSINE. What did you call me for?

ROKHL. Here, take a piece of bread and butter. You must be hungry.

TSINE. Fix my hair ribbon. My hands are covered with mud. (ROKHL *kisses her, braiding the ribbon into her hair.*)

DOVID-NOYEKH. You wanted to ask her something.

ROKHL. I can't while you're standing there.

TSINE. What is it?

ROKHL. Nothing. I just had a little run-in with Gitl.

TSINE. Why?

ROKHL. No reason. About you.

TSINE. About me?

ROKHL. Go on, Dovid-Noyekh, go into the garden.

TSINE. Oh, Mama, what is all this?

ROKHL. Nothing, child. Why do you look so funny? It's nothing.

DOVID-NOYEKH. First she quarreled and now she's sorry. (*Goes away.*)

ROKHL. Where is Hersh-Ber?

TSINE. Helping to plant.

ROKHL. What were you and Stere talking about?

TSINE. Me? Nothing.

ROKHL. Did you ask her to come help you? What's she doing now?

TSINE. She's planting potatoes.

ROKHL. Did you ask her to or did Hersh-Ber?

TSINE. She came herself. I told her that I'd help too. And if she came to help Hersh-Ber, so what? (*Sudden burst of laughter.*)

ROKHL. What are you laughing about? (TSINE hugs her mother, kisses her, and laughs.) Since I have to stick up for you anyway—

TSINE. It's because you're peeking where you shouldn't.

ROKHL. Ay, go away, get off of me. Maybe Gitl is right when she says that you're ruining Stere.

TSINE. Me? Too bad I wasn't there. I would have known how to answer her. She really believes that Stere is just a puppy. I can't hold a candle to her. (*Continues laughing.*)

ROKHL. What now?

TSINE. I'm laughing because you're mad about something, and you ask about such strange things.

ROKHL. Why not? I'm a mother, so I want to know.

TSINE. I invited her because I knew she wanted me to.

ROKHL. And here I believed that she came on her own.

TSINE. What's the difference? So long as she gave him a kiss.

ROKHL. Who?

TSINE. She thought I didn't see.

ROKHL. What?

TSINE. Both of them were bent over into the furrow, like this, side by side. I pretended I didn't see.

ROKHL. And him?

TSINE. He was embarrassed. He turned around to see if I saw.

ROKHL. I would never have believed it of her.

TSINE. There's a lot she can teach me.

ROKHL. Did Avrom-Yankev see, God forbid?

TSINE. He wasn't in the garden.

ROKHL. That's all I need, for him to see things like that, God forbid.

TSINE. Don't tell papa because—

STERE. (*Enters.*) Where did you hide yourself, Tsine? Do you want me to plant your garden by myself?

TSINE. Come here. There's practically no more to plant anyway.

ROKHL. Thank you very much, Sterele, for coming to help out a little. God willing, when you mow your hay, we'll all come help you out.

STERE. You know, I'm practically as strong as Hersh-Ber, maybe.

TSINE. Did you wrestle with him?

STERE. I rolled the big stone out of your furrow all by myself.

ROKHL. You shouldn't have lifted a weight like that. If something happened, God forbid, your mother would end up blaming me.

STERE. Nothing will happen.

ROKHL. I'll plant the few potatoes that are left. (*Takes on her shoulder a sack with a few potatoes and exits.*)

TSINE. Sterele, come right over here in front of me.

STERE. What?

TSINE. Why did you get so red?

STERE. What?

TSINE. Oh, Sterele, I saw everything.

STERE. What did you see?

TSINE. (*Hugs and kisses her.*) Silly, it doesn't matter. That's what I told Mama, too.

STERE. I swear I don't know what you're talking about.

TSINE. You told everyone that I asked you to come help me.

STERE. Who told you that? My mother told me to come.

TSINE. Your mother had a fight with my mother.

STERE. What are you saying?

TSINE. You got so scared. What do you care if my mother and your mother are mad at each other?

STERE. But what are you saying—that you saw everything?

TSINE. I really did see how you gave Hersh-Ber a kiss.

STERE. It's not true.

TSINE. I saw it myself, silly. If you had a big brother like that, I might have done it myself.

STERE. It's a lie.

TSINE. Sterele, silly, why are you so scared?

STERE. You're not nice, Tsine, I'm telling you.

TSINE. He's my brother after all, Stere.

STERE. I'll be mad at you my whole life.

TSINE. I can call Hersh-Ber and ask him.

STERE. Just try it.

TSINE. I even told Mama too.

STERE. Whose mama?

TSINE. My mama. What do you think, I'm so dumb I'd go tell your mama? I don't like your mother all that much that I'd go tell her such things.

STERE. No, you're lying.

TSINE. What's the matter with you, Sterele? I saw you myself.

STERE. It's a lie that you told your mother.

TSINE. Honestly, I told her.

STERE. (*Wiping tears.*) I won't ever speak to you my whole life.

TSINE. Sterele, you silly thing, why are you crying? I love you so much. Stere, why are you crying? (*Embraces her and wipes the tears from her cheeks with her apron.*)

STERE. You shouldn't have done a thing like that to me.

TSINE. I shouldn't have looked when you gave him a kiss? What a dummy—he waited for you to do it.

STERE. (*Bursts out into laughter.*) He got so red. (TSINE *also laughs out loud.*) All the same, I'm telling you that you're not nice and you want to spoil everything for me.

TSINE. I don't know what you're talking about.

STERE. How could you do a thing like that? I'll be ashamed to show myself in front of your mother.

TSINE. Maybe I really shouldn't have told.

STERE. Well, you see then.

TSINE. Don't look at me like that, Sterele. I really don't know why I did it. I heard that your mother quarreled with my mother, so I wanted . . . Oh, I don't know myself why I did it. Will you forgive me, Sterele?

STERE. I'm mad.

TSINE. You dope, it was bound to happen sooner or later.

STERE. (*Laughs and cries.*) I wouldn't have minded if he had done it. No, I ought to be mad at you forever. Forever.

TSINE. If you had a big brother, I'd let the whole world know that I love him. What is there to be ashamed of in that?

STERE. No, you little goat, it's better when no one knows. It would be so nice if no one knew. Now I'll be embarrassed even in front of him.

TSINE. I'll tell him what you said.

STERE. I might drown myself if you do that. Nobody can know.

TSINE. I never knew you were like this. (STERE *cries silently.*) You know, Sterele, maybe I really was dumb.

STERE. I wouldn't have minded the whole thing if your mother didn't hate me so much.

TSINE. Now that's not a nice thing to say.

STERE. I know that your mother can't stand to look at me.

TSINE. Go away now, just go. You know I envy you. So what if you cry? So long as it really makes you feel good.

STERE. (*Laughs through tears.*) Oh, I'll be so embarrassed.

TSINE. Sh! Look, who's Avrom-Yankev bringing over here? Look, in the garden.

STERE. It's a stranger? I'm going to run.

TSINE. Just look, a total stranger. (*Approaching from the garden come* AVROM-YANKEV *and a young man, who is piously dressed and has a pious face. He carries a pack on his back. Climbs clumsily over the fence.* TSINE *barely keeps herself from laughing.* STERE *lets out a laugh, then breaks it off.*)

AVROM-YANKEV. Here's the house.

STRANGER (LEVI-YITSKHOK). A good day to you.

AVROM-YANKEV. Mama said would you please go in the house. Come in. (*Both go into the house.* TSINE *and* STERE *grab each other and choke with laughter.*)

STERE. Maybe it's a sin to laugh like this at a stranger.

TSINE. Who can it be? He didn't even look at us once.

STERE. Shy.

TSINE. What a pale face he has.

STERE. Must wander around the world.

TSINE. Collecting for charity, you think?

STERE. I have a good mind to look in the window. (*Steals to the window.*)

TSINE. Well?

STERE. He put down the pack.

TSINE. He's talking with Avrom-Yankev.

STERE. He's looking around.

TSINE. Stay there and I'll sneak up behind you.

STERE. Look how Avrom-Yankev isn't afraid of him at all.

ROKHL. (*Enters.*) Why are you standing behind the window?

TSINE. Who's that, Mama?

ROKHL. A stranger. Asked to spend the night in our house.

STERE. You hear?

ROKHL. Looks like he hasn't eaten anything yet today. (TSINE *laughs.*) What strikes you so very funny about a strange man?

TSINE. He looks so strange. Just a boy still. I'm shy to go into the house.

DOVID-NOYEKH. (*Enters.*) Where is he, the man?

ROKHL. In the house.

DOVID-NOYEKH. Give him a proper welcome. Dinner, maybe. (*Goes into the house.*)

TSINE. There are strange people in this world. People who look altogether different from us. He has black hair, doesn't he?

STERE. Black eyes too.

TSINE. He kept his eyes down.

STERE. Probably he has black eyes.

TSINE. And such a pale face.

STERE. A fine face. City men are like that.

TSINE. And wanders around the world on foot.

STERE. Maybe he isn't a poor man at all? He may even be . . . What did you think of him, Tsine?

TSINE. Who can he be, really, the man? Maybe he heard me when I was laughing?

STERE. He must have heard. But he wouldn't have understood that it was him we were laughing at. (*Enter* HERSH-BER.) I beg you, Tsinele, don't tell him anything.

TSINE. Did you see the stranger?

HERSH-BER. I'm just on my way to take a look.

STERE. I'm mad at you.

HERSH-BER. You'll make up.

TSINE. Hersh-Ber, you're a dummy.

HERSH-BER. I'm what?

STERE. Remember, Tsine.

HERSH-BER. You're going to get it from me right now. (*He chases* TSINE *in fun. She runs away.*)

TSINE. You're a dummy.

STERE. I'll help you catch her. Head her off at the well. (TSINE *jumps over the fence and disappears.*)

HERSH-BER. She'll get hers from me yet. Say, what did she mean?

STERE. How do I know what she meant?

HERSH-BER. Will your father be here today?

STERE. I don't know. If you want to see him, you can come over to our house.

HERSH-BER. Your father thinks he's something, you understand? He's got flies up his nose. Let him just admit it's none of his business.

STERE. What do you mean?

HERSH-BER. I mean what I mean. Why do I need to keep hanging around, and you too, till our eyes fall out of our heads?

STERE. You really think I want you for a bridegroom? You were bending down right under my nose—so what could I do?

HERSH-BER. I know all about it. Come over here.

STERE. Tsine must have sneaked in somewhere and eavesdropped. She saw too, before, and she told her mother.

HERSH-BER. Sure she did.

STERE. Honestly. She told me herself.

HERSH-BER. Don't worry about it. She made a fool out of you. You still don't know her.

STERE. Are you coming over to our house today?

HERSH-BER. You say you don't care whether I do or not.

STERE. Just go a little away from in front of the window, just like that. (*Throws her arms around him.*)

TSINE. (*We hear her voice from beyond the fence.*) Hersh-Ber, you're a dummy.

STERE. Tsinele, now I really am mad at you forever. (*Embarrassed, confused, jumps over the fence and runs away.* TSINE *enters.*)

HERSH-BER. What are you doing spying?

TSINE. I'm ashamed really. She loves you so, and you make such a dummy of her. You'd have a long wait till I gave you a kiss. If it was me, you'd be running after me. You don't care.

HERSH-BER. Look at this. When did you get so smart?

TSINE. I told Mama that you gave her a kiss.

HERSH-BER. She was the one who gave it to me.

TSINE. See what a dummy you are?

HERSH-BER. But why are you spreading lies around?

TSINE. But you know it's the truth.

HERSH-BER. If it's the truth that you told mama, I'm going to shrivel you like an apple.

TSINE. We'll see about that.

HERSH-BER. You've got no excuse to spy on me.

TSINE. You can't stop me. If you make her run after you and cry, when you're in love with her, are you a dummy or not?

HERSH-BER. Who cries? (TSINE *laughs aloud.*) You're crazy and it's not worth talking to you.

ROKHL. (*Comes out of the house.*) Oh, what a man. A boy still, really. If you saw—pearls pour out of his mouth.

TSINE. Really? I'll go into the house.

ROKHL. If you behave yourself. You might laugh.

TSINE. I promise, Mama, I'll just pass through to the other room. (*Steals into the house.*)

ROKHL. Why are you standing there like that, Hersh-Ber?

HERSH-BER. She's just lucky you came out. I was ready to give it to her good.

ROKHL. Where is Stere?

HERSH-BER. Went home, probably.

ROKHL. Is it true what Tsine told me?

HERSH-BER. (*Confused.*) What?

ROKHL. She probably made it all up.

HERSH-BER. Made what up?

ROKHL. Nothing.

HERSH-BER. So what are you talking about? Anyone can believe anything.

AVROM-YANKEV. (*Comes out.*) You know, Mama, what his name is? Levi-Yitskhok.

ROKHL. A very nice name, really.

AVROM-YANKEV. Papa asked him what his name is, so he said.

DOVID-NOYEKH. (*Comes in.*) Where are you, Rokhl? Listen to me, I like that man.

ROKHL. Still milk on his mouth.

DOVID-NOYEKH. I talked it over with him. He would stay on here.

ROKHL. He'd do what?

DOVID-NOYEKH. You know what? An educated person. The children will pick something up from him. You should have heard how he talks.

HERSH-BER. I'll bet he does.

AVROM-YANKEV. I want to study with him.

HERSH-BER. Probably a dummy like the old teacher who couldn't tie a horse's tail.

DOVID-NOYEKH. If you didn't have such a stopped-up head, even that teacher would have been enough for you.

ROKHL. So what will be?

DOVID-NOYEKH. Meanwhile we'll put him up for the night.

AVROM-YANKEV. Really, Mama, let him stay with us.

ELKONE. (*Enters.*) Hello. Why are you standing around like that?

DOVID-NOYEKH. A man came by here. He talks like something solid. His head is full of fire. We're talking it over here about maybe taking him on as a teacher.

ELKONE. Who is he? I'll chip in.

DOVID-NOYEKH. A wonder. A real somebody.

ELKONE. I'll chip in. (LEVI-YITSKHOK *comes out.*) This is him? Just a kid.

ROKHL. But with God's presence resting over him, really.

ELKONE. Excuse me. How do you do?

LEVI-YITSKHOK. How do you do?

ELKONE. You come from far away?

LEVI-YITSKHOK. Not from nearby.

DOVID-NOYEKH. We can see that.

ELKONE. May I ask where you're headed?

LEVI-YITSKHOK. I am traveling around right now. When I come to a town of good Jews, then I will stop there.

ELKONE. Maybe stop here in this village?

DOVID-NOYEKH. That's just what I'm getting at.

LEVI-YITSKHOK. What is there for me to do here in the village?

DOVID-NOYEKH. There are more Jews around here, no evil eye. We have ten men and more, every Sabbath.

ELKONE. Good Jews around here. You could study with my children, with this man's children. We would treat you with respect. We would provide fine clothes, food, and also a little money into the bargain.

ROKHL. In my house, we never lack for food, praise God above.

ELKONE. Where do they lack for food in this village? Children, fine children, only somehow we haven't managed a good teacher.

DOVID-NOYEKH. Think it over. Here, my son, though he's a big boy, nevertheless he's got a not-so-bad head on his shoulders. He can still accomplish something too if he wants.

LEVI-YITSKHOK. The children are big and I'm—

DOVID-NOYEKH. For a serious person, that doesn't matter. They won't talk back to a teacher. You'll be respectful to the teacher, right, Avrom Yankev?

ROKHL. Have you forgotten that he has always wanted to study?

ELKONE. And the girls can learn their prayers.

LEVI-YITSKHOK. I don't have any lessons for them.

ROKHL. Women are sinful creatures, I have to admit it.

ELKONE. I'll give you my whip, and if my gang don't listen, you'll thrash their bones and that'll be that.

HERSH-BER. I'll do the thrashing.

AVROM-YANKEV. Nobody will have to thrash me.

LEVI-YITSKHOK. Are there are more Jews in the area?

DOVID-NOYEKH. Naturally. Where aren't there any Jews?

ELKONE. Respectable Jews. A fine group every Sabbath.

DOVID-NOYEKH. You eat till you're full in the village: milk, butter, cheese.

ELKONE. A potato isn't poison either.

ROKHL. A person could live just on what I throw out here.

ELKONE. My old lady will want him to spend Sabbath with us.

DOVID-NOYEKH. Listen, I'm not giving him up on Sabbath.

LEVI-YITSKHOK. I would want to have time for my own studying.

ELKONE. I swear this man will be a rabbi someday even.

DOVID-NOYEKH. A day is long. If a person isn't too lazy to get up at dawn, he can manage everything. Here the children have already planted a garden of potatoes and it's barely noon.

ELKONE. All right then, I'm going home, and this evening I'll bring my gang over here for him to examine them. You can talk it all over with him. However much it takes, I'll chip in. Good-bye. (*Goes.*)

DOVID-NOYEKH. Eat. Rokhl, go make some food. Maybe he'll eat something.

LEVI-YITSKHOK. (*Looks around him.*) A nice day here in your place.

DOVID-NOYEKH. Of course. Fine Jews in the country, no evil eye.

HERSH-BER. I really want to eat. Talking doesn't get anything done.

AVROM-YANKEV. (*To* LEVI-YITSKHOK.) Do you want to see the potato garden we planted today?

ROKHL. Go show the teacher the calves in the barn. (*Goes inside the house.*)

HERSH-BER. (*As he enters the house, to his mother.*) How long will it take you to fatten him up, Mama?

ROKHL. Am I going to be stingy with his food? (*They go inside the house.*)

LEVI-YITSKHOK. Who was your teacher till now?

AVROM-YANKEV. There hasn't been any teacher here for a long time.

LEVI-YITSKHOK. But who was the last one?

AVROM-YANKEV. An old Jew.

LEVI-YITSKHOK. You didn't respect him?

AVROM-YANKEV. We were little kids still. No sense.

LEVI-YITSKHOK. I like you.

AVROM-YANKEV. Come, we'll see the calves. Then we'll go eat. Come. (*Both go away into the barn.* TSINE *comes out. Steals up to the barn, looks through a crack.* LEVI-YITSKHOK *comes out of the barn with* AVROM-YANKEV *after him.*) We have another calf, a bigger one. Grazing on the meadow.

LEVI-YITSKHOK. A nice day here at your place. (*Doesn't notice* TSINE, *who hid behind the barn when the family passed on into the house.*)

TSINE. (*Comes out, calls quietly.*) Avrom-Yankev! Avrom Yankev! (*He doesn't hear. She remains alone. Gives a sudden movement as if she wants to run into the house. At the threshold stops and stays a while in thought. Takes a basket of potatoes and goes away into the garden.*)

ROKHL. (*We hear her voice calling from the house.*) Tsine! Tsine!

Curtain

ᘓᬀᘏ

Act II

Inside DOVID-NOYEKH's *house. Beginning of summer, around midday.* LEVI-YITSKHOK *sits buried deep in his studies. Rises, walks about.*

AVROM-YANKEV. (*Enters.*) Here I am. I didn't think we were studying today.

LEVI-YITSKHOK. Why is today different from all other days?

AVROM-YANKEV. We're mowing today.

LEVI-YITSKHOK. The peasants do that.

AVROM-YANKEV. But it's nice on the meadow. Why don't you ever go barefoot?

LEVI-YITSKHOK. There's a time for everything.

AVROM-YANKEV. So really are we studying today?

LEVI-YITSKHOK. If you don't want to, and your father won't mind—

AVROM-YANKEV. Papa doesn't know.

LEVI-YITSKHOK. Even I know that it's nice out. Do you think I don't know that?

AVROM-YANKEV. We won't study. We'll just sort of talk. Talk to me about something, Rebbe.

LEVI-YITSKHOK. Call me by my name. You're bigger than I am, after all. You want me to talk to you just idle words?

AVROM-YANKEV. You want to be a rabbi. Is it really good to be a rabbi or is it hard?

LEVI-YITSKHOK. Depends for whom.

AVROM-YANKEV. Could I become a rabbi?

LEVI-YITSKHOK. It's not too hard for anyone. But you love to be in the fields better, so that's good too.

AVROM-YANKEV. It's not that I love it. It's that in summer it's hard to be inside when it's so good out there. You're like an old man already.

LEVI-YITSKHOK. A person who wants to be a rabbi has to turn his mind away from idle thoughts.

AVROM-YANKEV. Talk to me about God.

LEVI-YITSKHOK. What do you mean? Don't you know that God is everywhere?

AVROM-YANKEV. Yes, he is in heaven and on earth. I believe that things would be bad without God. He makes the grass grow, after all. It's very good that there's a God in the world. If not for God, people might be thieves.

LEVI-YITSKHOK. Like wild beasts.

AVROM-YANKEV. Did you ever see a wolf?

LEVI-YITSKHOK. It is written: *z-ev toref,* "a wolf devours."

AVROM-YANKEV. Last year a wolf ripped up one of our horses.

LEVI-YITSKHOK. Really, ripped a horse.

AVROM-YANKEV. He was hobbled in the meadow grazing. In the night. Next morning we found him dead. His throat was ripped. We recognized the wolf's teeth.

LEVI-YITSKHOK. So you see.

AVROM-YANKEV. Wolves don't know that there is a God. Man is really a smart creature.

LEVI-YITSKHOK. It's written after all: *Ki betselem elokim nivro ho-odom,* "God created man in his image." God gave some of his greatness to human beings.

AVROM-YANKEV. But a person couldn't create a world.

LEVI-YITSKHOK. A person could destroy a world.

AVROM-YANKEV. Really?

LEVI-YITSKHOK. You know, Avrom-Yankev, that I may leave here.

AVROM-YANKEV. You don't like it here?

LEVI-YITSKHOK. It's not my real life here. Here I don't have any holy books. I don't have the things I need here. I miss the voices of the scholars in the study house early every morning. I miss the light in the faces of the pious Jews. It's for the sake of their merits that the world exists.

AVROM-YANKEV. I would so like to go with you. I would like to get up to study before dawn too.

LEVI-YITSKHOK. You just said that you're longing to go into the field.

AVROM-YANKEV. That's true. But I figure that there is something mysterious in the world. Sometimes it happens that a stranger goes through the world, and he looks so different. Last year some kind of rabbi came through here. He had this long white beard. I've never seen such a Jew in the village. A synagogue full of such Jews must really be beautiful

LEVI-YITSKHOK. Of course it's beautiful.

AVROM-YANKEV. Teach me how to write my name.

LEVI-YITSKHOK. For that you first have to know how to write the alphabet.

AVROM-YANKEV. I'll bring a board and a piece of chalk and you'll show me how. (*Runs out.* LEVI-YITSKHOK *looks out the window as if he notices something. Rushes to the table, buries his eyes in his book.*)

TSINE. (*Enters, barefoot. Her dress is pulled up on one side; she straightens it as she enters. Busies herself laying a fire. Approaches him.*) Mama wants to know if you want to eat.

LEVI-YITSKHOK. I'm fine as I am.

TSINE. You want to fast?

LEVI-YITSKHOK. A person shouldn't get so used to eating.

TSINE. If you ate as much as me, you'd have more strength.

LEVI-YITSKHOK. What does one need strength for?

TSINE. It's not good not to have any strength. You couldn't wrestle Hersh-Ber.

LEVI-YITSKHOK. A Jew shouldn't wrestle.

TSINE. Why not? A Jew should be just as strong as everyone else. (*She tries to break a branch over her knee, can't, and brings it to him.*) It's too long, it sticks out of the oven. Would you break it?

LEVI-YITSKHOK. Why break it over your knee if you can do it with an ax?

TSINE. If everyone did everything just the way they're supposed to—I'm not a city person.

LEVI-YITSKHOK. People have to behave decently in the city too.

TSINE. (*A little embarrassed.*) My mama does say that I am spoiled. Stere is better than me, it's true.

LEVI-YITSKHOK. Who?

TSINE. Stere. Elkone's daughter. She told me she talked to you. My brother wants to marry her.

LEVI-YITSKHOK. Which brother?

TSINE. The big one, Hersh-Ber.

LEVI-YITSKHOK. The parents have already come to an agreement?

TSINE. Why, do you like her?

LEVI-YITSKHOK. Hm?

LEVI-YITSKHOK. Do you like Stere?

LEVI-YITSKHOK. It's not nice to ask a question like that.

TSINE. Why isn't it nice? I don't understand what's not nice about it.

LEVI-YITSKHOK. Besides, I'm thinking about leaving.

TSINE. You don't like it here?

LEVI-YITSKHOK. It is very nice here, but I'm useless. The children don't want to learn.

TSINE. Teach me. I'll learn like a boy.

LEVI-YITSKHOK. Women are not required to learn. Their husbands learn for them.

TSINE. What?

LEVI-YITSKHOK. Hm?

TSINE. I'm telling you, teach me without anybody knowing. Of course nobody needs to know. You'll see how nice it will be.

LEVI-YITSKHOK. Not right.

TSINE. Why not? It's all right for my brother and Stere.

LEVI-YITSKHOK. What, he's teaching her?

TSINE. No, they're in love. They are very much in love. It's very nice being in love. Nobody will know that you're teaching me. We can hide in the field or in the attic maybe.

LEVI-YITSKHOK. I may leave today, even.

TSINE. I won't let you.

LEVI-YITSKHOK. You can't keep me here by force.

TSINE. No, but listen, tell me what you don't like here. Maybe your mattress isn't nice, maybe—is that it? If you like my bed, I'll trade with you. Tell me why you want to leave us.

LEVI-YITSKHOK. I'll tell your father. He's the one that invited me.

TSINE. But I'm begging you not to go away. I beg you, please.

LEVI-YITSKHOK. You aren't studying anyway, so what difference does it make to you?

TSINE. Oh, if only I could do something to make you be happy here with us. You know what - when you're done eating, you'll come out into the fields and see how I bundle up the hay. I take a bundle this big up on my head, and all you can see is my feet underneath. Tell me what you like to eat. (LEVI-YITSKHOK *hides a smile.*) Just pretend that you are my husband and I am your wife, and I love you very much, and I want you to tell me what tastes good.

LEVI-YITSKHOK. But it isn't true.

TSINE. What isn't true? Just pretend we're a married couple, and I'm standing at the oven, and I want to know what my husband likes. Oh, it's so nice. Oh, I'm talking silly. I see that my talking embarrasses you. Stay with us. I beg you.

AVROM-YANKEV. (*Enters.*) Here's a board with a piece of chalk. The teacher is going to teach me how to write my name.

TSINE. Me too, Rebbe. Write my name. I want to see how my name looks written. (LEVI-YITSKHOK *writes "Avrom-Yankev" in big letters.*) All that is my name—so long?

LEVI-YITSKHOK. That says Avrom-Yankev.

TSINE. I beg you, write my name: Tsine. (LEVI-YITSKHOK *writes it.*) Oh, my. Now I'll erase it and you write it again.

LEVI-YITSKHOK. That's crazy.

TSINE. Write it, please. (*He writes it. She rubs it out again.*) Now one more time. I just love to see you write.

LEVI-YITSKHOK. You're being silly.

TSINE. Me, I can see already that you're not going to leave.

ELKONE. (*Enters.*) Good day, Rebbe. I've come to bring you home with me.

TSINE. Why?

ELKONE. That's my business.

LEVI-YITSKHOK. I want to leave the village altogether.

ELKONE. My children go around empty-headed. I can't let you leave.

LEVI-YITSKHOK. They don't obey their elders.

ELKONE. I'll be there, and I'll give them the whip if they don't obey. What can I do? We're always so busy, there isn't even time for a spanking.

LEVI-YITSKHOK. Spankings are not necessary.

ELKONE. There, you see, I don't agree. I got spanked too. Otherwise it would really have been bad. (TSINE *says something quietly to* AVROM-YANKEV, *who exits. She listens uneasily to the conversation.*)

LEVI-YITSKHOK. You ought to get an older person for the children. Then they'll treat him with more respect.

ELKONE. But - may you be healthy! - how does my wife say it: why should I fool myself? In the country, plain Jews but decent. You can find a bride here, a fine Jewish girl. In the country you always make out all right. Sha, what's this on the board? You're teaching the boy to write? He wrote this himself, did he? (*Studies the board.*) A pity I don't have my glasses. (TSINE *looks at him angrily.*) Wonderful letters—they jump right out from the board. (DOVID-NOYEKH *enters.*)

TSINE. Papa, do you know that—

ELKONE. Hello, Dovid-Noyekh. I want to take the rebbe away with me.

DOVID-NOYEKH. The boy told me. What's going on?

ELKONE. He ran pretty fast.

DOVID-NOYEKH. What does he lack here in my house? A bad mattress? Or not enough to eat maybe? And what I promised, you can count on me for it. For education—no question.

ELKONE. But you're missing the point. I'm saying that it's more sensible for him to be with me.

DOVID-NOYEKH. I'm saying that I won't let him go.

ELKONE. My children are smart alecks, and if they have the teacher right there, they'll have some respect.

DOVID-NOYEKH. Respect? How can you not have respect? (AVROM-YANKEV *enters.*) Just tell me, are you the reason why the teacher is leaving? I'll take a stick and break your bones.

LEVI-YITSKHOK. No, not because of him. If only all children were like him.

ROKHL. (*Enters.*) Dear Father in Heaven, the teacher is leaving?

DOVID-NOYEKH. You heard, Elkone wants to take him to his place.

ROKHL. You wouldn't dare.

ELKONE. Let's ask the man himself. What do you say, Rebbe?

LEVI-YITSKHOK. I think it would be better to go where I should have gone. I've spent a month, maybe more than a month, here already. It's enough.

ROKHL. What do you mean?

LEVI-YITSKHOK. I'll send you somebody older.

DOVID-NOYEKH. We want you. Everyone all around here is talking about you.

ELKONE. That's what I'm saying too.

ROKHL. Go on, Avrom-Yankev, beg the teacher to stay here with us.

DOVID-NOYEKH. Oh, this is foolishness. Let things be. It's not right to go shaming country people.

ROKHL. That's what they say: in the country, people forget God and his commandments. I was in seventh heaven that in my own home I had ... I don't know what I had here.

DOVID-NOYEKH. You see? If you give a person bad food, he leaves.

ROKHL. I don't know what you're talking about. Did I take for myself first? Or maybe for the children first?

ELKONE. That's just what I'm explaining: if he isn't happy here, he should come to me.

DOVID-NOYEKH. Elkone, what you're doing isn't right.

ROKHL. Elkone wants to start up with us—all right, then.

LEVI-YITSKHOK. Jews, don't fight over me. I lack nothing with you. I like it here too much. I eat and drink without limits. It's not what I want.

DOVID-NOYEKH. So let it be. Shaming a country person. If I lived in town, we would have other chances to board a student in our house. I would go right into the study house and search, as you see me standing here. In the country, if a Jew wants to be a Jew, he can't. I had my older one crammed, and it didn't stick in his head.

ELKONE. He's got a horse in his head, and feed for the horse, and potatoes.

ROKHL. Why now? Maybe around the holidays.

ELKONE. I have no time—what's left to talk about?

DOVID-NOYEKH. You don't dare just dismiss a country person like that, with a wave of the hand. Go out and look around a little, go in the fields, see what country people do. They don't waste their time. They don't study Torah, but they don't waste their time. Go on, Avrom-Yankev, take the teacher out into the field.

ROKHL. Go on, child.

AVROM-YANKEV. Will you go, Rebbe?

LEVI-YITSKHOK. We can go a little. (*Both go out.*)

ROKHL. (*Yells after them.*) Show him, child, show him how beautifully the corn is growing.

ELKONE. Why so quiet, Tsine? Did you see Stere?

TSINE. No.

ELKONE. They're both a fine piece of goods.

TSINE. Just so my mama is satisfied with me.

ELKONE. You hear, Dovid-Noyekh. The way they learn to answer an older person. If Stere answered me like that, she'd sure get it from me. Children nowadays!. Come, Dovid-Noyekh. (*He and* DOVID-NOYEKH *go out.* TSINE, *her back turned to the room, looks out the window and wipes away tears.*)

ROKHL. I believed that he liked it here with us, God in Heaven, and in the end . . . there you are . . . Look now, why are you crying? (TSINE *sobs.*) Why are you crying, silly child? Did you listen to what Elkone was saying? I could hardly hold myself in. Somehow he hasn't been the same Elkone lately. Gotten so mean, somehow. I wouldn't mind being in his place, though. (TSINE *sits at the window, head hanging, and wipes her tears.*) I really don't understand why you're crying. Come on now, please, what is going on?

TSINE. Didn't you hear what Elkone was saying?

ROKHL. Then what were you doing? Don't you have a mouth? You could have answered him so that he'd have something to think about.

TSINE. Don't let him go away.

ROKHL. Is that any reason why you have to cry? It is a shame for Avrom-Yankev.

TSINE. (*Hides her head in her mother's shoulder.*) I want him to stay with us. He is such a fine person, Mama.

ROKHL. But you were the one who laughed at him.

TSINE. I didn't understand.

ROKHL. But what can I do? What can I do?

TSINE. But Mama, you don't understand.

ROKHL. What don't I understand?

TSINE. When he talks, I feel like dying.

ROKHL. So that's what you mean, my child?

TSINE. I'm not a child any more. I understand everything now. I've never seen anyone like that before.

ROKHL. I'm really scared to think so high.

TSINE. What's going to happen then? What's going to happen?

ROKHL. That man is going to end up a rabbi somewhere, and what are we worth, as they say, in the world?

TSINE. Well, why can't I be his wife?

ROKHL. Ha?

TSINE. If he leaves our house, maybe I'll die.

ROKHL. Child, my heart is shaking inside me. I hear what you're saying, God in Heaven.

TSINE. Aren't I good enough for a husband like him?

ROKHL. No, it isn't that, God in Heaven, but what is a country person?

TSINE. And if I am a country person, so what? What I'm told to do, I'll do it. If somebody tells me what you have to do to be pious—I'll do it.

ROKHL. In town a Jewish girl can pray, beg God, and here, as they say—

TSINE. So I'll be able to do that too. I wanted him to talk to me, I tore off grapes for him, I was ashamed to give them to him. I asked him what he liked so I could cook it for him.

ROKHL. Here you see what the story is. Now I finally understand why he wants to leave us. How in the world could you do that? Did you go to him barefoot like that, God in Heaven?

TSINE. Why can't I be with him the way Stere is with Hersh-Ber?

ROKHL. Jews don't act like that. I'm going to go whole nights without closing an eye now you've told me. I didn't look your father in the face before our wedding. (TSINE *sobs, wipes tears.*) God in Heaven, I am going crazy. Maybe I should tell your father. Maybe he'll know how to talk to him.

TSINE. No, don't. I'm afraid for him to know. If he goes away, maybe I won't be able to bear it.

ROKHL. First of all, my child, you shouldn't go around barefoot. You mustn't do that.

TSINE. Put on a different dress, maybe?

ROKHL. I don't know, maybe.

TSINE. (*Joyfully.*) Actually, now I do know what to do. I know.

ROKHL. What's the matter with you? What's this happiness all of a sudden.

TSINE. Now I know exactly all I have to do.

ROKHL. If you act immodest, he may not even want to look at you.

TSINE. Look, Mama, look, they're all coming. I can cook supper all by myself.

ROKHL. Shouldn't I tell your father anything?

TSINE. No, mama, I beg you. (ROKHL *wipes a tear. Goes to* TSINE, *gives her a kiss and blows three times. Goes out.* TSINE *washes her face and smoothes her hair. Puts a kerchief over her head so that no hair shows and looks into a pail of water to see her face there. Takes off the kerchief and looks at her reflection again. Winds her braids up on her head and looks again. Then it occurs to her to make them into one braid. She winds this braid up on her head, but then it occurs to her to let it fall onto her shoulder. Puts on shoes and stockings. Wipes her tears.*)

HERSH-BER. (*Enters.*) Food ready?

TSINE. It'll be ready soon.

HERSH-BER. I don't have time to wait.

TSINE. What are you doing?

HERSH-BER. I have enough to do. You think I hang around doing nothing?

TSINE. You're a bad brother.

HERSH-BER. I'll be back later.

TSINE. I really have something to tell you.

HERSH-BER. I know all about your stories.

TSINE. You don't know anything about it. You're going to beg me to tell you.

HERSH-BER. So don't tell. Am I worried?.

TSINE. You didn't see Stere yesterday at all.

HERSH-BER. You saw her?

TSINE. I talked to her.

HERSH-BER. Did she say anything?

TSINE. (*Takes him around his neck and looks into his eyes.*) She cries, she wails. She can't live without you.

HERSH-BER. Some girl!

TSINE. She says she may go crazy.

HERSH-BER. Now you're lying. How did you see her yesterday?

TSINE. Certainly. I was there.

HERSH-BER. You're lying. She asked me last night why you're acting so stuck-up to her.

TSINE. I didn't really talk to her.

HERSH-BER. You see, you just want to drive me crazy.

TSINE. Really, marry Stere. It'll make you happy.

HERSH-BER. You want to be a matchmaker? It won't do you any good.

TSINE. You're my own brother, after all.

HERSH-BER. So go talk to her then. Why talk to me?

TSINE. You know she's dying for you.

HERSH-BER. Everything all set already. Started acting stuck-up.

TSINE. Probably her father mixed in.

HERSH-BER. Say, how do you know that?

TSINE. I just know.

HERSH-BER. Why are you talking funny today? Have you cooked something up with Stere? Tell me. If you get in my way, I'm telling you, you'll get it all right.

TSINE. Dope. How you talk. You're my brother after all. Am I your enemy?

HERSH-BER. I know that you're not an enemy to me. That's exactly why I'm asking you—why is she stuck-up? I tell her that when we finish mowing the hay, we'll go into town and have her measured for a dress. So she stared at me with a pair of eyes—exactly as if she didn't even know me. And you say that you talked with her.

TSINE. I wanted to make you happy.

HERSH-BER. Well, you didn't. She thinks I'll just run after her. No lack of girls in this village.

TSINE. But a pearl like Stere—

HERSH-BER. Some pearl.

TSINE. Did you ever see how she washes the sheets? When she scrubs sheets in the river, you can hear it all the way up here. Now she's just shy. But when she's your wife, she will be so affectionate. She's maybe twice as strong as I am. Did you ever see her hands? They're maybe twice as big as mine.

HERSH-BER. If you're such a good sister, you talk to her.

TSINE. Me talk to her? You should be ashamed. Why do you lie around here at home every night? Can't you eat up your supper and go over there? Why does she need to sit alone and look at nothing with things going nowhere?

HERSH-BER. Look, how do you know all this?

TSINE. How do I know? I understand.

HERSH-BER. You are a good friend. I will tell her what you told me to do.

TSINE. You would certainly embarrass her if you told her that. Why does she have to know that I ordered you to go to her?

HERSH-BER. She is a flame of a girl. I know that.

TSINE. Make plans for her to come out to our hayfield tonight.

HERSH-BER. Will you come out too?

TSINE. What do you need me for?

HERSH-BER. She won't want to come out if you're not there.

TSINE. So you'll tell her that I'll be there.

HERSH-BER. But you'll come?

TSINE. Maybe I won't come. You'll talk it all over with me. We can celebrate the wedding this winter.

HERSH-BER. On my honor, you are some manager. And I believed that you were getting in my way. When I go to the fair, I'll bring you back some beads.

TSINE. Better off bringing them to her.

HERSH-BER. Plenty of time for that. Why should I bring stuff for no reason? I'll bring her something when the time comes.

TSINE. Tell her not to listen to her father if he mixes in.

HERSH-BER. You're really teaching me nice lessons.

TSINE. And you should tell her to come out in our hayfield. Sh! Here she comes.

STERE. (*Enters.*) Hello. My father isn't here?

TSINE. Came and left.

STERE. Long ago?

TSINE. You really need him so badly?

STERE. I saw Avrom-Yankev went with the teacher to the meadow.

TSINE. You like him?

STERE. I didn't look at him.

TSINE. Swear.

HERSH-BER. Look how red she is. (*He catches her, she tears herself away.*)

TSINE. Let me, I'll catch her.

STERE. (*Doesn't let herself be caught.*) Why do you want to catch me?

TSINE. Come on, Hersh-Ber, don't let her get away.

STERE. We'll see about that. (*Pulls herself away. With ringing laughter, runs out of the house.*)

TSINE. You're a dummy. Go out, tell her to come out in the hayfield.

HERSH-BER. I don't need her. She's bad. I tell you she is bad. Better give me something to eat, that makes more sense. (DOVID-NOYEKH *and* ROKHL *enter.*)

TSINE. Supper is done.

DOVID-NOYEKH. He's really not such a fool.

TSINE. Who do you mean, Papa?

ROKHL. He means Elkone.

TSINE. What is it, Mama? Please.

ROKHL. Oh, don't pester me. What was the girl doing here?

TSINE. She came looking for her father.

DOVID-NOYEKH. You could have told her that he already went home. Such a thing. You know it's not right, none of this. I believed that he was my good friend.

ROKHL. He's got more sense than you.

TSINE. What is it, Mama? What are you talking about?

ROKHL. Better for you not to know.

DOVID-NOYEKH. You'll make him another bed today. Stuff the sack with fresh hay. Let him have a softer mattress.

TSINE. Maybe he should just take my bed?

DOVID-NOYEKH. That might not be such a bad idea. Just put in fresh hay.

TSINE. Where will I sleep? Maybe I'll go back to sleeping with Mama.

HERSH-BER. Look what a fuss they make over him.

DOVID-NOYEKH. You've got a head like a peasant. You don't even know what a privilege we've got here.

HERSH-BER. What are you making there?

TSINE. Kasha porridge with milk.

DOVID-NOYEKH. Take a look, Rokhl, whether there's enough milk in the pot.

TSINE. Enough, enough. I know by myself.

ROKHL. Did you put on shoes? Well done, my child.

TSINE. I'll do the serving. (LEVI-YITSKHOK *and* AVROM-YANKEV *enter.*)

ROKHL. You can go wash now. (*Readies the table. Lays on black and white bread.*)

AVROM-YANKEV. The teacher says he likes it here.

ROKHL. Praise God on High.

LEVI-YITSKHOK. If it's what you really want, I might as well stay here till after the holidays.

DOVID-NOYEKH. You won't be sorry. (*Everyone washes, goes to the table, makes grace, and chews bread.* ROKHL *pours everyone a bowl of barley soup.* TSINE *serves with extreme care.*)

HERSH-BER. It's just like Sabbath, the way we're sitting at the table.

ROKHL. Praise God on High. (*Pours out a bowl for* LEVI-YITSKHOK. *When* TSINE *is halfway along to serving it, she calls her back with a wink and pours in another little bit of milk. Holding the bowl,* TSINE *bends over her mother and gives her a kiss. Carries it very carefully and reverently to the table.*)

Curtain

༄

Act III

In front of DOVID-NOYEKH*'s house. Late summer. Early evening.* LEVI-YITSKHOK*'s voice is heard from inside the house. He is studying.*

TSINE *sits in front of the threshold churning butter. She remains quiet a while and listens to the chanting coming out of the house. Something occurs to her, and she runs into the garden.*

LEVI-YITSKHOK *comes out, looks at the butter churn. Tries using the stick. Sees that there are bits of butter clumped around onto the stick. Hears from the garden* TSINE*'s cry and a noise from between the branches of a tree. He remains frightened a moment, takes a few steps toward the garden, climbs quickly over into there, but soon hurries back into the house.*

TSINE *appears, pale and holding her side. She climbs over the fence and approaches her former place at the threshold. Looks at the spot of blood on her arm.* LEVI-YITSKHOK *comes out, carrying water.*

LEVI-YITSKHOK. I brought you a drink of water. Did you hurt yourself? (TSINE *takes the water and drinks.*) You frightened me.

TSINE. I fell from the top of the tree.

LEVI-YITSKHOK. Ought to say the prayer for escape from danger.

TSINE. I got scared and fell down.

LEVI-YITSKHOK. There is blood on your hand there.

TSINE. My heart is beating so hard.

LEVI-YITSKHOK. Why climb a tree?

TSINE. I heard you studying, so I went to pick apples.

LEVI-YITSKHOK. What for?

TSINE. For you. Do you think I didn't get them? (*Takes two red apples out of her shirt.*) You see, like holiday apples. I fell off the tree for you. I could have been killed.

LEVI-YITSKHOK. God forbid.

TSINE. What do you care if I'm killed?

LEVI-YITSKHOK. I have a Jewish heart after all.

TSINE. Take the two apples.

LEVI-YITSKHOK. Not now. Not till after the New Year.

TSINE. What if you want an apple now, and you can't resist?

LEVI-YITSKHOK. One must conquer the evil impulse.

TSINE. Apples grow in summertime. Can a person really hold out that long? I eat maybe ten apples every day, easy. I had no idea that you weren't supposed to.

LEVI-YITSKHOK. I'm telling you now that one isn't supposed to.

TSINE. Who is he, this evil impulse?

LEVI-YITSKHOK. He sits in people. He's the one who sent you up the tall tree to pick apples, and in fact punishment came right away.

TSINE. Oh, you don't know why I fell down from the tree.

LEVI-YITSKHOK. What do you mean I don't know?

TSINE. You don't know. You really don't know at all. If you knew how I've become another Tsine entirely. Well, why did I fall from the tree?

LEVI-YITSKHOK. Certainly no answer in the Talmud. No one gets a bloody hand in the Talmud.

TSINE. I want to show you something. (*Runs into the house.* LEVI-YIT-SKHOK *looks at the two apples, which have remained on the ground near him. He smells them.* TSINE *comes out carrying a board with chalk letters written on it.*)

LEVI-YITSKHOK. What's this?

TSINE. Read.

LEVI-YITSKHOK. That's not Avrom-Yankev's writing.

TSINE. It's mine.

LEVI-YITSKHOK. (*Looks at the letters in amazement. Reads.*) "Tsine, daughter of Reb Noyekh."

TSINE. Well, who wrote it?

LEVI-YITSKHOK. Not Avrom-Yankev.

TSINE. Rub it out.

LEVI-YITSKHOK. What should I do that for? It's not good to rub out a name.

TSINE. I beg you, rub it out. Wipe it off, like this.

LEVI-YITSKHOK. (*Laughing.*) You're being childish. All right, there, I rubbed it out.

TSINE. Now close your eyes. (*He does so. She takes a piece of chalk out of her pocket and writes.*)

LEVI-YITSKHOK. Now?

TSINE. Just a little bit more, keep them closed. Now. Well, what does it say?

LEVI-YITSKHOK. My name. "Levi-Yitskhok." Who wrote it?

TSINE. Me.

LEVI-YITSKHOK. It's impossible.

TSINE. It is too possible.

LEVI-YITSKHOK. I'll rub it out and you write it again.

TSINE. Close your eyes again, then. (*He shuts his eyes. She writes his name again with big letters, and when he still keeps his eyes shut, she steals quietly up to him and gives him a kiss. She runs away into the house.* LEVI-YITSKHOK *is astonished by what has happened. He wants to go into the house but at the very threshold catches himself. He takes the board, wipes off his name and flings it away. Remains sitting on the same bench where she was sitting before. His head down, thoughtful.*)

ELKONE. (*Enters.*) Good day, Rebbe. All alone? (LEVI-YITSKHOK *looks at him distracted.*) What's this? They keep you home to churn the butter—very practical. (LEVI-YITSKHOK *looks at him uncomprehendingly.*) You're churning butter?

LEVI-YITSKHOK. It's permitted to churn butter. What's the matter?

ELKONE. I have come to ask you a question.

LEVI-YITSKHOK. I am not qualified to settle ritual questions.

ELKONE. This kind of question you can answer.

LEVI-YITSKHOK. For example?

ELKONE. What's to be done when a daughter doesn't obey her father?

LEVI-YITSKHOK. Ha?

ELKONE. My oldest child has taken something into her head—I don't know, I can yell from today til tomorrow.

LEVI-YITSKHOK. Maybe she's right.

ELKONE. What do you mean—a child right when the father says no?

LEVI-YITSKHOK. It happens sometimes that an older person makes a mistake.

ELKONE. But against a father, such boldness? That's what I'm asking.

LEVI-YITSKHOK. Sometimes parents have to listen to what a grown child is saying.

ELKONE. No, I don't agree with that. It's written in the Torah: "Honor your mother and your father." Isn't it true that's what's written?

LEVI-YITSKHOK. Who doesn't know that?

ELKONE. That's why I say that a girl must obey her father. Dovid-Noyekh isn't here?

LEVI-YITSKHOK. No.

ELKONE. I hate an ignoramus. Who am I fooling? I may not be educated myself, but I can tell who is a decent person and who is a scoundrel.

LEVI-YITSKHOK. One must not talk about a Jew that way.

ELKONE. Why should I be ashamed? Dovid-Noyekh is a nothing and his son is a nothing.

LEVI-YITSKHOK. Fine Jews. I have nothing against them.

ELKONE. It's actually because of you that I'm saying it. They don't show you enough respect. That's not the way to treat a person.

LEVI-YITSKHOK. They show me no disrespect, God forbid.

ELKONE. The boy really doesn't take after him. Avrom-Yankev, I mean. But he himself is a nothing. Spoiled his daughter. In my house, she wouldn't go around so light-headed.

LEVI-YITSKHOK. It is not permitted to listen to that. That's gossip.

ELKONE. You are a true scholar. A pious man. But you don't see what they're doing with you.

LEVI-YITSKHOK. What should I see? Jews, the same as all other Jews.

ELKONE. So what am I supposed to do if my daughter has already attached herself to his son the clod? I beat her, she just answers back. That's what I've come to talk over.

LEVI-YITSKHOK. He is a decent young man. He'll be a pious Jew.

ELKONE. The fact is I wanted you with me in my house. We'd look after you better in my house. Maybe the children would learn something. Well, they got to you first. Everything is a matter of luck.

LEVI-YITSKHOK. You are angry, Reb Elkone. And gossip is not permitted. You are a good Jew. Dovid-Noyekh is not your enemy. And the children live in peace. So why are you acting this way?

ELKONE. Maybe you're right. A Jew should act better. What am I supposed to do? My heart is burning up. Because I am an ignoramus. My sons—they're not going to turn into aristocrats. So why shouldn't I get for my daughter some different kind of person who would light up the house—make a holiday, make a Sabbath—and then really, if you go into town for the High Holy Days, so what? I would pay to my last shirt.

LEVI-YITSKHOK. So where is the difficulty? One makes the trip into town, one asks around. There are many fine young men in town.

ELKONE. Who knows how to go about it? Who could give me advice? Who even thought of such a thing? Here for the first time my eyes were opened.

LEVI-YITSKHOK. Ha?

ELKONE. You don't understand what I mean? I'm saying you should be my son-in-law. My Stere, the older one. A good heart. I wanted to beat her today, but I felt bad about it. It's not even my idea, it's my old lady. She sent me over here. Why should I deny it? If you told me where your parents live, I'm ready to harness the horse and make a quick trip. Maybe you'll tell me where they live?

LEVI-YITSKHOK. They are in the world to come.

ELKONE. You don't say.

LEVI-YITSKHOK. In the world to come. Long ago.

ELKONE. A total orphan! Such a thing! It would be very wrong to let you go.

DOVID-NOYEKH. (*Enters.*) Hello, Elkone. What are you doing here?

ELKONE. Just so, just chatting.

DOVID-NOYEKH. Who's churning butter? My old lady is home, I see.

ELKONE. I thought you were giving the teacher the honor of churning the butter.

DOVID-NOYEKH. (*Laughing.*) My old lady still knows how to treat a guest.

(LEVI-YITSKHOK *exits behind the house.*) So nobody at all is home? Let me see. (*Looks in through the window.*)

ELKONE. I think the girl is home.

DOVID-NOYEKH. Come inside. Why are you standing outside?

ELKONE. I was just leaving.

DOVID-NOYEKH. Where were you headed then?

ELKONE. Here, actually. I wanted to have a talk with the teacher.

DOVID-NOYEKH. Why? The children don't listen?

ELKONE. Something else entirely. Listen, he's a total orphan. Well, tell me—is it really absolutely necessary to have parents?

DOVID-NOYEKH. In town you can find everything.

ELKONE. He might think that I was gossiping about you.

DOVID-NOYEKH. Why in the world should he think that?

ELKONE. Where did he go off to? He's a big fool. I was just talking to him and he probably didn't understand.

ROKHL. (*Enters.*) A guest. Practically a week since we saw you. How is Gitl? (ELKONE *groans a little.*) Does her side still hurt her? You ought to go ask someone in town. She works too hard. (GITL *enters.*) Here's a guest. We were just talking about you.

GITL. What did my mother say: If God is in heaven, should I lie down on the ground? My daughter is giving me a black year.

ROKHL. What's the matter?

GITL. What's the matter—

ELKONE. Too bad I left the house. She would have gotten it from me good.

ROKHL. I should have as good a year as she is a good child.

GITL. I know that you like her.

ROKHL. Of course I like her. If I had, besides Tsine, another three daughters like Stere, what more would I want?

GITL. You hear, Elkone?

DOVID-NOYEKH. A wonderful child. What could anyone have against her? A year younger than Tsine and twice as big, no evil eye.

GITL. (*To* ELKONE.) What are you afraid of? I don't know what there is for you to be afraid of. I dropped everything at home and came over here because I don't want to leave things hanging.

ROKHL. I don't understand what you're talking about at all, Gitl.

GITL. I want Hersh-Ber to stop bothering her.

DOVID-NOYEKH. What do you mean, "bothering her"? What do you have against Hersh-Ber?

ELKONE. I have nothing against him. He's your son. You like him and I don't.

ROKHL. And I don't care whether you don't like him or not. Ever seen such a thing?

GITL. So then let him not get Stere all stirred up.

DOVID-NOYEKH. Elkone, I'm not good enough to be your in-law?

ELKONE. Your son isn't good enough to be my son-in-law.

DOVID-NOYEKH. Why did you come to tell me this? I don't know about anything. Don't let Hersh-Ber into your house. It's your business.

ROKHL. I don't know what you have against my child.

ELKONE. I'll talk plain talk.

GITL. What do you have to be ashamed of?

ELKONE. I want the young man, the children's teacher. You understand, he is a match for Stere.

GITL. And you grabbed him into your house.

ELKONE. Your daughter is ruining him.

DOVID-NOYEKH. What do you mean?

ELKONE. I found him sitting outside.

ROKHL. What outside? When outside? Don't start telling me your bad dreams. What do you want here? Why did you come to say wicked things about my children?

DOVID-NOYEKH. Sh! Don't yell. We can straighten this out nicely, like decent people. I don't understand the whole story here. He was talking about Hersh-Ber, not about the girl. What can he have against the girl?

ROKHL. You hear how some people talk? I would like to ask her. Tsinele? Just come outside a minute. (TSINE *comes out a bit confused.*)

ELKONE. Ah, why are you getting excited? Go into the house, Tsine. It won't do you any harm if I said something about you, God forbid. Your mama wouldn't let it.

TSINE. Why did you call me?

ROKHL. Where were you when Elkone arrived?

TSINE. In the house.

ROKHL. I wouldn't have believed it of you, Elkone.

GITL. So don't. My heart is breaking.

DOVID-NOYEKH. But what is there to fight about here? I say we should ask the children.

ELKONE. I don't need to ask anyone anything. My daughter will do what I tell her.

DOVID-NOYEKH. Fine.

ROKHL. Go in the house, my child.

TSINE. What did you call me for?

GITL. Just tell me, Tsine, what does Stere talk to you about?

TSINE. She talks to me . . . She talks to me about everything. How should I remember what?

ELKONE. You hear, my wife, how smart fine people can be. Whoever is teaching my girl to be wild, she'll learn from me what's right. I'm going home and let all my bad dreams out on her. (*Starts out.*)

DOVID-NOYEKH. Not right, Elkone. I considered you a better father. Where did he run away to?

TSINE. You go instead, Gitl. Don't let him get at her, because it isn't her fault at all.

GITL. I'm not saying anything to you, Tsinele, while your mother is standing right there. Later.

ROKHL. Be well and go away. I didn't send for you. I actually believed that you were my good friend. Come into the house, Dovid-Noyekh. I have nothing to say to her. (*Both go into the house.*)

GITL. Listen to me, Tsine. Your mother believes that I wish you harm. I am not your enemy. I want to tell you without your mother hearing that I know everything you told Stere.

TSINE. I'm not scared. I don't tell things that I need to be scared about.

GITL. And here comes Hersh-Ber. I want to talk plain talk with him.

HERSH-BER. (*Enters.*) What's Elkone mad about anyway? I called to him and he didn't look at me.

GITL. He has his reasons.

HERSH-BER. And why are you so stuck-up? I didn't throw any stones in your garden.

GITL. Yes, you are throwing stones, let me tell you.

HERSH-BER. Why are you getting excited? I'm asking you, do you have a better bridegroom for Stere? Why did you start interfering? What do you want—should I pay you for Stere? I should maybe go to market to get her?

If I love Stere and Stere loves me, what are you mixing in for, I'm asking you?

GITL. So that's how it is then? It's gone that far already?

TSINE. Yes, of course.

GITL. Just look at them. Do I deserve this, God in Heaven?

HERSH-BER. If you don't want it, then no. Then whatever you want. And tell Elkone that if he lifts a hand to her, I'll show him how to be a father.

GITL. Just listen, just listen, God in Heaven.

HERSH-BER. Don't listen then, if you don't want. I'm going to say it to Elkone. (*Exit.* AVROM-YANKEV *enters.*)

TSINE. Avrom-Yankev, good you've come. I looked my eyes out for you. Now here's a kiss for you and don't tell the teacher that you taught me to write his name and my name.

AVROM-YANKEV. What do you mean?

TSINE. I'm begging you. Look, here's another kiss. Good. Here he comes. Don't tell him anything. (*Runs into the house.*)

LEVI-YITSKHOK. (*Enters.*) Where were you, Avrom Yankev?

AVROM-YANKEV. I went to see whether the horse got itself into mud somewhere.

LEVI-YITSKHOK. Why did your sister learn to write my name?

AVROM-YANKEV. She told me that she envies me because I study with you. She said she wants to learn too.

LEVI-YITSKHOK. In other words, you taught her?

AVROM-YANKEV. Wasn't I supposed to? She wanted me to teach her to pray. I'm sorry. Maybe you're not supposed to.

LEVI-YITSKHOK. Women are permitted to pray. Women need to pray too.

AVROM-YANKEV. I'll go tell her.

LEVI-YITSKHOK. Wait a little.

AVROM-YANKEV. She'll be very happy. (*Runs into the house.*)

HERSH-BER. (*Enters.*) Good that you're here, Rebbe. I hope you don't mind, I want to ask you something.

LEVI-YITSKHOK. Why not?

HERSH-BER. You know about Torah. Tell me, where is the law for when I've chosen a wife and her parents have taken it into their heads and don't want it?

LEVI-YITSKHOK. What do you mean "they don't want it"? There must be a reason.

HERSH-BER. They don't want it and that's all. Go do something.

LEVI-YITSKHOK. One must make them happy.

HERSH-BER. They've got their heads turned around and—go do something.

LEVI-YITSKHOK. Jews can discuss things. Probably there is some reason.

HERSH-BER. What kind of reason? No reason at all. Her father is stubborn and her mother is a cow and that's all. No reason at all. They're stubborn.

LEVI-YITSKHOK. You should speak to them nicely. Explain so they understand.

HERSH-BER. Maybe you're right. Only it's hard to know what's going on. Maybe you would give me a hand, Rebbe. Maybe he would have respect for you, Rebbe. I mean Elkone. I want to marry his daughter. So he's all excited.

LEVI-YITSKHOK. How can I help?

HERSH-BER. He'll have respect. You know her, after all. You've seen her. We grew up together. I'll take her just as she is, no dowry. It's hard to do anything with them.

LEVI-YITSKHOK. Alone is simplest. You should speak to them alone, nicely, with sense.

HERSH-BER. With him it might even work out all right, but that mother of hers turns her nose up.

LEVI-YITSKHOK. Let your mother talk to her.

HERSH-BER. The mothers had a fight.

LEVI-YITSKHOK. Wait till the New Year. They'll make up. Between New Year's and the Day of Atonement. People think things over. They repent.

HERSH-BER. Rebbe, you talk like a saint. But I can't wait that long. I want to go to their house and they said I can't. I know why, Rebbe. Only I can't tell you. It's all right if you don't know.

LEVI-YITSKHOK. What is there for me to know?

HERSH-BER. I know you don't know anything about it, Rebbe, that's what I'm saying. She doesn't know anything about it either. It's them getting excited. She doesn't want to hear about it. You can be sure of that.

LEVI-YITSKHOK. I don't understand how I can help.

HERSH-BER. I wouldn't like Papa to hear. You understand, he wants you for a son-in-law.

LEVI-YITSKHOK. Who?

HERSH-BER. Elkone wants you for a son-in-law.

LEVI-YITSKHOK. What do you mean?

HERSH-BER. He has a daughter. You understand. Stere. You know her, Rebbe.

LEVI-YITSKHOK. I don't understand.

HERSH-BER. You don't understand he's always hanging around you? Why does he come around just when nobody else is home? That's the whole story.

LEVI-YITSKHOK. I don't think that that's what he has in mind.

HERSH-BER. Tell him you don't want his daughter.

LEVI-YITSKHOK. The whole thing is news to me.

HERSH-BER. I told my father and mother that you don't know.

LEVI-YITSKHOK. It's a great surprise to me. (TSINE *appears in the door, eavesdrops.*)

HERSH-BER. I agree that you shouldn't do such things without the parents. But go do something with them.

LEVI-YITSKHOK. It's a great surprise to me.

HERSH-BER. Don't take it as an insult, Rebbe. (DOVID-NOYEKH *enters. Catches* TSINE *eavesdropping. She is embarrassed, hides behind the door.* HERSH-BER *was going to say something more. Gestures with his hand and goes into the house.*)

DOVID-NOYEKH. A stubborn man, that Elkone. Imagine a Jew being so stubborn. I've fought with him a lot of times. The women the same. If not for the Day of Atonement, we'd go around mad forever. Why, I ask you? Can't we live in peace? Why in the world should Jews fight? What do you say, Rebbe?

LEVI-YITSKHOK. Harmony and peace are the pillars of the world.

DOVID-NOYEKH. I've heard that before. The rabbi from town said it in a sermon. But you don't have to remind me. I am a Jew that knows what's important in this world. My wife would jump out of her skin sometimes, but I don't allow it. When you live way out in the country, before you know it, you become like the Gentiles, God forbid. They fight, and Jews fight. I have my own ways.

LEVI-YITSKHOK. There are Jews like you in town too.

DOVID-NOYEKH. We get a little bit buried in the country. But when it comes to committing a sin, we catch ourselves. We know better, thank the Lord on High. Although no one in town has much respect for country people. Oh well, we can't compare ourselves to townspeople. A town person is a real Jew. Discusses things with the rabbi. Hears proper praying and can give a donation when God in Heaven helps.

LEVI-YITSKHOK. You are a good Jew. Nothing to be ashamed of about Jews like you.

DOVID-NOYEKH. My father, rest in peace, was a farmer too. Didn't know how to train the children. How could he? Barely learned to read Hebrew. He died in my house. I took him into town, and I didn't want to leave town. That must be how our Father in Heaven wanted it, that some of us live far from Jews. Just so we're buried among Jews. Can't be helped. So it goes. My older one has given up on fine ways already. But the boy could be somebody. I thought if Elkone wanted to chip in. Well, now I hear that his children make trouble. All the same, I'd like to say: don't go away. Let things remain as they are.

LEVI-YITSKHOK. I'm not going away, Reb Dovid-Noyekh. I was getting ready to tell you that maybe you should think it over.

DOVID-NOYEKH. What is there to think over? If not Elkone, then all by myself, with all my strength. What do you mean?

LEVI-YITSKHOK. I mean that you should think it over first.

DOVID-NOYEKH. I have nothing to think over.

LEVI-YITSKHOK. I mean whether to take me as a son-in-law. That's what I mean.

DOVID-NOYEKH. (*A bit confused.*) Ha . . . Bu . . .

LEVI-YITSKHOK. My parents are in the world to come. Otherwise I would have sent them to speak for me.

DOVID-NOYEKH. Yes. Tsine, my daughter.

LEVI-YITSKHOK. You understand. That if . . . You have to agree.

DOVID-NOYEKH. I agree, I agree. No need to ask her at all.

LEVI-YITSKHOK. You need to ask her mother.

DOVID-NOYEKH. That's what I mean, ask the mother. I mean my child will obey. A good child. Rokhl. Rokhl! Come out here a minute.

LEVI-YITSKHOK. Nevertheless—

DOVID-NOYEKH. (*Calls.*) Rokhl! Rokhl, please!

ROKHL. (*Comes out.*) Do we have a God in Heaven or don't we?

DOVID-NOYEKH. Here is the mother. He asks whether you agree.

ROKHL. God in heaven, what more can I wish for my child? (*Wipes tears.*)

DOVID-NOYEKH. You don't know what you're agreeing about.

ROKHL. You know, and I don't? How would a mother not know? I know everything. (*Embraces* LEVI-YITSKHOK *and kisses him.*) I will be like a mother to you. What more can I ask of him in heaven? How will I tell her? Mama mine, she might not be able to bear it.

ELKONE. (*Enters with* GITL *and* STERE.) Where is your son, Dovid-Noyekh?

DOVID-NOYEKH. I beg you, Elkone. Don't fight with me now.

ELKONE. Where is your son? I want Stere to tell him right in front of my eyes that she doesn't want to know him.

STERE. (*Her eyes show she has been crying.*) May I have sorrow if I know what they want from me. (HERSH-BER *enters.*)

GITL. Here he is.

ROKHL. Don't ruin my joy, Gitl dear.

GITL. Joy for you. Bitter and dark for me.

HERSH-BER. Stere, good you came. Tell the truth.

ELKONE. She's got nothing to say.

HERSH-BER. Tell the truth in front of the whole world, Stere. I'm not afraid.

ROKHL. Sh! Don't yell like that, my child.

HERSH-BER. Now I'm angry. Stere grew up in the village with me. Grew up in the same field, and she's mine. Say it, Stere, say it—don't be afraid.

ELKONE. What do you say about this blockhead, Gitl? He can't add two and two, but look what a mouth, how he can make speeches.

HERSH-BER. I don't know whether I talk good or bad. I asked the teacher. I said that I don't want to go against her parents. The teacher said be nice. I wanted to do it tonight. Why did you come over, drag her here with her eyes red? Why should you make her cry for no reason and no sense?

ROKHL. I have to say he's right.

HERSH-BER. (*Chokes on tears.*) You have no reason to make her miserable. I can't stand to see her cry. (STERE *weeps loudly.*)

GITL. Sh, dope. He spoke up and she—

ELKONE. I stand and I listen . . . What's the matter with you, Elkone?

HERSH-BER. We grew up in the same field. Why are you getting in the way? Ha? I'm taking her just as she is, no dowry, what more do you want? Enough of all this and an end to it.

ELKONE. You can have a dowry too, Hersh-Ber. When you talk like that, I like you. I thought maybe—well, there's nothing to say. My daughter will be taken care of. Well, all right, then. Don't cry. Who would dream that Hersh-Ber could cry? And I myself practically—(*All wipe their eyes.*) Give me your hand,

Dovid-Noyekh. (*Embrace. Sob. The women weep loudly.* TSINE *and* AVROM-
YANKEV *enter, stare in amazement, start wiping their eyes too.*)

ROKHL. (*Hugs* TSINE, *kisses her.*) My child, you have become a bride.

ELKONE. (*Goes over to* LEVI-YITSKHOK, *takes his hand.*) Good luck to you.
You'll have a decent Jewish girl. Even if she did grow up among peasants in
the middle of a field.

GITL. It goes to show: God looks out for us even in the country. (*Hugs*
ROKHL.)

Curtain

❧

Shop (Shap)
(1926)

H. LEIVICK

❧

The play was published in the New York journal *Der Hamer (The Hammer)* in 1927. It was published in full in Yiddish in Vilna in 1928 *(Vilner Farlag fun B. Kletskin)*. Also a Hebrew translation appeared in Vilna the same year.

The only name that might present problems is SHLOY-me KHAY-im. The single greatest stress is on the syllable KHAY. (See Note on Transliteration.) Reb simply means "Mr." It is not a form of address to a rabbi.

By the time Leivick wrote *Shop,* there existed the expression "potato Yiddish," to describe a Yiddish language corrupted by many English borrowings. The dialogue incorporates many English words, which were transliterated into Yiddish letters in the printed text. A list of such words, in order, may be illuminating. In act 1: shop, designer, operator, cutter, presser, electric, boss, businessman, Mister, strike, union, boys, pay, lollipop, corner, greenhorn, kikes, Miss, and of course the lyrics to "Yes sir, that's my baby." In act 2: pickle, pay packet, jazz, yes sir, "He is a gentleman," "a nice gentleman," scab, job, bunch, "I don't care too." In act 3: "Don't worry," settle, hall, please, "come here, Boys," candy, cake, "You can't," fun, raise, dollar, trimming. In act 4: queen, stop, party, meeting. Like many other Yiddish plays set in America, *Shop* was printed with a glossary of such English borrowings for the benefit of readers in Europe. The characters Sadie, Katie, and Gertie are actually named *Seydi, Keydi,* and *Goydi;* in other words, the English-language names (pronounced with Yiddish accents) were transliterated into Yiddish, and I have returned them to the originals.

Contrariwise, some Yiddish words have become familiar in English and would certainly have been part of the vocabulary of these people even when speaking English; "kvetsh" (complain) and "kosher" (here meaning "ritually pure") are two such words, and I left them both. Similarly I left a version of Leyzer's pun in act 3; "*oy vey*" (literally "oh woe" or "oh pain") is a familiar exclamation. "Socialism," "capitalism," and "machine" are Yiddish words as well as English. The dialogue also includes some Russian as part of the Operators' rough-and-ready cursing.

When I began to translate *Shop,* the sound of the dialogue, even in plain, direct translation, reminded me of something. Eventually I realized that what it reminded me of was Clifford Odets' plays *Awake and Sing* (1932–35) and *Waiting for Lefty* (1935): oblique, ranging from grunts and slangy exchanges to swoops of proletarian poetry and a yearning, stirring tone. I do not know that Odets was directly influenced by Leivick. However, Odets came from a Yiddish-speaking family, so in his youth he may have read or seen Leivick's work, which was already well known. At any rate, both he and Leivick were part of a political commitment that carried its own aesthetic. The First Operator's wedding ode, with its jerky, aggressive rhythm, typifies another approach of the day to creating "Jazz Age" poetry.

Though set in New York's Lower East Side, the play often makes reference to workers' lives in the Old Country. Although wagoner or teamster was traditionally a profession of low status, associated with physical strength but ignorance and vulgarity, wagoners are the subject of many Yiddish folk songs, which generally portray them affectionately. The Bund was the major Yiddish socialist workers' organization. Wolf was a Bundist hero but has betrayed the Bund by becoming a boss. The Lena River which they sing about in act 2 is in the Siberian region where Wolf—like Leivick himself—was imprisoned for Bundist activities. The song they break into at the end of Act 2 is the Communist anthem, the "Internationale."

Many references to religious and folk beliefs appear in the play. In act 2, for example, Raya says that the "black year" won't get her (this common expression for "bad luck" or "the devil" I rendered here as "evil spirits"). According to legend, the golem was a statue or robot created and animated in order to protect the Jews of sixteenth-century Prague from a pogrom. In slang, "golem" means someone mindless, a big dummy. All Jewish holidays and the Sabbath last from sundown to sundown. The evening which is the first part of the occasion is called its eve, as in Sabbath Eve. Thus, at the end of act 2, Gertie is applying to the strike the familiar terminology of religious ritual. In act 3, Gold assures Shloyme-Khayim that the food is kosher, meaning prepared in accordance to ritual law. Many folk tales like Shloyme-Khayim's in act 4 tell about saints who live unrecognized on earth as poor simple workingmen and through their good deeds redeem mankind. Also in act 4, the First Operator teases Gold with a toast to "next year, with God's help"—a wedding toast that usually means a baby, not a strike.

Songs in this play serve many purposes. They evoke a community in transition. Thus, Gertie sings Yiddish folk songs; she and Sadie and Katie sing American pop tunes; and the First Operator sings a Russian song. Yiddish-speaking American Jews drew naturally from all those sources. Songs underscore the political ideology which is in a sense the protagonist of the drama. They also provide movement and color.

Shop was first performed in 1926 in New York. Jacob Ben-Ami directed and played Wolf. Other members of the original cast who already were or were to become important actors were Lidia Pototska as Mina, Jacob Mestel as Shloyme-Khayim, and Stella Adler as Katie. A production by the Vilna Troupe followed the next year, and one in Hebrew at the Ohel in Tel Aviv in 1932. In 1981–82, the Folksbiene presented the play in New York, much compressed, with additional music by Zalmen Mlotek. Karol Latowicz played Wolf; Morris Adler, Gold; Moishe Rosenfeld, Lipman; and Zypora Spaisman, Raya.

H. Leivick (Leivick Halpern) (1888–1962) was respected for his life as well as for his writing. For his devotion to freeing the masses, he spent years in chains in prison and in Siberia, and although he was later disillusioned by conditions in the Soviet Union and by anti-Jewish pogroms in Hebron, he remained true to his original convictions. *Shop*'s characters may be said to represent a range of attitudes toward the revolutionary ideals of Leivick's youth, with the conflicted Lipman perhaps closest to Leivick's own position. Leivick wrote many plays and poems, in a variety of genres. His best known play, *The Golem,* explores in verse the philosophical implications of the golem legend. (The Introduction tells more about Leivick and more about *Shop.*)

Characters

LEYZER, the old watchman, a former revolutionary
WOLF, a boss, a former revolutionary
GOLD, a boss

LIPMAN, an operator

BARKON, a designer

PHILIP, a cutter

HYMIE, a cutter

LEYBL, a cutter, a young greenhorn

BER, a presser, a wagoner in the old country

SHLOYME-KHAYIM, a presser and pious old man

FIRST OPERATOR

SECOND OPERATOR (BENNY)

THIRD OPERATOR

YOUNG MAN

FIRST GOON

SECOND GOON

MINA, an operator, a former revolutionary

GERTIE, a finisher

SADIE, an operator

KATIE, an operator

RAYA, an operator, an old maid

YOUNG WOMAN

OTHER WORKERS

Scene

A garment-manufacturing sweatshop on the Lower East Side of New York City.
Act I. In the shop.
Act II. On the roof of the building where the shop is located.
Act III. In the shop.
Act IV. In the shop.

Time

The early 1920s.
Act I. Early morning, just before the shop opens.
Act II. Lunch break that day.
Act III. Six days later, late at night.
Act IV. Saturday, two days later, at noon.

Act I

Garment industry shop. It's dark. Right, two cutting tables: one where HYMIE *works and the other for* PHILIP *and* LEYBL. *Left, standing separately, the small table of* BARKON *the designer. A few lengths from him is the operators' table:* RAYA's *place is closest, and beyond her,* MINA *and* LIPMAN. *Between the cutters' and the operators' tables stands the table of the pressers* BER *and* SHLOYME-KHAYIM. *Between the pressers and the operators stands the small table where* GERTIE *works. Between the cutters and pressers stand tables piled so high with clothing and fabrics as to form a sort of wall dividing the shop in two. At the door, a big time-clock at which each entering worker stamps his card.*

The curtain rises to reveal an odd scene. Old LEYZER *is sweeping the shop with a long broom. The empty sewing machines turn noisily. It seems that the old man turned on the electricity and is enjoying his clever idea. He sweeps and dances with difficulty to the music, in a comic way. The clock shows 7:45* A.M. *Enter* WOLF, *one of the bosses.*

WOLF. What's going on?

LEYZER. (*Runs to shut off the electric power.*) Just nothing.

WOLF. What does that mean—"just nothing"?

LEYZER. I'm sorry. Silly. Sometimes it gets lonesome here. So I do it. Excuse me.

WOLF. No, I don't excuse you. What do you mean, turning on the *electric?* You'll break the machines. All the needles.

LEYZER. You're right, Wolf. Never again.

WOLF. (*Sets to work at a table. Spreads fabric, cuts with shears.*) How many times have I told you that a shop gets cleaned in the evening after work, not in the morning?

LEYZER. All right, my friend, don't yell.

WOLF. Again "friend," again "comrade." I've told you fifty times, don't call me "friend" or "comrade." So we were neighbors together in Siberia—so what? Such dust, damn it! If you clean up in the morning once more—

LEYZER. All right. sh! Don't yell.

WOLF. How many times have I told you you should speak to me properly. Call me "mister." People come in, businessmen, and there you are in the middle with your "friend." Why is it with Mr. Gold—

LEYZER. Mr. Gold is from here. What am I to him, and who am I to him?

WOLF. I'm from here too. No more "back in the Old Country." I'm like Gold too.

LEYZER. But how can I—?

WOLF. No arguments. Unless you don't care about your job. (LEYZER *laughs sadly.*) You're still laughing?

LEYZER. Not at all, just the opposite. Let it be "mister." (*They work in silence.*)

WOLF. They make me sick: pals from the Old Country. Tell me instead what the shop is saying. About the general strike?

LEYZER. What do I know?

WOLF. The workers must talk about me, probably. Don't they?

LEYZER. What's to talk?

WOLF. Just, I mean, about me. That is: a boss. The shop hates me probably, right?

LEYZER. I haven't heard that.

WOLF. You haven't heard? You don't want to say. You hate me too. I see that.

LEYZER. Not nice to make fun of an old friend.

WOLF. Enough clean-up.

GOLD. (*Enters.* LEYZER *escapes with his broom.*) What's the argument?

WOLF. Senile. I told him to listen to what the shop is saying about the general strike, but he—

GOLD. Not necessary.

WOLF. It's important to know what the shop is thinking.

GOLD. A shop doesn't think.

WOLF. But there's going to be a strike.

GOLD. So? I'm not letting any union in up here.

WOLF. You look so . . . (*Pause.*) But to come in in the morning to do the cutting out . . .

GOLD. Not necessary.

WOLF. Not necessary?

GOLD. As far as I'm concerned, they'll be working right through the strike. You, maybe . . .

WOLF. What—me?

GOLD. There's no union shop here and never will be. Maybe you feel like giving in to them. I don't have to. My conscience is clean.

WOLF. Who says I'll give in to them?

GOLD. The old Bundist is scratching inside you.

WOLF. Maybe I'm still a socialist.

GOLD. A socialist. No wonder the shop has no respect for you.

WOLF. Not everyone has a face like yours, that never smiles.

GOLD. You don't smile to a shop. What's a shop? Workers. (*Goes close.*) Look at the collar a person can wear. Dirty. A business establishment is a business establishment, not a little prayer house, not a Bund meeting.

WOLF. Stop it.

GOLD. And those greenhorns of yours. I'm not letting any union in up here.

WOLF. What can I do? Acquaintances, people from home. They come begging for work.

GOLD. A shop doesn't need acquaintances. Negroes, Italians, Chinese, Jews. A shop needs hands. Let the strike begin tomorrow, even. (BARKON *enters, says hello, goes to his place.* GOLD *speaks to him.*) I talked to you yesterday.

BARKON. Well—

GOLD. I'm being frank with you.

BARKON. Well—

GOLD. We're going to treat each other like gentlemen. (*Catches sight of* HYMIE *entering. Goes over to* HYMIE, *claps him on shoulder.*) How are you, Hymie?

HYMIE. Thanks, Mr. Gold.

GOLD. How's the family?

HYMIE. Thanks, Mr. Gold.

GOLD. You talked to me about a raise.

HYMIE. I'm a family man. Four children.

GOLD. Go in the office. (HYMIE *goes into inner office.* GOLD *sees* MINA *entering.*) Here's your lady with the gray eyes. The shop looks up to her. Go talk it over.

WOLF. Just ask if she's going to strike?

GOLD. Yes. Ask. Just ask. (*Exits into office.* MINA *tries to pass* WOLF.)

WOLF. Mina.

MINA. What do you want?

WOLF. Why so hard? Forget for a while that I'm a boss and you work for me.

MINA. Why should I forget?

WOLF. For the sake of our old friendship. You think that I've forgotten Siberia?

MINA. Oh, really? You haven't forgotten? Thank you very much. But once upon a time was Wolfson, not Wolf. Wolfson died.

WOLF. And Wolf?

MINA. A boss.

WOLF. It would have been better, you know, if you hadn't come to me in the first place asking for work.

MINA. That's what hurts. But I went around a whole year without a job. Anyway, what's the difference? Most bosses nowadays are the same kind of former so-called socialists as you.

WOLF. Mina—

MINA. My name is Miss Ghermann. What do you want?

WOLF. Nothing. (*She starts work. He exits. The workers have been entering and clocking in.*)

KATIE. (*Dances in with* SADIE, *singing.*) Where was you last night, Sadie?

SADIE. What's the matter?

KATIE. We was waiting for you. All the boys was waiting for you.

SADIE. Will they be there tomorrow too, the boys?

KATIE. Yeah. You should come. The boy with the glasses keeps asking about you.

SADIE. Your pa don't yell no more when the boys come over?

KATIE. No, he don't yell no more. I give him my whole pay. (*Singing.*) "Yes, sir, that's my baby."

SADIE. "No, sir, don't mean maybe." (*They dance over to their machines and sit down.* GERTIE *jumps hastily to her work table and sings so the whole shop can hear the folk song "Turn, little wheel, turn."* HYMIE *comes back out of the office with a happy face and takes his place.* GOLD *returns, spots* BER, *calls him aside and speaks to him.* LIPMAN *approaches his machine next to* MINA.)

LIPMAN. (*Quietly, as if to himself.*) Good morning, Mina.

MINA. Hello. Have you heard any news?

LIPMAN. No, and I don't expect to.

MINA. To just sit like this, to crawl into the machine body and soul, and drown in there—

LIPMAN. Ah, well—

MINA. And to die in there—

LIPMAN. To die, then—

MINA. You promised me something yesterday, Lipman. To be different, to be stronger.

LIPMAN. Well, I feel sad.

MINA. Still sad, after our talk yesterday?

LIPMAN. I'm working on myself. I want to obey you. I myself want to be different.

MINA. You must remember, Lipman. Be strong, in the name of our friendship.

LIPMAN. (*Grasps her hand.*) In the name of our friendship, more than friendship—more.

BER. (*Has been standing and talking with* GOLD, *jumps up angrily.*) What do you mean? Buy me with a five dollar bill? (GOLD *lets him go and exits.* BER *moves to his table. To second presser* SHLOYME-KHAYIM) Ever seen a thing like that? He thinks I'm some kind of a lowlife. Never mind, at home I drove a wagon, it's true, but even then I was as decent as an American boss.

LEYBL. (*He enters with* PHILIP, *a dandy, and hurries over to* GERTIE.) I'm mad at you.

GERTIE. Why?

LEYBL. Philip persuades you and you do what he says. He is a talker, a nothing. (*He goes to his place. The machines start up.*)

GERTIE. (*Sings.*)
"Turn, little wheel, turn.
Dance, little needle, dance."

PHILIP. (*To* HYMIE.) But what was Mr. Gold talking to you about?

HYMIE. Let me work.

PHILIP. You started it yourself.

HYMIE. Let me work.

PHILIP. You creep into the office too much.

HYMIE. (*Screams.*) Just let me work.

LEYBL. They're always quarreling. It's ugly.

PHILIP. Two months in the shop and already mixing in.

LEYBL. How long does it take to see something's ugly?

HYMIE. A little respect here for Barkon's cousin! (HYMIE *and* PHILIP *laugh.*)

LEYBL. A worker like all of you.

HYMIE. We're training him as a cutter, and he doesn't appreciate anything.

LEYBL. What's to appreciate?

HYMIE. (*Screams.*) Gertie, Gertie, Louie is mad again!

GERTIE. I like him.

PHILIP. Watch out, Hymie, he'll grab a shears again like yesterday because you're calling him Louie.

HYMIE. A man who can't bear to be called Louie.

LEYBL. (*Pale.*) I'm asking you to stop.

PHILIP. (*Stifles his laughter.*) Watch out for your bones, Hymie.

LEYBL. (*In tears.*) Like convicts in a jail.

GERTIE. (*Sings.*)

"What do I have? What do I need?

I have a looking glass. What do I lack?"

SHLOYME-KHAYIM. Sh! A little quieter.

GERTIE. You don't like the way I sing?

SHLOYME-KHAYIM. It hurts my ears.

GERTIE. (*Louder.*)

"Come, boys, dance.

Come, boys, carry on.

And buy me a lollipop."

(*Laughter.*)

SHLOYME-KHAYIM. Sure the shop spoils her.

GERTIE. Take me out tonight, Mr. Shloyme-Khayim.

SHLOYME-KHAYIM. Tfoo!

BER. Ask me, Gertele.

GERTIE. You've got to mean it for real.

BER. And what if I do?

GERTIE. I love young boys. (*Sings.*)

"I am a wagoner.

I have my horses."

BER. That's aimed at me.

SHLOYME-KHAYIM. That's what I'm saying—bad.

BER. A good girl. I love you, Gertie.

GERTIE. Oh, I'm so happy, he loves me.

BARKON. (*Harshly.*) That's enough.

GERTIE. (*Makes a face toward* BARKON. *Apart to* LIPMAN.) Mr. Lipman, are you still angry at me? (LIPMAN *doesn't answer.*) I offended you yesterday. I apologize, Mr. Lipman. (LIPMAN *doesn't answer.*) Mr. Lipman, I'm a bad girl. You are a quiet man—you're shy, a stranger.

BER. Lipman isn't angry.

GERTIE. When you talk to him, it's as if you're hitting him.

BER. But he is very smart. A scholar. Back home he was almost a rabbi.

GERTIE. Really! (*Calls.*) Mr. Lipman.

BARKON. (*Yelling angrily.*) Gertie, shut up!

GERTIE. (*Jumps up.*) I don't want you to speak to me that way.

BER. Good for you, Gertie, give it to him.

BARKON. (*To* BER.) Who are you?

BER. Who am I? I used to be Ber the Wagon Driver, and now I'm Ber the Presser. Good enough connections?

GERTIE. (*Sings.*)

"With my whip a twitch—"

BER. If only a strike would come. A little airing out here.

BARKON. (*Through his teeth.*) Kikes.

BER. (*Makes for him.*) What did you say? (*Almost hits him.*)

SHLOYME-KHAYIM. (*Holds him back.*) Let it go. Work. (*Everyone works.*)

GERTIE. (*Sings.*)

"I am a bad girl.

I dance on every corner.

Everyone is mad at me.

Come on, every mister."

(GOLD *enters and crosses the shop with rapid steps, noticing everything. As he passes, a "sshh!" passes through the shop. Everyone works busily and in silence.* GERTIE *catches on too late, when* GOLD *is already standing beside her, cutting her open with his eyes. Her singing breaks off suddenly.*)

GOLD. You are happy. (GERTIE *reddens. Her hands tremble on her work.*) A shop, not an opera.

BARKON. They carry on. They don't let you work.

GOLD. Who?

BARKON. Her, and that one, the greenhorn.

MINA. (*Jumps up.*) Low.

GOLD. (*Looks around.*) What? (*Nobody answers.* GOLD *looks at* MINA, *steps backward. To* BARKON, *pointing to the machine next to him, which is empty.*) Where is Raya?

BARKON. Not here yet. How should I know?

(GOLD *goes to the cutters' area. Meanwhile* WOLF *enters, moves around, searches among the bundles of merchandise.* HYMIE *and* PHILIP, *feeling* GOLD'S *gaze, begin to work rapidly.* PHILIP, *especially, practically dances, clacking with the shears.* LEYBL *keeps spreading out pieces of fabric, laying them one upon the other.* GOLD *doesn't seem to like the way* LEYBL *does this.*)

GOLD. (*Standing hands in pockets. Cold voice.*) Faster, Louie. Smoother. (LEYBL *gives a jerk but doesn't even turn around to* GOLD, *just keeps working.*) I'm speaking to you, Louie. (LEYBL *still ignores him and doesn't turn.*)

PHILIP. (*Heatedly*) Mr. Gold is speaking to you.

GOLD. Come over here, Louie. (LEYBL *still doesn't turn around. All the others watch.* GOLD *is pale.*) Louie. (LEYBL *ignores him.*)

PHILIP. When you call him Louie, he doesn't answer.

GOLD. What? (*To* WOLF.) What does that mean? I don't want a lunatic asylum here. This is a shop. Mr. Barkon. (BARKON *hurries over to him.*) This is your cousin? I don't want his kind. I talk to him, and he doesn't answer.

BARKON. Louie, have you lost your mind? (*Everyone's face is strained, including people in the other work area.* GERTIE *jumps up from her machine.* LEYBL *does his work and doesn't turn his face around.*)

GOLD. (*To* WOLF.) Get rid of him. Throw him out of the shop.

LEYBL. (*Suddenly turns around. Childishly, almost weeping.*) My name isn't Louie. My name is Leybl. I hate when people call me Louie. I don't answer when they call me Louie. I don't answer.

BARKON. What are you talking about?

LEYBL. (*Screaming.*) I've begged people a hundred times not to call me Louie. I hate it. I can't bear it. They all think it's a joke. Because I've only been in this country six months, they can have a good time with me. I won't stand for it. I have a name of my own. I hate Louie. I'll shear their heads.

BARKON. You're a greenhorn. Mr. Gold talks to you and you don't answer. (*Goes to his table.*)

LEYBL. So it's Mr. Gold, so what? Yes, I am a greenhorn.

GOLD. (*To* WOLF.) You deal with them. (*Exits.*)

WOLF. I've never seen such a thing in my life.

HYMIE. How a person can be so stubborn. About a name! Some precious bargain—a name. And where? In America. You've got to be crazy. Sell tickets, on my life.

PHILIP. Theater.

GERTIE. (*Back at her place.*) Bravo, Leybl.

WOLF. (*Quickly to* GERTIE.) Comedy. (GERTIE *takes a look at* WOLF, *can't keep from laughing.*) What am I to you?

GERTIE. You are what you are. (WOLF *goes out shrunken, saying nothing.*)

SHLOYME-KHAYIM. You'll lose your job, Gertie, like Leybl.

GERTIE. We'll make a match then, the two of us.

BER. What will Philip say?

GERTIE. Have you ever seen such a thing? Everyone wants to be boss. Every one of them. I should tell him. What is he to me? A pest, that's what he is. (*All work.*)

BER. Tell something, Reb Shloyme-Khayim, tell one of your little stories.

SHLOYME-KHAYIM. Ah, what are you talking about?

BER. You know you've got a lot of stories.

SHLOYME-KHAYIM. Today is not a good day for storytelling.

BER. Why not?

SHLOYME-KHAYIM. You see for yourself. A bad day. A difficult day.

BER. Tell me, Reb Shloyme-Khayim, in paradise are we still going to stand and press pants?

SHLOYME-KHAYIM. Oh, let it go.

BER. Or in paradise will clothes grow already pressed on the trees?

SHLOYME-KHAYIM. First make sure you have a place in paradise.

BER. What, they wouldn't let me into paradise? I'll drive in with two pairs of horses.

(*All laugh. Meanwhile,* RAYA *has entered: an old maid with a worn out, sickly, but not ugly face. She approaches her machine. She greets no one, and it is clear that she is not welcome. She goes to* BARKON. BARKON *feels uncomfortable at her approach.*)

RAYA. (*Quietly, through her teeth.*) You promised to pick me up in the car.

BARKON. I forgot.

RAYA. Sitting and waiting and waiting like a dummy. A whole hour.

BARKON. It slipped my mind.

RAYA. (*Tears.*) How can a person do such a thing?

BARKON. Not now, Raya, I beg you.

RAYA. (*Despairing.*) Now, not now—what's the difference?

BARKON. Not in the shop, Raya.

PHILIP. The old maid is sawing away again.

BARKON. Please, Raya.

RAYA. You always hurt me. (*She throws herself down beside her machine with a hysterical wail. A shiver runs through the shop.*)

BARKON. Work, work. It's nothing. (*To* RAYA.) Sh! Raya. (RAYA *controls herself, sits with head lowered.*)

WOLF. (*Runs in.*) What happened here?

BARKON. Nothing, Mr. Wolf.

WOLF. (*To* RAYA.) So late?

GERTIE. Late, late, late.

WOLF. (*To* GERTIE.) I'm not talking to you. Be quiet. (*He looks all around, lost. Suddenly he goes over to* MINA.) Why are you looking at me like that? Why?

MINA. (*Startled by suddenness.*) What do you want?

WOLF. (*No self-control.*) I won't have it. This is the devil knows what. I won't put up with it.

MINA. Mr. Wolf, you are out of your mind.

WOLF. (*Yelling.*) I'll chase you all out of here. I know you. I know you. If . . . if . . . if I am only a boss and that's all I am, then I have a right to yell, I have a right to not like your work. (*He grabs pieces of* MINA's *work and throws them to the ground.*) And in fact I do not like your work. I don't like it. Clumsy big stitches, worth ten thousand nothings. (*He smacks* MINA's *machine and starts for the exit. All are astonished by such an outburst from* WOLF. *Suddenly* LIPMAN *jumps up, runs to block* WOLF's *way, and yells out with a pale face.*)

LIPMAN. Stop, you!

WOLF. What is it?

LIPMAN. You are to turn around and apologize.

WOLF. What?

LIPMAN. This very minute. (*Grabs* WOLF *by the lapel. A confusion begins.* HYMIE *and* PHILIP *drag* LIPMAN *back.*)

WOLF. (*Stammering and lost.*) Silence.

LIPMAN. Don't be afraid. I've never lifted a hand to anyone. Even if he deserved it.

WOLF. You're standing up for your neighbor. She has a mouth of her own.

MINA. (*Runs up, takes* LIPMAN's *hand.*) Go to your machine.

LIPMAN. (*Pulls his hand away angrily.*) I've worked here a year already. You all think—such a quiet man, nothing matters to him. Nothing matters to you. It matters to me. The way a knot rips, that's how my quiet is ripping apart inside me. The devil! Grab for an iron and throw it through a windowpane. A boss is running around, and screaming a sick scream. I know your scream, you know, I know your scream.

WOLF. What do you know?

LIPMAN. (*Returns to his machine, speaks standing by it and gazing somewhere into emptiness.*) It has to rip open, in the end. It has to, in the end. Who are we all?

Sitting like dummies with our heads to the needles. All of us. And who is he, the so-called boss? Lost. A stammerer. A nothing.

WOLF. Talk. I'm not afraid.

LIPMAN. You are afraid. Always. Always. You're afraid right now. An insult—that's what you are to me. To everyone. A life gone to waste is wailing inside you, and it's our life wasted. Against a different boss one could struggle. Against you, one can't even struggle.

WOLF. Go on, struggle.

LIPMAN. Who is there to struggle against? You are our own everlasting defeat. You will always be there to remind us, to cancel us out. And we will always be beaten. Your sick conscience beats us worse than it does you. (WOLF *is silent.*) A lot of revolutionaries have become angry, sick bosses like you. Well, we work, we are quiet—you be quiet too. You think it's anger swelling inside me? It isn't anger, it's meaninglessness. The meaninglessness of all our lives. So you keep quiet the way we keep quiet. I've been sitting over your machine more than a year now. And everyone keeps chewing over your name. Your once-upon-a-time revolutionary life, it is actually disgusting. (*Indicates* RAYA.) And over here she sits and sobs like a person who has gambled her life away. (*Indicates* MINA.) And here another one sits and bites her lips.

RAYA. (*Tearfully.*) I beg you not to talk about me.

LIPMAN. You are to apologize to Miss Ghermann. (*Again jumps out from his place.*)

MINA. I don't want his apology.

LIPMAN. (*Beside himself.*) I demand it.

MINA. (*Places herself between* LIPMAN *and* WOLF. *To* LIPMAN, *commandingly.*) I order you to go back to your machine. (LIPMAN *sits back at his place.* MINA *looks at* WOLF *sharply and silently.* WOLF, *shaky and deadly pale, shuffles out of the shop.* MINA *goes to her machine, stands a long while paralyzed, gives herself a shake with her hand on the machine. She screams out.*) Is this how it's going to be? How much longer? (*All jump up with rage.*)

FIRST OPERATOR. (*Gives a bang with his chair and screams out.*) How much longer? To hell with them!

(*At that* GOLD *enters. With cold sharp eyes, silent and haughty, his gaze forces everyone to sit down and begin work.* MINA *is the last to sit. The scene ends silently. Machines make noise.*)

Curtain

❧

Act II

The roof of the building that the shop is in. Two big four-sided chimneys rise from the middle. The roof is surrounded by a low fence. On all sides, we see other shop buildings. Upstage, roofs and towers of the city.

Midday, between twelve and one. The shop workers come up here to relax, eat, chat, dance. From time to time, boys' and girls' heads look out of the windows of the shops across the way. They wave and flirt. When the curtain opens, a group of operators are sitting behind the chimney and eating, each by himself from his own little package. Downstage, on his side of the chimney, against the wall, sits LIPMAN, his knees up and his food on his knees. Next to him lies a bundle wrapped in newspaper. LEYBL stands in a corner facing the city skyline.

FIRST OPERATOR. (*Eats and gestures with a hand to the window opposite, from which girls' faces are looking out.*) Wait a minute, you sweet little apples, just let me swallow my pickle.

SECOND OPERATOR. The little apples can't wait. They can't restrain themselves.

THIRD OPERATOR. Here comes Benny with his wisecracks. (FIRST OPERATOR *stands and blows kisses.*)

SECOND OPERATOR. Kiss them for all of us.

THIRD OPERATOR. Not for me.

SECOND OPERATOR. He can do his own kissing.

THIRD OPERATOR. Put your tongues back in your mouths.

SECOND OPERATOR. A tongue isn't a needle. It doesn't break.

FIRST OPERATOR. And it doesn't need electricity, so it won't wear out. (*Yells.*) Hey, girls, where are you running, girls? Hey, Sweet-Lips! Doll-Face!

THIRD OPERATOR. Enough. Lipman is sitting right there.

FIRST OPERATOR. Let him sit. Attacked Mr. Wolf, but what, where, why? And now quiet again. So righteous, and said—what? Stammerings. With a boss you should talk hard talk.

THIRD OPERATOR. I'd love to hear that.

FIRST OPERATOR. I hate a lazy bum. If you want to be a ladies' man, let me tell you, you've got to take a chance. What's her name there—Mina—I'd look her in the eye. (*To* LIPMAN.) With a boss you should talk hard talk.

LIPMAN. What do you mean?

THIRD OPERATOR. Stop.

FIRST OPERATOR. I'm a plain human being. A machine is—What is a machine? It's a plague. It's hell. And so is a boss. Worse than hell. Not like you: fancy stitches and a lot of talk.

LIPMAN. Go to the devil.

THIRD OPERATOR. Enough now. (*Pulls the* FIRST OPERATOR *back.*)

LIPMAN. You're still talking? You'd all be better off quiet. You quarrel like cats over garbage, scratching and clawing. I wish you'd choke on your shop and your machines and your own guts!

FIRST OPERATOR. Holy man! Milk and honey flow from his lips. (*To the window.*) Girls, where are you, dollies? (*To* LEYZER, *who has come up.*) Hello, Mr. Leyzer, you hungry?

SECOND OPERATOR. When is he satisfied?

FIRST OPERATOR. Or Mr. Wolf?

LEYZER. Leave Mr. Wolf alone, little brothers.

FIRST OPERATOR. Your philanthropist, a plague on his bones. You guard the shop for him. You guard him. And what do you get? Fever. (*Gives him bread.*) Eat.

LEYZER. Thank you, little brothers. And leave him alone. Look, you respect Mr. Gold.

FIRST OPERATOR. Mr. Gold? Certainly. Yes. Mr. Gold doesn't make faces. Mr. Gold says: "work." Mr. Gold says: "machines, machines." Certainly—when the time comes, he'll get more than his pay packet, a plague on his bones. But that one, your wolf cub—he's got to creep into his little socialist actions, he was a socialist—makes him sick to pay you enough to eat, even.

LEYZER. I have nothing against him. I'm already old and sick. What am I worth? And he is a businessman. I'm grateful I have the shop to sleep in at least.

THIRD OPERATOR. You've really known him since Siberia?

LEYZER. (*Revives.*) Certainly. Worth telling. Ay, little brothers. Ended up in the same camp. Siberian region, Alexandrovsk, Buratish steppes. A kid, Wolf was. Handsome, devil-may-care.

THIRD OPERATOR. (*Sings.*)

"There, where the Lena River turns—"

LEYZER. (*In tears.*) Sing, little brothers. (*Sings.*) "There she stands before my eyes.

Drags her chained feet.

Drags—" Ah, little mother Lena. You curse Wolf—"Boss." What kind of boss? Ay, ay, ay. I know better.

FIRST OPERATOR. What do you know? We're striking him. We're going out on strike against your handsome devil. Well, what's the matter? You don't want any bread? (*Shares out to him.*) Take, take.

LEYZER. (*Takes and puts in pocket.*) Time to go clean up the shop. (*Starts off.*)

FIRST OPERATOR. So how do you like America, Mr. Leyzer, you watchman of capitalism?

LEYZER. Laugh, laugh. (*Exit.*)

THIRD OPERATOR. (*Sings.*)

"There stands a tiny nomad's tent—"

(*Noisy sounds of jazz carry in from somewhere.*) What tent? Some tent. There you have it. (*Beats out the rhythm.*)

FIRST OPERATOR. And when we strike, what will he do, your devil-may-care? He'll bring goons against us. Yes, sir. One man has a little shop. And another is a little watchman in the little shop. Hey, girls, proletootsies, when we make our little strike, then we'll have time for you, dollies.

THIRD OPERATOR. We'll go out, we'll go out. We won't be lazy. But you think the shop is with us? A ladies' prayer meeting. Katies and Sadies.

FIRST OPERATOR. We'll drag them out by the hair.

THIRD OPERATOR. Our men know how to scab just fine too.

FIRST OPERATOR. Won't live to see it. (*Stretches out.*) Catch a wink, brother. (*The others stretch out too.* MINA *enters, intends to go to* LIPMAN, *has second thoughts and starts to retreat.* LIPMAN *jumps up pale, his lips dry.*)

LIPMAN. Are you really angry?

MINA. Very.

LIPMAN. Why?

MINA. The way you jumped to attack Wolf was ridiculous.

LIPMAN. In your eyes too?

MINA. In my eyes most of all. You're looking for justice? Demand justice—from a boss?

LIPMAN. (*Quietly.*) From Wolf.

MINA. I say: "boss." Why do you answer me: "Wolf"?

LIPMAN. Wolf loves you.

MINA. I have asked you never to mention that to me.

LIPMAN. It boiled over in me. He insulted you.

MINA. It's a shop. One doesn't stand against a shop with talk. With strength! Such unproductive talk: "insulted." You expect decency everywhere. And the result is you get hurt. It's sickening to expose yourself to all kinds of people.

LIPMAN. Even when you expose yourself to someone you love?

MINA. (*She looks at him for a long while, laughs with happiness, pulls him toward her by the hand.*) That is good, Lipman, it's good.

LIPMAN. All the same, you fight with me constantly.

MINA. In the shop I will always fight with you. There you behave like a stranger. You don't understand what a shop is. For you, a shop just happens, or it's a misfortune; in any case it means nothing.

LIPMAN. And what is a shop to you?

MINA. (*Strongly.*) Class.

LIPMAN. Yes, yes.

MINA. And power. (LIPMAN *moves away to the wall. The bundle falls from his hand.*) What is in the bundle?

LIPMAN. (*Picks it up. Flushes. After a pause.*) A dress for you.

MINA. The dress you've been sewing in lunch breaks?

LIPMAN. You don't want it?

MINA. How strange you are.

LIPMAN. Strange how?

MINA. (*Happily.*) In a good way. No—I like it.

LIPMAN. You'll take it?

MINA. Of course. Of course.

THIRD OPERATOR. (*Sings, lying down.*)
"In the salty sea of human tears,
A terrible abyss . . ." (*Silence.*)

MINA. (*Goes to* LEYBL.) Why stand alone all this time?

LEYBL. I want to be alone.

MINA. You make yourself so lonely.

LEYBL. Loneliness comes all by itself.

MINA. You're still so young.

LEYBL. Well, so what? Young—so what? Tops of towers go crawling up to the sky there—in broad daylight. They're already old. So what?

MINA. But what are you looking at there so long?

LEYBL. The city. (*Meanwhile* RAYA *has come up, stands by the wall bent over with her head over it.*)

MINA. What are you doing? Don't lean over like that.

RAYA. (*Bitter.*) The evil spirits won't get me.

MINA. But don't lean over like that. You could—

RAYA. So another old maid would work my machine. (*Hastily runs off.* MINA, LIPMAN, *and* LEYBL *look after her, astounded. Jazz from opposite. Dancing couples can be seen like moving shadows.*)

LEYBL. (*Into the air.*) You can go crazy. (*Starts down.*)

MINA. (*Holds him back.*) What is all this, Leybl?

LEYBL. (*Distracted.*) There—that. Look. Listen. Dance. (*Exit.*)

LIPMAN. (*Shaken, confused.*) It really can drive you crazy. (*To* MINA.) We keep talking about working class, socialism. And there, Raya—it chills you through to the heart.

MINA. (*Looks at him sternly.*) It chills you? It's true, the shop really does need a fire in its bones. It needs a real strike.

LIPMAN. How can a strike help Raya?

MINA. What is Raya? Who is Raya? You don't believe in the working class.

LIPMAN. (*Excited.*) Oh, "believe." What does that mean? Look—such profound indifference to the fate of a fellow human being. And you're just as bad.

MINA. (*Quickly, angry.*) You are free with insults.

LIPMAN. Twenty years sitting at the machine. Everything gambled away. What is her life? A pauper thirsty for a little bit of leftover happiness. She's looking for a poor little crumb of happiness. Can anyone blame her for creeping and begging from a thing like Barkon? Look how the shop treats her.

MINA. The shop is right. The shop hates Barkon, so it hates Raya too. Very natural.

LIPMAN. Senseless. And if a thousand people do something, it's right? If twenty people sew sleeves or pants at the same time, so what? That makes them right? Just because there are twenty of them? You make fun of me because I look for decency. What else should I look for?

MINA. (*Firmly.*) If you weren't Lipman, I would—

LIPMAN. What?

MINA. I told you once that a shop is power. I say it again. And whose power? Ours—if we stand together. And a strike—our celebration—if we stand together. Not alone, like you, but a class.

LIPMAN. And class makes it all right to trample the suffering of someone like Raya under our feet?

MINA. (*Pale.*) If you weren't Lipman, I would— (*She slaps down the dress* LIPMAN *gave her, rushes off, leaving* LIPMAN *amazed.* KATIE *and* SADIE *come up. They start dancing, turning as if flying, around the chimneys and the* OPERATORS. LIPMAN, *dazed, smiling painfully, watches them dance.*)

KATIE. (*Dancing.*) The Prince Charmings are asleep.

SADIE. Some princes.

KATIE. Blue sky, look.

SADIE. And boys in all the windows, all of them. (*Blows kisses.*)

KATIE. (*To* LIPMAN.) Would you like to dance?

LIPMAN. No.

SADIE. And maybe yes?

KATIE. And maybe no?

SADIE. Maybe yes, maybe no, maybe yes. (*They dance in a circle around him.* LIPMAN *turns his back to the exit.*)

KATIE. Mr. Gold—handsome, right?

SADIE. Very. (RAYA *comes back up.*)

KATIE. She's an old maid already.

SADIE. Mr. Gold took me home yesterday in his automobile.

KATIE. Today he'll take me.

SADIE. He is a gentleman.

KATIE. Oh, a nice gentleman. (*To* RAYA, *making fun of her.*) Come dance. (RAYA *turns away from them.*)

SADIE. Dance with us, dance with us.

KATIE. Maybe no, maybe yes, maybe no. (*They dance away with teasing laughter. Meet* BARKON *in the doorway. Yell "Boo." Exeunt.*)

BARKON. (*To* RAYA, *not bold.*) I've been looking all over for you.

RAYA. (*Bitterly.*) All right, find me.

BARKON. You make the whole shop gossip about me.

RAYA. (*Hardens herself not to break down.*) My heart's blood is pouring out.

BARKON. "Blood. Blood." I hate that kind of talk.

RAYA. I know, you hate me.

BARKON. That's not what I said.

RAYA. You don't have to say it.

BARKON. Keep your voice down.

RAYA. Inside I'm screaming. You torture me. You've made me into a—

BARKON. Stop it.

RAYA. What am I asking for, after all? A little tenderness. A warm smile. (*In a choked voice.*) For everything, for everything, for everything.

BARKON. You make a big deal out of such a trifle, that I forgot to come for you.

RAYA. And what happened last night? (*She holds her head.*) I know that it's ugly for me to talk like this. A beggar. A whole life, alone with the needle, eagerly waiting for a man. First you also think: an old maid, anybody can do anything they want with her. And then later—

BARKON. (*He lays a hand on her shoulder.*) I am not so bad a guy as all that.

RAYA. Your promise of marriage—what do I want, after all? A corner of my own, a little rest.

BARKON. But I told you: first set up in business for ourselves. We'll open a shop of our own. I've thought about it. The season is starting. First of all, you've heard yourself, a strike is in the works. (*He looks around.*) And if there should be a strike—

RAYA. (*Jumping up.*) I understand what you mean.

BARKON. Why are you shaking like that?

RAYA. (*Fearfully.*) Scabbing.

BARKON. I knew you'd start in with your piety.

RAYA. (*Beside herself.*) We are workers. (*She catches his hand.*) Barkon!

BARKON. (*Tears his hand away.*) I tell you beforehand that I will not strike.

RAYA. (*Her hands on her head.*) Where will I end up with this man?

MINA. (*She comes up, sees how* RAYA *stands with her hands over her head.*) What's the matter with you, Raya?

RAYA. Let me alone. (*She goes off.* WOLF *enters.* MINA *paces back and forth.*)

WOLF. (*As if choking.*) I want to talk to you.

MINA. Talk.

WOLF. Forgive me.

MINA. (*Gestures with her hand.*) Ah.

WOLF. Even hate has its limits.

MINA. Let me alone.

WOLF. Why so much contempt?

MINA. It hurts you?

WOLF. Yes.

MINA. I have ripped you out of my heart.

WOLF. From so much love—

MINA. (*Trembling.*) Go away.

WOLF. All right, it's true. Business—money—dragged me in, dragged me down. Then my whole life from before shook and collapsed. And you weren't here. I was alone. What do I have from my money? I'm screaming. My life is emptied out. A boarder in Gold's house. Without a friend, without love.

MINA. You have plenty of money. Buy yourself love.

WOLF. (*His teeth chattering.*) All right, sell me you.

MINA. Go away.

WOLF. (*Tottering.*) You came slipping into my shop like a bad memory. As if you wanted vengeance on me. (MINA *turns away, covers her face.*) Twelve years gone by since we parted in that little village there in Siberia. Yes, it's true, it's a big fall from what I was once to what I am now. I let myself be swallowed up by the life here. And life here is bad, Mina. Bad, and it eats you up. (*Catches himself.*) No. No. I'm not asking you to forgive me. I don't want to excuse myself. Yes, I admit it. I forgot everything and everyone. Even you.

MINA. Good. Now we are getting to the real facts.

WOLF. (*Quietly.*) But since you came in to me in the shop, I feel that everything in me is tearing apart. Mina, you are like a sword at my throat. (*Pause.*) Fate, or chance, placed you at my machine so you could breathe on me, breathe hatred and contempt on me. Why did you come asking me for work?

MINA. (*Her face pale.*) For me you are a boss like all bosses.

WOLF. I order you not to come any more. Look for a job. Come into the office, I'll pay you off.

MINA. You have no right to fire me.

WOLF. (*Shouting.*) I have the right. I have. (*He goes to the door, remains standing there.*) And if I gave up the shop?

MINA. (*She looks at him sharply.*) Not for me. For yourself. (HYMIE, PHILIP, *and* BER *enter.* PHILIP *has a harmonica in his mouth.* WOLF *exits abruptly.*)

HYMIE. Just look at them, the operators. Stretched out in their daddy's wine garden.

BER. Up. Time to get up.

PHILIP. Time to dance. (*He drags the sleepers to their feet. All pull themselves together.*)

FIRST OPERATOR. Hell.

HYMIE. Call the girls from across the way. Give them a bear hug, Mr. Ber. (*All three wave at the girls from across the way. The* OPERATORS *join in too.*)

BER. Jump over. (*Stretches out his arms.*) I will catch you in my arms.

FIRST OPERATOR. The arms of a presser. He'll press you out flat, girls.

BER. Listen to the little operator.

PHILIP. The devil with it, I want to dance. (*To* MINA.) Do you dance?

MINA. Not now. (GERTIE *runs in, gasping with laughter.*)

PHILIP. Gertie, Gertie—let's dance.

GERTIE. A stitch in my side. I'll die. Such dummies.

ALL. What? What?

GERTIE. (*Laughing.*) Two new operators. A few days only. A young man and a young woman. Don't know each other.

FIRST OPERATOR. They sit next to me. So? Well?

GERTIE. We think they don't know each other. I go looking for a piece of fabric between the tables in back, so what do you think? They're sitting under a table, the two of them, hugging and kissing. The whole shop is wide awake. (YOUNG MAN *and* YOUNG WOMAN *run in. She is out of breath. The whole shop follows them, including* LEYBL. *Noise, laughter.*)

YOUNG WOMAN. (*To* GERTIE.) Stool pigeon.

GERTIE. (*Turns and yells.*) Dummies. If you're married and you want to kiss another man, do you have to hide under a table? Dummies.

YOUNG WOMAN. Not another man. He's my husband.

GERTIE. Your husband? And you're kissing him under the table? (*Much laughter.*)

YOUNG WOMAN. A bunch of murderers.

MINA. But why deny that you are husband and wife?

YOUNG WOMAN. I didn't want anyone to know that I'm still working after the wedding. You don't know what a shop is like? It's a wood full of bandits. I didn't want anyone to know that my husband can't support me. Don't you see? Are these workers? Bloodsuckers. (*She cries, points to* GERTIE.) It's her fault.

YOUNG MAN. If you weren't a woman, I would settle the score with you. (*He takes his wife by the hand.*) Come away from here.

LEYBL. (*Quickly to* GERTIE.) I thought you were better. Now you're the same as all the rest.

GERTIE. (*Confused.*) Leybl, what?

LEYBL. It's dangerous to love you. (*Exit.*)

PHILIP. Another county heard from.

HYMIE. A duel between Philip and Leybl.

MINA. You did wrong, Gertie.

GERTIE. (*She runs pleadingly up to* YOUNG WOMAN.) Please, please, I didn't mean anything.

YOUNG WOMAN. (*Pushes her away with a sob.*) Snakes. (*The couple exit.* GERTIE *stands as if she too is ready to collapse into weeping.*)

PHILIP. Spit at them, Gertie.

GERTIE. (*To* PHILIP.) Go away. (*She falls against chimney and weeps.*)

MINA. Crying is not productive, Gertie.

PHILIP. What did you howl for? Aren't we going to dance at all today, Gertie? (*Plays harmonica.*) Katie! Come on. (KATIE *and* SADIE *start to dance, most of the others with them. During the dancing,* LIPMAN, RAYA, *and* BARKON *enter but don't take part. Under the rhythm of the dance,* GERTIE *can't resist. Her body begins unwillingly to move, she tears herself from her place and lets herself go too.* PHILIP *grabs her and dances with her.*)

PHILIP. That's the way, Gertie, that's the way.

LEYBL. (*Suddenly runs in, a newspaper in hand, yelling excitedly.*) Strike. General strike. (*Silence.* BER *tears the paper from* LEYBL's *hand.*)

BER. Tomorrow! Hurray! (*All hurrah.*)

PHILIP. What's the big celebration?

MINA. Certainly it's a celebration, a great one.

BER. Oh, will we thrash them.

FIRST OPERATOR. Sharpen up these two little bombs. (*He raises his fists.*)

HYMIE. All the same, we have to talk it over.

MINA. There can't be any doubt at all that we'll all go out on strike.

HYMIE. Yes, but—

THIRD OPERATOR. There you have a "but" already. You think our shop is a shop? A prayerhouse for old ladies.

HYMIE. If you had to feed a wife and four children—

FIRST OPERATOR. Bury them.

BARKON. I don't have any children myself. Nevertheless I also wish they'd ask me first whether we need to strike now.

THIRD OPERATOR. Sure, they should come to you personally to ask.

BER. Take a look how important he is.

BARKON. They don't ask anyone, they just decide.

FIRST OPERATOR. Well, excuse me, Your Lordship the Designer. Hats off to the important Mr. Barkonunu.

BER. Tomorrow all the shops will be deserted.

THIRD OPERATOR. And we'll be on the picket line.

LEYBL. And just let somebody try to scab.

BER. Let them try.

GERTIE. We won't let each other scab. Leybl, you aren't mad at me any more. (*Hugs him.*) Boys, let's celebrate. What was, was. Now everything's different. Holiday. I love to strike.

BER. Hurray for Gertie. (*They all hug* GERTIE, *lift her into the air.*)

GERTIE. We have to choose strong comrades to picket.

RAYA. (*Who has been standing off on a side.*) We'll all picket.

BARKON. (*Mutters.*) Don't mix in.

RAYA. I say we should all picket.

MINA. Certainly, of course, all of us.

KATIE. I don't care, myself.

SADIE. I don't care too.

GERTIE. But first comes dancing. Truly, Leybl, will you dance with me?

LEYBL. (*He takes hold of* GERTIE *and dances till he's dizzy.*) Yes, Gertie. (*All applaud.*)

GERTIE. You too, everybody.

MINA. Now I'm dancing too. Dance with me, Lipman? (LIPMAN *moves back.*) I'm asking you. (*She takes hold of him strongly.* LIPMAN *joyfully follows her to dancing.*)

FIRST OPERATOR. Ha. A little New York. A village. (*All dance with great energy. From distant buildings in the distance comes a storm of jazz and also of shouts of "hurray"*)

LEYZER. (*Comes up.*) Mr. Wolf ordered me to say that it is already one o'clock. You have to start work.

GERTIE. Come here, Reb Leyzer. Come dance with us.

LEYZER. Mr. Wolf says that it's already one o'clock.

GERTIE. Let him. Tomorrow we strike, Reb Leyzer. This is Strike Eve. (*She grabs the old man and spins around with him.*)

LEYZER. Let go, daughter, I'm too old to dance. It's fine for you to say strike. But someone has to watch the shop.

GERTIE. Don't watch. You strike too.

LEYZER. And if there's a fire, God forbid?

GERTIE. Let it burn.

WOLF. (*Comes up.*) It's after one already.

GERTIE. Who cares?

WOLF. What do you mean?

GERTIE. Let it go, Mr. Wolf, come out with us. Strike together.

LEYZER. Who should Mr. Wolf strike against?

GERTIE. Against himself.

WOLF. (*Rigid.*) Leave your jokes for tomorrow. Today still belongs to me.

GERTIE. (*Venomously.*) Today still belongs to him.

WOLF. I say it is after one already. (HYMIE *and* PHILIP *hastily go down.*)

KATIE. I don't care.

SADIE. I don't care too.

GERTIE. Come on, boys, today still belongs to him.

ALL. (*Laughing.*) Belongs to him.

THIRD OPERATOR. (*Sings the "Internationale".*)

"Arise, ye prisoners of starvation . . ." (*All join in song. Raise their hands and move toward* WOLF. WOLF, *pale, draws back, presses himself against the wall, bent in on himself under the hail of the singing.*)

Curtain

৵৺৶

Act III

The shop. Late at night, during the strike. The windows are draped over. Dark, fearful atmosphere. PHILIP, HYMIE, BARKON, SHLOYME-KHAYIM, SADIE, KATIE, *and a few other operators are scabbing.* GOLD *helps out.* LEYZER *sits, broom in hand. Two* GOONS *stand at the entrance.*

BARKON. You know, I already asked you to cover the windows better, Mr. Leyzer.

GOLD. Go on, Mr. Leyzer. (LEYZER *climbs, busies himself at the window near* BARKON.)

LEYZER. It's all covered, look. Lord of the World, what do they all have against me with the windows? Six nights already. They shiver like in a forest. Don't work—you won't shiver.

BARKON. Nobody asked you. Don't mix in.

LEYZER. Take and break the panes with boards. That's all.

BARKON. You've been told, don't mix in.

LEYZER. A whole new kind of praying till dawn.

BARKON. The old man complains. That's all he does is complain. (*A bang is heard from somewhere. People get scared.*)

FIRST GOON. Don't worry.

LEYZER. Every rustle, the heart jerks.

BARKON. Go to your place. Go. (LEYZER *exits.*)

HYMIE. It would be good to settle already—get it over with.

PHILIP. Not that fast.

HYMIE. Well, I have no choice. A father of four. In your place, I wouldn't take the risk.

PHILIP. What risk? Let the greenhorns come and grab me.

HYMIE. That's all we need. I tell you the truth. I'm scared.

PHILIP. And you're a liar besides. You and Barkon. Every day you creep into the strike hall as if you were a striker, and every night—

HYMIE. What can I do? A father of four.

GOLD. Who wants a bite, boys? Mr. Leyzer, is the coffee ready?

LEYZER. It's been ready a long time already.

GOLD. Serve it, please. Come here, everyone. There's fruit, too, and candy. Sadie, Katie.

SADIE. I'm going home.

KATIE. I'm going home too.

GOLD. What's the matter?

SADIE. I'm scared. (*Sobs.*)

KATIE. I'm scared too. (*Sobs.*)

BARKON. Let them go and not report us.

GOLD. (*To* BARKON.) Please. (*To the girls.*) You can't go now. In one more hour I'll take you in the automobile. You see yourselves, everything is perfectly safe. Here is coffee and cake. Have some.

SADIE. I want fruit.

KATIE. I want fruit too.

GOLD. Good. Here's candy, too. (*Takes it around, offers everyone, everyone takes except* SHLOYME-KHAYIM.) Well, and you, Reb Shloyme-Khayim?

SHLOYME-KHAYIM. I also don't want to come work any more.

PHILIP. They work and they complain.

GOLD. Please, Philip. There's kosher meat here for you, Reb Shloyme-Khayim. Mr. Leyzer, you put out kosher meat?

LEYZER. It's out.

SHLOYME-KHAYIM. Thanks, I don't want to eat. (GOLD *pours coffee, serves everyone. All take and say thanks.*)

GOLD. (*To* SHLOYME-KHAYIM.) Really nothing for you?

SHLOYME-KHAYIM. Are we working much longer today?

GOLD. One more hour. (*To the* GOONS.) Come here, boys. Have some coffee. (*Both* GOONS *come over, take coffee and food.*) Take candy too, take some. (*Both take, say thanks, and return to their places.*)

SHLOYME-KHAYIM. Nice guards: Oy and Vey.

GOLD. Mr. Leyzer, go into the office and see whether Mr. Wolf is up yet.

LEYZER. I was there. He's not asleep.

GOLD. What is he doing?

LEYZER. He's lying there. Doesn't want to get up. Angry—terrible.

GOLD. Eat. I'll be right back. (*Off. The others eat and go back to work.* KATIE *and* SADIE *jump out and snatch a quick little dance.*)

SHLOYME-KHAYIM. One minute crying, the next minute dancing.

PHILIP. That's what I like. (*Dances along with them, by himself*)

LEYZER. (*Mutters angrily to himself.*) No shame. A disgrace. Wolf is angry. Embarrassed in front of me. Of course. Make coffee for them. Wait on scabs in my old age.

BARKON. All he can do is complain. (*Shouts.*) The window's pushed back again. Dammit. Mr. Leyzer!

LEYZER. (*Creeps to window, very angry.*) They want to drive me crazy. (WOLF *comes out with* GOLD, *angry, threatening, his face showing broken-off sleep.*)

WOLF. (*Darkly.*) No dancing.

GOLD. (*To* WOLF.) I'm begging you, don't make a scene here. (*To the girls.*) You want to dance a little? Dance.

WOLF. (*Darker still.*) No dancing. (*The girls go off to their places.*)

GOLD. (*To* WOLF.) Have you gone crazy?

WOLF. Not yet.

GOLD. Go home and sleep it off.

WOLF. I'm not asking for your advice.

GOLD. But this is no place—

WOLF. (*Screams.*) Enough working! (GOLD *pushes him back, covers his mouth.*)

GOLD. Stop it, I'm telling you!

WOLF. Close the shop. Go home. Everyone.

GOLD. You're making me lose my patience.

WOLF. Let it come to an end.

GOLD. Are you acting in a play, or what? Or did you have a bad dream?

WOLF. A nightmare. I still have some say here. (*Suddenly screams.*) Scabs! (GOLD *grabs hold of him, drags him with difficulty into the office. Everyone is startled.* GOLD *comes back out.*)

GOLD. Mr. Wolf doesn't feel good.

SHLOYME-KHAYIM. (*Puts away his work and starts out.*) I'm going home.

GOLD. (*Yelling.*) You are to go back to your place right now. Tomorrow, if you don't want to come, be my guest. I'll get someone else. But now, since you are here, you'll go home together with everyone else. I didn't force you to come here.

SHLOYME-KHAYIM. You talked me into it.

GOLD. Are you a child that can be talked into something?

SHLOYME-KHAYIM. It doesn't feel right to me. You're paying us to whore. I'm an old Jew. I am ashamed.

GOLD. (*To all.*) He wants to go home before you. Can you allow that?

HYMIE. (*Frightened.*) No, no. Everyone together. Don't let him, Mr. Gold.

BARKON. This was supposed to be decided on together. Well, go depend on people like that. Try and make an agreement with them.

SHLOYME-KHAYIM. What, maybe you want solidarity too?

GOLD. (*To the goons.*) Don't let anybody out.

FIRST GOON. (*To* SHLOYME-KHAYIM.) Go work, old man.

SHLOYME-KHAYIM. But I want to go home.

FIRST GOON. You can't.

SHLOYME-KHAYIM. But if I want to go home—

SECOND GOON. Go work, go on. (*They push* SHLOYME-KHAYIM *back. He is helpless. He goes to his table but doesn't work any more. He stands with his back to everyone, silent the whole time.*)

GOLD. (*To* SHLOYME-KHAYIM.) I wouldn't have expected it of you. What is this with you? (SHLOYME-KHAYIM *doesn't answer.*) You don't have to be afraid of pickets. If they did find out and come, you'd all go out the fire escape to the courtyard. You know where. (*All work in silence.*)

FIRST GOON. Losers.

SECOND GOON. Kikes.

FIRST GOON. The sixth night already.

SECOND GOON. Stand around and yawn.

FIRST GOON. The strike will be over without even a little bit of fun. (*Yawns.*)

SECOND GOON. Yes, give the fists a little airing.

FIRST GOON. Let's ask for a raise at least.

SECOND GOON. A ten-dollar raise. And if he doesn't give—

FIRST GOON. We let go and—

SECOND GOON. And we strike. (*They laugh.*)

FIRST GOON. Mr. Gold. (GOLD *comes over.*)

SECOND GOON. We want a raise.

GOLD. What do you mean?

FIRST GOON. No long negotiations. A ten-dollar raise.

SECOND GOON. And one word out of you, Mr. Gold—

GOLD. All right, boys. (*Claps their backs, starts off. All work. Suddenly there is a bang on the door. Fear grows.* GOLD *goes to door.*) Don't be afraid.

SECOND GOON. A quiet knock, somehow.

FIRST GOON. (*Opens door, looks out. Immediately.*) Not them, boys. You work. Some woman wants you to let her in.

BARKON. We shouldn't let anyone in. (*Falls to work with his face toward his table.* GOLD *goes out, returns immediately with* RAYA. RAYA, *pale, her eyes wandering, looks like a lunatic. All look at her silently. They start to work.* BARKON *pretends not to see her.*)

GOLD. What did you want?

RAYA. I want Mr. Barkon.

GOLD. Did they send you to spy?

RAYA. No, no.

GOLD. Are the pickets behind you?

RAYA. I am alone. I have to see Barkon.

FIRST GOON. Tell the truth.

RAYA. (*Crying.*) I am telling the truth.

GOLD. Mr. Barkon.

BARKON. (*Goes very close to* RAYA.) Why did you come? (*To* GOLD.) She has to talk with me about something. (GOLD *moves away.* BARKON *and* RAYA *remain in the other half of the room in the darkness.*)

RAYA. (*With energy and fear.*) Come home.

BARKON. You can find your way without me.

RAYA. I won't let go of you.

BARKON. Well, sit down there and wait.

RAYA. Barkon.

BARKON. Or sit down and work, then we'll both go home together.

RAYA. You're joking.

BARKON. What are you doing here?

RAYA. I can't bear the thought that you're scabbing.

BARKON. I don't want you spying on me. Go bring the pickets here.

RAYA. I'd rather you took shears and hit me over the head than say that to me. Anyway, they already know in the strike hall that people are working in Gold's shop. Pickets will come in any case.

BARKON. I wouldn't be surprised if it was you who reported it.

RAYA. Yes, I should have reported it, really. And if I don't report it, I am even lower than you. It's my duty.

BARKON. Go do your duty.

RAYA. Six nights already I haven't closed an eye. I am a liar. I know people are scabbing and I don't report it. And who is scabbing? Barkon. And Barkon has become everything to me. If you are scabbing—then I'm a scab too.

BARKON. I'm not a scab. I'm working, that's all. I don't have anything to do with the strike.

RAYA. (*Crushed.*) My God, why do I deserve this?

BARKON. Go home, I beg you.

RAYA. Yes, yes. I'm going. (*Starts off, turns back. Into* BARKON*'s face, with weeping and hatred.*) Scab.

BARKON. (*Grabs her by the shoulders.*) Be quiet.

RAYA. (*Suddenly, pleading tearfully.*) Barkon, dear, come home. I beg you.

BARKON. You love me. And you treat me like an enemy. Come help me instead. Sit down and work.

RAYA. My God.

BARKON. Do it for me, Raya. I'll be different. You'll see. I'll love you. We'll make a lot of money. We'll open our own business. Make a life for ourselves. Our own little corner. You want a home, don't you? You want to rest. (*Pulls her to him by the hand.*)

RAYA. (*Totally subjugated, lost. Follows him, in love. As if in a dream. Stammers.*)

Barkon. Barkon dear. (BARKON *leads her to her machine, sits her down. All act as if they don't see.*)

GOLD. (*Goes over to her.*) We'll make up, Raya.

RAYA. (*Stands up.*) No, no, let me go. (*Loud bangs are heard from outside, angry and stormy.*)

GOLD. Put out the lights.

GOONS. Don't be scared. We're here. (*Knocking grows louder. Sound of smashing as if something is breaking down.*)

WOLF. (*Comes in.*) No one is to fight.

GOLD. Go back where you were.

WOLF. No one is to think about lifting a hand to anyone.

GOLD. (*To GOONS.*) You take your orders from me. Put out the lights. (*They put out all the lights except a red light at the entrance. Dark in background.*)

WOLF. I say again: no fighting. (*Behind the door, pushing and tumult.*)

GOLD. And I say: open the door and give it to them.

WOLF. (*Stations himself at the door.*) I will not allow you to lift a finger against anyone. I have a say here too.

GOLD. Mr. Wolf, don't get in the way, I'm telling you.

FIRST GOON. Get away from the door.

WOLF. You get away, bums.

SECOND GOON. (*Grabs WOLF.*) Out of the way!

WOLF. I won't allow beating. I won't allow it.

(*Struggles with both GOONS. Old LEYZER wrings his hands. He mixes in, is immediately pushed away. The GOONS slam WOLF to the floor. He remains lying there. The GOONS open the door and throw themselves forward with their fists. We see nothing. We only hear voices. A few minutes of fighting. GOLD stands cold-bloodedly by and waits. The picketers behind the door win. The GOONS run away. MINA, LIPMAN, LEYBL, GERTIE, BER, and FIRST, SECOND, and THIRD OPERATORS come in ragged and disheveled.*)

BER. His goons will be more careful next time. Who's here in the shop? Put on the lights. (*Sees GOLD.*) Where are the scabs?

GOLD. Search.

BER. Smile, smile. Why aren't you a goon? (*Rummages around, drags out from somewhere a deathly pale LEYZER.*) Where are the scabs?

LEYZER. (*Crying.*) How is it my fault?

FIRST OPERATOR. A plague on his bones. Break his ribs.

MINA. (*Catches sight of* WOLF *with his face to the floor.*) Who is lying here?

GERTIE. It's Mr. Wolf himself.

LEYZER. They beat him up.

LIPMAN. Who?

LEYZER. They did. The young toughs. The handsome guards. Wolf didn't let them attack you. (*Kneels beside* WOLF.) Stand up. Oh, he's bleeding.

WOLF. Never mind, never mind. Don't yell. (*Gets up.*)

LIPMAN. Who beat you?

WOLF. Not important. What's the difference?

LIPMAN. No difference to me.

WOLF. No, not to you.

LIPMAN. Your forehead is bloody.

WOLF. It's not important. (*Takes out a handkerchief, covers his forehead.*)

FIRST OPERATOR. A nice little piece of trimming on your forehead, Mr. Wolf, huh?

LIPMAN. (*To* GOLD.) And you stand there so peacefully with your hands in your pockets?

GOLD. Yes. (*Exits into his office.* BER, LEYBL, GERTIE, *and the* OPERATORS *search the shop. They suddenly give a yell: "Raya!"*)

GERTIE. Raya is here. (*They lead* RAYA *out. She can hardly stand on her feet. Her face is stony.*)

MINA. Raya—you?

GERTIE. You picketed with us together last night.

LEYBL. Scab.

FIRST OPERATOR. Old plague. Scab-lady.

LIPMAN. I beg you to restrain yourself a little.

MINA. She scabbed.

LIPMAN. Mina . . . we have talked about Raya so many times . . . you know yourself . . . Mina.

MINA. There is no mercy.

LIPMAN. I want to hear it from you yourself, Raya. (RAYA *stands frozen and doesn't speak.*)

FIRST OPERATOR. Open your mouth, open it, Scab-lady.

WOLF. (*From the side.*) If I may be permitted, I would like to beg consideration for Raya. She did not scab.

MINA. You are permitted nothing—nothing.

WOLF. You can trust me.

MINA. It would have been better if you had stood stiff and smiling to yourself like the other gentleman. Who asked you to defend us and get beaten? It would have been better if you had done the beating.

WOLF. Mina.

MINA. I am not Mina now. We have broken your doors, we punched faces and we got punched. She—Raya—is a traitor. Here Gertie cried all day yesterday because she smacked a girl who was scabbing. It wasn't the one who got hit that cried, it was the one who hit, and her tears were ours too. And here Raya is crying and her tears are ours. But what kind of tears? You're not the one who should beg for Raya. Not you.

WOLF. Yes, yes. You are right. Not me. It must look a little comical in your eyes, right? Beaten by my own goons. (*Laughs crookedly.*) Yes, yes. Now everything's all right. The goons are gone. (*Starts for the door.*) And I thank you, Mina. I thank you. (*Exit.*)

LIPMAN. We'll let Raya go home. And we'll go to the hall.

MINA. Raya will go to the hall with us.

LEYBL. There must be an end to scabbing.

FIRST OPERATOR. You have to bring scabs in to the hall, and everyone should know—

LIPMAN. Mina, how do you allow this? You don't realize that Raya is different?

MINA. Everyone is different. One can find an excuse for everyone.

LIPMAN. This time, however, must be an exception. I demand it, Mina. Do I need to remind you what it means: hunger for a little bit of happiness?

MINA. I know what it means. No excuse. This is a strike. War.

FIRST OPERATOR. You don't stand on ceremony with scab-ladies.

LIPMAN. (*More and more upset. Heatedly, almost stammering.*) Be quiet. If anyone says one more bad word to Raya—I know what the story is here. You know too.

FIRST OPERATOR. We don't want to know.

LIPMAN. Why are you silent, Mina? What if a person struggles and doesn't have the strength to overcome? And you yourself, Mina . . . And I . . . Aren't we searching for personal happiness?

MINA. (*Looks at* LIPMAN. *Looks at herself, shivers. Suddenly cuts him off sharply as if with a chop.*) Enough backsliding. (*Turns away as if with disgust.*)

RAYA. Let them bring me. Let them sentence me. (*Her knees buckle. She lets herself down on the floor as if executed. All run to her, lift her.*)

LIPMAN. (*Pushes everyone away from her, including* MINA. *Takes her under the arm.*) Come with me. I'll take you home. (*Leads her after him. Exits with her. Pause.*)

MINA. (*After a long stony silence.*) And for us—back to the hall. (*All exit.*)

LEYZER. (*To himself.*) Oy, children.

GOLD. (*Comes out.*) Close all the doors. Pay attention. Be careful. A shop is still a shop.

LEYZER. (*Puts out the lights. In the dark.*) Pay attention. Be careful. A watchman—What kind of watchman? Guarding dirty money in my old age. (*Creeps to a window, tears off the hangings. Light of dawn strikes into the shop. With tears.*) Me—the watchman. The watchman.

Curtain

༄

Act IV

The following Saturday at noon. The shop is decorated with multicolored ribbons. As the curtain rises, everyone is in his place finishing work. Machines are coming to a stop. Before the workers have had time to stand up, BER *begins to speak, loudly enough to be heard all over the shop.*

BER. (*In the tone of an orator.*) I hereby announce and bring it to the attention of the rank and file- no one is to go home by himself. As you all know . . . However . . . To repeat . . . So here goes: I hereby announce and bring it to your attention—that today we are celebrating a shop party in honor of our Queen Gertie and in honor of Leybele. Which they became engaged during the strike. And whose wedding will be tonight following the approved procedure. (*Applause.*)

FIRST OPERATOR. Look who's a big-shot speech-maker.

BER. What can't you learn in America? And in a strike, what's more. Here it is a pleasure, I'm telling you, brothers, to strike and to win following the approved procedure. After serious theoretical consideration.

VOICES. Get to the point.

FIRST OPERATOR. Talk, talk, without the trimmings.

BER. So here goes. This is it. Together with the strike which we pulled off so nicely, we also pulled off such a sweet match. Yes. We're going to celebrate an extra lucky and happy occasion, following the approved procedure. And although our Gertie isn't saying farewell to us altogether—

GERTIE. Of course not. I'm not stopping work yet.

BER. So there it is. Yes. Our Gertie isn't the kind that's embarrassed to work after the wedding. Yes. Brothers and sisters, but we have to give our party following the approved procedure. Yes, as a general principle— (*The group starts to get restless.*) So here goes, brothers. Order, order. This isn't a union meeting. Now, all of us in the rank and file—after serious theoretical consideration—notwithstanding the general principle—we've got good things to eat. We've got presents. The shop is decorated, but not enough. Yes, and furthermore—we should decorate the machines too and decorate the bride too, following the approved procedure. And I am therefore announcing and bringing it to the attention of the membership that Lipman will be the best man. (*Applause.*)

LIPMAN. No, no.

BER. Today you have to obey me, that's the approved procedure.

LIPMAN. I can't. I beg you.

BER. And Mina the maid of honor.

MINA. I accept. (*Applause.*)

FIRST OPERATOR. Give us any job. We'll do it.

BER. All right. All right. I demand silence. Yes. Go in back, girls. You decorate the machines. And bring flowers. And you, Gertie dear, don't you mix in. Be quiet, that's the proper thing for a pretty bride like you. Do what you're told. After serious theoretical consideration, let them dress you up as nice as they can. And you too, Leybl, yes sir, as a general principle, don't mix in. (*Sees* SHLOYME-KHAYIM *entering.*) Here is Reb Shloyme-Khayim too. Came to the party, huh? Go back, all of you. All of you. (*All go up into background.* BER *and the girls start decorating the tables.* BARKON *moves around. It can be seen that he doesn't feel comfortable. We see that he wants to approach* RAYA *and can't manage it.* RAYA *sits in a corner turned away and doesn't look at him.* LIPMAN *is unhappy too, stands on the side deep in a newspaper.* MINA, *on the contrary, seems excited, takes part in the dressing-up, but we see that she notices every movement* LIPMAN *makes.* LEYBL *goes to* LIPMAN, *places himself behind his shoulder, looks into newspaper too.*)

LEYBL. I'm not bothering you, Comrade Lipman?

LIPMAN. (*With good-humored smile.*) No, you're not bothering me.

LEYBL. You're smiling that I called you Comrade, aren't you? (*Flushes.*)

LIPMAN. You don't have to blush about it.

LEYBL. Even before the strike I took a liking to you. (*Stammering.*) Compared to you I'm still a kid.

LIPMAN. Well?

LEYBL. You were so active. Everyone was amazed by you. Then suddenly you got quiet. You don't take part in anything.

LIPMAN. I'm an old man already, Leybl.

LEYBL. You don't like something here, probably, or you don't like us.

LIPMAN. I like you all. I have gotten quiet, you say. What do you mean: "got quiet"? The machines are turning again and we are all back in our places.

LEYBL. But we won so much. We ought to be happy.

LIPMAN. (*Smiles wanly.*) I am happy. You are still a very young boy and you're already getting married. You love Gertie very much?

LEYBL. Yes.

LIPMAN. She loves you too. She's a fine girl. Do you have money to get settled?

LEYBL. We'll both go to work and earn.

LIPMAN. Yes. That's the way. Be happy, both of you.

LEYBL. Thank you.

LIPMAN. Here in the paper is the whole description of Tuesday night. (*Jumps up.*) Look, Mr. Wolf withdraws from the business.

LEYBL. (*Over the whole shop.*) Just listen, Mr. Wolf is leaving the business. (*The news makes an impression. The crowd run around* LIPMAN, *look in the paper.*)

LIPMAN. Don't tear the paper.

BER. (*Pushes the crowd back.*) Out of the way, please. (*To old* LEYZER, *who is also pushing among the crowd.*) You'll get your turn. Go on.

LEYZER. Wolf is abandoning us. Who is he abandoning me to—his old friend?

BER. Go away. (LEYZER *exits.*)

LEYBL. (*Looks again at* LIPMAN.) Mina would like to see the newspaper for a while.

LIPMAN. (*Frightened.*) What do you mean: she would like to see it? Does one need a messenger for that?

LEYBL. I don't know.

LIPMAN. (*Goes to* RAYA.) Is it all right to sit next to you?

RAYA. (*Between her teeth*) I don't need pity.

LIPMAN. Why so angry?

RAYA. Why do you keep watching me? You're guarding me.

LIPMAN. Why should I guard you?

RAYA. I see. You watch me. Guarding me is not your job. (*Off angrily.*)

LIPMAN. (*To* LEYBL.) I'm afraid of her. You should have seen her eyes.

MINA. (*Comes over.*) You begrudge me the newspaper?

LIPMAN. (*Smiles.*) Has it become so unpleasant to you to come near me?

MINA. You've been avoiding me so in the two days that we've been back working. It's strange.

LIPMAN. You avoid me.

MINA. You exaggerate your quiet out of all proportion.

LIPMAN. And you exaggerate your joy out of all proportion.

MINA. You're determined to fight.

LIPMAN. (*After a pause.*) You want to read about Wolf. (*Hands her the paper.*)

MINA. (*Takes the paper. Reads.*) Fine. A good deed. It should make you happy.

LIPMAN. I am happy. And you?

MINA. Very. This is much more than gestures of pity for undisciplined misery.

LIPMAN. (*Sharply.*) For human misery. To you a human being is nothing.

MINA. Yes, in himself man is nothing. He suffers? A worm suffers. To conquer—that is what makes him great. You've been angry at me since that night with Raya. You have withdrawn from me. That gives me pleasure because I know how much that withdrawal costs you.

LIPMAN. You know?

MINA. Yes. But you also know what it cost me to tear the name Wolf out of my heart. I tore it out forever. And you even know, I think, how much your withdrawal costs me. Or don't you know it?

LIPMAN. Do I know it?

MINA. Well, all right then. I'll tell you. It was strange when you talked to me that night. I was tempted. You don't know yourself how sharply you cut my heart.

LIPMAN. (*Pleadingly.*) Mina.

MINA. It wasn't the first time. Don't answer.

LIPMAN. I love you.

MINA. I know that. You also know that I love you. Nevertheless we are in opposite camps.

LIPMAN. Are we?

MINA. Yes, opposite camps. (PHILIP *and* HYMIE *pass by.*)

PHILIP. (*To* HYMIE.) Come home.

HYMIE. I'll wait. Do you think the shop doesn't know who scabbed? I'm embarrassed.

PHILIP. I'm going home. (*He exits. So does* HYMIE. RAYA *comes, followed by* BARKON. *In the background people are making noise and singing.*)

BARKON. (*To* RAYA.) But let me say one word.

RAYA. You have nothing to say to me. (WOLF *approaches.* BARKON *exits.*)

WOLF. (*To* RAYA.) How are you, Raya?

RAYA. Let me alone.

WOLF. (*Lost.*) We won't see each other again.

RAYA. (*Looks at him sharply.*) Never again.

WOLF. (*Can't find a place for himself. To* BER.) You're running around, huh?

BER. Yes, Mr. Wolf.

WOLF. May I bring flowers for you?

BER. Why not?

WOLF. I'm leaving soon. That makes you happy?

BER. For the shop, it makes no difference.

WOLF. (*Lonely.*) Right, no difference.

MINA. (*Passes nearby, approaches unwillingly. To* WOLF.) It makes me very happy.

WOLF. Yes?

MINA. I practically feel like thanking you for it.

WOLF. That's all you feel?

MINA. You don't expect payment for your good deed?

WOLF. No.

MINA. You ought to feel glad.

WOLF. About what?

MINA. About yourself, your own strength.

WOLF. I am glad.

MINA. And you look so tired, pale—excuse me, I am busy. (*Bows, exits.*)

WOLF. (*Confused. To* BARKON, *who is approaching.*) May I bring flowers?

BARKON. (*Wildly.*) What do you want?

WOLF. Nothing, nothing. It's not important. Yes, for the shop it makes no difference. (*Exits ashamedly.*)

BARKON. (*To* RAYA, *who stands against the wall.*) Raya.

RAYA. Call the whole shop together and apologize to everybody.

BARKON. (*Wide-eyed.*) What?

RAYA. Apologize and beg them to forgive you.

BARKON. I should beg them to forgive me?

RAYA. Clear away the shame off yourself and also off me. I've kept my mouth shut. I've taken everything on myself. And I could have carried the burden, too, if you didn't also mock me for it.

BARKON. Who tells you to make such a burden out of it?

RAYA. I am a worker. Twenty years now. (*Shuddering.*) Barkon, this is my last request. My last hope.

BARKON. What a thing to ask.

RAYA. (*Takes his hand.*) The world would become full of light.

BARKON. What am I, a kid? I should beg the shop to forgive me!

RAYA. We both sinned. Left to itself, the shop will never forgive. The shop will take revenge.

BARKON. Let them try.

RAYA. I won't forgive either. Not you, not myself. I am the shop.

BARKON. Oh, you drive me crazy. I'm going home. (*Exits hastily.* KATIE *and* SADIE *dance in and cry, "Finished, finished."*)

BER. Over here, gang. Lead in the bride and groom. Operators, you be the musicians. Use the shears, and irons, and thimbles.

(*The machines are decorated, the tables decked with red flowers, fruit, candy.* GERTIE *and* LEYBL *are led in.* GERTIE *is dressed in white with a red crown on her head, a wreath of buttons at her throat. The* OPERATORS *bang and clang with irons, shears, and other tools. All the others hold strings of thimbles which ring like bells.*)

FIRST OPERATOR. (*Steps forward and sings satirically.*)

> Dear little groom, darling little bride,
> Thimbles and buttons—
> Against your little throats, shears,
> Against your little heads, an iron.
> Turn, little machine.
> Sing, little machine.
> A pull on the little strap—
> Into the little finger, a needle.

(GERTIE *and* LEYBL *are seated at the decorated table.*)

BER. (*Presents a bouquet of flowers to* GERTIE.) This is from all of us. After serious theoretical consideration.

GERTIE. Thank you. Thank you. You say thank you too, Leybl, don't be shy.

LEYBL. I really do thank you.

GERTIE. Well, let's dance.

BER. Wait, Gertele. You're a bride, so obey. We'll get to the dancing. First comes a little speech-making. On general principles. I honor Mina with a toast. (*Applause.*)

MINA. (*Hides her face. Stands a long while sunken into herself. Tears her hands away from her face.*) What should I say? Maybe say the simplest thing. You are dear to us, Gertie. You are a beautiful bride. You are young, and you are ours. You too, Leybl—we love you. After such a great victory, such a precious celebration. Today our shop is singing. Some people say that a shop has no meaning. A lie. Work is what gives meaning to the world. Like beauty, like love. We workers must be the meaning of the world. If inside your heart something grieves, tear it out. Because if not, I tell you openly, I myself might run away somewhere— (*Her voice begins to wobble. Catches herself.*) No, no. (*Grabs GERTIE and squeezes her to herself.*) Be happy, happy. It's so good to be young.

GERTIE. Are you crying, Mina?

MINA. (*Weeping quietly.*) It's good near you.

BER. And now Lipman.

LIPMAN. I can't talk today.

VOICES. Lipman! Lipman!

FIRST OPERATOR. Enough. Enough. Let's eat.

BER. Well, all right. Help yourselves. (*The crowd help themselves to fruit and candy.*)

FIRST OPERATOR. Come here, Mister Leyzer. Don't stand far away.

LEYZER. Oy, little brothers, a little schnapps would go down nicely.

FIRST OPERATOR. All ready. Here. (*Pulls a bottle out of his pocket. Pours into glasses, serves everyone.*) Drink, little operators. Down those aristocratic little throats. (*To LEYZER.*) That's the way. Make speeches—what for? All the words—it's only trimmings. You got married—all right, so what? Everyone has to get married. And boys, so you were good strikers—do you deserve a thank-you? How could it be any different? Would you scab? You'd get your ribs broken. We've got enough scabs.

VOICES. Enough. Enough.

FIRST OPERATOR. (*Sees GOLD coming out of his office. Jumps to him with a glass in hand.*) Drink, Mr. Gold. (*GOLD, embarrassed, after hesitation takes the glass.*) Next year, with god's help—another strike. (*Burst of laughter. GOLD exits.*)

LEYZER. (*Tipsy.*) Oy, little brothers, so Wolf is going away. Maybe to you that's nothing, little brothers? Give me another little glass. Give. A long time since I had a drink. To you, it's nothing, maybe. I am left alone with the machines. At night. Alone. Maybe to you that's nothing? And how about if I go and die, ha? If I go and die among the machines? Is that maybe nothing to you? (*Weeps.*)

FIRST OPERATOR. Sh! sh! Drink another glass. (*The old man drinks. To* SHLOYME-KHAYIM.) Why do you stand far off, Reb Shloyme-Khayim? Come here nearer, tell one of your stories.

SHLOYME-KHAYIM. Well, what is there to tell?

FIRST OPERATOR. Tell. Sit yourself right there and tell.

SHLOYME-KHAYIM. (*Sits down and tells.*) So then—what? A story they tell about the holy little operator. Mm. The story goes like this. Once upon a time there was a little operator. It was decreed from above, all the way above, that he, the little operator, will bring the Messiah. So then—how? Altogether simple. That he will sew so much and so many pants—namely, a million, or two, maybe three million pants—it should be the necessary number—and as soon as he gets to the necessary number, the Messiah will come. Well, so the little operator sewed and sewed and sewed his whole life, and managed to sew barely ten thousand pairs of pants, and suddenly he went and died. Ay, ay. What would be? How would Messiah come? Earth and heaven started in weeping, and they wept so hard that their weeping reached all the way down to the little operator in his grave. And when the holy little operator heard the weeping of the world, he rose up from his grave in the middle of the night and came back to his little shop. He sat himself down at his machine, and he started sewing the pants that still remained to sew. And when cocks began to crow, back he went back to his own grave. And on the second night back he came again. And that way night after night, still till today, he gets up from his grave and comes in to his little shop, and he sews and sews and sews. And still is far from the decreed number. Ay, far, far. So then—what? Mm. That's how the story goes.

ALL. Bravo. Bravo.

FIRST OPERATOR. Some operator. The hell with him. Well, and what we sew, that doesn't get counted, huh? Drink a glass, Reb Shloyme-Khayim, and if the holy little operator comes in, he'll get a glass too—and the hell with him. Drink, drink. (LIPMAN *rises from his place, goes up to* RAYA, *sits next to her.*)

BER. You have to sit next to the groom.

LIPMAN. I want to sit next to Raya.

RAYA. (*Jumps up.*) I beg you not to sit next to me.

LIPMAN. Calm yourself.

RAYA. (*As if she has been waiting a long time for an opportunity to jump up. Her face alters, steely and drawn, lips dry and pale. She speaks in a voice that seems about to break. All look at her with amazement.*) I am calm. I beg you not to soothe me. Go away from me. I don't need any pity. Nobody speaks to me, don't you speak either. I am not your job.

LIPMAN. What is it, Raya?

RAYA. I hate you. All of you. Spiders. You caught me the way spiders catch a fly and fight over which one will eat it.

LIPMAN. (*Takes her hand.*) You shouldn't talk like that.

RAYA. (*Storm.*) You all look at me like a crazy woman. You're crazy yourselves. You dance, you celebrate. On other people's flesh, you dance. On other people's bones, you celebrate. You're big laughers. Go on, laugh. Judge me. You're such saints, why don't you judge me? You've got shears in your hands— cut. Hit with the irons. Why have mercy? I am a scab, saints. An old maid and a scab.

GERTIE. Who is judging you?

RAYA. You—be quiet. They put the crown on your head, so sit. Why did you decorate the machines with false ribbons? They should stand naked. (*Tears the ribbons from the machines. They catch her by the hands. She tears herself away, fights them, hurls words at* GERTIE.) Tear the crown from your head. Tear it off.

GERTIE. Don't judge her. Let her go. (*Embraces* RAYA *warmly.*) Sh! Calm down. (*Bows her head.*) You want to tear it off—here, tear.

RAYA. (*Suddenly tired and quiet.*) No, no, I don't need to—forgive me, everybody.

GERTIE. (*Sits down next to her.*) We forgive you. Calm down.

RAYA. I am already calm. Don't hold it against me. Somehow everything went dark in front of my eyes. Now I'm fine.

GERTIE. We're not mad at you.

RAYA. Then go on with your party. (*Strokes* GERTIE*'s head.*) Dear Gertie, pretty Gertie, I thank you.

GERTIE. What for?

RAYA. For everything. Because you are so pretty. I thank everyone. Everyone. And I thank you, too. Everything has become full of light. Dance some more.

GERTIE. You dance with us.

RAYA. (*As if entranced.*) Dance the dance of the machine and the needle.

GERTIE. The dance of the machine and the needle.

BER. Everyone here. Turn on the electric. The dance of the machine and the needle.

(*All start to dance. This is a couple dance. Straight vertical movements up and down, mixed with sudden turns, one partner up and the other down like movements of the needle. The machines are abandoned. The noise becomes controlled, cut off and reawakened according to the rhythm of the dancers. Increasingly fast and energetic. The dance spreads over the whole shop. No music except the machine rhythm. All draw the others in as if into a spell. The pattern of the dance is transformed into something which welds the people with the machines. Severe and inhuman from the start, it changes increasingly into a storm. Hands outstretched and faces like fire. At its greatest heat, as the dance reaches ecstasy, screams and whistles are suddenly heard from the street.* LIPMAN *runs in from behind and shouts: "Raya fell off the roof!"*

The dance is interrupted. The machines are turned off. All remain frozen, then suddenly rush out. GERTIE *remains alone until she pulls herself together, tears off her decorations, and runs out too. We hear the sounds of an ambulance and of heavy tread. It becomes silent outside.*

LIPMAN *and* MINA, *who didn't run out, remain like stone.* WOLF *rushes in. Looks at* MINA, *goes to her with outstretched hands and wants to say something.* MINA *turns away from him decisively. She goes to* LIPMAN, *lays a hand on his shoulder.*)

MINA. Lipman. Comrade. (LIPMAN *looks at her in sharp pain.*) Lipman, the struggle needs us both. (*Takes his hand.* LIPMAN *lets her lead him. Both off.*

WOLF *seems half-crazy. His face contorted, he leaps at the machines and turns on the electric power. A wild laugh tears itself out of his heart. He runs from the shop, kicking out of the way everything that he meets. The shop is alone. The machines make noise; they make noise.*)

Curtain

✧

The Treasure (Der Oytser)

(1906)

DAVID PINSKI

ംﻪﯩﻪ

I derived this text from Volume 2 of a series entitled *Dovid Pinskis Dramn* (David Pinski's Dramas) (New York; Poaley Tsion, 1919) and made it percepti- bly shorter by editing out repetitions. Yakhne-Brayne keeps groaning and curs- ing; Khonye keeps swearing and cursing; both use virtually the same few words over and over. So I took a good deal of that out. Also I omitted a num- ber of repetitions of the same exchanges of dialogue, such as "Give me all the money" and "Give it here right now." These were only meant to give actors scope for comic business, infinitely expanded. I also eliminated some repeti- tions of various versions of the question "Who has the treasure?" asked in the last act by crowd members or by individual or grouped anonymous voices. It is impossible to know how many of these repetitions were actually said onstage in various productions. However, the copyright is in Pinski's own name, so pre- sumably he made those final printing decisions himself.

Syllables of names are stressed as follows (in order of appearance):

> YAKH-ne BRAY-ne
>
> TIL-ye
>
> YUD-ke (nickname for Yehude-ye-HU-de; YUD-ke-le is another diminutive.)
>
> ZHUTSH-ke
>
> KHON-ye (nickname for Khonon-KHON-en)
>
> SOS-kin
>
> MIR-kin (diminutive: MIR-ke)
>
> NA-khum KHAY-im MORD-khe ZAKH-haym

The following names are mentioned in act Two:

SHO-lem ba-LASH-nik
LEY-ye
FREY-de
GEL-ye
BEN-det
IT-she (nickname for Yitskhok or Isaac)

The name Yehude (ye-HU-de) appears in act 3, as do the following words:

TFI-lin (means phylacteries)
MAZ-l tov ("congratulations"; sometimes anglicized as "mazel tov")
le-KHAY-im (toast meaning "to life"; sometimes written "Lechaim")
TISH-e-bov (annual Tisha b'Av observance, mentioned in every act; see below)

(See Note on Transliteration.) Also, please note that *Reb* simply means "Mr." It is not a way of addressing a rabbi.

I made some specific translation decisions for the sake of characterization and dramatic verisimilitude. Yakhne-Bryne is a stock figure of Yiddish comedy: an ignorant old lady gabbling, cursing, and spitting superstitiously for protection from evil. To maintain this cartoon quality, I retained for her the most exclamations and the most heavily Yiddishized diction. Not only does Yiddish integrate elements of other languages, but in addition it is plausible for characters to know several languages. I left Tilye's show-off scraps of French and German. German was associated not just with the wide sophisticated world but also with Enlightenment intellectuals; that is why the lawyer is addressed as Herr Mirkin as a compliment. In the original, Tilye, the Matchmaker, and others occasionally use Russian words and exclamations. In act 3, committee members greet each other sometimes as *Reb* So-and-so and sometimes with the Polish *Pani*. "Princely raiment" is a biblical phrase for which Tilye uses the Hebrew original. As religious functionaries, the First Member of the Burial Society, Khonye, and the Matchmaker all use Hebrew phrases. Finally, gold *greber* is plain Yiddish for gold "diggers"; however, I translated it as "grabbers" for the sake of Yudke's incantation.

The way Pinski identified speakers in act 4 is confusing. In the cast of characters, he listed several groups, such as Scared Group and Merry Group. In the text he listed Homegoers, which does not appear in his cast list, but indicated most other speakers by numbers (First Man or First Woman and so on), with the numbers starting all over again from one several times. I changed the number indications of all such numbered men and women so that they are consecutive up to Fifth Woman and Sixth Man. In a few places where I was sure I was clarifying, I actually changed speakers' names. For example, Pinski identified the Schoolmaster sometimes as both Schoolmaster and Third Man and sometimes just as Third Man; I made him simply Schoolmaster. Pinski called the Writer just Young Man, but there are a group of Young Men earlier in the act, and this individual is the only Writer, so I named him that. Similarly the Mother, the Pregnant Woman, and several other individual female characters were all called Woman. In clear cases like these, I specified the individual identities and added them to the cast list. One of the Dead is identified in dialogue as a surgeon, and one is twice identified in a stage direction as having a harsh voice, so I distinguished them as separate characters. But I left the original ways Pinski grouped the speeches of the Homegoers, the Dead (both dead rich men and dead paupers), and the various Voices and Screams (some of which are printed as dialogue and some as stage directions), in case a director has insight into the way Pinski intended them to be orchestrated. For an amateur reading that I myself organized, I divided up all the characters listed from Pregnant Woman down, plus all the Voices, among eight actors and six actresses, doubling some of the actors who had already appeared as committee members in act 3.

The play takes place in a village in the hinterlands in late-nineteenth-century eastern Europe. The characters' religious practices, superstitions, and social organization were all recognizable elements of such a world.

Religious observance is an integral part of the community's life, though not everyone in town lives up to the clearly prescribed ideal. Tisha B'Av (literally: the ninth day of the month of Av) is the anniversary of the destructions of the First and Second Temples in ancient Jerusalem, and according to tradition also the anniversary of many subsequent catastrophes. It usually falls in August. It is marked by fasting and by such rituals of mourning as sitting on low stools and abstaining from bathing and combing one's hair. On Tisha B'Av, in synagogue or at home, one reads the Book of Lamentations, which begins: "How doth the city sit solitary . . ." Although Lamentations is written in Hebrew and would be chanted in Hebrew by men and by particularly well-educated women, Yakhne-Brayne like most women reads it in Yiddish translation.

Much dialogue in the play derives from familiar religious practice. Khonye wears his *arbe kanfos* (a small fringed prayer shawl, cut like a rectangular poncho and worn under the shirt) and recites blessings before and after every meal. He prays morning and evening (wearing *tfiln,* or phylacteries, every morning), preferably not at home but at the synagogue where there will be a quorum of ten men. Synagogues are always built so that the ark holding the Torah scrolls is toward the east, facing toward Jerusalem, and the congregation faces in that direction; thus, the east wall is the prestigious place to stand when praying. A snack of brandy or whiskey and cake often follows fasts and other prayer services as well. In act 3 the mathematical calculation sanctioning drinking uses a common technique of interpretation of sacred texts, but uses it playfully. There is a specific blessing to be recited in thanksgiving for having escaped danger. The incantation in the Second Boy's story in act 4 is derived from the story of Samson told in *Judges* 14:14 and would have been recognized by many in Pinski's audiences.

Because *The Treasure* is set in a cemetery, the characters mention many customs involving mourning, some of which are still observed. Mourners went to and from the burial in processions, for example, stopping seven times along the way to recite Psalm 91, and when leaving the gravesite passed between a double line of people.

Country people held a number of superstitions associated with the dead. These superstitions, traceable to the Middle Ages and even in some cases to the Talmud, were familiar to Pinski's audiences, though already considered quaint. For example, the spirits of the dead were thought to come out of their graves at night to pray or converse. They might be seen on occasion in a cemetery in the form of flickering lights. There was a danger that they, or some other kind of evil spirits, might pounce upon a person alone outdoors in the dark. Among lower-class eastern European Jews, spitting was a superstitious (not a religiously sanctioned) gesture intended to keep such evils away.

Khonye's treasure unsettles a community typical in the complexity of its governing structure. Eastern European Jews even in small towns were often highly organized in a network of committees integrating civil and religious functions. Getting poor girls married and paupers decently buried and visiting the sick are still considered important specific charities; fundraising for the first two and organizing for the third are still the formal responsibilities of many Jewish communities.

The town is provincial. There were certainly illiterates who paid to have letters written or read. There were also people like Soskin who were better educated and more cosmopolitan. In such regions, peasants might still farm using
pre-industrial tools, but trains and telegraphs made connections with the larger
world.

Today the character of Yudke poses difficulties for both audience and actor.
We are no longer comfortable with the half-wit, the village simpleton, either as
a reality of village life or as a conventional nineteenth-century stage presence
embedded in a universe of old-world grotesques. In addition, the parents' attitudes toward him are difficult to accept. (I have heard of a recent adaptation of
the play that made Yudke not simpleminded but just young and irresponsible.)
However, in the past Yudke was played by actors in a position to choose roles.
Jacob Ben-Ami, who was known for intelligence and sympathy, sometimes
played Yudke and sometimes Khonye. Ludwig Satz, beloved for gentle comedy,
actually chose to play Yudke for a personal benefit: an evening designed to
showcase his talents, for which he kept the entire profit. At the play reading
that I organized, the audience was surprised to find how touching a figure Yudke (played by my husband William Meyers) turned out to be. So the character
must be acknowledged to offer opportunities for pathos and laughter, once we
get past our initial distaste.

A footnote to the history of the play is worth mentioning. Pinski wrote *The
Treasure* in 1906. In 1908, when he was about to try to get it produced, he
learned that Sholom Aleichem had just finished a very similar play, which also
depicted a town hunting for treasure in the cemetery. Sholom Aleichem's play
even had the same title. Anxious to prove that he had not plagiarized, Pinski
sent his play off to a St. Petersburg journal, asking for it to be published as
soon as possible. Later Sholem Aleichem changed his own title to *Di Goldgreber
(The Gold-Diggers)*. This play was produced several times, though it is stronger
on amusing, folksy characters than on plot. Another difference between the
two plays is that *Di Goldgreber* is rather jolly and affectionate (though certainly
not simpleminded), in typical Sholom Aleichem tone, whereas *The Treasure* is
rather nasty—a tonic corrective to seductive sentimentality about the old days
in the Old Country.

The Treasure was first performed in 1912 in New York as a benefit for Yiddish writers. It was directed by Joseph Schildkraut, with Rudolph Schildkraut
as Khonye, Mark Schweid as Yudke, and the popular soubrette Clara Young as

Tilye; most of the other roles were played by writers, including Pinski himself. In 1918, Ludwig Satz chose it for his personal benefit performance at the Irving Place Theatre in New York; he played Yudke. In 1922, Maurice Schwartz produced it at his Yiddish Art Theatre and himself played Khonye, with Bina Abramovitsh as Yakhne-Brayne and Celia Adler as Tilye. The VYKT Theatre performed it in Warsaw in 1927, directed by Zigmund Turkov and starring Moyshe Lipman and Ida Kaminska. The next decade brought major productions in Philadelphia, Chicago, Detroit, and Buenos Aires. The Yiddish Theatre Project of the WPA included *The Treasure* in its repertory. In 1942, Menashe Skulnick and Miriam Kressyn played father and daughter at the Second Avenue Theatre. For several of these productions, Pinski himself provided revisions.

In 1918, *The Treasure* was produced in German translation in Vienna, directed by Egon Brecher, with Schildkraut again playing Khonye. The following year Max Reinhardt produced it in German in Berlin and the Theatre Guild produced it in English in New York. Celia Adler, who had already played the role in Yiddish, played Tilye, and Dudley Digges played Khonye. That year *The Treasure* was performed in Hebrew translation as well.

David Pinski (1872–1959) wrote many other successful plays as well as critical commentary on Yiddish drama and literature and on other subjects. (The introduction to this book tells more about Pinski and more about *The Treasure*.)

Characters

KHONYE, the Gravedigger
YAKHNE-BRAYNE, his wife
TILYE, his daughter, a young woman
YUDKE, his son, a half-wit

MATCHMAKER
REB SOSKIN, a rich man
HEAD OF THE COMMUNITY COUNCIL
REB MIRKIN, his lawyer (non-speaking)

TWO MEMBERS OF THE DOWRIES-FOR-POOR-BRIDES COMMITTEE
TWO MEMBERS OF THE VISITING-THE-SICK COMMITTEE
FOUR OR MORE MEMBERS OF THE BURIAL SOCIETY

YOUNG PREGNANT WOMAN

YOUNG PREGNANT WOMAN'S HUSBAND

OLD MAN

OLD WOMAN

THREE YOUNG MEN

FIVE WOMEN

SIX MEN

MOTHER

LITTLE GIRL

FOUR BOYS

SCHOOLTEACHER

MAN BEING LED AWAY

WIFE OF MAN BEING LED AWAY

WELL-DRESSED MAN

WRITER

THE DEAD

DEAD SURGEON

HARSH VOICE AMONG THE DEAD

DEAD SAINT

In Act One: WIDOW'S VOICE

In Act Four: MEN, WOMEN, ONLOOKERS, VOICES, HOMEGOERS

Scene

The Jewish cemetery of a small town in Eastern Europe
Act I. The poverty-striken hovel of Khonye the Gravedigger,
at the edge of the cemetery.
Act II. The same house.
Act III. The same house.
Act IV. Outside the house.

Time

During and after the religious observance Tisha B'Av, late summer,
late nineteenth century.
Act I. Afternoon of Tisha B'Av.
Act II. That evening.

Act III. Early the next morning.
Act IV. Late that night.

༺✺༻

Act I

A whitewashed room in the home of KHONYE, *the Gravedigger. Two windows in the back wall overlook the cemetery. Between them, a worn old leather sofa. In the left wall, a door leads to the kitchen and the outer door. Left of the door is the wall of the oven, which stands in the kitchen, with a sleeping place on top. Right of the door stands a cupboard with drawers below. Down on the right wall stands a bed over which hang clothes draped with a sheet. Behind the bed, a door leads to the inner rooms. In front, a sofa and a wing chair. There are four more chairs in the room, arranged in no order at all. Great disorder reigns. The bed is unmade, and bedding lies on the sofa.*

YAKHNE-BRAYNE *sits down stage center on a little stool. She wears stockings with the toes poking out, a dirty red kerchief over her bonnet, and a dirty torn skirt and top. She is reading the biblical book of Lamentations and weeping hard.* TILYE *sits to the right by an open window, leaning over the back of her chair. She wears a faded old green jacket. Her hair is combed and wound up into a knot with spit curls. She is looking into a little hand mirror in front of her on the window and fixing up her spit curls. Through the window we see many passers-by in the cemetery.*

YAKHNE-BRAYNE. (*Reading slowly and with difficulty so that the words run together in a monotone.*) "And God caused the Temple to be destroyed and said, 'I will remember your sins and you will devour your children's flesh.' And because the daughters—" (*Through the window, the sound of wailing voices.* TILYE *checks herself in the mirror, fixes her spit curls, and looks out the window.*) Here comes the funeral. And this one keeps on admiring herself. It's a widow left single, not a widower. (*Back to book.*) "And because the daughters of Jerusalem boasted of their beauty and said, 'When the Babylonians come they will take us for wives,' therefore did God bring sorrow upon them. And when the Babylonians saw this, they cast off their wives, and the chariot wheels rode over their heads and crushed their heads and—" (*Interrupts herself.*) You should listen to this. Sits and admires herself! (*Back to book.*) "And because the daughters of Jerusalem boasted—" (*Interrupts herself.*) Doesn't pick up a comb for days on end, but today when we read Lamentations, that's her day for a hairdo. (*Back to book.*) "And said, 'When the Babylonians come they will take us for wives,' and—" (*Interrupts herself.*) Get away from the window. Get away! There are no Babylonians around here. Nobody comes to the cemetery on Tisha B'Av to find a wife. (*Funeral procession is heard passing outside window. Widow wails: "Who is left for me? Who? Seven little orphans. Take me away, my God." Funeral recedes.*)

TILYE. Seven orphans. What will the poor thing do? Starve, probably. Be a widow forever. Who's going to marry a widow with seven children?

YAKHNE-BRAYNE. Especially when there are so many girls just sitting at their window making eyes.

TILYE. Ah, stop it. Is that what's written in your Lamentations?

YAKHNE-BRAYNE. What's written in my Lamentations is you should put down the mirror—put it down!—and get away from the window.

TILYE. What do you care if I sit here? I don't go out in the street. I can't show myself because I've got nothing to wear. So at least I can sit by the window and look at people. And when can I do that except when there's a funeral, or on Tisha B'Av when a lot of people come to the cemetery?

YAKHNE-BRAYNE. When people come, she's got to sit herself down in a show window.

TILYE. And really why not? Come and see, come here. There goes a good-looking young man. Just looking at him is a pleasure. And I do believe he noticed me. He's looking. He's looking. He can't take his eyes off me. He is beginning to approach, closer and closer . . .

YAKHNE-BRAYNE. Get away from that window right now!

TILYE. He isn't looking. He isn't looking. He doesn't see me at all. Ah, you don't have one little crumb of imagination. You have no idea what it's like to dream.

YAKHNE-BRAYNE. All my bad dreams on your head!

TILYE. Daydreaming. Daydreaming. You just sit and dream.

YAKHNE-BRAYNE. Stop talking nonsense and let me read. And get away from the window. You don't have to do your daydreaming there. Dreaming! (*Reads.*) "And when they saw . . . they cast out—"

TILYE. It's so good. Like a lovely storybook. You forget yourself. You make yourself up. You become somebody else entirely. I think hard, and imagine, and think. And I become absolutely a Lady Rothschild.

YAKHNE-BRAYNE. No more and no less.

TILYE. The bride of Rothschild. Why not? He doesn't need a dowry. He's rich. I can imagine how he pours whole sacks full of gold and goes wandering all alone, far and wide, till he comes at last to our town and he sees me. He came to see our cemetery, and I was sitting at the window.

YAKHNE-BRAYNE. We should lock you up in a crazy house.

TILYE. And he falls on his knees to me and cries out, "I adore you. I am Rothschild. Will you be mine?"

YAKHNE-BRAYNE. I'm going to throw something at your head.

TILYE. But isn't that nice? And then sometimes I imagine that a count comes—

YAKHNE-BRAYNE. This one isn't even Jewish?

TILYE. It's only fantasy. I can fantasize anything.

YAKHNE-BRAYNE. "Pantasize!" You're no better than the daughters of Jerusalem. "When the Babylonians come—" A dark end is what's coming to you. Tisha B'Av and she has nothing else to do but sit and imagine demons-only-know-what.

TILYE. Demons only know? Marriage is a Jewish thing. So is needing money. And I'm imagining about getting married and getting money. Listen, Mama, what I would do if I had money. I'm telling you, Mama, I would rule the whole world. I feel I'm getting so clever—

YAKHNE-BRAYNE. (*Begins repeating angrily, with energy.*) "And he strengthened my sufferings, and I was scorned upon the ash heaps of Jerusalem—" (YUDKE *enters, wailing. He has a crooked hand, a crooked foot. Perpetually saliva in mouth. Overgrown, sparse little beard. Big tufts on his head under a torn old hat. Dressed in rags.*)

TILYE. What is the matter with you, Yudke?

YAKHNE-BRAYNE. (*Angry.*) What are you crying for this time?

YUDKE. Zshutshke buried. Zshutshke buried.

YAKHNE-BRAYNE. There's a new Tisha B'Av for you. (TILYE *laughs.*)

YUDKE. (*Throws her an angry glance and yells out, full of rage.*) Zshutshke dead. Zshutshke buried. You not laugh. (*Weeps more, going to stand with his face to the oven.*) I this way hold him. (*Breaks out in wail like the mourning widow's wail.*) Who is left for me? Who? (*With a cry, he falls with his face to the oven sleeping place.* TILYE *starts to laugh again, catches herself immediately and puts her hand to her mouth.* YUDKE *goes to her with his face distorted by anger.*) I you kill. I you strangle. (*Gnashes his teeth and stretches out toward her his healthy right hand with the fingers crimped.*)

TILYE. (*Jumps up and begins to stroke and soothe him.*) No, no, no, Yudke. I'm not laughing. I didn't mean to laugh. It just . . . It popped out by itself. Don't be mad. And don't cry, Yudke. Don't cry, poor thing.

YUDKE. You still laughing. I see. Your eyes.

TILYE. I'm not laughing. My eyes laugh all the time. But I'm not laughing. I mean it seriously. It really is a pity.

YUDKE. I this way held him.

TILYE. He really was a good little dog.

YUDKE. On back legs stood. Paw gave.

YAKHNE-BRAYNE. Ever heard such yelling?

YUDKE. (*Angry.*) You fault, Zshutshke dead. You his foot broken.

YAKHNE-BRAYNE. I should have broken your feet too.

YUDKE. Wait. I money found, you nothing give. I Zshutshke's grave dug and gold money found. (*Takes from his pocket and holds in both fists.*) See? But I—

YAKHNE-BRAYNE. (*Screams.*) You found what?

TILYE. (*Looks into his hands.*) Some kind of golden coins. Really. I could swear they're imperials.

YAKHNE-BRAYNE. Imperials, did you say? Imperials? A lot?

YUDKE. (*To* YAKHNE-BRAYNE *with clenched teeth.*) Heh. (*Quickly hides his hands in his pocket.*)

YAKHNE-BRAYNE. Where did you find them? A lot?

YUDKE. (*As before.*) Heh.

YAKHNE-BRAYNE. (*To* TILYE.) A lot? He's got a lot of them?

TILYE. A fistful. More than ten anyway. (*To* YUDKE.) Show me. Let's count them.

YUDKE. No. Her see.

YAKHNE-BRAYNE. You'd better show me. (*To* TILYE.) How much is an imperial? A lot?

TILYE. I wish I knew as much about money as I do about fasting. A great lot, probably. Fifteen rubles, for sure.

YAKHNE-BRAYNE. Fifteen rubles, my God. How many did you say he has? More than ten?

TILYE. More than ten for sure. A lot more, maybe. A full fistful. Two hundred rubles for sure.

YAKHNE-BRAYNE. (*Stands up and goes very determinedly to* YUDKE.) You'd better give me what you found right now. You hear what Mama is saying to you or not? You'd better give it to me. Two hundred rubles, oh my God in Heaven. You'd better give it to me nicely. Because I will take a stick, I won't leave you a single bone in one piece.

YUDKE. (*Screams as if possessed, eyes wild and foam on his lips.*) No, no, no, not give!

TILYE. (*Whispers to* YAKHNE-BRAYNE.) Just let him alone now. He'll hand it over later.

YAKHNE-BRAYNE. I'm getting dressed and running straight to the police.

YUDKE. (*Altogether beside himself.*) I you strangle.

TILYE. Look at that. Why do you have to fight with him? Don't you want to get anywhere with him? (*To* YUDKE.) You don't have to be scared, Yudke. She won't run to the police.

YAKHNE-BRAYNE. Who knows, maybe he stole them somewhere.

TILYE. Why do you have to talk like that? You know he didn't steal them.

YUDKE. Not steal. You steal. I not steal. (*To* TILYE, *quickly pulling his hands out of his pocket and giving her handful after handful.*) Take. You everything. You take. Her nothing. Give nothing. I her strangle. She, she steal. (*Falls against cupboard in a convulsion.* TILYE, *who has been standing astonished with both hands full of money, quickly stuffs it into her skirt pocket. She rushes over to* YUDKE, *unbuttons his shirt, runs quickly into the kitchen and comes in with a dipper of water.* YAKHNE-BRAYNE *rummages through his pockets meanwhile, opens up his hands, then sneaks into* TILYE'*s pocket.*)

TILYE. (*Busying herself around* YUDKE, *pushes* YAKHNE-BRAYNE'*s hand away with an elbow.*) No creeping. Wait. There's time.

YAKHNE-BRAYNE. Give it here.

TILYE. There's time. We'll sit down. We'll talk it over. (*Stands up and puts the dipper away on the cupboard.*)

YAKHNE-BRAYNE. Are you crazy or what? What's to talk over? Are you going to give me the money or not?

TILYE. If I feel like it. Anyway, I don't dare. You heard yourself how he ordered me not to give you anything.

YAKHNE-BRAYNE. You don't mean that.

TILYE. If he gave the money to me, the money is mine, and if he ordered me, I have to obey him. But because I am good . . . just put down your hand and I'll count into it. (*She takes* YAKHNE-BRAYNE'*s hand and counts into it.*) One. Two. Three. You see? Gold. Imperials. Now you are a rich lady. But keep it quiet. Don't say anything to him. And wait. Here you have another one. Four. Now you are very rich. And here's another one for you. Five. Now say thank you.

YAKHNE-BRAYNE. (*Holds her hand stretched out still.*) And this is all?

TILYE. (*Nods.*) No more.

YAKHNE-BRAYNE. I'll grab a stick and split your head. Five pieces she slipped me.

TILYE. You don't want them? Give them back.

YAKHNE-BRAYNE. I'll give you a give-back so you won't know where it came from. You're going to give me the whole money right away.

TILYE. Some people are never satisfied.

YAKHNE-BRAYNE. All the money! Out with it. I'm going to get you.

KHONYE. (*Without a jacket, pants tied up with a strap,* arbe kanfos *over shirt. Comes in rapidly.*) You can hear the yelling from outside. What money? What's going on?

YAKHNE-BRAYNE. Tell her to give me the money. Two hundred rubles, oh my God in Heaven. (TILYE *goes to the window and closes it.*)

KHONYE. What two hundred rubles? What are you raving about?

YAKHNE-BRAYNE. Yudke found them. What right does she have to take them?

TILYE. I didn't take them. He gave them to me himself.

KHONYE. Will you for once talk plain sense?

YAKHNE-BRAYNE. Look at him, he suddenly stopped understanding. What don't you understand, what? When Yudke buried his Zshutshke, he found golden imperials. Is that sense? Do you understand yet? So just tell her she should give them back. What right does she have to take them? Now do you understand? Then why are you standing there like a stick? Why don't you deal with her? (*To* TILYE.) You hear? Get me out the money.

KHONYE. So then wait—so then let's get this clear. Yudke buried Zshutshke and found golden imperials. Where did he bury him? Where did he find them?

YAKHNE-BRAYNE. How should I know?

KHONYE. (*Moving his gaze to* TILYE.) Where did he bury him? Where did he find them?

YAKHNE-BRAYNE. (*Imitating.*) "Where did he bury him? Where did he find them?" What do you care? He found them. Now look—

KHONYE. You're so smart, and what if—

TILYE. Oh, that's true. (*Rushes to* YUDKE.) Yudke. Yudke.

YAKHNE-BRAYNE. What "what if—"

KHONYE. (*Looks around to make sure that there are no strange ears and whispers.*) And what if this is a treasure?

YAKHNE-BRAYNE. A . . . A . . . (*Lets herself down on a chair.*) Oh my, I don't feel good. My feet can't hold me up.

TILYE. Yudke. Yudke. Do you hear me? He hasn't come to himself yet.

KHONYE. How come it didn't occur to you right away to ask? May you burn! All you can do is tear at each other. I will destroy you both, I will crush you to ashes. And so many people in the cemetery today, too.

TILYE. He must certainly have filled the grave back up, so what are you yelling so loud for?

KHONYE. She's right. What am I yelling for? Now you'd better get me out that money right away. (*To* YAKHNE-BRAYNE.) How much did he find? How much?

YAKHNE-BRAYNE. Did I count it, then? Did I see it? Here I have five.

TILYE. I'm the one who gave them to her.

YAKHNE-BRAYNE. She did me such a big favor. She's still got a great pile. More than ten for sure.

KHONYE. (*Hungrily grabbing the five coins, stares at them.*) Imperials. Imperials. A treasure. Certainly a treasure. Oh, I should bury you all in one day. (*To* TILYE.) Out with the money. You better get out that money right away.

TILYE. Do you really mean it? Go on. You're teasing.

KHONYE. You're going to take all the money out of your pocket. (*Clenched teeth.*) Out with the money.

TILYE. I should be such a fool. (KHONYE *makes a snatch at her.* TILYE *quickly puts herself between table and divan.*) I should give you all the money and then die for a kopeck and beg you for every little thing. Yudke gave the money to me, so it's mine. You're not going to take it away from me. This is my dowry now. Have you put away a dowry for me? I'm not going to be left sitting with a long gray braid. I need to have a dowry. Out with my dowry. Out with my dowry.

KHONYE. Why should you grab the whole thing? We need some too.

TILYE. I didn't grab anything, and I didn't take the whole thing. You have your share.

KHONYE. The five imperials?

TILYE. It'll be enough for you. You'll be rid of me soon. And if you do need more, you can always get it from me. I'd give it to you. And what am I doing so bad? I want to look after myself. I want to buy myself a small husband, at least.

KHONYE. (*To* YAKHNE-BRAYNE.) What do you say to your daughter, hah?

TILYE. And in any case all your fuss is a sin. You know yourself nobody takes back from the cemetery. (YUDKE *stands up suddenly.*) But here Yudke is up. Ask him.

KHONYE. You're not going to wriggle out of it with me. Yudke! (YUDKE *goes to door.*) Yudke, where did you find the imperials? (YUDKE *keeps going.*) Get over here, I'm telling you. Where did you bury Zshutshke?

YUDKE. (*At the door.*) Not tell.

KHONYE. What do you mean, not tell?

YUDKE. Not tell.

KHONYE. In the cemetery? Behind the cemetery? In the old field? In the new field?

YUDKE. (*Through clenched teeth.*) Heh.

KHONYE. (*Takes belt from his trousers.*) You'd better tell. If not—you see the belt? I'll skin you.

YUDKE. Not tell, not tell. I you strangle all. (*Runs out.*)

TILYE. (*Moves to leave.*) He'll tell me. I'll go after him fast.

KHONYE. You want to wriggle away from me?

TILYE. I don't have to wriggle away from you. But we do need to know where the grave is, after all. We do have to see what's doing there, after all. Imagine if there's a whole treasure there.

KHONYE. But I want the money that you've got.

TILYE. There he goes again. Meanwhile Yudke will go off and we won't be able to find him. (*She comes out from behind the table and tries to get to the door.*)

KHONYE. (*Blocks her way.*) I'm not going to let you out of the house till you put down all the money.

TILYE. He may start to dig there and people will see.

KHONYE. Put down the imperials.

TILYE. I'm talking for your own good. After all, I've got money already.

YAKHNE-BRAYNE. So let her alone for now. He could begin to dig, it's true, and other people will see.

TILYE. There's a whole treasure lying there, maybe, but he's got to have the very imperials that I have.

YAKHNE-BRAYNE. You better run after Yudke, and let her go too.

KHONYE. First I want the imperials that she's got.

TILYE. I could jump out the window anyway, only if he doesn't mind losing the whole treasure, I don't mind either. My goodness, a whole treasure. No, I am going to jump out the window. (*Makes a move toward the window.* KHONYE *moves toward* TILYE. YUDKE *comes in howling. The others freeze in their movements and turn their wondering, inquiring gazes toward him.*)

YAKHNE-BRAYNE. (*First to come to herself.*) What's the matter with you now?

YUDKE. Zshutshke's grave can't find.

YAKHNE-BRAYNE. (*With fear.*) You hear?

KHONYE. What do you mean you can't find it?

YUDKE. Forgotten where.

YAKHNE-BRAYNE. Oh my God in Heaven.

TILYE. So there's your treasure for you.

KHONYE. What do you mean forgotten?

YAKHNE-BRAYNE. He must be lying.

YUDKE. (*Angry.*) Heh.

TILYE. Why should he lie? He never forgot anything before?

YAKHNE-BRAYNE. (*Discouraged.*) Start up with Crazy Yudke.

KHONYE. You don't remember at all? More or less in the cemetery? Behind the cemetery?

YUDKE. Deep in ground. Covered. A little board put. A stone put. With knife cut out "Zshutshke." And . . . anymore don't know where. Wall maybe, tree maybe.

TILYE. Should we help you look?

YUDKE. Don't know where. No more find. (*Stretches out on the sofa and cries. Through the open door on right are heard from the street the cries and noise of voices.*)

TILYE. Now we'll have to go over the whole cemetery and everywhere around the cemetery and look for the board.

YAKHNE-BRAYNE. That's ridiculous.

TILYE. Not worth the trouble?

KHONYE. Are there still imperials in there or did he take them all?

TILYE. Who could get anything out of him?

KHONYE. (*Angrily.*) Get something useful out of him, that you can't do. All you can do is drive him into fits.

TILYE. You're screaming for no reason. I didn't drive him into fits.

KHONYE. You had to start up with him. You had to grab the imperials away from him.

TILYE. Again and again, I didn't grab. It was Mama—

KHONYE. A plague should hit all of you in one day. (*To* TILYE.) I have no time and no energy for you right now, but you are going to lay all that money on the table in front of me. I will kill and murder you.

TILYE. Yes indeed.

KHONYE. You will give me the last groschen. I'm going to dig another grave now—I should only dig a grave for you and soon! And don't you go running around the cemetery now hunting. Too many people. And don't think about having a chat with anybody in the meantime, you smart people. (*Exit.*)

TILYE. I'll give him plenty. (*Jumps up onto bed, takes down a jacket and hat—old, worn things—and starts putting them on in front of the mirror.*)

YAKHNE-BRAYNE. Where are you running to?

TILYE. I'm going to take care of the money. And take care of myself.

YAKHNE-BRAYNE. You're running into town? Better give the money to me.

TILYE. Don't start all over again, Mama. Don't. Ah, I'm telling you, it's a very strange feeling to have money on you. Listen, Mama, money makes you warm. If you only knew how strangely warm I feel. I feel like another person entirely. In a whole new skin. Tilye, Khonye the Gravedigger's daughter, the everlasting pauper, has got some money. (*Slaps her pocket.*) You hear how it rings? And Yudke will remember yet, and we will find a whole treasure. A whole treasure, Mama. It makes me dizzy. We could actually become gloriously rich. I'll turn the world upside down yet.

YAKHNE-BRAYNE. Talked herself into something. Wait till you have to talk yourself out of it.

TILYE. There, now I'm ready. All dressed and all dressed up. Maybe the hat should have been thrown out in the garbage long ago. The jacket too. And the skirt for sure. But now I've got the goods. Mama, I can't help it, I have to give you a kiss. (*Runs over and hugs her.*)

YAKHNE-BRAYNE. (*Pushes her away.*) Get away from me. You might as well get started. (*Meanwhile tries to sneak her hand into* TILYE*'s pocket.*)

TILYE. Ah, ah, that is stealing. (*Pushes away her hand.*) Mustn't do that. Well, good day to you. And a good day to you, Yudkele. And remember. (*To* YAKHNE-BRAYNE.) And if he goes out into the cemetery, you have to go after him. Forget your Lamentations. *Auf wiedersehn.* (*Hurries out.*)

YAKHNE-BRAYNE. What a girl. Oh my God in Heaven, oh great God in Heaven. (*The same wail as before now comes in from the cemetery side. She groans and goes slowly to the window and opens it. The wail now comes in with all its frightfulness. She looks outside, groans, and goes to her seat.*) Treasures, treasures. There goes another funeral. Ah, ah, ah. (*Sits and begins to read.*)

Curtain

❧

Act II

The same room. Early evening, between afternoon and evening prayers. A lamp burns on the table. Also on the table are an old cloth, a samovar and a loaf of bread. At the sides of the table: plates, forks, knives, and glasses.

YAKHNE-BRAYNE. (*Sits at the window, one hand supporting her head.* YUDKE *sprawls on the bed above the oven.*) Your father will be home from evening prayers soon. Where could she have disappeared to? Maybe you should go ask at Auntie's.

YUDKE. She come.

YAKHNE-BRAYNE. My heart tells me that she'll blab it all over town. We'll probably have the whole town here hunting. What are you sitting for? Why don't you go hunt?

YUDKE. Not find. Not remember. Forgotten.

YAKHNE-BRAYNE. Worthless children. That girl . . . that girl has certainly blabbed it all over. Will her father give it to her. (*We hear a carriage driving up and then a knock on the outer door.* YAKHNE-BRAYNE *jumps up.*) Who can be driving up here? (TILYE *enters. She is dressed up in a silk skirt and blouse made in the latest style, a tiny hat with big feathers, with a parasol and white gloves in one hand and a cardboard box and a big package in the other. Rings on two fingers of the left hand and earrings in her ears.* YAKHNE-BRAYNE *and* YUDKE *remain totally dumb with amazement.* TILYE *bursts into loud laughter.* YAKHNE-BRAYNE *finally comes to herself.*) Heavens, look at her! That wasn't you that drove up?

TILYE. (*Still laughing.*) Who else? And in a carriage, mind you. Now, Mama, bring on the bridegroom, the wedding gown is ready. (*Begins twirling around with the posture of a grand lady.* YUDKE *bursts into laughter and continues to do so from time to time.*) How do you like me now? How do you like my dress? Zeldovitsh the Tailor.

YAKHNE-BRAYNE. Zeldovitsh the Tailor?

TILYE. What do you think, I'd go to just anyone? He made it for Shmerling's daughter, who died a week before her wedding. I got it for half price. Just look at my hat—special from Paris Millinery.

YAKHNE-BRAYNE. My God, how does a person treat themself to a hat like that? It must have cost—

TILYE. What do I care, I've got money. But look how becoming. Chic, no? (*Unpacks the box.*) And here you have—behold the queen!—a cloak. I went specially to Geshrunsky.

YAKHNE-BRAYNE. They didn't kick you out of there?

TILYE. Nobody who pays good money gets kicked out. Just look how it drapes on me. Like made to order, isn't it? You'll see, I'll put on the dress and the cloak and the hat—and here I have something else—just look what a parasol. Silk. Just look at the lace. And there's more too. Just look at this pair of gloves, real high-quality leather.

YAKHNE-BRAYNE. (*Blurts out.*) You spent all the money.

TILYE. Hold on, I'm just getting to the good part. Look here. (*Shakes her ears, showing off earrings.*) And look here. Diamond ring number one and diamond ring number two. And now—what time is it? (*Takes out a golden watch on a golden chain.*) And you think that's all? I ordered myself another dress from Zeldovitsh.

YAKHNE-BRAYNE. (*Screams.*) All the money! All the money!

TILYE. This is for you. (*Unwraps the package of fabric.*) See, a dress for you too. Really fine wool. Eight yards. It cost a lot of money. Just look what fabric. (*Brings the wool to her.*)

YAKHNE-BRAYNE. (*Pushes it aside.*) Break your head and the fabric together! Who asked you to buy it? Who?

TILYE. My good heart. Because I'm a good daughter. How can a person buy only for herself? (*Picks it up from the ground and arranges it.*) You've never in your whole life worn such wool, and you push it on the ground. What a sin. Come, Yudke, look. Suits for you and Father. "Princely raiment."

YUDKE. (*Jumps up and looks, bursts into laughter, strokes the fabric.*) Pretty. Pretty. I pretty clothes. We walk both. (*Grabs her under her arm and promenades with her through the room. Then remains, wondering at her new things, often laughing.*)

YAKHNE-BRAYNE. All the money. All the money And what's the sense of it?

TILYE. Does everything have to make sense?

YAKHNE-BRAYNE. "Give me my dowry. Give me my dowry." And goes and throws the whole money out the window to the devil and all the ghosts. Naturally you've blabbed the news all over town by now?

TILYE. Naturally. Ah, you should have seen—the street got packed with people. From all sides and corners, people came running to stare at the imperials.

YAKHNE-BRAYNE. Ah, I'm going to kill myself. I'm going to grab something—anything—and smash your head! Now the whole town will come looking for the treasure.

TILYE. Don't worry, nobody will come. I wouldn't be such a fool as to say that the treasure is still somewhere in the ground. Better to say we already found it. You should see, now the whole town believes that we're millionaires.

YAKHNE-BRAYNE. Aren't we lucky. Did you give a thought what harm you could do spreading that?

TILYE. I already have a thousand excuses for you. First of all, there is such a thing as stingy millionaires. So we'll be stingy millionaires. Second,—

YAKHNE-BRAYNE. Some good stew you've cooked up. Your father is going to lose his job yet. Some chance the town will want a stingy millionaire for a gravedigger. Because of you we'll be begging house to house.

TILYE. Spare me the Lamentations. Why should they kick him out of his job? Is he taking anything away from anybody? Is he going to ask for more wages? So he's a stingy millionaire—is he hurting anybody? And besides, don't forget, meanwhile we'll be looking for the treasure. And Yudke will probably remember by himself.

YUDKE. Not.

YAKHNE-BRAYNE. And what will happen if all you find there is Zshutshke's corpse? If the whole treasure is only the imperials that Yudke brought home—that are already gone?

TILYE. Then wait for the Messiah. (*Stands quiet a while.*) Ah, for a little while, at least, to be the daughter of a millionaire, even a stingy one. I'll dress up in my dress and cloak and hat, with the earrings, with the gloves and the parasol and the watch. I won't put the gloves on, I'll just hold them in my hand, like this, so they can see the rings. Will I dress up, positively chic! And I will promenade through the streets and on the boulevard. You'll see, the world will come to an end. Chick and child will run after me.

YAKHNE-BRAYNE. I swear she's crazy.

TILYE. Oh, at least for a while to feel like a millionaire's daughter, to feel that everyone is looking at you, everyone is running after you!

YAKHNE-BRAYNE. They run after Tsipe the Idiot too.

TILYE. You should have seen how they looked at me, how they made way for me. And I kept going, this way, my head haughty, with an expression—oh, if only I could be a millionaire's daughter. You would see how I live up to it.

YAKHNE-BRAYNE. And if everything turns out to have been a dream? How will you look then? How will you show yourself in the street?

TILYE. How and what and who and whom—let tomorrow take care of itself. Meanwhile I'll be a millionaire. Oh, what a dress I ordered! I myself don't know how I come to understand so much about fashion. Evidently the way it works is that when money comes, taste comes.

YAKHNE-BRAYNE. And you couldn't find any other time to dress yourself up? It had to be Tisha B'Av?

TILYE. What, didn't the shopkeepers sell to me? Aren't they sitting in their shops today? And in fact, if not for them, I might not have bought anything. Because I was going along and struggling with the idea whether to spend the money or put it in the bank. But as I was passing by Zeldovitsh, there in his window was Shmerling's daughter's dress for half price, and I said to myself, "Ah, you only live once. And where is it written that Tilye the Gravedigger's daughter must live out her whole life as a pauper? What will be, will be. The money is only found money anyway, after all."

YAKHNE-BRAYNE. A fine practical thinker, no doubt about it.

TILYE. And "suddenly it came to pass"—the thought sort of floated by me—and the shops around were all open—

YAKHNE-BRAYNE. I thought you were fasting. Where did you find the energy a whole day?

TILYE. Millionaires don't fast. From Paris Modiste, I went in to Leon's restaurant and treated myself.

YAKHNE-BRAYNE. You should have choked on the first bite.

TILYE. (Laughs.) Do you want to break your fast? Come with me, I'll treat you.

YAKHNE-BRAYNE. Death should treat you, God in Heaven! He should serve you a four-pound ulcer. What a girl, God in Heaven!

TILYE. Ah, is it good to have a lot of money! And oh a secret, a secret, a secret, Mama! Now, if I want, I'll have boys ten for a penny.

YAKHNE-BRAYNE. That's what's on her mind, that's all: boys.

TILYE. Mama, that is the whole point. Don't you know anything?

YAKHNE-BRAYNE. You're just lucky I don't have any strength now, otherwise—(*A knock is heard on the outside door.*) Lord, here comes your father from evening prayers.

KHONYE. (*In a worn black stained overcoat over his* arbe kanfos *and with a stick in hand, enters, extremely upset.*) Ha, what did I tell you? (*Sees* TILYE *and remains standing, mouth open.*) Well, it's true. She really is dressed up. (TILYE *laughs. To* YAKHNE-BRAYNE.) You don't know what she's started. She'll throw us in the fire.

YAKHNE-BRAYNE. What now?

KHONYE. (*To* TILYE.) I'll tear it off you to the last thread and throw you out of my house.

TILYE. Why yell so? What have I done wrong, what?

KHONYE. No shame. She spread it over the whole town that we found a treasure, she threw money around exactly as if it was true—and then she asks what she did wrong.

TILYE. Well, what?

KHONYE. You cabbage with eyes, you cow in horse form, you—I'm going to murder you.

TILYE. Yes, you will, you certainly will. But first sit down, drink a glass of tea, and have something to eat.

KHONYE. You already broke your fast, didn't you? In the restaurant there?

YAKHNE-BRAYNE. You already know that too?

KHONYE. What do you mean? The whole town is ringing with her. The synagogue is upside down. You think I could pray? You think anybody else could either? All anybody could talk about was her and the treasure. Who didn't come over to me and ask? The whole synagogue was around me. They made me stand at the east wall next to Soskin.

TILYE. Next to the rich man? So listen, why are you yelling? Didn't you get respect because of me? When did you ever dream of praying at the east wall next to a rich man?

KHONYE. Thank you very much for the favor, my smart daughter. You should have broken your head and your feet before you set out to do me such a favor. What will I do tomorrow when they discover that I didn't find a treasure?

TILYE. You'll go back to praying by the door. But meanwhile, you stood at the east wall next to a rich man. What's the harm in that?

YAKHNE-BRAYNE. She says that about everything: "what's the harm in that?"

KHONYE. I can do without your east walls, do you understand? Who told you to blab it all over? Why did you go off all of a sudden to dress yourself up and eat in a restaurant and travel in a carriage? What makes you the owner of the money?

TILYE. We already settled that.

KHONYE. What do you mean, settled? Who settled? You'd better hand over all the money. Take back all these things and bring me the money.

TILYE. Yudke, the money is mine, right?

YUDKE. Yours. I you. I you. All.

KHONYE. But I will—

YAKHNE-BRAYNE. Khonye, you fasted today. Go, wash and eat. Drink a glass of tea. (*Pours for him.*) Lord, Lord, and I don't have strength to move a finger. This is a fine way to end a fast.

KHONYE. I'm already full. I'm full of misery is what I'm full of. (*Sits down at the table, drinks tea.*) And besides, after prayers the beadle brought brandy and honey cake and we made a blessing and ate, the rabbi and I, and the rich man, and the sexton.

TILYE. See? See? You ought to thank me.

KHONYE. I'll thank you. Over the head I'll thank you. Would I mind it if it was true, if the treasure was in my pocket? But what will happen tomorrow? When I heard people talking about the treasure, the world got dark in front of my eyes. At first I thought they knew that we haven't found it yet.

TILYE. You thought the whole town was running to the cemetery to hunt.

KHONYE. Of course. My hands and feet went numb. First I hear, people are talking to me about a treasure. I try to deny, stone and bone, that there is any such thing. They say that it's too late to hide because my daughter—I should only be rid of her and soon—

TILYE. Amen.

KHONYE. Shut up, or—

TILYE. I mean that you should marry me off soon. Why do you need to get so angry?

KHONYE. Marry you off, yes, to the angel of death. They tell me that my daughter spent masses of money on all kinds of clothes and jewelry in the best, most expensive, stores. I open mouth and ears. I don't know what to say. I say the truth: I know about a few imperials. I am embarrassed to say that I don't even know how many because my daughter grabbed them for herself— bad luck should grab her!—

YAKHNE-BRAYNE. Amen, it should only happen.

KHONYE. So I say that I know about ten, fifteen imperials. And maybe less. They laugh at me: "You can't tell a lie, Reb Khonye." "Reb" Khonye! That's what they all call me now, not plain Khonye.

TILYE. (*Laughs.*) Hooray.

KHONYE. (*Throws her an angry glance.*) "You can't lie to us," they tell me, "your daughter spent many times that much today." So then I don't know what else to say, I stutter, and they all wish me "Mazl tov." They all shake my hand, and I stand there and I don't know whether I'm dreaming or I'm crazy. And here the rabbi says he wants to talk to me.

TILYE. (*Bursts out into laughter.*) He probably wants you to take his side against the other rabbi they wrote to.

KHONYE. And here Soskin says he wants to talk to me.

YAKHNE-BRAYNE. (*She is eating.*) Soskin! I practically choked.

TILYE. To make you a partner, probably.

KHONYE. I should know as little about you as I know about why they want to talk to me. (*Suddenly yelling.*) I'll gut her like a fish. What a stew she cooked up. (TILYE *laughs.*)

YAKHNE-BRAYNE. And she laughs.

TILYE. What's not to laugh? After all, now we are somebody.

KHONYE. (*Jumps up toward* TILYE, *holds himself back.*) Tell me straight how much money you had.

TILYE. More than I have now.

KHONYE. Tell me in plain words.

YAKHNE-BRAYNE. Why should you mind telling?

TILYE. Because the money is mine and I don't have to give you an accounting. And it's just more interesting if you don't know.

KHONYE. I'm going to make you tell. (*Takes his stick.*) Are you going to tell?

(YUDKE *growls at* KHONYE *angrily.*)

YAKHNE-BRAYNE. Let's finish eating in peace.

TILYE. (*Tranquilly.*) Don't waste time. Finish eating and let's go out and hunt for the treasure.

KHONYE. You'll tell me right now.

TILYE. All right. What's mine—let that go. In order not to lose any of the treasure, I will tell you everything—how much money I had—and I will give you an accounting of everything.

KHONYE. (*Bangs with his stick.*) Right now. I want to know what I'm going to say to people.

TILYE. You're going to tell them the whole truth?

KHONYE. Not your worry what I'm going to tell them. How much money did you have?

TILYE. Exactly what you see on me is everything that I had.

KHONYE. How many imperials was it? Fifteen?

TILYE. Fifteen.

KHONYE. Twenty?

TILYE. Twenty.

KHONYE. (*Makes for her.*) Are you making fun of me?

YAKHNE-BRAYNE. (*Jumps up and blocks his way.*) You see that she won't tell you anything.

KHONYE. She'll tell me.

YAKHNE-BRAYNE. Wait a day or two, till we know how it turns out with the treasure. Better sit down and eat.

TILYE. That's just what I say. We should finish eating fast and go outside. It's a bright night. And I'm hungry myself too. In the restaurant was only an appetizer. (*Sits down at table.*)

KHONYE. (*Cooled down, throws her a glance full of hatred and suspicion.*) On Tisha B'Av is when she goes into a restaurant. I'm only a fool for putting the stick away. (*Goes into next room.*)

TILYE. (*Makes a face.*) Ah, after those hors d'oeuvres, radish with sour cream makes you feel like throwing up.

YAKHNE-BRAYNE. (*Taking the samovar from table and putting it on the cupboard.*) The millionaire's belly got so delicate all of a sudden. (KHONYE *enters with wet hands, says blessing, dries hands, says blessing, sits at the tale, says blessing and eats.*)

TILYE. Those preserves were so delicious.

YAKHNE-BRAYNE. (*Sitting at table.*) She's still teasing.

KHONYE. Haven't you choked yet?

TILYE. See for yourself. (*They eat. Silence.*)

KHONYE. Went shopping. What did she buy?

TILYE. Now that's a different way of talking. (*Jumps up, poses and turns for* KHONYE.) You see? Chic, right? (*Shows rings.*) And you see? (*Shows earrings, shaking her head.*) And you see? (*Watch and chain.*) And you see? (*Grabs hat and puts it on.*) And you see? From the Paris Modiste. (*Opens the parasol.*) And you see? (*Poses.*) Well, now how do you like your only daughter? (*Suddenly grabs cloak and opens it.*) And see more. (*Throws it on his shoulders, picks up her train and promenades about like a lady.*)

KHONYE. (*Angry.*) What games is she playing?

TILYE. Let's just find the many many thousands—then you'll see what games I'll play. But look what I bought for you. For suits for you and Yudke and a dress for Mama. Just look what goods.

KHONYE. (*Looks angrily at the fabric and then immediately at her jewelry.*) And those are really genuine diamonds?

TILYE. Your only daughter should wear fakes?

KHONYE. (*Finishes eating.*) Some daughter, no doubt about it. Does what she feels like, respects her parents like the cat.

TILYE. (*Sits down at table.*) When the treasure is found, Dad, I'll start calling you paPA. (*French pronunciation, accent on second syllable.*)

KHONYE. (*Indicating* YUDKE.) And he still hasn't remembered anything.

YAKHNE-BRAYNE. Sure he'll remember, you can wait for it.

KHONYE. (*Groans. To* YUDKE.) Were there a lot more golden coins like this there?

YUDKE. (*Meanwhile has been eating very hungrily, never taking his eyes from his plate.*) Not tell. Not talk.

(KHONYE *groans and begins reciting blessing after meal.*)

TILYE. Talk, Yudke. Be nice. Would you like more radish? What more do you want to eat?

YUDKE. Nothing.

TILYE. Were there more golden coins?

YUDKE. Nothing.

TILYE. A sin. Such a good little dog Zshutshke was, and not even to know where he is buried.

YUDKE. (*Hits himself in head.*) Why not remember? Why not remember?

TILYE. Sh! Don't be crazy. When you get a good night's sleep, then you'll remember. (YUDKE *sits a while. Then takes suit fabric, climbs up to bed on top of oven, strokes fabric and laughs. Soon falls asleep.* KHONYE *finishes blessing. Knock on outer door.*)

YAKHNE-BRAYNE. Someone's coming.

MATCHMAKER. (*Enters.*) A good evening. A good break-fast.

KHONYE and YAKHNE-BRAYNE. (*Amazed.*) Good evening.

TILYE. Good evening. Here's a guest.

YAKHNE-BRAYNE. A matchmaker wandered over to us at last!

MATCHMAKER. You know yourself that everybody postpones wandering into the cemetery as long as they can.

YAKHNE-BRAYNE. That means gravediggers' daughters end up old maids.

TILYE. Your daughter is no old maid yet.

MATCHMAKER. That's what I think too. It was hot today, a hard fast. Jewish luck—fasts fall on the longest, hottest days.

KHONYE. Plenty of fast days in winter too.

MATCHMAKER. I just mean that fast days in the summer are unnecessary. And in the winter too. When is a Jew not hungry? A Jew is always hungry, thank God: summer and winter, long days and short days.

YAKHNE-BRAYNE. (*Sighs.*) Yes, that's true. (*Starts clearing the table. Takes the plates out to the kitchen, puts the bread away in the cupboard, takes off the tablecloth, shakes it out in a corner and lays it back on the table.*)

MATCHMAKER. You have a lot to do today?

KHONYE. Work is never lacking.

MATCHMAKER. In other words, the world is dying little by little.

KHONYE. And not so little by little. Four graves today.

MATCHMAKER. Yes, people die. But God sends a medicine for every plague. People die, so he sent down matchmakers to the world, and they make matches, and the world becomes pregnant, and that's how it goes around. (*Laughs.*)

TILYE. Still it's better to be a matchmaker than a gravedigger.

MATCHMAKER. And it's better still to be somebody with a match, isn't it? (*Laughs.*)

TILYE. It always was.

MATCHMAKER. (*Takes out a cigarette and offers the cigarette-holder to* KHONYE.) Help yourself, Reb Khonye. People are talking about you. (*Laughs.*)

KHONYE. I figured you heard something.

MATCHMAKER. What do you mean? The whole village is ringing. (*Laughs.* YAKHNE-BRAYNE *groans.*) Is this your daughter? You have one daughter, I believe.

YAKHNE-BRAYNE. You've had enough time to find that out.

MATCHMAKER. A matchmaker, forgive me, is not a gravedigger. He makes his living off the living, not the dead. Although paupers have been compared to corpses. (*Laughs.*)

TILYE. And for poor girls nobody makes matches?

MATCHMAKER. I, you understand me, I am a matchmaker. I have made the biggest matches in the richest households. I have bridegrooms worth five, ten, twenty thousand rubles, and more, too. I have doctors, lawyers, engineers, and just plain nice young men, scholars, of wealthy families, who have nice fortunes themselves. Right now I'm looking for a bride for a chemist—

YAKHNE-BRAYNE. A what?

MATCHMAKER. A chemist. A kind of educated person who makes paints. You've probably heard of Sholem Balashnik's son? A thinker—one in the world—can figure out deep things—there is nobody to compare to him. Now he has figured out a kind of something, a kind of paint, that they're trying to buy from him for hundreds of thousands, but he doesn't want to sell. He would rather set up his own paint factory and in two, three years he'll be a millionaire. That's the kind of paint it is. You understand me, for that he needs about twenty-five thousand rubles, but since he doesn't have any money of his own, he's looking for a bride with that kind of dowry. I'm a kind of a banker that lends young people money, without interest, and with a wife into the bargain. (*Laughs.*)

TILYE. Is he handsome?

MATCHMAKER. Who, the chemist? Handsome! And if he isn't handsome, so what? Since when is that so important for a man? The main thing for a man is to be a good breadwinner—

TILYE. If I'm giving twenty-five thousand rubles dowry, I only want a handsome one.

MATCHMAKER. Girls all make the same mistake. A handsome man is not a good buy at all. A handsome man takes too good care of himself, and nowadays, because of our sins, you have to watch a handsome man at every step. (*Laughs.*) The main thing is—this. (*Strikes himself on the forehead.*)

TILYE. No, for me the main thing is handsome. I'll make sure he watches me, not the other way round.

MATCHMAKER. You hear? She's something, this girl of yours.

TILYE. For twenty-five thousand rubles dowry, he doesn't have to be such a scholar.

MATCHMAKER. But that's what counts. Take my chemist, for example. In two, three years, a millionaire. Somebody else, in two, three years he might drop the twenty-five thousand rubles so that no one would even know where they'd gone.

TILYE. So then poverty—but with a handsome man.

MATCHMAKER. Now, you see, you should forgive me, you're talking just like a child.

TILYE. And what will I do when my scholar loses the money? Then there'll be nothing to eat and nothing to look at.

MATCHMAKER. What do you mean loses the money? A chemical thing that they're offering him hundreds of thousands for!

TILYE. He's the only one on your list?

MATCHMAKER. What? As many—you should have found as many treasures as I have bridegrooms on my list. And such handsome ones. I'm only talking about the chemist because—

TILYE. Better talk about the handsome ones. Tall, strong, with black burning eyes.

MATCHMAKER. We should only live but I've got one exactly like that. He's an engineer. But let's talk plainly. (*To* KHONYE.) How much dowry do you want to give?

KHONYE. Me—dowry?

YAKHNE-BRAYNE. Us—dowry?

TILYE. (*Serenely.*) Depends on the bridegroom.

MATCHMAKER. Five, ten, twenty, fifty thousand? They say that your treasure comes to close to a million or more.

YAKHNE-BRAYNE. All bad dreams in my enemies' heads!

KHONYE. I feel sick when you start to talk about it.

MATCHMAKER. I know that what other people have always looks bigger. If they're saying a million, probably it's less, but how much less can it be? We all know about treasures. I don't want to steal it, God forbid. Keep it in good health. Today it was your fate to find a treasure, so you found it. Another time it may be my fate to find one, so I will find it. In fact, personally, I am happy it was you that found it and not someone with no children. You, I can earn something from. You have a son too, I think—a cripple they say—that's him, lying on the oven? We'll marry him off too, it'll just be a little more difficult. The main thing that I need to know is the price, the value, you understand me. Once and for all, exactly how much do you want to give—a thousand more, a thousand less—and done.

YAKHNE-BRAYNE. Oh, my heavens above.

KHONYE. Tell me, do you know what you're talking about?

MATCHMAKER. I understand you, I understand what's bothering you. In your place, I wouldn't behave any differently. Maybe you believe that I would blab it all over town: I found this much and this much? I would never do that because one-two I would have the whole village here with everyone begging and everyone trying to tear it out from my pockets. Because everyone's an in-law when it comes to money. I would keep quiet just like you. And if I did have to give a number, I'd give it ten, twenty times less. But here between you and me, it's a totally different matter. Hide your money as much as you want and good luck to you, but how much dowry you want to give your daughter— that I do, after all, have to know.

TILYE. I told you already—the dowry depends on the bridegroom. The main thing is—handsome.

KHONYE. Am I crazy or are you?

YAKHNE-BRAYNE. Father in Heaven!

MATCHMAKER. I'd better talk to your daughter alone. There's a limit to everything. You must marry off your daughter; you're not going to put her into a convent. And anyway I don't think she's the kind of child that would let herself be put into a convent. So, I think, the sooner you marry her off the better.

KHONYE. But—

YAKHNE-BRAYNE. Lord of the World—

MATCHMAKER. And if you believe that another matchmaker will bring you a better match, you're making a big mistake. Once you know what matches I have arranged, you can feel confident that I will bring your daughter a match.

KHONYE. Lord of the World, this is some kind of a plague.

MATCHMAKER. Who's a plague? I'm a plague? Nobody has ever called me such a thing since I started coming into Jewish households. It really is obvious that we are dealing here with paupers who just came up in the world. And you know what? Soon I'm not even going to believe in your treasure at all. That must be a pretty small treasure, a few measly little imperials.

KHONYE. Don't believe, I'm telling you. Don't believe. (TILYE *has stood up, pulled the dress in at the waist, put out her hand with the rings, turned her head with the earrings in the ears.*)

MATCHMAKER. (*Changes his tone.*) Me a plague. You'd think I came to beg a handout.

TILYE. Don't get mad. It's better to talk with me. You just find a handsome bridegroom.

MATCHMAKER. But the number, I need to know the number. Ten—twenty—fifty—a hundred thousand?

TILYE. (*Calmly.*) Ten—twenty—fifty—a hundred thousand.

KHONYE. Wha . . . wha . . . ? (YAKHNE-BRAYNE *opens mouth and sits as if turned to stone.*)

MATCHMAKER. Now that's plain talking. But what if your father doesn't want to give?

TILYE. Leave it to me.

MATCHMAKER. I see you're the boss here, right? So should I actually telegraph?

TILYE. Actually telegraph. But a very handsome one, you hear?

MATCHMAKER. Leave it to me. You could travel the world. Can't take your eyes off him. The engineer it is. But he won't go below thirty thousand.

TILYE. Fifty thousand even, so long as he's gorgeous.

KHONYE. (*Grabs his forehead.*) Father in Heaven.

MATCHMAKER. Tall, broad—a palace guard. With black burning eyes.

TILYE. (*Breathless.*) You can telegraph. Does he live far away?

MATCHMAKER. If I telegraph him right away, he'll be here eleven o'clock tomorrow night.

TILYE. So then go telegraph.

MATCHMAKER. I just wanted to tell you his family connections. He is well connected too. But I'll go telegraph. Will you give me for the telegraph?

TILYE. Certainly. (*Hurries out to next room.*)

MATCHMAKER. She won't have to watch her husband. (KHONYE *and* YAKHNE-BRAYNE *sit open-mouthed.*)

TILYE. (*Enters, gives* MATCHMAKER *a five-ruble note.*) For the telegraph. Probably it will cost less, so you can keep the change for your trouble.

MATCHMAKER. She understands business, on my word. She herself will be a treasure for her husband. Now I'm really running. Have a good evening. May I come back later and go over the whole matter with you?

TILYE. Not necessary. After a fast, people need to rest. You'll be coming with him. The main thing is that I should like him.

MATCHMAKER. Wisdom, as I am a Jew. Well, have a good evening. You'll see—gorgeous. You'll smack your lips. Good night, all. (*Exit. Pause.*)

TILYE. (*Bursts into laughter, claps hands, jumps.*) A millionairess! A millionairess! It's working!

YAKHNE-BRAYNE. If I didn't have a stroke, I am stronger than iron.

KHONYE. (*To* YAKHNE-BRAYNE.) Who knows, maybe she does have a million there. Did you hear how she dropped: "Five—ten—fifty—a hundred thousand rubles"? (*To* TILYE.) You tell me right now how much money you have, hear me? Now you won't get away from me. (*To* YAKHNE-BRAYNE.) Where has she been? Where is she hiding her money?

YAKHNE-BRAYNE. Somewhere on her, probably.

TILYE. I'm a millionairess. Oh, you never get a joke.

KHONYE. I'm taking off all your clothes. You'd better give me all the money. I won't take it away from you, all right? I just want to see what it looks like. In my whole life I never saw what a lot of money looks like. I want to take a look. (*A knock is heard on outer door.*)

TILYE. (*Teasing.*) Sh! Somebody's coming to the man with the treasure.

KHONYE. (*Whispers between clenched teeth.*) You'll hand over the money, don't you worry.

SOSKIN. (*Enters. Very nearsighted. Expensively dressed. Importantly.*) Good evening. (YAKHNE-BRAYNE, *scared and dumb, leads him in.* TILYE *bites her lips to hold in laughter.*) It was a difficult fast, wasn't it? (*Takes a chair and seats himself expansively.*)

KHONYE. A fast like any other fast. (*Slowly sits down.* TILYE *takes a book from the shelf and sits at the table to read it.*)

SOSKIN. Any graves today?

KHONYE. We have graves almost every day. No lack, thank God.

SOSKIN. Yes, but today you dug up something for yourself as well. (*Laughs.* KHONYE *looks at him dumbfounded.* TILYE *glances up from her book, then down and smiles.* YAKHNE-BRAYNE *looks meaningfully at* KHONYE *and then at* TILYE. *Shakes her head angrily and sighs.*) Where did you dig it up—the old field or the new? (KHONYE, *in extremis, can't speak.*) I think I might have asked you that in synagogue. You answered me that it was in the new, if I am not mistaken.

KHONYE. How could I have answered you that?

SOSKIN. I don't know how. But you did.

KHONYE. May I know as much about that as I do about evil.

SOSKIN. What I don't understand is what you are afraid of and why you regret saying it.

KHONYE. What do you mean regret? When I couldn't have told you anything.

SOSKIN. Why couldn't you have told me anything? If you found it in the new field, you found it in the new field.

YAKHNE-BRAYNE. (*Sighs.*) You see us, Father in Heaven.

SOSKIN. How many graves today?

KHONYE. (*Carefully.*) Four.

SOSKIN. Where were you digging?

KHONYE. I ... in ...

SOSKIN. Where?

KHONYE. (*Altogether lost, to* YAKHNE-BRAYNE *and* TILYE.) Where was I digging today?

YAKHNE-BRAYNE. There you have it, he asks me where he was digging today.

TILYE. In the old field, seems to me.

SOSKIN. Why do you ask them? You did the burying, you should know. But we can easily find out. Correct, Reb Khonye? We can find in the records who was buried today and then we'll know where you were digging. But—

TILYE. Why do you need to know that so badly?

SOSKIN. (*Ignores question.*) But a blind man could see that you were digging in the new field today. Otherwise, you would have said so right away, not discussed it first with your wife and daughter.

KHONYE. But really, what does it matter to you?

SOSKIN. To me? Not at all. I was just wondering why you want to conceal the truth here. If you found your treasure in the new field, say so: simply say that you found your treasure in the new field.

TILYE. Actually it must matter a great deal to you. Otherwise you wouldn't take the trouble to come late in the evening after a fast to find out where Khonye the Gravedigger found his treasure. Because why isn't it all the same to you?

SOSKIN. In proper households, when one speaks to the parents, the children don't mix in.

TILYE. (*Offended, mutters to herself.*) You won't do any business with us.

KHONYE. Hold your tongue, you.

YAKHNE-BRAYNE. She should burn.

SOSKIN. (*To* KHONYE.) Can we go in to another room and talk things over?

TILYE. (*Puts book away.*) You don't have anything to talk over with Father because I found the treasure, not him.

SOSKIN. I should believe that.

TILYE. Don't believe if you don't want to.

SOSKIN. (*To* KHONYE.) I would like to talk to you alone.

KHONYE. If you want to know the whole truth, it is that, as I am a Jew, I am not the one that found it.

SOSKIN. Who then?

TILYE. You heard.

SOSKIN. How did she come to be digging in the cemetery?

KHONYE. She's right here, let her tell.

SOSKIN. In other words, you have agreed not to tell where you found it.

KHONYE. Why would we have to agree?

SOSKIN. I don't know. I wasn't eavesdropping behind your door.

TILYE. But you agreed among yourselves that we found it in the new field, and you want to persuade us that we found it there. It must really be important to you.

SOSKIN. (*To* KHONYE.) I don't remember now whether it was in synagogue that you told me clearly and specifically that you—you yourself, that is—found the treasure in the new field.

KHONYE. But . . . see . . . how . . . what . . . How could I have said that when . . . when I didn't find it and I don't know where it was found.

SOSKIN. You mean you totally deny what you said? But how can you, when other people heard it and I will have plenty of witnesses?

TILYE. Witnesses? (*Looks at him sharply, putting something by.*)

KHONYE. You hear?

YAKHNE-BRAYNE. What kind of witnesses?

SOSKIN. You know what? Come show me the grave where the treasure was lying.

TILYE. (*Thoughtfully.*) The grave was filled in long ago.

SOSKIN. Why did you need to fill it in?

TILYE. So a blind horse wouldn't fall in.

SOSKIN. (*Jumps up.*) Be aware that you will stand trial for this.

KHONYE. Stand trial?

YAKHNE-BRAYNE. I'm dying.

TILYE. What kind of trial?

SOSKIN. You'll find out.

TILYE. Aha, I know. The Council bought the new field from him. Now I understand why he wants so badly for us to have found the treasure in the new field. (*Laughs.*) You understand, he wants a share.

SOSKIN. If not the whole thing. Since you are so smart—

TILYE. I had totally forgotten. That's what he wants, a share.

SOSKIN. You found the treasure in the new field. I sold the congregation a field, but not what is buried in the field.

TILYE. It wasn't you that buried the treasure. You didn't even know about it.

SOSKIN. You think you're a whole lawyer. But I am as smart and as experienced in these matters as you. You're going to have to hand it over to me to the last kopeck. If not—

TILYE. If not—?

SOSKIN. I'll see you all rot in jail.

KHONYE. Father in Heaven.

YAKHNE-BRAYNE. I can't bear this any longer with my health.

TILYE. Jail? I'd really like to see that.

SOSKIN. You'll see it and how.

TILYE. Fine, go make your trial. We can afford to hire a lawyer as well as you can, and we will prove with signs and wonders that I did not find the treasure in the new field. Go, hold the trial. We'll see who ends up looking silly.

SOSKIN. But I have witnesses that your father said that he found a nice few hundred thousand in the new field.

KHONYE. But if there couldn't be . . . ? But if I could never have said . . . ? If I'm telling you the whole truth that I . . . ah . . . that I—

TILYE. Good, what do you care, let him bring his witnesses. Because even if you did say it, so what? Did you mean to lie, didn't you want to tell the truth?

KHONYE. But I didn't say it. I couldn't have said it.

YAKHNE-BRAYNE. How could he have said it, how?

SOSKIN. You'll see what your daughter will bring you to. Good night. (*Goes to door.*)

KHONYE. You hear this, lord of the World?

YAKHNE-BRAYNE. (*Breaks into wailing.*) A misfortune,

SOSKIN. (*Remains standing in door, turns back.*) Still and all, let us deal with each other decently. Without trials. A private settlement. I know for certain that you found the treasure in the new field.

TILYE. A lie.

SOSKIN. On condition that you cooperate—if not, you will bring worse troubles upon yourselves. The penalty for perjury is hard labor.

TILYE. Your witnesses are the ones who will perjure themselves.

SOSKIN. The best thing is for us to agree between ourselves in good faith.

TILYE. Aha, what did I say? He wants a share.

SOSKIN. Why shouldn't I? The treasure was found in my land.

TILYE. Snow in July. You can talk from today till tomorrow, the treasure was not found in the new field.

YAKHNE-BRAYNE. (*Tearfully.*) Where treasure? When treasure?

KHONYE. It's enough to drive you crazy.

SOSKIN. So you don't intend to settle?

TILYE. Not even a hair.

SOSKIN. I ask you, Reb Khonye. You are getting on in years, after all. Would you rather stand trial than arrive at a settlement?

KHONYE. If I know absolutely nothing about . . . I didn't—

SOSKIN. Settle, I'm telling you. (TILYE *laughs.*)

KHONYE. I didn't—

SOSKIN. All right then. We will meet again elsewhere. But I'm telling you, you should think it over carefully. A good night. (*Exits.* TILYE *laughs.*)

KHONYE. I'll murder you. Didn't I say she'd get us burned alive? Because of her, we'll come to a bad end.

YAKHNE-BRAYNE. Because of her we'll rot in jail.

KHONYE. And she laughs. You should laugh bloody laughter, Lord of the World. Look what a stew you've cooked up. You had to get dressed up right away.

YAKHNE-BRAYNE. Doesn't ask anybody. Does whatever it wants.

KHONYE. When I don't even begin to know, when except for the five imperials I haven't even seen anything more, when I don't know where, what—

TILYE. So laugh with me, then. Why are you so scared?

KHONYE. You should be scared of the angel of death and soon, Lord of the World. He's going to get me thrown in jail.

TILYE. Why should he throw you anywhere? Did you really find a treasure? Do you really know where Yudke found the imperials? (*The outside door opens and closes.*)

YAKHNE-BRAYNE. (*Helpless.*) Sh! Here comes another one.

HEAD OF COMMUNITY COUNCIL. (*Enters.*) Good evening.

KHONYE. (*Crushed.*) Good evening. (YAKHNE-BRAYNE *groans.* TILYE *laughs silently.*)

HEAD OF COMMUNITY COUNCIL. (*Sits down.*) I come to you, Reb Khonye, directly from the Community. The Community Council held a special meeting just now this evening. Probably you can guess why.

KHONYE. (*Exhausted, can hardly speak.*) I can guess, I can guess.

HEAD OF COMMUNITY COUNCIL. About your treasure.

YAKHNE-BRAYNE. Ah.

KHONYE. Oh.

HEAD OF COMMUNITY COUNCIL. What do you have to groan about, Reb Khonye? God has shown you great kindness such as he has shown to no one else. And if what you guess is that the Community wants to take it away from you—

KHONYE. Take away what?

HEAD OF COMMUNITY COUNCIL. Let me explain everything to you. Today you found a treasure of many thousand rubles, a hundred thousand. (YAKHNE-BRAYNE *groans.* KHONYE *throws a wild glance at* TILYE.) When someone is suddenly blessed by God, he doesn't forget his Community. And the more he shares what God sent him, the more God blesses him. But your case is altogether different.

KHONYE. Lord of the World.

HEAD OF COMMUNITY COUNCIL. Don't groan, Reb Khonye. The Community is no thief. The Community wants no more than is right. You yourself must understand, Reb Khonye, that you found the treasure on the Community's land, and furthermore you are still the Community's employee, someone who serves the Community, and on that basis the Community is entitled to demand that you hand over the entire sum. But as I said, the Community is not a thief, and the Community Council has simply concluded that you must share. Now isn't that generous?

KHONYE. (*Can hardly groan.*) I don't know what to say any more.

TILYE. Father had a very difficult fast, and on top of that at synagogue people offered him liquor.

HEAD OF COMMUNITY COUNCIL. Perhaps we should postpone our discussion till tomorrow.

KHONYE. I don't know anything, I don't know anything.

HEAD OF COMMUNITY COUNCIL. We can postpone it till tomorrow, although I would strongly have preferred the matter to be dealt with and not postponed.

TILYE. You held a meeting. We have to hold a meeting too.

HEAD OF COMMUNITY COUNCIL. What do you have to talk over? Surely you wouldn't want to go against the Community?

TILYE. Nevertheless we too have to clarify things, and at the moment Father can't even speak.

HEAD OF COMMUNITY COUNCIL. So good, let it be tomorrow. But I want to tell you, Reb Khonye, that the Community will demand what is coming to it and won't come down even a groschen from its rightful share. And I will further inform you that you shouldn't hide some of the treasure and pretend that you found less. Because that would be robbery pure and simple, and the Community would certainly not suffer it in silence.

TILYE. We are as honest as anyone else.

HEAD OF COMMUNITY COUNCIL. Fine, then. (*Stands up.*) So good night to you all. And tomorrow morning you will be so kind as to appear before the Council. We will wait for you there immediately after morning prayers. Good night.

KHONYE. (*Totally crushed.*) Good night.

YAKHNE-BRAYNE. Good night. (HEAD OF COMMUNITY COUNCIL *exits.*)

TILYE. The pack has scented money.

YAKHNE-BRAYNE. They have scented sorrows for you.

KHONYE. What should I tell the Council?

TILYE. If you are a good man, you'll give them half your treasure.

KHONYE. Half of the five imperials? (TILYE *laughs.*)

YAKHNE-BRAYNE. May she laugh for the last time, Lord of the World.

KHONYE. I don't know what they're going to do to me. If I tell them the truth, are they likely to believe me? Here she bought herself diamonds and jewelry and watches and I don't know what, for I don't know how much money. She told the matchmaker, "Five—ten—fifty—hundred thousand rubles dowry." She told Soskin, "We are as rich as you." If I come and put down the five imperials and say: "Here, this is the whole treasure, and I am nice enough to give you three-quarters—"

TILYE. (*Laughing.*) You won't be telling a lie.

KHONYE. (*Screams as if possessed.*) I will kill you. I will murder you. What did you lay on my old age? Why are you driving me crazy? I will—where is my stick? (*Grabs his stick.*) Out with all the money now. Hand me over all the money right now. (YUDKE *jumps up from sleep and gazes wonderingly at his screaming father.*) All the money, the hundreds of thousands, the whole million. I won't wait a single minute. This time you won't get away from me.

TILYE. (*Laughs.*) The hundreds of thousands. Here, Yudke is up, ask him how many imperials he brought home.

KHONYE. Hand me over all the money you've got on you.

TILYE. It's inside my corset.

KHONYE. Undo yourself right away and give me the money.

TILYE. If that's really what you want. (*Begins unfastening her blouse.*)

YUDKE. Tilye, slept but not remember.

TILYE. But you should understand that this is my money I'm giving away. (*Takes a few bills from inside her corset.*) There you have all the money, the hundreds of thousands, the million.

KHONYE. (*Jumps on the money, counts with nervous hands. Yells.*) Thirty-five rubles. (*Throws the papers around as if he doesn't believe his eyes and is searching for more.* YAKHNE-BRAYNE *helps him.*)

TILYE. (*Fastening herself up.*) You don't have anything to look for. It won't grow.

KHONYE. I don't believe you. You have more. All the—

TILYE. Should I strip to the skin for you?

KHONYE. Then what was the game with the matchmaker?

TILYE. What do you care if I had a little fun? It wasn't me that called him, after all. He invited himself. If he believes that we're rich, well, let him go on believing.

YAKHNE-BRAYNE. Eleven o'clock tomorrow night the groom is arriving here.

TILYE. So what? If we find the treasure, no harm done. If not, then—I won't like him. All gone bride, back to a spinster. And he'll go home.

KHONYE. Meanwhile Soskin will have us arrested.

YAKHNE-BRAYNE. Help us, Lord of the World.

KHONYE. And the Community Council? What should I do about the Council? (*Scratches his head.*)

YUDKE. (*Crawls down from his perch.*) I go look for. (*Exit.*)

TILYE. Yudke went hunting. You go too.

KHONYE. What should I go for, what?

TILYE. He's giving up entirely. And what if there happens to really be a treasure?

KHONYE. You think I have the strength to move a foot?

TILYE. It's really a pity. It's a sin to waste the night. So light out. I'll just change and go right out. (*Takes a skirt and goes into the other room.*)

KHONYE. (*To* YAKHNE-BRAYNE.) And what are you sitting for, my princess?

YAKHNE-BRAYNE. I can barely stand up. A fast day on top of everything else.

KHONYE. And I have strength? My head is turning upside down. Come on, the both of us. I feel like I'm falling off my feet.

YAKHNE-BRAYNE. Come on then, come on.

KHONYE. Oh, Lord in Heaven. (*Both drag themselves to the door.* KHONYE *remembers the money lying on the table, turns back and puts it in his pocket with a groan.*) Oy. (*Both out.*)

TILYE. (*Enters wearing an old skirt and carrying the new one. Looks around.*) Gone. Both of them. (*Strokes the new skirt, contemplates it, picks off a speck of dust, hums a tune. Cannot tear herself from admiring the skirt and finally hangs it up behind the sheet. Does the same with her cloak. Contemplates and admires her hat and takes it, with parasol and gloves, into other room. Comes right back and admires her earrings in mirror, still humming. Finally calls out aloud.*) Ah, for one day, at least, to pass for a millionaire. (*Hurries out.*)

Curtain

✿

Act III

Same room. A sad, rainy morning peeps in through the window. Bedding lies on the sofa. KHONYE, *wearing his phylacteries, is preparing to say morning prayers. He takes the prayer book from his prayer shawl bag and starts to mumble into it.* YAKHNE-

BRAYNE, YUDKE, *and* TILYE, *who is in morning negligee but wearing all her jewelry, are drinking tea from the samovar that stands on the table.* YAKHNE-BRAYNE *sighs often.*

KHONYE. (*Breaks off.*) There you have it. Praying at home, not going to synagogue, hiding out. All came from her head—she should break it on a stone!

TILYE. The curses keep pouring out. Before breakfast even. That's how he prays.

KHONYE. I'll pour you out. If not for you, I wouldn't have any of these troubles. So all right, then, I haven't shown myself in public, I haven't gone to synagogue, and I won't go to the Council either. But what if the Council sends for me?

TILYE. You won't go.

KHONYE. What do you mean, I won't go, if the Council sends for me?

TILYE. When they call, you won't be home.

KHONYE. Where will I be, then, dead and buried?

TILYE. You'll be sitting in there (*Indicates the other room.*) or out in the shed where you wash the bodies, and we'll say that you've gone away.

KHONYE. All right, then, but what if the Council comes to me? Then what will I do?

TILYE. You know what? I have the best advice of all. You don't have to hide, you don't have to run away, you don't have to do a thing. Just get sick. (YUDKE *bursts into laughter.*)

YAKHNE-BRAYNE. (*To* TILYE.) You should only get sick yourself, God in Heaven.

KHONYE. What do you mean, sick? How am I going to just get sick, all of a sudden? (YUDKE *laughs again.*)

TILYE. You go lie down in bed or on the sofa, you cover yourself up, and when anyone comes, we say that you don't feel good. Doesn't matter what: you caught cold, the fasting weakened you, or—I know—it's the excitement.

YAKHNE-BRAYNE. From you a person really can get good and sick.

TILYE. And if anyone comes and starts talking to you, you keep quiet, you pretend you don't understand, you don't hear, you can't talk. Let them talk to the wall. If there has to be any talking, I'll talk for you.

YAKHNE-BRAYNE. Your tongue should only fall off.

KHONYE. And so we'll end up having to fool the whole world. But how will it all end, I ask you? All right, so I'll pretend to be sick, I'll lie in bed, but then what? I can't lie there my whole life. I'm going to have to get up some day.

TILYE. We need time. Meanwhile we'll hunt the treasure.

YAKHNE-BRAYNE. In this pouring rain, when it would be a sin to drive a dog outside.

TILYE. You dig graves in rain and snow and frost. But stay indoors, you two. Who's asking you to go? Yudke and I will go out hunting. Right, Yudke, the two of us? We'll wrap ourselves up well. Right? And if we get wet, so what, right?

YUDKE. You go. I go.

TILYE. Because it's so important, you understand?

KHONYE. But afterwards? What will happen afterwards, when the treasure isn't found?

TILYE. Why shouldn't it be found? We'll hunt, and Yudke is sure to remember.

YUDKE. Remember, yes, remember.

YAKHNE-BRAYNE. (*Sarcastic.*) He's going to remember!

TILYE. If he doesn't, so what? You've got the five imperials? And you've got the thirty-five rubles? So you're rich. What more do you want?

KHONYE. But why did you have to blab it around so fast?

TILYE. You shouldn't have made such a fuss yesterday. Besides, I slipped up. I didn't think ahead that there would be so many people wanting a share. Over and done with. Now what's important is time to hunt.

KHONYE. Did somebody open the door? (*Jumps up.*)

TILYE. Lie down on the sofa, quick! (KHONYE *stretches himself out on the sofa.*)

YAKHNE-BRAYNE. Lord God, Father in Heaven.

TILYE. (*After a while of listening tensely, goes to kitchen door and looks out.*) No one. Must have been the wind.

KHONYE. (*Sits up.*) Nice morning prayers! I'll have to lie down every time the door bangs, right in my *tfilin*.

TILYE. Well then, you know what? Go pray in the shed.

YAKHNE-BRAYNE. Drink your glass of tea first, at least. I'll bring you something to eat in there. Otherwise, you'll have to eat lying down. (*Pours* KHONYE *a glass of tea.* TILYE *takes down her new dress, and starts putting it on. Looking at her.*) Rubbing it in.

TILYE. I want to try it on again. Doesn't it fit me as if I were poured into it? I think this button needs to be moved. What do you think? It gaps a little here. (*Turns and bends, looks at herself from all sides.*) Ah, if you want something done right, you have to go to the best shops. They charge a lot, but you get your money's worth.

YAKHNE-BRAYNE. You'll see what you get when you have to pawn everything or sell it. You'll get a lot back then, my practical lady. (KHONYE *groans.*)

TILYE. Don't you worry. Yudke will remember, and we really will find a great treasure, and we'll be so rich—so rich—we'll be the richest people in town! We'll move into a great big castle on the hill, and we will live high! Ah, me and my tall, handsome engineer.

YAKHNE-BRAYNE. Crazy and that's all.

TILYE. If you can think about things one way or the other, why think the worst?

YUDKE. We rich get. (*A carriage is heard.* KHONYE *jumps up.*)

TILYE. (*Goes to him.*) Lie down quick. Why did you get up? (*Pushes him down.*) Quick! Quick! (*Pulls off his boots and covers him.*) You can close your eyes, too.

KHONYE. You'll be closing your eyes, for good. Lie down healthy and be sick.

YUDKE. We rich get. (*Lies down on oven.*)

TWO MEMBERS OF THE DOWRIES-FOR-POOR-BRIDES COMMITTEE. (*Enter.*) Good morning.

FIRST MEMBER OF THE DOWRIES-FOR-POOR-BRIDES COMMITTEE. And mazl tov to all of you.

SECOND MEMBER OF THE DOWRIES-FOR-POOR-BRIDES COMMITTEE. And mazl tov to all of us.

FIRST MEMBER OF THE DOWRIES-FOR-POOR-BRIDES COMMITTEE. Look, here's Reb Khonye lying down. Why is he lying down? Good morning, Reb Khonye. Why are you lying down?

KHONYE. (*Barely groans it out.*) Good morning.

SECOND MEMBER OF THE DOWRIES-FOR-POOR-BRIDES COMMITTEE. Good morning, Reb Khonye, and mazl tov.

YAKHNE-BRAYNE. Mazl tov, no less. What kind of a mazl tov?

FIRST MEMBER OF THE DOWRIES-FOR-POOR-BRIDES COMMITTEE. I'd say you were entitled to the biggest mazl tov that anyone can imagine.

If not you, who? A pauper having his tenth child?

SECOND MEMBER OF THE DOWRIES-FOR-POOR-BRIDES COMMITTEE. Every Jew should only get a mazl tov like yours. It should only happen to me.

TILYE. (*Has seated herself close by* KHONYE.) See, and you have to go and get sick. (YAKHNE-BRAYNE *groans.* KHONYE *throws* TILYE *an angry glance.*)

FIRST MEMBER OF THE DOWRIES-FOR-POOR-BRIDES COMMITTEE. (*Takes a stool and sits near* KHONYE.) Probably the day you had yesterday, the excitement.

TILYE. What else? (KHONYE *groans.*)

SECOND MEMBER OF THE DOWRIES-FOR-POOR-BRIDES COMMITTEE. Such luck. When a poor man gets money, he has to go lie down.

FIRST MEMBER OF THE DOWRIES-FOR-POOR-BRIDES COMMITTEE. Probably he'll feel better soon.

SECOND MEMBER OF THE DOWRIES-FOR-POOR-BRIDES COMMITTEE. The simplest thing is just to send for the doctor.

TILYE. What he needs is rest, a good rest.

FIRST MEMBER OF THE DOWRIES-FOR-POOR-BRIDES COMMITTEE. Rest, yes, certainly, rest. A good rest. Well, of course, you don't need any advice from us. So, do you know why we've come, Reb Khonye? You know that we're from the Dowries-for-Poor-Brides Committee?

KHONYE. (*Nods and groans.*) Yes.

FIRST MEMBER OF THE DOWRIES-FOR-POOR-BRIDES COMMITTEE. In other words, I don't have to tell you who, what, and how, and I will only tell you that as soon as it became known in town that God had blessed— (YAKHNE-BRAYNE *groans.*) And what a blessing! And if he's not feeling so healthy? He'll feel healthy again soon enough. It can happen to anybody, even without a treasure. As I was saying, as soon as it became known in town, right away we said to each other that our committee has to be the first to enjoy God's loving-kindness that he has shown to you. Because first of all, the absolutely most important and most beautiful deed for Jews is helping brides; after all, it leads to the very first commandment: be fruitful and multiply. And second of all, our committee has always had our eye on you, so we are entitled to your first donation. What does that mean, you ask, that our committee has had an eye on you? I'll explain, only you mustn't be offended. (YAKHNE-BRAYNE *groans.*)

SECOND MEMBER OF THE DOWRIES-FOR-POOR-BRIDES COM-
MITTEE. Poverty is no shame. People from very fine families, from the best
families, have come to our committee.

TILYE. This is about me.

FIRST MEMBER OF THE DOWRIES-FOR-POOR-BRIDES COMMIT-
TEE. We always had in mind that our gravedigger had a daughter to be
brought under the wedding canopy, no evil eye, but he was a very poor man,
no longer to be thought of. And we always expected that when God sent him a
life partner for his daughter and he came to us, we would provide with a generous hand.

TILYE. See, Dad, did I have anything to worry about?

FIRST MEMBER OF THE DOWRIES-FOR-POOR-BRIDES COMMIT-
TEE. May God help us and may poor brides be brought to the canopy if that's
what we always intended. And now, when God has helped you so much, and
you can give your daughter a dowry of thousands of rubles, you really ought
to pay us back for our good intentions, with interest. So here is our book, Reb
Khonye, and write down, if you can, as much as your heart commands you,
and naturally the more the better, and God will send you a total recovery.
(*Leafs through the book to a page and lays the book and a pencil before* KHONYE *on the
table.*)

KHONYE. (*Groans.*) Tilye, I don't feel good.

YAKHNE-BRAYNE. (*Had been sitting on the bed, drags herself to the sofa.*) Look,
he really looks sick. Oh, he's getting good and sick.

TILYE. (*Busies herself around him.*) You should have slept a good long sleep.
He hardly closed an eye all night.

SECOND MEMBER OF THE DOWRIES-FOR-POOR-BRIDES COMMIT-
TEE. From pure excitement. That always happens. I know a case where a man
went crazy from a surprise like that. He was a poor man, suddenly he learned
he inherited a fortune, and he went crazy right on the spot.

YAKHNE-BRAYNE. Not to be thought of, not to be thought of for any
Jew.

SECOND MEMBER OF THE DOWRIES-FOR-POOR-BRIDES COMMIT-
TEE. I'm talking about what excitement can do to you.

TILYE. The best thing for him now is rest. He shouldn't see anybody or
hear anybody.

SECOND MEMBER OF THE DOWRIES-FOR-POOR-BRIDES COMMIT-

TEE. Who could have known that he would go get sick all of a sudden? Especially since yesterday he was in the synagogue for evening prayers.

FIRST MEMBER OF THE DOWRIES-FOR-POOR-BRIDES COMMITTEE. (*Stands up.*) It can't be helped. We'll have to meet another time. Never mind, Reb Khonye won't run away from us.

SECOND MEMBER OF THE DOWRIES-FOR-POOR-BRIDES COMMITTEE. (*Also stands up. To* TILYE.) How about you? We wouldn't turn down a donation from you either.

TILYE. Think about it, is that what's on our minds right now? Just let Papa get well. (*We hear a carriage coming.*) Maybe it's the doctor. (KHONYE *groans loudly.* YAKHNE-BRAYNE *wrings her hands and drags herself back to the bed.*)

SECOND MEMBER OF THE DOWRIES-FOR-POOR-BRIDES COMMITTEE. Really? You really sent for the doctor? (*Both Jews move from the table to the left side of the room.*)

TWO JEWS OF THE VISITING-THE-SICK COMMITTEE. (*Enter, astonished to see the first two and take a moment before speaking to consult privately.*) Good morning. (*A little confusion of greetings: "Reb Itshe!" "Reb Yosef!" "Reb Rabinovitsh!" "Reb Fayvish!"*)

FIRST MEMBER OF THE DOWRIES-FOR-POOR-BRIDES COMMITTEE. (*To* KHONYE.) Here are the Visiting-the-Sick Committee too. (KHONYE *grabs at his head.*)

FIRST MEMBER OF THE VISITING-THE-SICK COMMITTEE. Look, he's lying down.

SECOND MEMBER OF THE DOWRIES-FOR-POOR-BRIDES COMMITTEE. (*Gravely.*) They've sent for the doctor.

SECOND MEMBER OF THE VISITING-THE-SICK COMMITTEE. Really? He's that sick?

FIRST MEMBER OF THE VISITING-THE-SICK COMMITTEE. It's very foolish of you to go and get sick now, Reb Khonye.

FIRST MEMBER OF THE DOWRIES-FOR-POOR-BRIDES COMMITTEE. That's what I just said. It's a great sin. (*All four around the table.*)

FIRST MEMBER OF THE VISITING-THE-SICK COMMITTEE. A person with money is not supposed to get sick.

YAKHNE-BRAYNE. (*Groans.*) A person with money—

FIRST MEMBER OF THE VISITING-THE-SICK COMMITTEE. What you mean is that sickness doesn't ask who it should visit. But I can tell you that your old man has gotten off easy. I read in the newspaper not long ago that in a town, I don't remember which, in Krementshug I think, or in—yes, in Krementshug, a Jew received a telegram that he had won fifty thousand rubles, so then, as soon as he finished reading the telegram, so then, boom! Dropped dead. Had a stroke.

SECOND MEMBER OF THE DOWRIES-FOR-POOR-BRIDES COMMITTEE. And I know a case—

TILYE. What kind of stories are you telling?

FIRST MEMBER OF THE VISITING-THE-SICK COMMITTEE. Not to be thought of, not to be thought of for any Jew. I only meant that you can all recite the blessing for escaping danger. So he had to lie down—he'll be up soon enough. Isn't that right, Khonye—Reb Khonye? Just come on now and get up and let's make a toast instead. And here is our book, and you'll write down a nice, a fine, a magnificent donation to the Visiting-the-Sick Committee.

FIRST MEMBER OF THE DOWRIES-FOR-POOR-BRIDES COMMITTEE. Visiting the sick compared to dowries for poor brides! Dowries come first.

FIRST MEMBER OF THE VISITING-THE-SICK COMMITTEE. No. Visiting the sick comes first. We have an account with Reb Khonye. We are kind of relatives by marriage, you might say.

FIRST MEMBER OF THE DOWRIES-FOR-POOR-BRIDES COMMITTEE. Because you provide work for him? (*All laugh.*) All the same, Reb Khonye will inscribe his first donation in our book. If for no other reason than that we got here first.

SECOND MEMBER OF THE VISITING-THE-SICK COMMITTEE. All right, then, you win, what can we do? Let him give you first and give us most.

FIRST MEMBER OF THE VISITING-THE-SICK COMMITTEE. What do you mean, most? Is Reb Khonye going to measure out more to one and less to the other?

SECOND MEMBER OF THE DOWRIES-FOR-POOR-BRIDES COMMITTEE. He'll give everyone the most. There will be enough for everyone. Isn't that so, Reb Khonye?

KHONYE. My head is splitting. My head is splitting.

TILYE. You need a lot of sleep, Dad. Why doesn't the doctor come already?

SECOND MEMBER OF THE DOWRIES-FOR-POOR-BRIDES COMMITTEE. It's true, we ought to let Reb Khonye get some rest.

FIRST MEMBER OF THE VISITING-THE-SICK COMMITTEE. Oh,

don't worry. The Talmud says, when you visit a sickbed, you relieve one-sixteenth of the sickness. So we are relieving four-sixteenths. And if the old lady will be good enough to put out something to drink, I, for my part, will relieve at least thirteen-sixteenths all by myself. (*To* KHONYE.) Well, why are you lying there that way, you old thief, and shaking your head? You don't know what to do with your money? Trust me, you'll figure it out soon enough. You just get well. (*Many voices are heard outside.*)

MEMBERS OF BURIAL SOCIETY. (*Entering the kitchen noisily.*) Make way. Make way. Make way. The Burial Society is coming. Here's the Burial Society. Mazl tov. Mazl tov. Where's the schnapps?

SECOND MEMBER OF THE DOWRIES-FOR-POOR-BRIDES COMMITTEE. Sh! Reb Khonye isn't well.

FIRST MEMBER OF THE BURIAL SOCIETY. What? Isn't well? (*Pushing his way to* KHONYE.) What do you need, Khonye? You need a fever?

SECOND MEMBER OF THE BURIAL SOCIETY. Come on, get up, we came for a drink.

THIRD MEMBER OF THE BURIAL SOCIETY. Drag him out of bed. What's he doing lying there?

FOURTH MEMBER OF THE BURIAL SOCIETY. Never mind, he'll be fine. He doesn't dare be sick when we're here.

TILYE. Have mercy, let him rest. You see how he looks.

SECOND MEMBER OF THE DOWRIES-FOR-POOR-BRIDES COMMITTEE. From excitement. They've sent for the doctor.

FIRST MEMBER OF THE BURIAL SOCIETY. He doesn't need any doctor. "All Israel are brothers," so he's our brother, and for our brother, the best medicine is brandy. Isn't that right, Khonye? What are you lying there for like an old lady, with your teeth chattering?

KHONYE. My head. My head.

FIRST MEMBER OF THE BURIAL SOCIETY. "He whose head aches, let him busy himself with Torah." If your head hurts, sit and study Torah. And studying means drinking. Get up, no tricks.

FIRST MEMBER OF THE VISITING-THE-SICK COMMITTEE. That's right, you give it to him.

SECOND MEMBER OF THE BURIAL SOCIETY. It's an insult for our gravedigger to treat us like this. Goes and lies down when he should be bringing out the liquor.

FIRST MEMBER OF THE BURIAL SOCIETY. You should have invited us last night already, right after the fast.

SEVERAL. Bring out the schnapps. Bring out the schnapps. Let him lie, and we'll drink. We'll drink double: for him and for us. (*They fall on* KHONYE *and begin dragging and shaking him.* KHONYE *groans, closing his eyes and holding his hands over his pocket.*)

FIRST MEMBER OF THE BURIAL SOCIETY. Just look how the patient holds his hands over his pocket so you can't tear them away.

KHONYE. Tilye! Tilye!

FIRST MEMBER OF THE BURIAL SOCIETY. We've got the money. We've got the money. (*He holds in his hand several bills and a few imperials and displays them high in the air.*) Here they are, the golden honeys, the pretty little papers.

TILYE. (*Goes up behind him and grabs away the money.*) What is this? Picking pockets? Where are you—in a tavern? The man is sick.

YAKHNE-BRAYNE. (*Can barely talk.*) You drunks. (KHONYE *groans. A carriage arrives.*)

SECOND MEMBER OF THE DOWRIES-FOR-POOR-BRIDES COMMITTEE. They've sent for the doctor. (*It immediately becomes very quiet. Everyone starts moving away from* KHONYE *and taking off their hats. People are pushing each other. Enter the* HEAD OF THE COMMUNITY COUNCIL.)

BURIAL SOCIETY. Our chairman. Our chairman.

HEAD OF COMMUNITY COUNCIL. There's a whole meeting going on here. (*Looks around.*) Look, he really is lying down. (YAKHNE-BRAYNE *groans in a wail.* YUDKE *laughs.*)

A MEMBER OF THE BURIAL SOCIETY. He got sick from excitement.

SECOND MEMBER OF THE DOWRIES-FOR-POOR-BRIDES COMMITTEE. They've sent for the doctor.

HEAD OF COMMUNITY COUNCIL. (*Sits on chair near* KHONYE.) What is the matter with you? (KHONYE *groans.*)

TILYE. You saw yourself how he felt last night. And the whole night he practically didn't close an eye. He should have gotten a good rest, but since two o'clock people haven't stopped pouring in. (*The crowd makes movements but remains in the same place. A carriage arrives. All look at the door in suspense.*)

SOSKIN. (*Enters, followed by his lawyer,* MIRKIN, *and nods to some people in the room.*) A real crowd, no evil eye. (*To* HEAD OF THE COMMUNITY COUN-

CIL.) You're here too? (*Indicating* KHONYE.) And he just lies there. (YUDKE *laughs*.)

HEAD OF COMMUNITY COUNCIL. The best thing is for us to leave. We have to let them rest up, get hold of themselves.

SOSKIN. Reb Khonye, I am accompanied by my lawyer. When he explains everything, you will see that I am right.

HEAD OF COMMUNITY COUNCIL. Leave him alone now, leave him alone now. What is your business with him, anyway?

SOSKIN. The treasure was found on my land. This is Herr Mirkin. (*The lawyer makes a gesture to say something*.)

HEAD OF COMMUNITY COUNCIL. (*To* SOSKIN.) Ah. Well. Then. But let him alone now. Well, Reb Khonye, get well, lie there and get a good rest. You don't need to dig any graves. In your own mind, when do you expect to be able to move out of here?

YAKHNE-BRAYNE. (*With fear*.) God in Heaven.

KHONYE. (*Barely speaking*.) What do you mean, move out?

HEAD OF COMMUNITY COUNCIL. You are not going to be a gravedigger anymore, after all. We already have another man to take your place.

KHONYE. (*Sits up*.) What do you mean, another man to take my place? (*Stronger*.) I'll be left without bread? (*Movement in crowd*.)

YAKHNE-BRAYNE. (*Weeping*.) Struck by lightning.

HEAD OF COMMUNITY COUNCIL. What do you mean, you'll be left without bread? What are you talking about, Reb Khonye?

VOICE. He's delirious.

VOICE. He's forgotten all about the treasure.

KHONYE. Where treasure? What treasure? I have no treasure. I'll be left without bread.

YAKHNE-BRAYNE. A plague.

VOICES. What? What? No treasure at all? That's a good one.

HEAD OF COMMUNITY COUNCIL. Silence! Reb Khonye, foolishness. You won't wriggle out of it that way.

SOSKIN. Obviously. A pretense. They have the treasure.

KHONYE. What "wriggle out of it?" What "pretense?" Yesterday my son was digging a hole for his dead dog, so he found a few imperials. I don't even know how many, because she, my little daughter, grabbed almost all of them and went running out to spend them on herself, and she also spread the news that we found a treasure because she wanted to make out that she was a rich lady.

HEAD OF COMMUNITY COUNCIL. (*Ironically.*) Oh, is that so? So then what were you telling us last night?

FIRST MEMBER OF THE DOWRIES-FOR-POOR-BRIDES COMMITTEE. And the show he put on here?

FIRST MEMBER OF THE VISITING-THE-SICK COMMITTEE. The whole story is a lie. They have the treasure.

SOSKIN. Sh! So then tell me where he buried his dog.

KHONYE. Do I know where? (*All laugh.*) Do I know how much he found? Look, here he is, let him tell you himself.

YUDKE. Cemetery.

SOSKIN. In the cemetery where? The old field or the new field?

YUDKE. Not remember. (*Laughter.*)

KHONYE. Nothing to laugh at. He really has forgotten.

HEAD OF COMMUNITY COUNCIL. Well, how can one not laugh? What do you mean, he has forgotten?

KHONYE. May I live so long, plain and simple forgotten.

YAKHNE-BRAYNE. It happens very often. Especially after a fit. He does a thing and he forgets it and he can't remember no matter what.

HEAD OF COMMUNITY COUNCIL. So why didn't you tell us all this last night?

KHONYE. Because . . . Because . . .

VOICES. Aha. Aha. Mirke, speak up.

TILYE. (*Has been standing and watching the crowd as if frozen. Says tranquilly.*) Because I wanted to make myself out to be a rich lady and catch a husband. All right?

VOICES. What do you say to her?

HEAD OF COMMUNITY COUNCIL. Foolishness. (*To* KHONYE.) Because . . . ?

KHONYE. Because we wanted time to hunt for the grave in case there really is a treasure there.

HEAD OF COMMUNITY COUNCIL. So how did you intend to hunt the grave?

TILYE. If you search, you find.

HEAD OF COMMUNITY COUNCIL. One little grave in the whole cemetery?

VOICES. Aha. Excuses.

KHONYE. He put up a marker. This misery you see here, he put up a marker for his dog, a board, and he even cut into it with his pocket knife "Zshutshke Deceased." (*Laughter.*)

SOSKIN. (*Yells.*) This is contrived. Not a single word of truth. Yesterday she was supposed to have found it, and today it's him. They have the treasure.

TILYE. And in synagogue Dad said he found it. You heard him yourself. Don't believe him now. Really, don't. We have the treasure and we won't give you any of it.

KHONYE. (*Jumps up and pounds table.*) Shut up, you. You'd better shut up.

FIRST MEMBER OF THE BURIAL SOCIETY. Look, he's healthy.

KHONYE. That's her smart idea. She made me lie down.

VOICES. He was acting sick. A comedy.

KHONYE. Because she wanted time to hunt. If not for her—

HEAD OF COMMUNITY COUNCIL. There is nothing further to discuss. We understand the whole history now. And I want to tell you, Khonye, that if your son remembers where he buried his dog, or you find it for yourself, you are not to think that the found money is yours and belongs to you. The cemetery belongs to the Community, and the treasure belongs to the Community.

TILYE. (*Sarcastically.*) A righteous judgment. (SOSKIN *begins talking heatedly to the* HEAD OF THE COMMUNITY COUNCIL, *who looks around and seems not to hear him. Several* MEMBERS OF THE BURIAL SOCIETY, *standing near the door, steal out. The* FIRST MEMBER OF THE VISITING-THE-SICK COMMITTEE *puts on a serious expression, gazes down at the floor, and leaves.*)

FIRST MEMBER OF THE DOWRIES-FOR-POOR-BRIDES COMMITTEE. (*Looking out window, says to* SECOND MEMBER OF THE DOWRIES-FOR-POOR-BRIDES COMMITTEE.) The rain seems to have stopped. (*Hurries away.*)

SECOND MEMBER OF THE DOWRIES-FOR-POOR-BRIDES COMMITTEE. (*Also looks out the window and says to no one.*) Yes. (*Hurries away.*)

HEAD OF COMMUNITY COUNCIL. (*Raises his voice as if to those who have left.*) Whoever finds it will have to share it with the Community and according to the Community's wishes. (SECOND MEMBER OF THE VISITING-THE-SICK COMMITTEE *coughs and leaves.*)

SOSKIN. (*Also raising his voice.*) Pardon me, but with one exception: if it is found on the new field. The new field was sold to the community by me. However I sold the land, not what lies in the land. Here I am accompanied by my lawyer. (*The lawyer wants to say something.*)

HEAD OF COMMUNITY COUNCIL. Later. First kill the bear, then sell the fur.

SOSKIN. Herr Mirkin, come. (SOSKIN *and the lawyer off.*)

FIRST MEMBER OF THE BURIAL SOCIETY. Well, I'm going too. (*Exits, the rest of the* BURIAL SOCIETY *after him.*)

TILYE. Crawling all over the cemetery, those locusts, those gold-grabbers.

HEAD OF COMMUNITY COUNCIL. (*To* KHONYE.) Well, I believe you heard me and understood me. I mean all of you.

KHONYE. Of course. If I had found the treasure, wouldn't I have shared with the community?

HEAD OF COMMUNITY COUNCIL. All the better. And since you aren't sick, you can still move out today.

KHONYE. What do you mean?

YAKHNE-BRAYNE. Moving out again?

HEAD OF COMMUNITY COUNCIL. Didn't I tell you that we have another gravedigger? We already have another gravedigger.

KHONYE. What? No treasure and no job? (YAKHNE-BRAYNE *weeps.*)

HEAD OF COMMUNITY COUNCIL. Nobody is taking away the treasure. You haven't found it yet. What your daughter bought for herself, may she wear it in good health, and the little bit of money that you have, keep that too. Nobody is asking you for any of it.

KHONYE. And that's all, and I am left without bread?

HEAD OF COMMUNITY COUNCIL. The Community never signed a contract that you would be grave digger forever.

YAKHNE-BRAYNE. Gravedigger fourteen years, and now in old age without bread, to beg from house to house.

HEAD OF COMMUNITY COUNCIL. Well, there's nothing more to talk about. (*Moves to leave.*)

KHONYE. (*Pounds the table angrily.*) I won't move. I'm not moving. The world can turn over. Fourteen years I've been gravedigger, and you can't throw me out.

HEAD OF COMMUNITY COUNCIL. Oh no? In that case, hurry and get a wagon and move yourself out.

KHONYE. I won't move, if I die on the spot.

HEAD OF COMMUNITY COUNCIL. Fine, then. (*Hurries out.*)

YAKHNE-BRAYNE. (*Runs after him weeping.*) Where is your heart? We have to find a home first.

KHONYE. (*Yells after her.*) You won't go look for a home. I won't let them kick me out, they can . . . We still have a rabbi, we still have judges. I'm not going to be a gravedigger for fourteen years and then just— (*Turns to* TILYE.) See what you've done? Where is my stick? I'll murder you.

YUDKE. (*Jumps up.*) Remember!

TILYE. Grab a stick. Grab a knife! But you've got nothing to complain about. You're an important man now. You have a lot of money. And if you need more, there'll be more. You can count on it that—

YAKHNE-BRAYNE. (*Enters.*) Here come the relatives: Leah, Freyde, Gelye, Bendet,—

KHONYE. (*Grabs at his head.*) Lock the door. Lock the door.

Curtain

༺❀༻

Act IV

The cemetery late at night. The rain has stopped, but it is still cloudy, with a few stars showing through here and there. On the left we see two sides of the gravedigger's house, with a side door and two windows in each side. There is a porch under one of the windows and a tree in front. Behind the house, a little removed, is the purifying shed where KHON-YE *prepares corpses for burial. A gate separates the house and the shed. A broad path, crossed by small side-paths, leads away into the distance. To the right of this main path, beyond the purifying shed, stand rows of trees and various monuments: little buildings, fenced-in family plots, grave stones, wooden triangles, board markers.*

KHONYE*'s furniture has been thrown out in front of the house. The cupboard lies on its side all the way in front of the porch. A bed has been lifted and propped against the tree. The sofa is diagonally at the corner of the house, with its head to the cupboard and its base on the path, pointing away. The table stands in front of it; the chairs are scattered over the path. Bedding and clothes lie on the sofa and cupboard.*

The cemetery is alive with people. We hear the noise of innumerable voices. We see the wandering fires of lights, lanterns, and torches. Dark figures holding lanterns come and go through the gate or into the purifying shed. A burning lantern stands on the table. By its shine we see YAKHNE-BRAYNE *lying on the sofa. From time to time, we hear her groaning.* YUDKE *is sitting on the front of the porch, making gestures and occasionally laughing as if very pleased with himself. The* YOUNG PREGNANT WOMAN *and her* HUSBAND *come out of the furthest side-path, carrying lanterns.*

YOUNG PREGNANT WOMAN. I'm exhausted. My whole back hurts from bending over.

YOUNG PREGNANT WOMAN'S HUSBAND. You told me already, you told me already. We'd better sit down. (*They sit on two chairs.*)

YOUNG PREGNANT WOMAN. What a nuisance. Just today it had to rain all day so we couldn't sit on the grass.

YOUNG PREGNANT WOMAN'S HUSBAND. The air feels a little damp. Maybe you want to go into the purifying shed?

YOUNG PREGNANT WOMAN. I would die of fright. Out here is bad enough. My legs are shaking with fright from going around the graves at night. But at least outdoors, I don't know, with a lot of people around— (YAKHNE-BRAYNE *groans.* YOUNG PREGNANT WOMAN *jumps up.*) Oh my God!

YOUNG PREGNANT WOMAN'S HUSBAND. It's just the gravedigger's wife.

YOUNG PREGNANT WOMAN. (*Sitting back down.*) All my blood drained out of me. I thought it was a corpse.

YAKHNE-BRAYNE. I wish I was a corpse, God in Heaven. I'm worse than a corpse. A corpse can rest, at least, and I can't even rest.

YOUNG PREGNANT WOMAN. I shouldn't have come. The bending is bad enough, but getting scared is terrible. If I don't miscarry, it will be a miracle from heaven.

YAKHNE-BRAYNE. A pregnant woman goes hunting for treasure.

YOUNG PREGNANT WOMAN. And if I find it, it will come in very handy.

YOUNG PREGNANT WOMAN'S HUSBAND. Are you rested? We didn't come here to sit.

YOUNG PREGNANT WOMAN. All right, come on then, come on. (YUDKE *laughs.* YOUNG PREGNANT WOMAN *screams, shakes, grabs the* MAN *with both hands and looks around, confused. Spots* YUDKE, *spits.*) Tfoo! It's just the loony, the half-wit. (*They go off and disappear among the gravestones, the* YOUNG PREGNANT WOMAN *groaning loudly.*)

YAKHNE-BRAYNE. (*Looking after them.*) Ah, ah, ah. Pregnant. They're going to kill that baby. And are you ever going to stop laughing over there? What possessed you to laugh like that, all of a sudden? (YUDKE *laughs briefly. Again we hear the noise of many voices and see the movements of dark figures.*)

KHONYE. (*Enters from the gate, holding something in his hand. Goes to* YAKHNE-BRAYNE, *not altogether steady on his feet, and bends over her.*) Here, here's a glass of something warm.

YAKHNE-BRAYNE. (*Jumps.*) You scalded me.

KHONYE. For luck. Well, go on, take it.

YAKHNE-BRAYNE. Can't you see how you're spilling? (*Takes the glass of tea from him.*) And you stink of brandy. You're drunk. I lie outside in the rain and the damp, and you sit in the tavern and get drunk.

KHONYE. (*Lets himself down on the cupboard.*) Go complain to your little daughter, go on. Don't complain to me. (*Lies down.*)

YAKHNE-BRAYNE. Old drunk.

KHONYE. Complain to your little daughter, not to me.

YAKHNE-BRAYNE. May the angel of death complain to you both.

KHONYE. Go find her and complain. Go find her. She's hunting. She stirred up the whole town, and now she runs around like a poisoned mouse from one end of the cemetery to the other, and she hunts. Let her hunt her own old age! She's hunting the marker, that's what she's hunting. Zshutshke's monument. I should have taken all the money away from her. Then I wouldn't have had all this trouble. I should have choked her. Broken her legs. I should have twisted her head off, together with yours.

YAKHNE-BRAYNE. Why mine, you drunk? And who stopped you from finding a house?

KHONYE. Tell your daughter the millionaire, she'll build you a castle. Now shut up. Let me sleep. (*To laughing* YUDKE.) And you, stop laughing. Who tickled you? (*Kicks at him.*) Let me sleep.

YAKHNE-BRAYNE. Go to sleep, drunk. How will it all end? (KHONYE *turns his back to her. An* OLD MAN *and* OLD WOMAN *appear, carrying lanterns.*)

OLD MAN. No, it's not for our strength and not for our eyes. We may have passed the marker twenty times without seeing it.

OLD WOMAN. If only we could have sat down on the grass, at least. (*They sit down on the chairs.*)

OLD MAN. I wish I knew what time it is.

YAKHNE-BRAYNE. The town clock struck eleven not long ago.

OLD WOMAN. I totally forgot she was there.

OLD MAN. So did I. Tfoo!

YAKHNE-BRAYNE. Lord, what have I come to, to lie outdoors and scare people. (*Weeps.*)

OLD WOMAN. If you really must lie there, you could at least lie with your mouth shut. You scare people with your talk.

OLD MAN. After eleven already. We've been going around a good three hours.

OLD WOMAN. So what?

OLD MAN. So go home. What does the town need you for?

OLD WOMAN. You said yourself that this isn't for our eyes.

OLD MAN. I'm going to find it anyway, just for spite.

OLD WOMAN. Snow in July.

OLD MAN. So why did you come?

OLD WOMAN. You were hunting, so I hunted too. Not that we could use the money, could we?

OLD MAN. I'd sure be glad of a glass of something warm. (*Remains sitting peacefully a while.* OLD WOMAN *lets out a little snore.* YUDKE *laughs.* OLD MAN *looks around in fright, spies* YUDKE, *spits, and starts shaking his wife.*) Don't you fall asleep now.

OLD WOMAN. I can't keep my eyes open.

OLD MAN. Do we have any coals for the samovar?

OLD WOMAN. Where? Here?

OLD MAN. At home. At home.

OLD WOMAN. So what?

OLD MAN. Will you open the jar of raspberry jam?

OLD WOMAN. Will you look at this greedy old drunk. I'm falling on my nose, and he—

OLD MAN. If you promise you'll open it, I'll go home.

OLD WOMAN. (*Stands up.*) And what about the treasure? You were going to find it yourself, just for spite.

OLD MAN. Tea with raspberry jam. You'd better remember. If not, I'm staying here. (*They walk a few steps, the* OLD MAN *illuminating the sides of the path and looking. As they turn to the exit, he balks and pleads.*) What if we looked a little while longer, ha? Just, I don't know, just for spite, ha? What if?

OLD WOMAN. (*Angry.*) There he goes again. Come home, come on. (*They go. A few dark figures appear, one by one, with lanterns. They sit down on chairs and on the fence. They sit a while, jump up and disappear. Finally three* YOUNG MEN *come out from among the graves. Arguing hotly, they go directly to the side porch.*)

FIRST YOUNG MAN. It makes no sense to start looking by the gravestones.

SECOND YOUNG MAN. The porch is damp.

THIRD YOUNG MAN. Let's not work so hard. My feet are giving out already.

FIRST YOUNG MAN. Aren't you listening? It makes no sense to search near the gravestones. It stands to reason that the loony buried his dog either next to the fence or under a tree, so—

SECOND YOUNG MAN. How does that stand to reason?

FIRST YOUNG MAN. Simple. He's not all that much of a loony as to bury his dog among graves or on top of graves.

THIRD YOUNG MAN. And to write his dog a grave marker with "Here Lies"—is he enough of a loony for that?

SECOND YOUNG MAN. It takes a loony to ask a question like that. It could have occurred to him to bury the dog next to his grandmother. (*Catches himself.*) You know that's a good idea. Honestly, I wouldn't mind knowing where his grandmother is lying.

FIRST YOUNG MAN. And I'm telling you, listen to me and let's search only under trees and near the fence.

SECOND YOUNG MAN. We already looked under the trees and at the fence and behind the fence.

THIRD YOUNG MAN. You know that the whole town must be here?

SECOND YOUNG MAN. The whole town? I bet you'd find all the villages around as well. (*Suddenly a woman's hysterical cries are heard coming nearer and nearer. The* YOUNG MEN *jump up and go toward the voices. A young woman is carried on with a circle of* ONLOOKERS *after her.*) What is it?

ONLOOKER. She got scared. She thought a dead man was standing behind her.

ONLOOKER. Take her into the shed.

OTHER ONLOOKERS. No, no. She'll get scared all over again. Take her home. Take her across to the tavern. (*They carry her out the gate. Soon her cries are not heard. A few of the onlookers remain sitting on the porch. They sit a while, jump up in haste, and disappear among the graves.*)

THIRD YOUNG MAN. Well, never mind, come hunt again.

FIRST YOUNG MAN. You'll see. I'm going to look under the trees and at the fence.

SECOND YOUNG MAN. Under the trees, on top of the trees, just so we find it. (*Their voices are soon lost beyond the graves.*)

YAKHNE-BRAYNE. (*Groans.*) We'll have more hysterics here, we'll have deaths here, we'll have everything. Ah, ah, ah. (*The sky becomes clear and starry. The moon shines over the cemetery.* YUDKE *suddenly laughs out loud and jumps up.*) What's the matter with you today? You haven't stopped laughing since six o'-clock.

YUDKE. (*Goes to her and speaks as if telling a secret, laughing hard.*) You see. I remember, oh, I do thing. Ah, Tilye taught. Tilye told. Ah, remember, I do. Ohh.

YAKHNE-BRAYNE. (*Ironic.*) You'll remember, certainly you'll remember.

YUDKE. I remember. I strong. I think. Oh, I do. (*Laughs, returns to his place.*)

YAKHNE-BRAYNE. What will you do? What has she taught you now?

YUDKE. (*Laughing.*) You now see. You see. Ah, I— Tilye smart. (*A woman runs out from the furthest side path, carrying a sleeping child on one arm and with the other hand dragging along a sleepy little girl. The little girl carries a lantern.*)

LITTLE GIRL. I wanna go to sleep. I wanna go home. I wanna go to sleep. I wanna go home.

MOTHER. You should go to your grave. Just when there's a chance I might be released from all my troubles, she has to start passing out. Come on. (*Disappears through the gate. Four* BOYS *run in with paper lanterns. Three sit on chairs. The fourth lies down on the table.*)

FIRST BOY. (*Finishing a story.*) And when he saw him, he took off his left boot and threw it at him and yelled, "*Hushim ben Dan,* you are mine." And right away the fire disappeared, and a great hole appeared under the boot, and in the hole was lying the treasure.

SECOND BOY. And my grandfather told me a different thing. Once upon a time there was a big big woods with big trees so thick that you could hardly get through them. And out of that woods you used to hear a singing, such a pretty, delightful singing like the most beautiful voice. And the singing was so sweet that nobody could tear himself away from it and everybody wanted to see who it was that was singing. But it was hard to get through the woods, and when there were people who could get through the trees, a big snake used to come and kill them. So nobody could get to where someone was singing so beautifully, and they were just dying to know. And in the town there lived a great saint, and once upon a time the great saint dreamed that the one who could arrive at the place where the singing was coming from, he would find a treasure. And in the same dream he was told that he himself should not go, and he shouldn't tell anyone until the right one came. And in the town there lived a man who was very poor but was also very righteous. And once the poor man came to the saint, crying tears, "Dear rabbi, help me." So the saint said, "How shall I help you, my son?" So the poor man answered, "I gave my shirt away to a man who didn't have any shirt, I gave away my last little bit of straw to someone who didn't have any mattress. Now I am naked and bare and have nothing to give for charity." When the saint heard this, he understood that this is the right one, so he spoke to him this way: "Fast three days and three nights, and recite psalms three times each day, and on the fourth day in the morning enter the woods at the place where the singing is heard, and on the way count the stones that you step on, and count up to as many as equal the number value of the letters that spell *shaddai,* the name of God, and pick up the last stone and take it with you. And when you enter the wood and see the snake, you must not be afraid and must not want to run away, you must only recite seven times, "Out of the eater came forth food, and out of the strong came forth sweetness," and throw the stone at the snake, and you will see for yourself what happens next." And the poor man did what the saint told him. He fasted three days and three nights and recited the psalms three times each day, and on the fourth day in the morning he went into the wood to the place where they heard the singing. He counted off the stones to equal *shaddai* and picked up the last stone and entered the wood. He could barely creep between the trees. The branches struck him on his body, and the thorns tore his skin and his face and . . . and . . . and everything. But he kept on deeper and deeper, nearer and nearer to the place that the singing came from. And when he was very close to the place, he heard the singing, and out of a cave sprang a big, big snake and opened up its big, big mouth and wanted to swallow him. But he remembered what the saint had told him, and he didn't get scared and didn't run away. He just recited "Out of the eater came forth food, and out of the strong came forth sweetness" seven times and threw the stone at the snake. And suddenly the snake melted into a big heap of gold, a big mountain of golden coins. (*Falls silent.*)

FOURTH BOY. (*On table.*) Oh boy, are my pants wet.

THIRD BOY. Well, then what happened?

SECOND BOY. Nothing. The poor man probably took the money home and became very rich. Grandfather didn't tell any more.

THIRD BOY. He must have divided the whole treasure among the poor.

FIRST BOY. Oh sure he did. A treasure is no little bundle of straw. You don't give a treasure away.

FOURTH BOY. (*On table.*) Is my mother going to whip me! She told me to sit home and watch my little sister and she herself came here. Oh, is she going to whip me! (*Kicks his feet and throws himself around.*)

YAKHNE-BRAYNE. You, off the table! You're going to break my table. (BOYS *jump up scared and disappear into the bushes. The* HEAD OF THE COMMUNITY COUNCIL, SOSKIN, *and their whole retinue come out of the purifying shed.*)

HEAD OF THE COMMUNITY COUNCIL. I keep explaining to you, why should we quarrel now? Time enough when this is over.

SOSKIN. This is a legal matter.

HEAD OF THE COMMUNITY COUNCIL. That is the twentieth time you've said that. What time is it now, ha?

ONE OF THE GROUP. Past eleven.

HEAD OF THE COMMUNITY COUNCIL. I have already had them announce three times for people to stop searching in the dark. They'll destroy the whole cemetery, and they won't find anything anyway. But nobody moves. I don't want to call the police. We'll have to make another announcement. (*All go.*)

YAKHNE-BRAYNE. (*Speaking after the people who are leaving.*) After fourteen years of penal servitude, for people to be thrown out and have to wander around outdoors. You must have the heart of a thief. Who ever heard of such a thing?

ANNOUNCEMENT. (*Among the graves.*) By order of the Council, the community is to go home now and come back tomorrow morning. (*The voices recede further and further. Men and women come from various directions. Some go to the gate, others into the purifying shed, still others remain sitting on the porch and chairs.*)

FIRST MAN. (*From the porch.*) And if the Council makes announcements from today till tomorrow, is anyone going to leave? Foolishness. Especially now that the moon is out.

SECOND MAN. (*From a chair.*) Here I can hardly stand on my feet, and even so I don't want to leave. I'll tell you the truth, I'm very sorry that I'm sitting here now. I feel as if, if I were searching right now, I would find it. And in fact, I'm running back to look some more. (*Jumps up and hurries off.*)

THIRD MAN. Now for myself I would be very glad to go home and sleep, but only if everyone else went too. If everyone else went home, I'd go too. Oh, am I sleepy. And besides I had a hard fast yesterday. (*Yawns.*)

FOURTH MAN. And it really is late already too. Almost midnight already. Soon the dead will wake up and go pray in the synagogue.

FIRST WOMAN. Oh, be quiet. As it is, my soul is shaking. I hunt and I'm scared to lift my eyes. I keep thinking there's somebody dead standing next to me.

SECOND WOMAN. Why did so many people come here dressed in white?

FIRST MAN. At least when you're hunting, you hunt. But just sitting and looking straight ahead—dead people really do start to appear before your eyes.

SECOND MAN. Who was the smart guy who started talking about the dead?

FOURTH MAN. Whoever is afraid should go home.

FIRST WOMAN. For god's sake, stop talking. I feel like I'm about to—

SECOND WOMAN. So why are we sitting here? Let's go hunt instead. Let's all go together, ha?

THIRD WOMAN. Right, all together. Whoever finds will find. (*All stand up to go.*)

FIRST WOMAN. I'm afraid to look around me. And behind . . . behind . . . oh, my.

THIRD MAN. (*Hard.*) Don't talk. Stop talking.

SECOND MAN. A Jewish woman has to talk. Has to talk. Don't look. Better to hunt. We're all afraid. But we have to keep our mouths shut. Keep your mouth shut and hunt. (*Disappearing. Silence falls.* TILYE, *in her new clothes, a veil over her face, comes from the gate side, goes to* YAKHNE-BRAYNE *and bends over her to see if she's sleeping.*)

YAKHNE-BRAYNE. (*Jumps.*) Oy, who is it? (TILYE *laughs and lifts her veil.*) Tfoo, on your head, your hands, and your feet. What is this veil, a masquerade?

TILYE. This is how I went to see my bridegroom, the engineer with the thirty thousand rubles dowry.

YAKHNE-BRAYNE. What?

TILYE. (*She lets herself down on the sofa at* YAKHNE-BRAYNE'S *feet.*) You remember, he was supposed to arrive at eleven o'clock. So off I went to the station to meet him. That's why I put on the veil, so the matchmaker wouldn't recognize me. I wanted to see what my tall, handsome engineer looked like, that I could buy for thirty thousand rubles. But the matchmaker wasn't at the station. So I don't know whether he fooled me, put the money in his pocket and didn't telegraph at all, or whether he telegraphed a second time for him not to come. Or whether he was simply afraid to show himself, so my handsome, tall, thirty-thousand-ruble bridegroom, poor thing, had to go off to a hotel all alone, without a welcome, and tomorrow, poor thing, he'll have to search for the matchmaker all over town—

YAKHNE-BRAYNE. (*Pushes at her with her feet.*) Oh, get away from me. She's still laughing.

TILYE. Don't kick. You can see that I put myself in his situation. It really is a shame, what they call cruelty to God's helpless creatures. Comes for thirty thousand rubles, with a bride thrown in besides, and poor thing goes away with nothing. I am sure that he is here, that he came. A few young people got out of the train, and all of them were handsome. Each one handsomer than the next. That's how it seemed to me. Sometimes all young people look gorgeous to me. But now I am terribly tired and there isn't even anywhere to lie down and sleep. And those locusts don't get tired of searching. Yudke, why don't you remember by now? You haven't remembered yet?

YUDKE. I strong. I look. I remember. I make. Look. (*Begins making crazy faces and laughs.*)

TILYE. But you don't remember. I'm not waiting for you. I'll do some tricks myself.

YAKHNE-BRAYNE. Not enough tricks for you yet?

TILYE. (*She stands up, takes lantern from table, goes off right.*) There's no place to sleep in any case. (*She disappears.*)

YUDKE. (*He jumps up.*) I see trick. (*He limps after* TILYE. YAKHNE-BRAYNE *groans. Silence. Soon five people come to the porch from various directions: three* MEN, *one of them a* SCHOOLTEACHER, *and two* WOMEN.)

FIFTH MAN. Hunt snow in July.

SIXTH MAN. Just so long as you hunt.

FOURTH WOMAN. My feet have already fallen off.

SCHOOLTEACHER. And the sad thing—you hunt till you're blind, you break your back, and someone may have already found it somewhere else.

FIFTH WOMAN. And what if someone really did already find it?

FIFTH MAN. Then someone really does have it.

FIFTH WOMAN. Very nice. And meanwhile we keep hunting.

SIXTH MAN. If someone did find it, he wouldn't be able to hide it so easily. A treasure is no wallet, he can't just pick it up and put it in his pocket. He's got to dig it out first, and then starts the whole Torah chapter of taking it away with him. And meanwhile hundreds of people are milling around, no evil eye.

FIFTH MAN. Hundreds? Thousands of people.

SIXTH MAN. So much the better. Each one watches the next, so that even swiping something from him wouldn't work.

FIFTH WOMAN. And what if somebody finds it and doesn't begin to dig right away, just makes himself a good marker and comes back for it another time?

FIFTH MAN. You're figuring out my whole plan for me.

SIXTH MAN. So long as the treasure isn't found, we'll keep on watching the cemetery.

SCHOOLTEACHER. I believe that people will never stop hunting.

FIFTH MAN. I certainly won't. As it is, I walk the streets in circles every day of my life, and sniff, and search, and all I find is a fever. Here at least, if I search, maybe I'll find a treasure.

SIXTH MAN. And you're not the only one of God's children. People rushed to close up shop today exactly like on Friday afternoons when Sabbath falls early, and they all ran straight to the cemetery. And I bet you that tomorrow half the stores won't be opened because all the Mr. and Mrs. Storekeepers will still be in the cemetery.

SCHOOLTEACHER. What do you expect? I'm a schoolteacher, so today I let the children out at midday, gave them recess. Oh, what I could do with that treasure.

FIFTH WOMAN. You wouldn't get to keep it all.

SCHOOLTEACHER. My share would do. What do you care?

FIFTH WOMAN. Meanwhile it's lively here.

SIXTH MAN. I should have as many thousands as the number of sins that will be committed here today.

FOURTH WOMAN. The cemetery is so packed.

SIXTH MAN. I myself saw—

FIFTH WOMAN. Let's hear.

SCHOOLTEACHER. Waste of time. (*He stands up and hurries away.*)

FIFTH WOMAN. So, what did you see?

SIXTH MAN. You seem to want to know very badly.

TILYE'S VOICE. (*Heard far to the right.*) Here. Here. Here. Found. Found.

FIFTH WOMAN. You hear? Found. (*All four hurry toward the voice. In cemetery, a great rush in the direction of the voice. The noise of voices rises.*) Found. Found. Found.

YAKHNE-BRAYNE. Khonye. Khonye. Get up. They found it. Get up. Look at the drunk. Khonye. Khonye. (*She gets up from the sofa and shakes him.*) Get up. They found it.

KHONYE. (*Asleep.*) Complain to your daughter. Don't complain to me.

YAKHNE-BRAYNE. What complain, what, you drunk? They found the marker, the treasure. Look how he lies there. It's got nothing to do with him at all. Are you going to get up?

KHONYE. I'm not moving from here.

YAKHNE-BRAYNE. Oh, you drunk. (*She shakes him, so he almost falls off the cupboard, and goes toward the voice.*)

TILYE'S VOICE. (*Moves closer upstage.*) Here. Here. Here. The marker. The marker. (*There is a running in that direction. We hear screaming: "There!" "It's there!" "There!"*)

YAKHNE-BRAYNE. (*She wrings her hands and slowly lets herself back down onto the sofa.*) A plague on her. Oh, she should break her head. Oh, they should break all her bones. Oh oh oh (*She sits on sofa and shakes her head.*)

TILYE. (*Voice from behind the purifying shed.*) Here, here, here. Behind the shed. Behind the shed. (*The running goes that way.*)

VOICES. This can't be right. First here, then there, and now all the way over—this must be somebody's joke. (TILYE *steals in on tiptoe past the wall of the purifying shed and the porch, jumps onto the sofa face down, laughing.*)

YAKHNE-BRAYNE. (*Shakes her fist over* TILYE'S *back.*) You, you, you. (*Noise of many voices approaching. A big crowd emerges from behind the purifying shed onto the main path. In the front row they are bringing someone who tears himself from their hands. Next to him, wailing, walks a woman with a little boy.*)

MAN BEING LED AWAY. I won't let you find the treasure. It's my treasure. I buried it. Don't you dare dig it up. A curse from God will come down on you. I won't let you. What do you need treasures for? You've got the whole world, and you're still not satisfied. Why do you need to make me miserable? I won't let you. I won't let you.

WIFE OF MAN BEING LED AWAY. Help, Jews, help me. He's crazy. Help, save me. (*The screams fade in the distant street.* TILYE *stops laughing and sits up, looking in the direction of the group.*)

YAKHNE-BRAYNE. You're not laughing. Why aren't you laughing? (*A new group enters on the same path. Men and women carry a woman who groans bitterly.*)

VOICE FROM EXITING GROUP. Look, here comes something more.

VOICE FROM ENTERING GROUP. A woman gave birth, or she had a miscarriage. (*They carry her out to gate.*)

YAKHNE-BRAYNE. What do you say to that, ha? (TILYE *stretches herself out face down on the sofa, throwing her hands over her head.* YAKHNE-BRAYNE *pushes her.*) Move over, you took my place.

YUDKE. (*His voice is heard from up right.*) Remember. Remember. Remember.

WOMAN'S VOICE. (*From same place.*) The gravedigger's son.

SCREAMS. He remembered. The gravedigger's son remembered. Yudke remembered. (*The screams move far and wide over the cemetery.* TILYE *jumps up and moves upstage.*)

YAKHNE-BRAYNE. My hands and feet are shaking.

YUDKE. (*Closer.*) Remembered. Remembered.

YAKHNE-BRAYNE. Khonye, get up, Yudke remembered. Khonye, get up. Look at the drunk. It's nothing to him. (*Screams.*) Khonye, wake up! Yudke remembered.

KHONYE. (*Raising his head.*) What do you want there, what?

YAKHNE-BRAYNE. Yudke remembered.

KHONYE. (*Lifting himself higher.*) Eh?

YAKHNE-BRAYNE. (*Imitating him.*) "Eh?" Drunk.

TILYE. (*Enters tired and disappointed.*) Too late.

YAKHNE-BRAYNE. Does he have to yell it out so everyone hears? May he burn.

TILYE. Well, that's life.

KHONYE. Aha, my little daughter, my millionairess. (*He wants to lie back down.*)

TILYE. Don't you lie down now. You're about to see something. You'll enjoy it.

YAKHNE-BRAYNE. He's got to lie right down, the drunk.

YUDKE. (*A great crowd around him, he enters from among the gravestones, jumping and yelling.*) Remember. Remember.

BUNCH OF VOICES. Where then, where? Tell. Where?

TILYE. (*Standing up and leaning against the table.*) Don't crowd him. (HEAD OF COMMUNITY COUNCIL *and* SOSKIN *push their way up close to* YUDKE.)

HEAD OF COMMUNITY COUNCIL. You have remembered where you buried your dog?

YUDKE. Yes. Remembered. Remembered.

HEAD OF COMMUNITY COUNCIL. Where is it?

SOSKIN. In the new field?

YUDKE. I tell. But I ... I ...

HEAD OF COMMUNITY COUNCIL. "I ... I ..." what?

YUDKE. (*Blurts.*) I not tell.

HEAD OF COMMUNITY COUNCIL. What kind of a business is that?

YUDKE. Yes tell, but you what I want.

HEAD OF COMMUNITY COUNCIL. (*To* TILYE.) Do you have any idea what he wants?

TILYE. Probably he took something into his head. He'll tell you. (KHONYE *sits up, rubs his eyes.*)

VOICES. Well, let's hear what he wants.

HEAD OF COMMUNITY COUNCIL. What do you want?

YUDKE. I want—all take places. All, all, just like that, just like that. All, all. And I do, and all do same. (KHONYE *laughs drunkenly and starts filling his pipe.*)

HEAD OF COMMUNITY COUNCIL. You want what? I'll slap your face right now.

VOICE. Evidently he wants to make fun of us.

ANOTHER VOICE. The lunatic wants to have fun. Obviously some crazy idea of his.

ANOTHER VOICE. Somebody must have coached him. (KHONYE *laughs.*)

VOICES. You'd better show the place right now, otherwise we'll make ash of you. (*They close in around him.*)

YUDKE. (*Face contorted with anger.*) I never show. Never. Forgot again forgot. (*Crowd moves away from him in fear.*)

TILYE. Are you the bosses of him to hit him? What's all this to you anyway? What do you care where the treasure is?

VOICES. What do you mean, what do we care? What have we been doing here half the day and all night?

TILYE. You won't get any of the treasure no matter what.

VOICES. Yes, but . . . but we just want to know.

YUDKE. I run away. Never not tell.

HEAD OF COMMUNITY COUNCIL. Start up with a lunatic.

VOICES. So then, why not? Take places everybody, let's do what he thought up. What more can happen if we act a little crazy? We're dying to know where the treasure is and how big it is. Take places. If we could only get half of it, at least. Take places.

YAKHNE-BRAYNE. You can go crazy from what comes into his head.

KHONYE. (*Laughs.*) Good.

HEAD OF COMMUNITY COUNCIL. It is the truth that we are about to go crazy here.

VOICES. Take places already, why not? Places for the standing prayer. Time to recite the blessings. Listen, soon it really will be time for morning prayers. Sh! Silence, the general takes command. (*They start placing themselves.*)

YUDKE. I show. I make, I say, you copy same do. You do.

KHONYE. (*Laughs.*) Good.

YUDKE. (*To* HEAD OF COMMUNITY COUNCIL, SOSKIN, *and a few well-dressed Jews who stand with their backs turned away.*) All. All. I want. (KHONYE *laughs. They join the crowd, a little to one side.* YUDKE *screams.*) Heh, heh, heh! (*The* CROWD *is silent.*) You too make "Heh, heh, heh."

CROWD. Heh, heh, heh. (KHONYE, *pipe in mouth, sits as though frozen and watches the crowd.*)

YUDKE. Heh, heh, heh.

CROWD. Heh, heh, heh. (YUDKE *starts making various faces and movements and the crowd copies him.*)

YAKHNE-BRAYNE. Crazy. (TILYE *signals to her to be quiet.*)

YUDKE. Heh, heh, heh.

CROWD. Heh, heh, heh.

YUDKE. Thieves.

CROWD. Thieves.

YUDKE. Locusts.

CROWD. Locusts.

YUDKE. Gold-grabbers.

CROWD. Gold-grabbers. (YAKHNE-BRAYNE *gestures with her hand to* KHONYE *and shakes her head.* KHONYE *gestures with his hand for her to leave him in peace.*)

YUDKE. Heh, heh, heh.

CROWD. Heh, heh, heh.

YUDKE. Hypocrites.

CROWD. Hypocrites.

YUDKE. Heh, heh, heh.

CROWD. Heh, heh, heh.

YUDKE. All of us.

CROWD. All of us.

YUDKE. Heh, heh, heh.

CROWD. Heh, heh, heh. (YUDKE *starts making movements again.* CROWD *copies him. In the back of the* CROWD, *the weeping of a hysterical woman breaks out.*)

YAKHNE-BRAYNE. God in Heaven, they're all going crazy. (YUDKE *laughs his most unpleasant laughter. The* CROWD *hardly moves.*)

VOICE. We really are going crazy.

VOICE. Our luck, we needed to know where the treasure lies.

VOICE. Do you understand what he talked us into here?

VOICE. But now he'll certainly show.

TILYE. (*Still leaning against the table, hands on her breast, she speaks up calmly.*) He's not showing yet. (*All eyes turn to her in wonder.*)

VOICE. Here comes the next chapter.

VOICE. First the brother, then the sister.

TILYE. (*To* KHONYE, *who is sitting and wondering.*) Dad, do you want to be gravedigger again?

KHONYE. (*He opens his mouth wide as if he wanted to catch on. He stands up, goes slowly to the table and lays his pipe down, speaking out firmly.*) He won't show. I won't let him show.

HEAD OF COMMUNITY COUNCIL. What does that mean: "He won't show"? Are we to allow you to drive us crazy for nothing? What can you possibly mean?

KHONYE. What can you possibly mean? Throw me out of gravedigging and then take away the treasure too?

HEAD OF COMMUNITY COUNCIL. "Take away"? Wouldn't you get a share, after all?

KHONYE. It's my treasure altogether. My son found it, so the treasure is entirely mine.

HEAD OF COMMUNITY COUNCIL. He found it on community land.

SOSKIN. And perhaps in the new field, what's more.

KHONYE. If you want him to show, I want to be gravedigger again.

VOICE. Foolish man. With the share of the treasure that he'll get, he'll still need to dig graves?

HEAD OF COMMUNITY COUNCIL. You renounce your share of the treasure and prefer to be gravedigger again instead?

KHONYE. What does that mean, renounce my share of the treasure? The treasure is entirely mine. You're the one that'll get a share.

HEAD OF COMMUNITY COUNCIL. Are you drunk?

VOICE. He has to ask? That one can barely stand up on his feet.

KHONYE. Not your granny's business what I am. I know very well what I'm saying. You go hunt. He won't show you where.

HEAD OF COMMUNITY COUNCIL. (*To* YUDKE.) Don't listen to your daddy. He is drunk. You tell me. I am the head of the Community Council.

KHONYE. He won't tell, I'm telling you.

TILYE. A pious Jew, a righteous man. Teach him not to listen to his father.

VOICE. Let him be gravedigger, and let his son show, and an end to the story. Why should we stand here? And we made ourselves crazy too.

VOICE. And what will we get if his son does show? I'll go hunt instead.

HEAD OF COMMUNITY COUNCIL. That's what you should all do.

TILYE. And if you hunt, that means you'll find?

VOICE. The whole town is searching and can't find.

VOICE. We'll search another year and a day and we still won't find anything.

VOICE. Let him be gravedigger. Let him be gravedigger.

SOSKIN. (*To* HEAD OF COMMUNITY COUNCIL.) What do you care? Let him be gravedigger again.

KHONYE. Fourteen years I've served faithfully. Can anyone say a word against me? The opposite. The whole town is here. Can anyone say a word against me?

VOICES. True. He's right. What did they have against him?

KHONYE. Should I let myself be thrown out on two splinters after fourteen years? I want to be gravedigger again, and I want to be gravedigger for as long as I want.

VOICES. Of course he should be gravedigger again. He should be gravedigger again.

HEAD OF COMMUNITY COUNCIL. (*To* CROWD.) Who's asking for your opinion? Silence.

VOICES. Oh, is that so? There you have him. Boss of the town.

SOSKIN. Really, what is the issue here? Let him be gravedigger again.

HEAD OF COMMUNITY COUNCIL. And what if the whole story is a swindle? We make him gravedigger again, and it turns out again that his son doesn't know and never did remember.

TILYE. That is an excuse, pure and simple.

YUDKE. Remember. As am a Jew, remember. See I tell.

KHONYE. Yudke. Quiet.

SOSKIN. If he swindled us, no more digging.

VOICE. If I were Khonye, I wouldn't bargain now. Some big treasure the Council would see from me.

TILYE. You see? We are righteous people.

HEAD OF COMMUNITY COUNCIL. All right, fine, let him be gravedigger. (*To* YUDKE.) Now tell.

KHONYE. Oh, that's how it is, is it? Say yes, say no, just like that?

HEAD OF COMMUNITY COUNCIL. What more do you want?

KHONYE. I want it black on white.

HEAD OF COMMUNITY COUNCIL. And if I say it in front of the whole town, that's not enough for you? What do you think I am anyway?

SOSKIN. You shouldn't let him offend you. You see after all that he is drunk.

KHONYE. Drunk or not drunk, I know what I want. I want to have it black on white that Khonye the Gravedigger must be gravedigger as long as he lives or as long as he wants to be. I don't want anybody to be able to throw me out whenever he happens to feel like it. I myself refuse.

VOICES. He's not so drunk after all. What do you know, the man understands a business deal.

KHONYE. I know what I want. My head hasn't shrunk. Write this down: "If Khonye's son Yudke shows correctly where he buried his dog, Khonye is to become gravedigger again and be gravedigger as long as he lives or as long as he wants to be. And if it happens that the treasure is found in the dog's grave, or any amount of money, half of it belongs to Khonye and half to the Community."

SOSKIN. Ridiculous. That you may not write down. The treasure may happen to lie in the new field.

KHONYE. In that case you can go to trial with each other.

SOSKIN. I'll tear you apart.

VOICES. What does that one there want? Why does he push himself in?

The whole world isn't enough for that one.

HEAD OF COMMUNITY COUNCIL. Incomprehensible insolence. He wants half the treasure, no less.

KHONYE. And say thank you that I was good enough to give up half.

HEAD OF COMMUNITY COUNCIL. I'll say that you're a big thief.

KHONYE. And I'll say that you're a bigger one. With fine people I can behave fine, but with a person like this, I don't mind being a pig.

WELL DRESSED MAN. (*To the* HEAD OF THE COMMUNITY COUNCIL.) You are surely not going to start quarreling with him. You see yourself that he is intoxicated.

KHONYE. What if I am?

VOICE. He's managing better than somebody sober.

HEAD OF COMMUNITY COUNCIL. And that's what I should give in to? That's what I should enter into a written contract with?

KHONYE. As you wish.

VOICES. So how will this all end? You could give in to the lunatic and not to him? What are we going to put up with here?

HEAD OF COMMUNITY COUNCIL. Who's telling you to stand here? Better go hunt.

VOICE. And so in other words we're supposed to find the treasure for him for less than a half?

VOICE. He'd be lucky to get a half from me.

VOICE. Easy for him to say, "go hunt." What does he care if we all close our businesses and go around the cemetery day and night and hunt, and then he comes and gives his opinion how much of the treasure he gets.

WELL-DRESSED MAN. (*To* HEAD OF THE COMMUNITY COUNCIL.) He wants a signature, give him a signature.

HEAD OF COMMUNITY COUNCIL. (*To* KHONYE.) But I will remember this against you.

KHONYE. Let's worry about that later. (*To* CROWD.) Who has paper and pencil with him?

VOICES. Who has paper and pencil with him?

WRITER. Me. (*Young man pushes through.*) I have paper and pencil.

KHONYE. Can you write?

WRITER. Why else would I carry equipment? I am a real writer. A writing teacher.

KHONYE. In that case, sit and write. (*Makes a place on the table, on which people set a few lanterns, and puts a chair there.*) Wait, what did I say before? Yes, write: "If the son of Khonon son of Reb Yehude, the gravedigger, shall show the place where he buried his canine Zshutshke, then must the aforesaid Khonon son of Reb Yehude, the gravedigger, again become gravedigger in our cemetery, and be gravedigger so long as he lives and so long as he himself wishes. And if in the aforementioned location where the canine is buried are found coins or the equivalent of coins, then one half is for the aforementioned Khonon son of Reb Yehude, the gravedigger, and half for our Community." All written?

WRITER. All written.

KHONYE. (*He takes the paper, puts on the eyeglasses and looks it over. To* HEAD OF THE COMMUNITY COUNCIL.) Now sign.

HEAD OF COMMUNITY COUNCIL. The first time such a thing has ever happened in my life. (*He looks over the paper and signs.*)

VOICE. He's a good guy, our old man. We didn't know he had it in him.

KHONYE. That's the way I am. If you don't bother me, I don't bother you. But if you— (*He takes up the writing and reads.*) Nakhum Khayim son of Reb Mordkhe Zakhhaym, Head of Community Council.

SOSKIN. I'll tear you apart.

VOICE. Here he goes again.

KHONYE. (*He folds the document and puts it away in his pocket.*) Yudke, go show.

YUDKE. Heh, heh, heh. (*He goes running off along the main path as far as the second side-path, where he turns. The* CROWD *breaks out into a cheer and runs after him with yelling and laughter.*)

TILYE. But it was nice, though. Now the treasure, fast. (*She runs after the crowd.*)

KHONYE. (*He starts running too, then remembers something and stops short.*) Yakhne-Brayne, move back in again. I'm running for the treasure. (*He hurries off.*)

YAKHNE-BRAYNE. Ah, ah, ah, what has God sent us now, ah, ah, ah? (*She picks up a pack of clothes and carries it inside the house.*)

VOICES. He buried his dog in the saint's grave. In the saint's grave. God in Heaven, in the saint's grave. Father in Heaven, what a terrible lunatic.

YAKHNE-BRAYNE. (*She comes out and shakes her head.*) He should die a terrible death.

VOICE. (*Nearby.*) He must have wanted his dog to have a glorious paradise.

VOICES. The marker. The dog is there all right. What about gold? And the treasure?

YAKHNE-BRAYNE. (*Picking up a bundle of bedding.*) My feet are breaking under me. (*She lets herself down on sofa.*)

VOICES. There you have it: burying a dog in the saint's grave. There you have it: your burial. There you have your crazy trick.

YUDKE. (*He comes running with the dead dog in his hands, panting.*) Let me. Let me. (*He runs off through gate.*)

VOICES. How many imperials? Four imperials. Four imperials?

YAKHNE-BRAYNE. (*Groans with disappointment.*) Oh.

VOICES. No more there? That's the whole treasure. Some treasure. They should dig deeper. Probably there's more money in there. Meanwhile they're digging up the saint's grave. (YAKHNE-BRAYNE *weeps out loud hysterically as if at a funeral.*) They're digging in another corner. They're digging in another corner. Oh, oh, in the saint's grave. Aren't they ashamed? They're not afraid of God? They're still digging in the corners. Nothing, snow in July. Only the four imperials. (*The* CROWD *begins to pour home. Various voices, laughter, lip-smacking from the* HOMEGOERS *among the trees.*) A treasure. There's a treasure for you. A whole night lost, for what and for when? Meanwhile the saint's grave is entirely dug up. How could anybody ever possibly do such a thing? (*A group of* HOMEGOERS *come out from among the trees.*)

FIRST HOMEGOER. What won't people do for money?

SECOND HOMEGOER. And for whose money? Who would have had anything from that money?

FIRST HOMEGOER. The town would have had.

SECOND HOMEGOER. The town would have had? A lot the town would have had, with Khayim Zakhhaym standing at the pot.

THIRD HOMEGOER. And if the town did have anything, what good would that have done me? (HOMEGOERS *disappear.*)

FOURTH HOMEGOER. (*In a different group.*) Where a lunatic buries his dog.

FIFTH HOMEGOER. (*In this new group.*) That's why Khonye shouldn't be gravedigger.

FEMALE HOMEGOER. It's not his fault he has a crazy son.

THIRD HOMEGOER. If they found it in a different corner, Khonye would certainly not have gotten a share, because that would have been— (*These* HOMEGOERS *disappear. The* HEAD OF THE COMMUNITY COUNCIL, SOSKIN, *and others pass by.*)

HEAD OF COMMUNITY COUNCIL. What legal, when legal? Not a single groschen.

SOSKIN. And I'm telling you that I— (*They disappear.*)

LAUGHING HOMEGOERS. (*A group of various* HOMEGOERS *in small and large groups pass by on various paths, rolling with laughter, repeating with variations.*) A treasure. There's a treasure for you. Four imperials a treasure. And what had to be done for it. What a treasure. Some treasure. And how we drove ourselves crazy. Ever heard of a treasure like that? What a girl. She deserves a bridegroom. If she just had a dowry, I would take her myself.

KHONYE. (*He comes from down right as if stealing in and goes over to the weeping* YAKHNE-BRAYNE.) A treasure, ha? A great treasure. Well, just so long as we didn't lie down for him and besides, I'm still the gravedigger. So what are you howling for? Enough howling. Come move back in. (*He puts various things together.* YAKHNE-BRAYNE *is in tears.*) What she can find to cry about. (TILYE *comes from behind, laughing.*)

YAKHNE-BRAYNE. Won't be able to show her face on the street, and she laughs.

TILYE. What do I have to be embarrassed about? Let all of them be embarrassed. I led them by the nose. I'll go out on the street, and with my head high too. After all I was a millionaire for a day. And . . . and . . . I still have money in the bank too.

KHONYE and YAKHNE-BRAYNE. What?

TILYE. Not so very much, but enough to hook a bridegroom anyway. A teeny bridegroom. Or maybe a big one. After all I'm so famous. And so well dressed.

KHONYE. (*Excited.*) Yakhne-Brayne. Yakhne-Brayne.

YAKHNE-BRAYNE. Why didn't you tell me that sooner?

KHONYE. I'll drink to that. Let's go in. (*To* TILYE.) Oh you . . . Oh you . . . What you just . . . Well, you deserve a spanking.

TILYE. (*She stands up to him.*) Give. (KHONYE *bursts into such a big peal of laughter that he almost falls. Laughing they go into the house with their bundles. They light a lamp; its weak shine can be seen through the windows. The sound of their voices carries faintly through the closed windows. Laughter is heard from very far away. Silence.*)

THE DEAD. (*In shrouds and prayer shawls, they begin to show themselves among the graves, one by one and in groups, first whispering and then aloud.*)

Quick into the synagogue.

Quick into the synagogue.

Midnight long past.

Quick into the synagogue. (*They hurry to the gate, gray silhouettes under the flat shine of the moon, which is veiled through clouds.*)

I thought we wouldn't get out tonight at all.

The dead are afraid of the breath of the living.

More than the living are fearful of us. There is no peace between living and dead.

A FEW. There is no peace. There is no peace.

Life teased at me terribly today.

For me, "teased" is not the word at all. I lived along with life and it made me shudder.

Shudder? Maybe you were just missing your money. (*A laughter-breath passes among the* DEAD.)

The high ones, the rich ones, certainly had a bad day today.

The smell of money all around, and they, poor things, were lying with the worms.

Ah, they were throwing themselves out of the grave, poor things.

A FEW. Money . . . money . . . money. (*Laughter-breath.*)

You paupers didn't have it any better. The smell of money, and you couldn't beg any donations. (*Laughter-breath.*)

HARSH VOICE AMONG THE DEAD. It's high time for all of you to forget about life. Quick, into the synagogue.

A FEW. It raised me from the grave.

How could they have had no mercy at all on us?

Don't scold. We wouldn't have been any better.

We were no better. (*Laughter breath.*)

ANOTHER FEW. Money . . . money . . . money.

That is life . . . that is life . . . that is life.

DEAD SURGEON. It brought me up out of the grave too. A lot of women were moving around my grave—young ones too, I could swear. (*Laughter-breath.*)

HARSH VOICE AMONG THE DEAD. Who is over there talking like that? Who is opening his mouth to speak obscenity?

A FEW. (*Pious.*) It's the surgeon who's buried near the fence.

THE SAINT. (*He enters with his prayer shawl barely hanging off his left shoulder.*) They dug my whole grave. They dug up my right arm. Father in Heaven, how will I put my prayer shawl on now? (*They encircle him and help him. Great move-*

ment of contemplating his missing arm, smacking their lips.)

God in Heaven, Heavenly Father.

Money . . . money . . . money.

THE SAINT. (*The prayer shawl on both shoulders, he moves off.*) Now I go to stand before God. Now I will ask him— (*He disappears through the gate.*)

A DEAD MAN. (*Behind him.*) He gets no answer. He gets no answer.

ANOTHER DEAD MAN. (*Declaiming.*) Life remains forever fixed. Generation after generation dies, but life remains unchanged. As it was long ago, so it was in my time, so it is still.

A FEW. Money . . . money . . . money.

But it's leading to something. It must be leading to something.

That only the one God knows.

The living must find it out.

That will be the greatest victory.

People's greatest victory.

A FEW. The living . . .

ANOTHER FEW. And what about us? (*A breath, as of laughing or groaning, sounds through the words.*)

THE FIRST FEW. The greatest victory.

Curtain

❧

Bronx Express (Bronks Ekspres)
A Dream in Three Acts with a Prologue and Epilogue
(1919–1926)

OSIP DYMOV

❧

Bronx Express was evidently never published. There are several typewritten scripts in the YIVO archives. One is dated 1925–26; the others are undated but seem to be from the 1919 production or some other production in the early 1920s, probably the Schildkraut production. The scripts are so scribbled over and pasted onto that in places they are illegible. The scribbles may have been added by Dymov himself, a director, an actor, or someone else. Differences between the versions—sometimes a word or two, sometimes as much as a page at a time—appear throughout. I felt free to choose whichever bit seemed funnier, taking sometimes from one and sometimes from another. The Nestlé Baby, for example, shows her lack of a good family life in 1919 by playing pinochle and later by union activities; I chose the latter.

The only obvious differences between the two versions were dictated by history. For example, Vanderbilt and Rockefeller were crossed out in one script, and Wendell Willkie and Ford were added. Stalin appears only in the 1925–6 version, and the names of both Roosevelt and Coolidge are scribbled in at various points. It was Wendell Wilkie that Khatskl didn't vote for, but I made it Coolidge because the name is more familiar.

The syllables in the characters' names are stressed as follows:

KHATS-kl
YAN-kl (in act 3 also called YAN-ke-le)
REY-zl
YO-se-le

sma-ro-ZHAN-ski

MOY-she POL-I-shook

(See the Note on Transliteration.) English-speaking readers may be interested to know that Yankl is the diminutive of Jacob, Yosele is the diminutive of Joseph, and Moyshe is the Yiddish version of Moses. Hungerproud's name is actually *Hungershtolts,* and Flames' name is *Flyamkes;* I gave literal translations of the names.

The Yiddish speech of *Bronx Express* has shed much of its Old-World sub-texts and echoes. Characters use many actual English words interpolated con-sciously or semiconsciously in Yiddish dialogue. This reflects the way many Jews actually spoke by the time the play was written: what intellectuals dispar-aged as "potato Yiddish." Some English words recur often, like "millionaire," "bluff," and "good-bye." There are whole English sentences every once in a while, such as "Good-bye Bronx, take care of yourself." And there are even longer sections. At the start of act 1, the sentence that Yosele reads about the Board of Estimate is an English sentence, including the word "requires," and when the teacher asks what it means, he simply reads the sentence all over again, translating a few of the prepositions into Yiddish. Almost the entire phone conversations in act 2 are conducted in English. All the English borrow-ings were transliterated into Yiddish letters in the play texts. (This was com-mon; plays published in America were sometimes printed with glossaries so that European readers could understand all the English borrowings.)

In fact, the sound of English spoken by characters like the people in *Bronx Express* was less "potato Yiddish" than "potato English," still a mixture of the two languages but by now predominantly English. I tried to recreate that sound by preserving in the dialogue some of the Yiddish words that are in rather common usage among speakers of English: *bar mitsva* (the occasion when a thirteen-year-old Jewish boy joins the community as an adult), *kosher* (ritually correct), *nu* ("Well"), *nudnik* (nuisance; irritating, nagging person), *rebbe* (teacher), *shlimazl* (loser), *schmaltz* (chicken fat). I also kept the old-fashioned Yiddish exclamation *vey iz mir* ("woe is me"), which conveys distress though it has come to sound funny in an English context.

All the advertisement characters were familiar figures advertising familiar products. Pluto Mineral Water's logo was a devil; Murad Chewing Tobacco's, a harem girl; and Arrow Collars', a handsome, blond, nattily dressed young man.

Nestlé used to be primarily known for baby food, symbolized by a baby. Aunt Jemima's logo is still a black woman in an apron, but she used to be older and fat; Wrigley's chewing gum's, twins; and Smith Brothers' cough drops, two solemn bearded brothers. To these, various productions added such up-to-date advertisement characters as Lily of France corsets, a seductive French woman; a Flit insect repellent figure, and Miss Chesterfield. No one remembers what Flit or Miss Chesterfield looked like, but the latter (perhaps a cigarette pack with legs) replaced Miss Murad as a love interest. The Folksbiene production in 1968, an adaptation by Abraham Schulman, substituted Miss Clairol, a model with beautiful hair, as Hungerproud's romance and added Miss Subways 1968 and the Marlboro Man, a cigarette-smoking cowboy, to the list of advertisements.

Hungerproud brags that he is "all the way left," but he is obviously kidding himself. People "all the way left" repudiated sectarian community and tradition in favor of solidarity with all working classes, and considered religion an opiate of the people. It is safe to say that a majority of *Bronx Express*'s audiences considered themselves on the left somewhere. Zionism was a separate political position from socialism; some zionist groups were hostile to socialism, and some parties combined the two. The Prologue's choral invocations of money, being both expressionist and anti-capitalist, were something of a cliché on the intellectual Yiddish stage. For example, similar passages were added to the Moscow Yiddish Art Theater GOSET's production of Sholom Aleichem's *200,000* to express the soulless capitalist bourgeoisie among whom the poor tailor finds himself when he wins the lottery. A closed shop requires all employees in a place to belong to the union.

Smarozhanski's refrain at the opening of act 1—"Is it good for the Jews?"—is a cliché question, the basis for a joke as often as for serious discussion. The question being asked here is "Is it good for the Jewish worker?" or simply "Is it good for the decent human being?" But the setting and the terms of the answer are all Jewish.

Sholom Aleichem, known by then as the Yiddish Mark Twain, was a beloved author and moreover a pioneer of the development of Yiddish as a literary language. Many Yiddish-language schools and cultural institutions in America and elsewhere took his name. He represented many of the soundest elements of Jewish and Yiddish tradition. *Sholem aleykhem* literally means "Peace be upon you," which is a common greeting. When characters use the phrase as a greeting, I transliterated it rather than spelling it as the writer did his nom de plume, and in act 1, Yosele plays with the double use of the phrase.

Yom Kippur, the Day of Atonement, is the major solemn holiday of the Jewish year, part of the High Holy Days marking every New Year. One fasts on Yom Kippur, as Flames mentions in act 3, and spends the day in prayer and in repentance for sins committed in the preceding year. Many Jews who observe no other ritual occasion visit synagogue on Yom Kippur.

Sabbath lasts from sundown Friday to sundown Saturday. On Sabbath observant Jews do not work. Work is defined to include lighting fires, which includes lighting cigarettes, so they do not smoke on the Sabbath. When Sabbath begins, the woman of the house lights candles, usually in special candlesticks, and makes the appropriate blessing. Then there is usually a special meal. The Hungerprouds' entire dinner is a conventional lavish eastern European Sabbath dinner, including chalah, compote, and such delicacies as stuffed derma (intestine stuffed with meat and bread or potatoes), jellied calves feet, and fish roe.

A production of *Bronx Express* that aims at verisimilitude would include some ceremony, however perfunctory or even pantomimed, before the family begin their meal in act 1. A household that observes so many particulars of ritual law, and even uses the customary greeting "Good Sabbath," would never begin Sabbath dinner without blessing first the wine and then the chalah.

The characters are constantly referring to Jewish laws and customs. I have left most of these in the text because I think that they are understandable in context and give a sense of time and place. In the prologue, for example, Khatskl is interested in whether food is kosher (prepared according to the dietary laws); in act 2, in the restaurant, he orders not only a combination of dairy foods and meat but even lobster and ham—all strictly forbidden. But then he doesn't eat any of it. It is clear that he has taught his son to use *tfilin* (phylacteries); in act 2 he imagines Yosele doing this for the first time at his bar mitsva. (A director who believes his audiences would be baffled by the reference could substitute the word "phylacteries" or the whole new sentence: "In synagogue he put the prayer shawl over his shoulders for the first time.") Khatskl and his family live by the Jewish calendar, and holidays are mentioned by name. Sukkos is the autumn holiday following Yom Kippur; Passover is the springtime holiday that commemorates the exodus from Egypt. On Passover it is customary for each man to lean on a cushion on his own chair, symbolizing that he is no longer enslaved but free.

In addition to familiarity with Judaism, it is useful to be familiar with the geography of New York City. Wall Street, location of high finance, is downtown in Manhattan. So is Canal Street and the rest of the Lower East Side. Broadway, a lively thoroughfare, passes diagonally through Manhattan and the Bronx, offering commerce, theater, and night life. Fifth Avenue is the place for elegant shopping. (Later versions added Madison Avenue as well.) The phrase "high windows" does not actually refer to buildings on Wall Street or anywhere else but is instead a Yiddish expression meaning the domain of rich and powerful people. The subway train still goes north, up past 14th Street, through Harlem, till it reaches the north end of the line, which is in the Bronx; it begins underground, but the last part of its route runs outside on an elevated track. At the time the play was written, Prospect Avenue housed a thriving Yiddish-speaking neighborhood, close to parks and tree-lined streets and altogether a move up from the Lower East Side where Hungerproud works and where he probably used to live. Schildkraut's Theatre, which Hungerproud dismisses in the epilogue, is the very place where *Bronx Express* was playing in 1923! A modern adaptation could substitute the name of its own theater.

The dialogue contains a number of specific references which people may not get. Several public readings have proven to me that the play goes over with total success even so. Audiences do not seem to miss a thing. Nevertheless, performers will want to understand all allusions, and for their convenience I supply explanations in the order in which they occur.

Prologue: Flames insults Hungerproud in several common, humorous ways. *Galitsianer* means a Jew from Galicia, a region that belonged to Austria till Partition made it Poland. People joked about a legendary feud between Galicians and *Litvaks,* Jews from Lithuania. Calling someone a *Galitsianer* was humorous in somewhat the same way that mentions of Brooklyn used to get a laugh. Note also that Atlantic City had only recently become a popular resort.

Act I: Lakewood was a community in New Jersey where many Yiddish-speakers lived. Also, people bonded on the long anxious trip to America. "Ship-brother" and "ship-sister" were expressions in common usage to express such a bond.

Act III: Yiddish papers used to carry a regular feature helping women to trace husbands who had disappeared, accidentally or on purpose, usually in the process of immigration. The joke here is that the norm was "disappeared" husbands, not wives. The expression "beyond the Pale" refers to the Pale of Settlement, the crowded area of czarist Russia where almost all Jews were forced to live. Sara calls Murad "Miss Purim Player" because on Purim, people dress up in silly costumes to perform, and she's all dolled up in her harem outfit.

The first production of *Bronx Express* opened on December 31, 1919, at the Naye Yidishe Teater (New Jewish Theatre). The theater was under the direction of Jacob Ben-Ami and Dymov himself. Ben-Ami got a lot of laughs as the shy young man, and Henrietta Schnitzer was admired in her harem costume as Murad. In his review in the *Forward,* Abraham Cahan explained that although it was a "vaudeville," it was nevertheless a "better" play, a play worthy of respect, because it treated a serious concern. Four years later Dymov and Rudolph Schildkraut took over an intimate theater in the Bronx, that had earlier been dedicated to serious repertory. They changed its name from Unzer Teater (Our Theatre) to The Schildkraut Theatre and opened it with a revival of *Bronx Express*. Schildkraut himself played Hungerproud. An English version, translated by Samuel Golding and adapted by Owen Davis, Sr., was produced by Mr. and Mrs. Charles Coburn at the Astor Theatre in 1922. A German translation was produced at Max Reinhardt's Theatre in Berlin in 1927, and a Polish one at the Athenaeum in Warsaw in 1929. The Folksbiene revived it in New York in 1968.

This rendering of the prologue of *Bronx Express* was originally prepared for *Vagabond Stars,* the revue that I wrote with composer Raphael Crystal and lyricist Alan Poul. It was performed at the Berkshire Theatre in New York City. I worked on an early version of the entire *Bronx Express* with support from Richard Siegel and the National Foundation for Jewish Culture.

Osip Dymov or Dimow, whose real name was Yosef Perlman (1878–1959), was best known for his romantic *Yoshke Muzikant (Yoshke the Musician)*, also known as *The Singer of His Sorrow.* (The introduction to this book tells more about Dymov and more about *Bronx Express*.)

Characters

KHATSKL (later: HARRY) HUNGERPROUD
YANKL (later: JAKE) FLAMES

SARA, Hungerproud's wife
REYZL, his daughter (eighteen years old)

YOSELE, his son (going on thirteen years old)
REB LIPE-KALMEN SMAROZHANSKI, his old teacher
("Reb" means "Mr." not "Rabbi")
MOYSHE POLISHOOK, Reyzl's young man, an intellectual

SUBWAY CONDUCTOR (later appears as WAITER)
WOMAN PASSENGER WITH BABY

MR. PLUTO, devil in red with a tail, advertising mineral water
MISS MURAD, exotic dancing girl in harem pants, advertising Turkish cigarettes
ARROW COLLAR MAN, blond and handsome, advertising collars
AUNT JEMIMA, black cook in apron, advertising pancake mix
TUXEDO TOBACCO MAN, wearing elegant tuxedo and eye patch,
advertising tobacco
NESTLÉ BABY, baby girl, advertising baby food
WRIGLEY TWINS, twin youngsters, advertising chewing gum
SMITH BROTHERS, bearded old men, advertising cough drops

PASSENGERS and VOICES on subway train
YOUNG PEOPLE on beach

Scene

New York and Atlantic City, real and in HUNGERPROUD's dream.
Prologue. On the northbound Bronx Express train.
Act I. Hungerproud's working class apartment in the Bronx.
Act II. A luxurious room on Wall Street.
Act IV. The boardwalk in Atlantic City and a restaurant on the boardwalk.
Epilogue. Back on the northbound Bronx Express train.

Time

A summer evening in the early 1920s.

◈

· Prologue

Subway car on the Bronx Express line. Afternoon rush hour of a hot day in August. The car is packed with people: men, women, and children, old and young. Some sit, some stand. Many read newspapers. The familiar overhead advertisement placards can be seen very distinctly: Pluto Mineral Water (a devil), Tuxedo Tobacco (an elegant gentleman with an eyepatch), Arrow Collars (a handsome, blond young man), Aunt Jemima Pancake Mix (a black woman in an apron), Murad Turkish Cigarettes (an exotic woman in harem pants), Wrigley's Chewing Gum (twins), Nestlé's Baby Food (a baby), Smith Brothers Cough Drops (two tall men with big black beards). The train is going fast. Through the noise of the wheels and talking, voices can be heard distinctly.

VOICES. Twenty-five dollars.

It cost twelve hundred dollars.

Made a few bucks.

Ended up without a dollar.

Eighteen dollars, not bad.

Two dollars and forty cents.

Five million dollars.

So he gave me six bucks.

(*We hear the motif of the song "America." Curtain rises slowly. The train stops.* CON-DUCTOR *appears.*)

CONDUCTOR. -eeeennnth Street next! (*Disappears.*)

VOICES. Which street?

CONDUCTOR. Fourteenth Street.

WOMAN'S VOICE. Fourteenth Street?

CONDUCTOR. Fourteenth Street.

WOMAN'S VOICE. Fourteenth Street?

CONDUCTOR. Yes, Ma'am. (*Some people leave, others enter. The* CONDUC-TOR*'s voice is heard.*) Let them out. Let them out.

VOICES. Bronx Express? Let me out. Getting off. Getting off.

CONDUCTOR. Bronx Express. Let them out. Watch your step. Step lively.

WOMAN WITH BABY. Is this the Bronx train?

CONDUCTOR. Bronx train. Step lively.

WOMAN WITH BABY. Excuse me.

CONDUCTOR. Certainly. Move inside, please. Step lively.

VOICE. Fourteenth Street?

CONDUCTOR. Fourteenth Street.

VOICE. Bronx Express?

CONDUCTOR. Bronx train. Watch your step. Move inside. Don't block the door. Bronx train.

(*Among the incoming passengers are* KHATSKL HUNGERPROUD *and* JAKE FLAMES. *However, we hardly notice them among the crowd.* HUNGERPROUD *pushes in, carrying a Yiddish newspaper.* FLAMES *wears a nice suit, a gold watch, a diamond ring. He is smoothly shaven. He looks about thirty-six but is older.* HUNGERPROUD *is a garment finisher, a workingman, not well groomed and poorly dressed. Dirty hands. A little beard and mustache. Bent over and exhausted. The train jerks.* HUNGERPROUD *and* FLAMES *grab simultaneously for the same strap. They stand with their backs to each other, unable to turn around because of the press of people surrounding them.*)

HUNGERPROUD. Please, Mister, that's my hole.

FLAMES. (*Doesn't let go.*) You bought it?

HUNGERPROUD. Yes, I paid a nickel for it. I have to hold on, or I'll fall.

FLAMES. The hole you bought is in the next car.

HUNGERPROUD. Wise guy.

FLAMES. Galitsianer.

HUNGERPROUD. No-good.

FLAMES. Peddler.

HUNGERPROUD. Loafer.

FLAMES. Bolshevik. (*Both turn around, excited, confront and recognize each other. Mutual delight.*) Khatskl Shlimazl!

HUNGERPROUD. Yankl Bluffer.

FLAMES. Twenty-two years since I saw you last.

HUNGERPROUD. I see you've done all right.

FLAMES. Cleaned twenty thousand dollars in the last two months.

HUNGERPROUD. So you're rich. You making a living?

FLAMES. And you?

HUNGERPROUD. Working. At buttons.

FLAMES. Still in the same shop on Canal Street?

HUNGERPROUD. You should see the shop. Big! A whole building now.

FLAMES. All this time with the buttons.

HUNGERPROUD. Today is my "universary". Twenty-five years today I started working in that factory. I've made seven and a half million.

FLAMES. Seven and a half million?

HUNGERPROUD. Buttons. Some record, huh?

FLAMES. Your record is missing one button.

HUNGERPROUD. Which one?

FLAMES. (*Points to* HUNGERPROUD*'s coat.*) That one.

HUNGERPROUD. My wife forgot to sew it on.

FLAMES. So you're married then.

HUNGERPROUD. Sure. I have a boy and a little girl. The boy's going to be bar mitsva three weeks after Yom Kippur.

FLAMES. When is that?

HUNGERPROUD. You don't know when Yom Kippur is?

FLAMES. On Wall Street we're not interested in such things.

HUNGERPROUD. And the little girl has a young man.

FLAMES. How old is she?

HUNGERPROUD. Eighteen, she should live long. He's a Zionist. But nobody's supposed to mention it.

FLAMES. That he's a Zionist?

HUNGERPROUD. No, that he's her young man.

FLAMES. Why not?

HUNGERPROUD. Bashful.

FLAMES. Eighteen years old and she's bashful?

HUNGERPROUD. No, he's bashful.

FLAMES. Why? Zionism is no crime.

HUNGERPROUD. No, he's not bashful about the Zionism. It's that he's her young man.

FLAMES. So let the girl explain it to him.

HUNGERPROUD. Nowadays is a new generation. They're crazy with love, suffragism, Zionism, psychologism. Let him be bashful—just so he marries her. A fine boy. Moyshe Polishook, his name is. He'd make good speeches if he could only open his mouth.

FLAMES. Does he make a living?

HUNGERPROUD. Sure he makes a living. That is, right now it's a small living. You might say very small. But he's busy though.

FLAMES. What line is he in?

HUNGERPROUD. He's interested in literature. You know what? Come home with me to my apartment. Moyshe will be there too. He comes every Friday night for the gefilte fish. And the chicken soup, and the pot roast, and the stuffed derma. At home they don't know about my universary, it'll be a surprise party.

FLAMES. I have an appointment on Broadway. Maybe I'll come later. Where do you live?

HUNGERPROUD. In the Bronx, Prospect Avenue. Five blocks from the station. Yes, you'll meet the rebbe too.

FLAMES. Which rebbe?

HUNGERPROUD. My old teacher, who taught me in school, in Polishani. He came to America too.

FLAMES. What's his line now?

HUNGERPROUD. Also in business. He works for Moyshe.

FLAMES. And you, you're a Zionist too?

HUNGERPROUD. I'm a socialist. All the way left. An extremist.

FLAMES. A socialist keeps bar mitsva and Yom Kippur?

HUNGERPROUD. Well, Yom Kippur is Yom Kippur, for the proletariat too.

FLAMES. How come you read the Yiddish paper, not the English?

HUNGERPROUD. Yiddish is better. I'm on the way home, I feel like forty winks. I open the Yiddish paper. I read the editorial, and I'm asleep from 14th Street to Harlem 160th. I walk in for supper refreshed.

FLAMES. In other words, all in all you're a happy man.

HUNGERPROUD. Who?

FLAMES. You.

HUNGERPROUD. Me?

FLAMES. Yes.

HUNGERPROUD. What about me?

FLAMES. You're happy.

HUNGERPROUD. Sure. Aren't I?

FLAMES. I tell you that with your buttons and your bashful young man and your pot roast and your editorials, you don't know what happiness is.

HUNGERPROUD. What do you mean?

FLAMES. We came over on the same ship twenty-five years ago. We both began to struggle. You went your way, and I went mine. Take a look at yourself, and take a look at me. What do you see?

HUNGERPROUD. You've gained a little weight.

FLAMES. Who's talking about weight? I became a real American, and you stayed a Jew from the Bronx. Am I right or not? Look at it another way. Seven million buttons you made, and you go around with a button missing.

HUNGERPROUD. My wife forgot.

FLAMES. That's secondly. And fourthly, what do you need a wife for anyway?

HUNGERPROUD. I don't know. To cook supper?

FLAMES. Go to a restaurant.

HUNGERPROUD. To have children?

FLAMES. You've already got children.

HUNGERPROUD. Well . . . to sew on buttons?

FLAMES. But she doesn't sew them.

HUNGERPROUD. Well, a wife . . . To go down and get the ice, the meat, the milk . . . You have to have someone to work for.

FLAMES. But if you'd married a rich American girl, you wouldn't need to work.

HUNGERPROUD. That's true.

FLAMES. That's sixthly. And eighthly, what are you doing in the Bronx with all the Jews? Why don't you go to Broadway, and Wall Street, to the high windows, to the Americans, where people make five million, ten million, fifty million, like me? Why not?

HUNGERPROUD. You're right. Why not?

FLAMES. What do you know about America? Between 14th Street and Harlem 160th is exactly where America is. You've been sleeping through America, and under America, your entire life.

HUNGERPROUD. My entire life?

FLAMES. Yes, sir. That's where life is, not by you in the Bronx. On Broadway, on Wall Street. Aha, it's cooking, it's burning, it's setting off sparks. They're running, they're grabbing, they're pushing. Hoo-ha! There a friend is no friend, a word is no word, a wife is no wife. That's life!

HUNGERPROUD. What do you mean, a wife is no wife?

FLAMES. One wife today, another one tomorrow. How do you do, good night, take care of yourself. Go to the Americans, I'm telling you. You get an idea, one new thought, a little gimmick, that's all—they drown you in gold. They buy, they sell, they jump up and down and ring bells. Bluff! Hoo-ha! Business!

HUNGERPROUD. What have I got to sell?

FLAMES. Buttons, cotton, silk, milk, yourself, your wife, your people.

HUNGERPROUD. Sell my people? Who'd buy?

FLAMES. People are making millions like fish cakes.

HUNGERPROUD. If everyone's making millions, where do all those millions come from?

FLAMES. From buttonmakers like you. There they are, the millionaires, right over your head. (*Points to subway ads.*) Do you see that Pluto Mineral Water?

HUNGERPROUD. The red devil with the tail?

FLAMES. Yes. Twenty-five million. I know him—he's a buddy of mine. Or Tuxedo Tobacco, "Your nose knows," forty million. Or Arrow Collars—he was a telegraph messenger boy. Who needs a collar? Do I need one? Do you? Bluff. Now he's worth one hundred million. Or Aunt Jemima Pancakes, "Delicious, economical, convenient," ten million.

HUNGERPROUD. No!

FLAMES. No? And people don't go every year to Atlantic City to the beach? And football and bathing suits, moving pictures and chewing gum, and ice cream, and shoeshine every minute. Do you have any idea what's going on with the Americans? Nestlé? That baby? Two hundred million. And chewing gum, Wrigleys, three hundred million. And Smith Brothers Cough Drops, three hundred fifty million.

HUNGERPROUD. Both brothers together?

FLAMES. Each brother separately. Both together, five hundred. Murad Cigarettes?

HUNGERPROUD. The pretty girl, Turkish, in pants?

FLAMES. Fifty-five million.

HUNGERPROUD. Nice girl, very beautiful girl. How many times I've looked at her. I had no idea she was so rich.

FLAMES. Too bad you didn't marry her instead of your old lady.

HUNGERPROUD. I never dreamed that crowd were so important.

FLAMES. What do you mean? They hold onto the whole country, just like this. (*Holds subway strap.*)

CONDUCTOR. (*Off-stage.*) Grand Central. Change for the shuttle.

FLAMES. Go to the high windows and rake in the gold pieces like me. By the way, can you lend me five bucks?

HUNGERPROUD. All I have is my pay envelope, and my wife is waiting for it. But here's a dollar.

FLAMES. All right. Maybe I'll come to your home. If it doesn't rain. Bye-

bye. (*Disappears.* HUNGERPROUD *glances up at the ads, shakes his head. He takes out the Yiddish paper, sits down in a corner, starts to read an editorial, slowly falls asleep. A baby wails loudly.*)

Curtain

༄

Act I

HUNGERPROUD's *dining room in the Bronx. Very clean and homey.* YOSELE, *thirteen years old, lies on the floor reading something that makes him laugh out loud.*

SMAROZHANSKI. (*Enters, almost falls over* YOSELE.) What's this? Who left this lying here?

YOSELE. Listen! He doesn't need any socks, and everybody's bringing him socks. So he yells, "Oh, no, not more socks!" And they answer him, "Here are your socks." Is that funny! Gee!

SMAROZHANSKI. You're reading Sholom Aleichem stories. Yosele, read me what they're saying in the English papers.

YOSELE. (*Reading entirely in English.*) "The Board of Estimate, which was working overtime this week to get the budget into shape before midnight tonight as the law requires, was twice interrupted yesterday."

SMAROZHANSKI. What does that mean: "requires"?

YOSELE. That means that the Board of Estimate, which was working overtime the whole week to get the budget in shape before midnight tonight as the law requires, was twice interrupted yesterday.

SMAROZHANSKI. Is that so? Is it good for the Jews?

YOSELE. Okay, sit down. Why don't you go to night school?

SMAROZHANSKI. The desks are too low. So is it?

YOSELE. I don't know.

SMAROZHANSKI. Budget? Money. If people are making a few dollars, Jews are earning too. It's good for the Jews. Go on.

YOSELE. "Expulsion of the members of the house of the King of Siam."

SMAROZHANSKI. The king himself? Is it good for the Jews?

YOSELE. It has nothing to do with the Jews.

SMAROZHANSKI. Everything has something to do with the Jews, and this is bad for the Jews.

YOSELE. How?

SMAROZHANSKI. Because if they kick out a king it's bad for the Jews.

YOSELE. And if they don't?

SMAROZHANSKI. It's worse. Go on.

YOSELE. "Earthquake took place on Java Island. Fifty killed."

SMAROZHANSKI. Is that good for the Jews?

YOSELE. Aw, gee.

SARA. (*Offstage.*) Reyzele, set the table. Your father will be home from the shop any minute.

REYZL. (*Offstage.*) All right, Mama. (*She enters, trying unsuccessfully to fasten the back of her dress. She is eighteen and pretty.*) Please button me up, Yosele.

YOSELE. You see I'm busy. Ask Mama. (SARA *enters, carrying plates.*)

REYZL. Button me up, Mama.

SARA. You see I'm busy. Ask Yosele.

REYZL. Button me up, Yosele.

YOSELE. Ask Mama.

SARA. (*Looking at clock.*) Your papa is getting out of the train now.

SMAROZHANSKI. I still remember how I whipped him in school. (SARA *lights the sabbath candles and makes the blessing.* REYZL *tries to button her own dress up behind.*)

SARA. Good Sabbath.

SMAROZHANSKI. Good Sabbath.

REYZL. Good Sabbath. Button me up. (SARA *off.*) Button me up, Yosele.

YOSELE. (*His eyes still on his reading, he buttons the dress with one hand.*) "Last week a seventeen-year-old girl got married, and they gave socks—" (*He reads and laughs.*)

SMAROZHANSKI. What I'd like to know is what the king of Java thinks about it.

REYZL. Papa's grandmother got married at fourteen.

SMAROZHANSKI. Yes, I remember how I whipped him in school.

REYZL. (*To* YOSELE.) Thanks.

SMAROZHANSKI. You don't need to thank me. He earned it. (SARA *enters with plates, goes back and forth setting the table with chala and so on.* REYZL *helps, and as she turns we see that her dress is buttoned wrong.*)

REYZL. Mama, did your grandmother marry young too?

SARA. My grandmother, may she bring you long life, was exactly—(*Disappears into kitchen, reappears immediately, still talking.*)—two months old at the wedding.

REYZL. How old?

SARA. I just told you. Right after Sukkos she was— (*Again disappears into kitchen and reappears immediately still talking.*) —burned up in the fire. You've been talking to me lately about marrying young—what's going on?

REYZL. Because I've decided— (*Disappears into kitchen and reappears immediately.*) —and nobody else.

SARA. What are you saying?

REYZL. I am saying that I want to— (*Again disappears into kitchen and reappears immediately.*) —and spend the winter in Lakewood.

SARA. Your grandmother's younger sister— (REYZL *goes off.*) —who had trouble with an ear—not trouble exactly, she was born that way— (*Exits.*)

REYZL. (*Enters.*) . . . and after that two rooms and a kitchen with nice curtains at the window and— (*Exits.*)

SARA. (*Enters.*) . . . God forbid, it has to be kept a secret, because a thing like that for a girl, and especially in a place like that where it's very important— (*Exits.*)

REYZL. (*Enters.*) . . . fifty dollars a month, and gas and electricity and laundry, and a shave at least two times a week— (*Exits.*)

SARA. (*Enters.*) The guests arrive, the bridegroom is waiting, the ear is sort of covered over. Up springs the bridegroom, and— (REYZL *returns. They collide.*) I go this way; she has to come the opposite.

REYZL. I need to get in.

SARA. Why do you keep moving while you talk? A person can't understand a word you're saying. (*Doorbell rings.*)

REYZL. Here he is. (*Goes to open door.*)

SARA. Here comes your father. (SMAROZHANSKI exits. MOYSHE enters.)

MOYSHE. Good Sabbath.

SARA. It's you, Mr. Polishook? Where is Papa? (*Exits.*)

MOYSHE. Sholem aleykhem.

YOSELE. Here's Sholom Aleichem. (*Exits.*)

REYZL. I've been wanting to ask you something very important. How many times a week does a person need to shave?

MOYSHE. I think you don't need to shave yet.

REYZL. It's not for me. My girlfriend really wants to get married, so she wants to know what things cost, by the week.

MOYSHE. Certainly. Did you read what Itsik Bitterzon said? Stalin and the troops went in—

REYZL. Because marriage to a man who wears a beard, that I absolutely do not want, I promise you.

MOYSHE. Comrade Stalin, he said . . . Comrade Stalin and his troops—

REYZL. Here he goes again! (*Knocks the newspaper out of his hands.*)

MOYSHE. When I come to your house, I remember when I lived in Shepetovke together with my mother, may she rest in peace. I was a child then, and I believed that there was no one more beautiful in the whole world.

REYZL. Once you told me that I look like your mother.

MOYSHE. (*Looks down, embarrassed.*) Did I really say that?

REYZL. If you want to make sure, you can always take another look.

MOYSHE. I can always take another look. (*He doesn't.*)

REYZL. You've got eyes.

MOYSHE. I've got eyes.

REYZL. So look at me and say: do I look like your mother?

MOYSHE. That's the best way: take a look and see.

REYZL. So look!

MOYSHE. I'm looking. (*He isn't.*)

REYZL. Here in America we look with our eyes. I don't know about Shepetovke.

MOYSHE. Shepetovke. If you make jokes, it's really hard to—

REYZL. I'm quiet. Well?

MOYSHE. Yes, you look like her. (*He finally looks.*) Yes. (*Sits down, exhausted.*)

REYZL. But if she was the most beautiful woman in the world, and I look like her, then you must think that I'm—

MOYSHE. Bitterzon says . . . Comrade Stalin . . . Comrade Stalin—

REYZL. I'm asking you something.

MOYSHE. You don't know, Reyzele, how you make my heart heavy. But at the same time, somehow, light.

REYZL. Is there something you're trying to say?

MOYSHE. I'm trying to say that if I could only . . . if I could only hope that I . . . that you . . . that your father . . . and my mother . . . that you and I together could . . . Excuse me, your dress is buttoned up wrong.

REYZL. Really? Then fix it.

MOYSHE. But . . . but I've never . . . never— (*Fastens her dress with shaking hands.* HUNGERPROUD *enters and sees.*)

HUNGERPROUD. Leave her alone! Leave her alone! I need this? A man comes home exhausted, what does he find? The bashful boy is hanging around his daughter. Let go of her.

MOYSHE. Good Sabbath. I wanted to—

HUNGERPROUD. I know what you wanted to. American nightclub tricks. Good Sabbath.

REYZL. Good evening, Papa.

HUNGERPROUD. Good evening. Broadway tricks! Broadway makes them all crazy. That's enough.

SARA. (*Enters.*) Good Sabbath, Khatskl. We have fish with roe tonight.

HUNGERPROUD. Again fish, and again stuffed derma, and again pot roast. Sure, I'm lucky. Good Sabbath, roe. (SMAROZHANSKI *and* YOSELE *come to the table.*) Ever since Passover I've been begging for a cushion, but there aren't any in the house.

SARA. I forgot.

HUNGERPROUD. You forgot. If I'd only married a rich American girl (*Goes off to wash his hands, grumbling as he washes.*)

SARA. What?

HUNGERPROUD. A wife with fish, no less.

YOSELE. Papa isn't cheerful today at all.

SARA. He's worn out from work, poor thing.

REYZL. But why is he mad at you?

SARA. You must never fight with your husband when he's hungry. First serve him his dinner. Stop up his mouth.

MOYSHE. Your father . . . Excuse me.

REYZL. Eat fish.

HUNGERPROUD. (*Returns from washing, still grumbling.*) Take a look how he grabs, Mr. Bashful from Shepetovke. Nobody's gotten near the fish yet, and he's already gobbling a second helping. (MOYSHE *chokes on a bone. Everyone helps him.*) That's all I need, someone chokes to death in my house, then I'll never get to Fifth Avenue. (*Eats some chala.*) Better?

MOYSHE. (*Hoarse.*) Better.

HUNGERPROUD. Don't talk. Keep quiet. (MOYSHE *tries to begin: "Hmm, Hmm".*) God is punishing you for your Broadway tricks and your bathing suit.

SARA. What bathing suit?

HUNGERPROUD. He knows.

MOYSHE. I never had a bathing suit.

HUNGERPROUD. Sure I'm lucky. Put down your book, bar mitsva boy.

YOSELE. What's the matter with you, Pa?

HUNGERPROUD. "What's the matter with you, Pa?" Would a millionaire's son answer his father that way? What kind of book is that? (*Takes the book.*)

YOSELE. Sholom Aleichem. Gee, it's funny. "You need socks . . ."

HUNGERPROUD. "Socks." "Gee." Sholom Aleichem. Sure I'm lucky. (*Reading. Starts to laugh.*)

"Here's your socks." (*Everyone joins him laughing.*)

SARA. Thank God that's over. Honestly, Khatskl, what is the matter today? (*Doorbell rings.* YOSELE *goes to open it.*)

HUNGERPROUD. Some kind of bluffer confused me today in the subway. A hustler, a liar, a good-for-nothing— (*Enter* YOSELE *and* FLAMES.) We were just talking about you. This is Yankl Flames. We came over on the same ship.

FLAMES. No more Yankl. Jake Flames now. Pleased to meet you all.

SARA. Is this the same one who snatched your life preserver when the ship was in danger?

FLAMES. My dear lady, if a man cannot swim, he shouldn't have a life preserver. He would only suffer needlessly.

HUNGERPROUD. It's true, I can't swim. Sit down.

FLAMES. But if it had been necessary, I would have sprung into the water for your husband.

HUNGERPROUD. Really, into the water? Eat some fish.

FLAMES. I just now ate, on Broadway. (*Eats.*) There they serve a man breakfast for five dollars, dinner for ten dollars, with music, with cigars.

HUNGERPROUD. Kosher?

FLAMES. Who notices on Broadway: kosher, not kosher? Details! When you eat just one meal there, you'll realize that all your life you've been hungry.

SARA. Meanwhile you look as if you've been hungry yourself.

FLAMES. I'm only eating this because we haven't seen each other for twenty-two years.

HUNGERPROUD. God brought us together today in the subway.

FLAMES. This is the child, the daughter? How do you do?

REYZL. How do you do?

FLAMES. And this is the bashful one. And this is the old teacher. You whipped him in school?

SMAROZHANSKI. You heard about it?

FLAMES. You whipped him so hard, they could hear it in the next town.

HUNGERPROUD. And this is my Yosele. He'll be bar mitsva after Yom Kippur. He reads Sholom Aleichem all day.

FLAMES. Yiddish? Why doesn't he read English?

SARA. Why not Yiddish?

HUNGERPROUD. (*To* FLAMES.) Why not Yiddish, in fact?

FLAMES. Because we live in America, that's why.

HUNGERPROUD. (*To* SARA.) Because we live in America, that's why.

SARA. And just because we're in America, should we be ashamed of Yiddish?

SMAROZHANSKI. True.

HUNGERPROUD. I'm talking to you.

FLAMES. In other words, you want to make your son unhappy the way you made your husband?

SARA. I made my husband unhappy?

HUNGERPROUD. What are you talking about? What do you mean, she made me unhappy?

FLAMES. (*To* SARA.) You keep him in darkness, in iron chains you keep him.

HUNGERPROUD. In iron chains she keeps me?

FLAMES. Today makes twenty-five years in the same factory.

HUNGERPROUD. Not the same. Bigger now—our own building.

FLAMES. Where is his career? Where is his automobile? Where are his millions?

HUNGERPROUD. (*To* SARA.) Where are my millions?

SARA. What millions?

HUNGERPROUD. (*To* FLAMES.) What millions? What are you blabbing about?

FLAMES. With his talents, with his brain, with his iron will, he could have been the biggest man on Wall Street.

SARA. How is it my fault?

FLAMES. To hold a person in the Bronx.

HUNGERPROUD. (*To* SARA.) A big person like that you hold in the Bronx?

SARA. I see just one thing: you are coming between a husband and wife.

HUNGERPROUD. (*To* FLAMES.) It's true, why are you coming between husband and wife?

FLAMES. (*Standing between them.*) Who's coming between? I'm talking like a friend.

HUNGERPROUD. (*To* SARA.) Jumping on a man! He's just talking like a friend.

SARA. Some dear friend: tears the life preserver out of your hands!

HUNGERPROUD. (*To* FLAMES.) Why did you have to tear it away? You could have taken another one, after all.

FLAMES. I already explained that if a person can't swim—

HUNGERPROUD. He can't swim. Go talk to women, they just can't grasp the idea. Sara, give him the roe.

SARA. It wasn't enough you confused him in the subway, you had to come here and try to insult me and say that I can't cook.

FLAMES. All I said was that on Broadway among the Americans—

SARA. Wait! On Broadway the Americans will leave you without a shirt on your back. You remember what I said. (*Cries.*) I can't cook!

REYZL. Mama! Mama!

YOSELE. Don't cry, Mama. Gee whiz.

HUNGERPROUD. What's going on here?

SARA. I can't cook! I cook a fish, even the fish enjoys it. I bake chala light like a feather.

HUNGERPROUD. He said you couldn't cook? He said—

MOYSHE. He talked against everybody.

HUNGERPROUD. (*To* FLAMES.) Out of my house.

FLAMES. Listen to me. Don't do this. Listen to what I'm telling you.

HUNGERPROUD. I don't want to listen. Out!

FLAMES. Your only friend, who is opening your eyes for you?

HUNGERPROUD. Out this minute, together with your eyes.

FLAMES. All right. Your stuffed derma, Mrs. Hungerproud, I can do without. (*Snatches some food from the table as he exits.*)

SARA. He ought to be lynched. Lynched for ten years.

SMAROZHANSKI. Well, I ask you: is such a thing good for the Jews?

HUNGERPROUD. Mixing in in my family life. You don't know how to cook!

REYZL. Papa, you're great.

MOYSHE. In another moment I'd have pushed him out.

SARA. May I live to cook for strangers if you weren't right, Khatskl.

YOSELE. (*Imitating.*) "Out of my house!"

HUNGERPROUD. (*After a pause.*) Why did you drive away my friend?

SARA. What are you talking about? Again?

HUNGERPROUD. The only friend who tells the truth and opens my eyes, you drove away.

SARA. What truth?

HUNGERPROUD. Such a man you hold down in the Bronx, with a dumbwaiter, without a cushion. Oh, my God, my God. A fine life!

SARA. What kind of a life do you want?

HUNGERPROUD. On Broadway they really live, on Wall Street, among the Americans, it's cooking, it's setting off sparks, gold lies around in the streets. A friend is no friend, a wife is no word, today one, tomorrow another. "How do you do, good-bye, take care of yourself." Where are my millions? I ask you, where are my millions? (*Exit.*)

SARA. Where are you going? You haven't eaten your pot roast. My God, what's going on here?

MOYSHE. It's all my fault. I'm the guilty one. I'm going to go tell him so.

REYZL. What are you going to tell him?

MOYSHE. That I didn't eat the dress. And if it's gone that far, I'm ready to make good the disgrace and marry her. And enough of my suffering.

REYZL. Papa, papa, open up.

SARA. If he would just hear this.

YOSELE. Pa, Pa! (*Bangs on door.*)

HUNGERPROUD. What's going on?

SARA. He wants to talk it over.

REYZL. He wants to talk to you.

SMAROZHANSKI. To talk to you, that's what he wants.

MOYSHE. I want to put an end to it.

HUNGERPROUD. Put. (*Takes* MOYSHE *back into the other room, closes door behind* THEM. *The others stand near door and listen.*)

REYZL. Shepetovke.

SARA. Shepetovke.

SMAROZHANSKI. Shepetovke.

REYZL. The dress.

YOSELE. Didn't fasten the dress.

SARA. Didn't fasten it, did something else.

REYZL. Loves—

SARA. Loves—

YOSELE. Loves—

REYZL. Shepetovke. Marry—

SARA. Marry—

YOSELE. Marry . . . marry—

SARA. Shepetovke. We heard this already.

REYZL. Marry.

SARA. Marry.

REYZL. Quiet. (*A slap is heard.*) What is it? (*Door opens,* MOYSHE *rushes out smeared with black shoe polish, tries to take his hat.*) Well?

SARA. What's he doing in there?

MOYSHE. He's shining his shoes.

REYZL. Why is your cheek black?

MOYSHE. When a person shines shoes, he gets polish on his hand.

REYZL. He slapped him. (HUNGERPROUD enters.)

HUNGERPROUD. I don't need that kind of son-in-law. For my daughter I'm getting a Broadway millionaire.

SARA. Khatskl, where are you going?

HUNGERPROUD. I am going to the high windows, to the Americans.

SARA. Khatskl! Don't let him go!

REYZL and YOSELE. Papa! Papa! Papa! (*He tears himself away from them and exits. They weep.*)

SARA. Children, Broadway has stolen your father.

CONDUCTOR. Don't block the door. Let them out. Let them pass. (HUNGERPROUD *enters the train.*)

HUNGERPROUD. Hey, Mr. Conductor, which stop for the big shots?

CONDUCTOR. Which big shots do you mean?

HUNGERPROUD. The Broadway millionaires, the cream of America.

CONDUCTOR. You're already there. Creep under the turnstile to get to the stage. How old are you?

HUNGERPROUD. Three times bar mitsva.

CONDUCTOR. Old enough to pay. (HUNGERPROUD *drops a nickel in his collecting machine.*)

HUNGERPROUD. Pay and pay is all they know. All right, I paid my nickel. (CONDUCTOR *exits, curtain opens on an office.*)

Curtain

Act II

Big parlor, exaggeratedly luxurious. Lamps, carpets, pictures, very high windows, golden chairs, big sign: "Mr. Pluto Corporation." Evening. Offstage, a storm. The stage is empty. HUNGERPROUD *appears.* FLAMES *enters.*

FLAMES. Well say, you showed up after all. Attaboy, Khatskl.

HUNGERPROUD. No more Khatskl. Harry Hungerproud, if you please. Twenty-five years' work, seven and a half million buttons, and a button missing. That is beyond the Pale. I want my millions. How do you make millions?

FLAMES. By bluff.

HUNGERPROUD. Who should I bluff?

FLAMES. Anyone you see. Otherwise they'll bluff you first. And remember: five percent commission for me.

HUNGERPROUD. Where am I? Who lives here?

FLAMES. This is the house of the director of Pluto Water. He's in conference with his friends the millionaires. They're figuring out how to get more millions.

HUNGERPROUD. More? Don't they have enough?

FLAMES. A millionaire is always a million short.

PLUTO. (*His voice from offstage.*) Who are you talking to, Jake?

HUNGERPROUD. Is that the old Pluto? (PLUTO *enters, dressed like a devil as in the ads.*)

FLAMES. With my friend, Mr. H . . . h . . . hungerproud, Mr. Pluto. A very smart businessman.

PLUTO. Glad to know you, Mr. Hungerproud. Won't you try my water? First thing in the morning. Or what can I do for you, sir?

HUNGERPROUD. My twelve-cylinder motor car broke down right in front of your door. May I use your telephone?

PLUTO. Help yourself.

HUNGERPROUD. Thank you. (*Moves toward phone.*)

PLUTO. Not that one. This one will be more comfortable. (*Shows him another phone.*)

HUNGERPROUD. What's the difference: this one, that one? I have no secrets. (*Speaks into phone.*) Wall Street one-two-three. Mr. Morgan? Mr. Hunger-proud speaking. How do you do? Mr. J. P. Morgan is not in? What is this in reference to? He'll know. It's about the six railroads. I'm ready to buy all six or more, but I'm not paying a million apiece. Tell that to the old nudnik. That's no bargain. Good-bye. (*Hangs up.*)

PLUTO. Which Morgan is that?

HUNGERPROUD. The one who calls himself a banker. But I don't go for monkey business.

PLUTO. I see.

HUNGERPROUD. (*Dials.*) Wall Street one-two-three-four . . .

FLAMES. (*To* HUNGERPROUD.) Go on, you've got him.

HUNGERPROUD. Hello, is this Mrs. Coolidge? I didn't recognize your sweet voice. This is Mr. H., who has spoken to your husband so many times. How do you feel? Your husband is well? Whenever you like. Whose? Chopin? I've heard him a hundred times already. All right. Next Tuesday, sharp. *Auf wiedersehn.* The same to you. (*Hangs up.*)

FLAMES. Khatskl, what are you doing?

HUNGERPROUD. I want to show you that when it comes to bluff, I can bite everyone into pieces, even you. (*Dials.*) Hello, Wall Street one-two-three-four-five?

PLUTO. Excuse me, I have an important meeting with my friends. Be careful, you're playing against the devil.

HUNGERPROUD. (*Dials.*) Rockefeller's apartment? Johnny? Is that you, Johnny? It's Harry. Hello. How's business? How much did you make today? Twenty million? Is that all? You're getting lazy. I see. Of course, if a person doesn't feel good . . . You didn't eat anything, a whole day? Ts, ts, ts. Just one soft-boiled egg? How much did you pay for the egg? For one egg? Listen, Rocky . . . Where am I at the moment? In somebody's house, nothing special. Listen, Rocky, you were going to send me Mexican oil stock. Send me ten thousand. All right, make it fifteen. How much? Two hundred and five? Two hundred five and a quarter. Forty-six. Forty-eight and a half. Three hundred. All right. Take care of yourself. (*Hangs up.*) That was John D. Rockefeller.

PLUTO. I see.

FLAMES. Khatskl, that was great.

HUNGERPROUD. All you have to do is hold the receiver. Thank you very much, Mr. Pluto. I must go.

PLUTO. Why are you in such a hurry? My friends and I would be very happy if you would spend the evening with us.

FLAMES. You got him in your pocket. Ten percent commission for me.

PLUTO. Do you know these people well?

HUNGERPROUD. Do I know them? Jack, do I know them?

FLAMES. My God, he knows them as well as he knows me.

HUNGERPROUD. Coolidge sounded a little miffed at me. He must know that I didn't vote for him.

FLAMES. He wouldn't have voted for himself. But he likes you.

HUNGERPROUD. He likes me very much.

FLAMES. Between two big men—jealousy, you know.

HUNGERPROUD. If he knew that I talked to his old lady on the phone, he would kick up some fuss.

PLUTO. He'll never know.

HUNGERPROUD. You mean it, Mr. Pluto?

PLUTO. Certainly. Because that telephone has no wires. That's a dummy. I keep it specially to outbluff people who want to bluff me. (*Laughs diabolically.* HUNGERPROUD *collapses onto stool.*)

FLAMES. Nu?

HUNGERPROUD. Nu, nu.

PLUTO. (*Imitates.*) "Mrs. Calvin Coolidge, I didn't recognize your sweet voice." "Wall Street one-two-three-four-five."

FLAMES. Idiot! How many times have I told you: don't go creeping off to the Americans. Stay in the Bronx.

HUNGERPROUD. I see that I'm no good at business. I'll go home. (*Starts out.*)

PLUTO. (*Intercepts him.*) Go home just when you were starting out so well? Bluffed me the very first time you saw me? A man like that belongs on Broadway. I sense that there is an idea inside you, and I am going to pull it out.

HUNGERPROUD. I've never had an idea.

FLAMES. Never.

PLUTO. I can smell out an idea in a person even when the person himself knows nothing about it. (*Loud coughing is heard offstage. Enter the two* SMITH BROTHERS.) The Smith Brothers, from the cough drops. You must know them.

HUNGERPROUD. Three hundred fifty. (WRIGLEY *twins enter.*) God in

Heaven, they look so familiar to me somehow.

WRIGLEYS. "Sealed tight, kept right, the flavor lasts."

PLUTO. Permit me to introduce to you Mr. Hungerproud, a captain of industry, a man with great ideas.

FIRST SMITH BROTHER. An original idea is the fundament of success. When my younger brother and I opened our business in 1847, he's the one who began the idea of cough drops.

SECOND SMITH BROTHER. I only added glycerine and sugar.

FIRST SMITH BROTHER. No, it was your wonderful idea to conquer coughs with candy. (*Coughs.*) An original idea. (*Coughs.*)

SECOND SMITH BROTHER. (*Coughing throughout.*) Glycerine . . . 1847 . . . brilliant. (*Both cough.*)

HUNGERPROUD. Have you had that cough a long time?

FIRST SMITH BROTHER. Since 18—

SECOND SMITH BROTHER. —47. (*Enter* AUNT JEMIMA, *carrying pancakes.*)

AUNT JEMIMA. Mr. Smith, specially for you. Just try it, Mr. Smith.

SMITH. I don't want to. I'm not hungry.

AUNT JEMIMA. Nice and hot, Mr. Smith.

PLUTO. (*Introducing.*) This is Aunt Jemima's Pancakes.

HUNGERPROUD. I never tasted you, but I am very glad to meet you.

FLAMES. Ten million.

HUNGERPROUD. No!

AUNT JEMIMA. "Delicious, economical, convenient." Specially for you, sir.

ARROW COLLAR MAN. (*Enters.*) Is she here yet?

PLUTO. Meet Mr. Hungerproud, Mr. Arrow.

HUNGERPROUD. You're the one from the Arrow Collars? You know, you and Miss Murad are the best looking of the bunch.

ARROW COLLAR MAN. But I'm not good enough for her. I'm not rich enough for her. New millionaires come around, richer than I am.

PLUTO. Yes, that's true. New millionaires, too many millionaires.

HUNGERPROUD. The trouble with you millionaires is that you have an open shop. Why don't you make a closed shop of millionaires? Organize. Millionaires of the world, you have nothing to lose but your chains. Fight for your rights. Make a union.

PLUTO. A closed shop. An inspiration! A closed shop.

MURAD. (*Enters.*) Who is this man?

PLUTO. Come on, we need to talk over this closed shop. (FLAMES, HUNGERPROUD, *and* MURAD *remain alone onstage.*)

HUNGERPROUD. How beautiful she is!

FLAMES. (*Dragging him over to her.*) Permit me to present Mr. Harry Hungerproud, a captain of industry. (*They say "Sholem aleykhem" to each other.*)

MURAD. I heard how wonderfully you spoke. What business are you in?

HUNGERPROUD. Buttons.

FLAMES. Buttons.

HUNGERPROUD. Buttons.

MURAD. You've made a success of your button business?

HUNGERPROUD. Sure. All these buttons that you see are mine. This button is mine, and this button is mine.

MURAD. In that case, you must be a very rich man.

HUNGERPROUD. Who, me?

FLAMES. Sure he is. (*To* HUNGERPROUD.) Sit down, idiot. Fifteen percent commission for me. (*From the door, the crying of a child is heard. In comes the* NESTLÉ BABY *crying.*)

NESTLÉ BABY. Everybody went away and left me by myself.

HUNGERPROUD. Sh! darling. Don't cry, baby.

FLAMES. Khatskl, that's no baby.

HUNGERPROUD. What is it then, an ox?

FLAMES. That's the Nestlé Baby. "Wholesome nourishment." Two hundred million.

NESTLÉ BABY. I'm hungry.

HUNGERPROUD. Two hundred million and still hungry. Where's his mother? Where's her father?

FLAMES. Never had any.

HUNGERPROUD. What good is money without a mother or father? Poor little orphan.

MURAD. Miss Nestlé, all our friends are in conference discussing a closed shop.

NESTLÉ BABY. Oh, I want a closed shop too. (*Exits.*)

HUNGERPROUD. I ask you, such a little baby and already for a closed shop.

MURAD. You are so fond of children, I hope you're not married.

HUNGERPROUD. Me? What makes you say that?

MURAD. You have that look.

FLAMES. He's not nearly so married as he looks.

HUNGERPROUD. Not nearly so.

MURAD. That's very nice of you.

FLAMES. Just a touch married.

HUNGERPROUD. Just a touch married.

MURAD. I understand.

FLAMES. Besides, a millionaire is never married.

HUNGERPROUD. A millionaire is never— (*To* FLAMES.) What are you babbling about? (FLAMES *withdraws into a corner.*)

MURAD. So then, you're in the button business. Unfortunately I don't use buttons. In my costume, everything is tied together.

HUNGERPROUD. What a pity. I work twenty-five years in buttons, and here the person who I would most love to serve does not need buttons.

MURAD. You wish to serve me? Have we met before?

HUNGERPROUD. Have we met! How many times, when I was tired from work, have I taken one of your cigarettes and looked at your picture. But I never dreamed that I would ever say all this right to your beautiful face.

MURAD. How wonderfully you speak. As soon as I entered and heard your voice, I began to tremble. I was electrified. Oh, how you understand women!

HUNGERPROUD. That's the truth. Many times in the subway a woman is sitting opposite me and I think to myself: she will certainly get out at 110th Street Harlem, and she really does get out at 116th—what's the difference, a few blocks?

MURAD. Don't tell me about your experience with women. You'll make me jealous. When I fall in love with a man, I want to be not his hundred and twentieth but his only one. I want to dance for him the dance of love. I see my beloved, how he sits before me like a young god, and I dance. Every muscle in my body trembles with longing, and he trembles too. I want to take your hand, pull it to my hungry heart and never let it go.

HUNGERPROUD. For the first time I hear such talk from above the earth to me down below.

MURAD. Ah, Harry.

HUNGERPROUD. Miss Murad.

FLAMES. They're coming. (FLAMES *and* MURAD *run off.*)

HUNGERPROUD. Who? (*Enter* MOYSHE *and* SMAROZHANSKI, *both wet from rain.*)

SMAROZHANSKI. I still remember how I whipped you in school.

HUNGERPROUD. This is no place to talk about it.

SMAROZHANSKI. You talk, Moyshe.

MOYSHE. But if it's not going to help—

SMAROZHANSKI. Talk.

MOYSHE. But if I know beforehand that it won't help at all—

SMAROZHANSKI. Talk.

HUNGERPROUD. What can you lose? Talk.

MOYSHE. What is there to talk about? You know better than I. You left home; you didn't finish supper.

HUNGERPROUD. I hate stewed prunes.

MOYSHE. And we need somebody with flaming words to persuade you to come home. Somebody strong with an iron will.

SMAROZHANSKI. So we came.

MOYSHE. Yes, in a word. I've explained everything. Now do whatever you want. Good-bye.

SMAROZHANSKI. What do you mean "Good-bye"? And his wife?

HUNGERPROUD. What about my wife?

MOYSHE. Nothing. She cries. She's a woman—she cries.

SMAROZHANSKI. Nu, and Yosele?

MOYSHE. What does he understand? A child. Come on.

SMAROZHANSKI. Wait. Nu, and Reyzele?

HUNGERPROUD. What's the matter with Reyzele?

SMAROZHANSKI. She's unhappy.

MOYSHE. You never know. There could be another reason entirely. She could be in love with a young man from Shepetovke.

SMAROZHANSKI. Are you finished talking yet? Now I want to talk.

MOYSHE. What for? It won't help.

HUNGERPROUD. Are you going to let him talk or not?

SMAROZHANSKI. I still remember how I used to whip you in school.

HUNGERPROUD. How many times do we need to remember it?

MOYSHE. He thinks it's really so pleasant to hear somebody remind a grown-up person, "I whipped you in school, I whipped you in school."

HUNGERPROUD. Who asked you to translate?

MOYSHE. I'm saying it so he won't talk any more about whipping in school.

SMAROZHANSKI. I understand. I would whip you again today with great pleasure.

MOYSHE. Again?

SMAROZHANSKI. I'm only saying that I would.

MOYSHE. It's all the same thing. If you tell somebody you would whip him, he immediately remembers that you did whip him. Isn't that true?

HUNGERPROUD. Sure. But why should you care?

MOYSHE. You shouldn't talk about whipping.

SMAROZHANSKI. Enough, I'm not talking any more. Khatskl, Khatskl, what have you done to your wife? Do you want her to go cook for strangers? And your daughter: to drive out such a bridegroom, such a fine young man, such an intellectual, such a great speaker?

MOYSHE. A girl like that won't have to wait for suitors.

SMAROZHANSKI. (*To* MOYSHE.) Sh, idiot! (*Back to* HUNGERPROUD.) Nu, and Yosele?

HUNGERPROUD. A child—what does he understand?

SMAROZHANSKI. Three weeks after Yom Kippur is his bar mitsva, and bar mitsva without a father is no good. Next Yom Kippur he already won't fast, and when Yom Kippur goes, everything goes: no holidays, no religion, no traditions. Everyone all mixed up in the American schmaltz pot.

HUNGERPROUD. But according to proletarian class consciousness—

SMAROZHANSKI. What do I care about class? What do I care about consciousness? It isn't good for the Jews. Remember my words: Your Yosele will end up shining shoes in the streets and whistling American tunes, and then you'll have class and consciousness. Remember!

HUNGERPROUD. She cries, you say?

SMAROZHANSKI. Such tears! (*Shows how big.*)

HUNGERPROUD. Tell her I'll just make a million or two and come right home. Meanwhile she should warm up the stewed prunes. Now leave.

MOYSHE. It's raining very hard. We'll wait under the high window, and if I whistle, it means that we're waiting.

HUNGERPROUD. Yes, fine, you can whistle for me.

SMAROZHANSKI. In other words, it wasn't worth whipping you in school?

MOYSHE. You shouldn't talk about whipping. (*They leave.* ARROW COLLAR MAN *enters.*)

HUNGERPROUD. What did they decide at the meeting?

ARROW COLLAR MAN. The closed shop is already organized. Mr. Pluto is the delegate. Wait a minute. I have something to say to you. I know everything.

HUNGERPROUD. What everything?

ARROW COLLAR MAN. Mr. Hungerproud, try to make her happy. But remember, she is very expensive. Here is her picture. I don't need it any longer. (*Gives him cigarette box with* MURAD*'s picture on it.*) I am off to Palm Beach to convalesce from heartache.

HUNGERPROUD. Good-bye, go in good health.

ARROW COLLAR MAN. By the way, here is my bill. (*Gives it.* FLAMES *enters.*)

HUNGERPROUD. What bill? I don't owe you anything.

ARROW COLLAR MAN. Four hundred dollars and thirty-five cents. For my broken heart.

FLAMES. Ten percent commission for me.

HUNGERPROUD. What have you told him? I haven't done anything to her.

FLAMES. It's all right, you can bargain with him. Leave it to me. (*Enter* MURAD.)

MURAD. Mr. Hungerproud, why do you look so worried? Smoke one of my cigarettes and forget all your troubles. (*Gives him a cigarette.*)

HUNGERPROUD. Thank you, but I don't smoke. (*All return from meeting.*)

MURAD. But earlier you told me that you smoke.

HUNGERPROUD. What I mean is, I do smoke, but today is Sabbath. We're forbidden to smoke on the Sabbath.

TUXEDO. That's it. An old story. Jews don't smoke on Sabbath, they don't buy tobacco, and that's how they spoil our business.

FIRST SMITH BROTHER. And because they don't smoke, they have good hearts and don't cough.

AUNT JEMIMA. They don't eat my pancakes either.

FIRST WRIGLEY. And because they don't eat pancakes, they don't suffer indigestion, so they don't—

SECOND WRIGLEY. . . . don't buy our chewing gum.

PLUTO. And if they don't suffer from indigestion, they don't need my water.

ARROW COLLAR MAN. Millions of them work in factories, don't need my collars, and spoil my business.

PLUTO. Jews stick together. That's the trouble. (*An uproar, all yelling at* HUNGERPROUD.)

HUNGERPROUD. I stick together. I spoil business. I see your faces every morning on my way to work. In the evening coming home, I see you again. Twenty-five years I've been traveling like that. Some of you have disappeared, others come—new ones. But you all keep yelling at me: "Buy, buy, two for a quarter, ten for a nickel, five for a dozen. A dime. A dollar. First thing in the morning. The best thing for children. You like to touch it. You love to wear it. Buy. Buy!" You have confused my mind with your yelling. I hid from you under the ground. I needed peace from your yelling and from the hard work that I do for you. For you, not for myself. But you found me and dragged me out, you tear at me and yell: "Buy! Buy! More! Money! Don't spoil the business." Some fine bunch you are.

ARROW COLLAR MAN. What do you mean: you worked for us and not for yourself? You didn't make seven and a half?

HUNGERPROUD. Not dollars, just buttons. And not even that, either. After twenty-five years work, you have the dollars and millions, and I have the envelope with forty-three dollars and thirty-seven cents. (*To the* WRIGLEYS, *who are pulling at him.*) Don't pull me, let go of me.

AD CHARACTERS. Buttons.

Faker.

A poor man.

Disgusting.

(*They exit.* HUNGERPROUD *and* FLAMES *remain.*)

FLAMES. Some nice party you threw. Who told you to flap your tongue?

HUNGERPROUD. What, they insult Jews and I should keep quiet? No sir. I'm getting out of here altogether. (*Goes to the door.*)

FLAMES. How about my commission?

MURAD. (*Enters.* FLAMES *hides.*) You wanted to go and leave me here all alone? Don't go. Stay here with me. I'll make you happy as a young god. Ah, Harry, I love you so. (*Kisses him and runs off.*)

HUNGERPROUD. What's going on here?

FLAMES. Luck is flying into your hands. Listen to me. Make a million. Marry Murad. Twenty-five percent commission for me. Adopt Nestlé, and good-bye, Bronx, take care of yourself.

HUNGERPROUD. Good-bye, Bronx, take care of yourself. How do you make a million?

FLAMES. Just one thought, one idea. That's all. Give me an idea and I'll sell it, even on Yom Kippur.

HUNGERPROUD. Yom Kippur! Yankl!

FLAMES. What?

HUNGERPROUD. I have it. For the first time, I have got an idea in my head.

FLAMES. Hold everything. Thirty percent commission for me. Thirty-five percent. Fifty percent. My God! Mr. Pluto, the man's got an idea. (*Off.*)

HUNGERPROUD. (*Alone.*) No. No. Get out of here.

FLAMES. (*Returning with* PLUTO.) A real idea. You'll make a fortune. (PLUTO *takes a million from his safe.*)

HUNGERPROUD. No. No. I'm not going to sell my soul to the devil. Escape. Escape.

PLUTO. Here's a million. Where is your idea?

HUNGERPROUD. (*Dazzled by the million.*) Uhhmm . . . uhhmmm . . .

PLUTO. What?

HUNGERPROUD. Americanization. Americanize them.

PLUTO. Who?

HUNGERPROUD. The ones who spoil business and stick together.

PLUTO. The Jews?

HUNGERPROUD. The Jews.

FLAMES. A marvelous idea. Listen. Listen.

PLUTO. How do we Americanize them?

HUNGERPROUD. Let me go home. Please.

PLUTO. I asked you how.

HUNGERPROUD. Don't look at me like that. I'll tell you everything. Yom Kippur is coming soon. A big holiday. No Jew works that day, none. You're not supposed to work.

PLUTO. I know that. Go on.

HUNGERPROUD. Make the Jews work on Yom Kippur. (*Thunderclap.*) Make an agreement with all the shops, all the factories, downtown, uptown, that day they pay the Jews double, triple, ten times. They'll work Yom Kippur too.

PLUTO. Jews love money.

HUNGERPROUD. Sure, Jews love money. This one has a sick child and has to buy medicine. That one has an old father or mother or just an old rebbe who can't work but he wants to eat anyway, or a wife exhausted in the kitchen from hard work. Or relatives in misery back home. Yes, yes, Jews do love money. They'll work Yom Kippur too.

PLUTO. Go on, go on.

HUNGERPROUD. Yom Kippur breaks down, everything breaks down. No holidays, no religion, no tradition. Everything one pot of schmaltz. Everyone cooked in the same pot. The iron grinder grinds them all up together, with the Poles, Italians, Chinese, Japanese, Negroes—everyone thrown in the iron wheels. Wheels and people—a machine with no holidays, no language, no traditions—a great mass of workers that works and buys, works and buys, and eats, and chews, and swallows. Two for a quarter, five for a dozen. The nicest, the best, delicious, you need it. Historical process, capital and labor.

PLUTO. (*Laughing diabolically.*) That's it. That's the big idea. Sign it over to me. (*Thunder and lightning. Outdoors, whistling.*)

HUNGERPROUD. They're out there. I won't sign, no, I won't.

(PLUTO *makes a sign. Oriental music.* MURAD *comes, dances the dance of love.* HUNGERPROUD *doesn't notice that* FLAMES *takes his hand and with it signs the contract. The whistling is heard from outdoors.* MURAD *falls into* HUNGERPROUD*'s arms, kneels before him. He embraces her.*) Good-bye, Bronx. Take care of yourself. (PLUTO *pours money over him.*)

Curtain

৵৺৶

Act III

A fine resort at the beach in Atlantic City. We see a part of the boardwalk. Occasionally young and old people pass by, being pushed in rolling chairs. To the side, a rich restaurant. A lifeguard, later revealed to be FLAMES, *sits with his back to the audience. A light melody is playing. Young men and girls are dancing, some in bathing suits. People are eating ice cream. People are playing ball.*

HUNGERPROUD *enters in white summer clothes.* MURAD, *richly dressed, leads him by the arm. He pushes* NESTLÉ, *who is screaming, in a baby carriage. He soothes* NESTLÉ.

HUNGERPROUD. Sh, sh! What's the matter with her? I'll catch you a fish. The food must not agree with her.

MURAD. I told you we should adopt the child later, after the honeymoon. Who goes on a honeymoon with a child?

HUNGERPROUD. Eat, for God's sake, eat. (NESTLÉ *quiets down.*)

MURAD. How funny you are. What do you understand about children?

HUNGERPROUD. I don't understand? Of course not . . . of course not . . .
ah, children . . .

MURAD. Deep in thought again?

HUNGERPROUD. It's nothing. Business. Do you want ice cream?

MURAD. Thanks. I've had ice cream.

HUNGERPROUD. Have it again. Big deal. Have a shoeshine.

MURAD. You're so good to me. (SMAROZHANSKI *appears as a messenger boy
in a uniform, gives* HUNGERPROUD *a telegram.*)

HUNGERPROUD. Wait, boy, I'll give you an answer. They don't let me rest
a minute. All the time business. (*Reads.*) Three percent? Tell it to your granny.
Please, darling, write: "President Lincoln Bank. Tell it to your grandmother.
Respectably yours, Hungerproud, Esquire." (*Opens another telegram.*) One hundred twenty million. Actually I asked for one hundred twenty-five. They'll
come through. (*Dictates.*) "Steel Corporation, Pittsburgh, Pa." (NESTLÉ *cries.*)

MURAD. Quiet.

SMAROZHANSKI. Ah.

HUNGERPROUD. (*Dictates.*) "Don't spit in my kasha. Very truly yours."
Take it, boy. Fast.

SMAROZHANSKI. All right, sir. I still remember how I whipped you in
school. (*Exit.*)

HUNGERPROUD. (*Recognizes him.*) Oy, *vey iz mir.*

MURAD. What's the matter, Harry, Honeybunch?

HUNGERPROUD. What's this new custom to make old people into messenger boys? Shame! It's a disgrace! (*Yells into the wings.*) Hey, you! (MOYSHE *appears, pushing a rolling chair. He is tattered and exhausted from the work.*) Push us.

MURAD. Stop. We can't abandon the child, after all. (*They climb in.* MOYSHE
pushes them.) Isn't it delightful to watch the young girls swim?

HUNGERPROUD. Yes, yes. A friend of mine also had a daughter, a wonderful girl. Reyzele her name is. I would like to know where she is now. (MOYSHE
weeps silently. His tears fall on HUNGERPROUD*'s head.*) What's the matter? It's
raining?

MURAD. The sky is clear blue.

HUNGERPROUD. Somehow I thought a few drops fell on me. Yes, a pretty
girl. She already had a bridegroom. A fine boy, quiet, intelligent, a very good

talker. He had only one failing: he tried to fasten up her dress, and he grabbed first for the fish. (MOYSHE *weeps.*) Positively, it's raining.

MOYSHE. Mr. Hungerproud, I . . . I . . . ah . . .

HUNGERPROUD. What is it? (*Recognizes him. Gives him money.*) Go! Go!

MOYSHE. I really did not fasten up the fish. (*Falls over* HUNGERPROUD*'s feet.*) I mean, I didn't eat the dress. (*Exit.*)

MURAD. What is it? Your dear little foot hurts?

HUNGERPROUD. He ruined my whole shoeshine. (*Enter* YOSELE *as a shoeshine boy, whistling.*)

MURAD. Hey, shoeshine. (YOSELE *shines his shoes, whistling.*) Are you worrying again?

HUNGERPROUD. Don't you understand? The friend I'm telling you about has a boy too, and this very day is his bar mitsva, and I promised him I'd be there. A fine young boy. I can see how he got up very early this morning. Went to synagogue. The rebbe went with him too. No, but the rebbe is . . . Sending old people to carry telegrams—-shameful, a scandal! In synagogue he rolled up his left sleeve and wound the *tfilin* straps for the first time. I see it before my eyes, how he stands and sways and prays out loud, and— (*To* YOSELE.) Stop whistling.

YOSELE. You talking to me? (*Recognizes him.*) Gee whiz, you bet your life.

HUNGERPROUD. Oy, *vey iz mir.*

YOSELE. Well, I couldn't help it.

HUNGERPROUD. Go away. (*Gives him money.*) Go! (YOSELE *goes.*) There's a fine bar mitsva boy for you.

MURAD. You know, Harry dear, the elder Smith Brother wants to get married.

HUNGERPROUD. What? Smith?

MURAD. To a young girl.

HUNGERPROUD. I can imagine the girl. That old nudnik.

MURAD. Why not? You made him richer. Now the girls run after him.

HUNGERPROUD. I made them all richer: so many new customers—opened up a whole new market.

MURAD. Oh, Harry, you are a great man, a genius. By the way, where has your friend Jack Flames disappeared to?

HUNGERPROUD. Some friend. He wanted me to pay him commission. For what? I don't know where he is.

MURAD. But he introduced us.

HUNGERPROUD. I'm very grateful. I don't know where he is.

MURAD. (*Speaks to someone in the wings.*) Hello. (*To* HUNGERPROUD.) Just look, there's Aunt Jemima taking a dip. (*Speaks off.*) How's the water, Auntie? Fine? (*To* HUNGERPROUD.) I'm going in the water.

HUNGERPROUD. I'll come with you.

MURAD. No, darling, it's deep here and you can't swim. And if a person can't swim—

HUNGERPROUD. —he can't swim. I know. But there's a lifeguard sitting there. (*Music.*)

MURAD. I won't permit you, sweetheart. Stay here with the child, my beauty. Darling, I am going to put on my bathing suit. (*Kisses him, exits.* NESTLÉ *cries.*)

HUNGERPROUD. Again? Already? It's not a child, it's a victrola. Sh! (*Sings a lullaby.* MOYSHE *appears pushing a rolling chair in which sit* SMITH *and* REYZL, *who wears a bathing suit.*) Just don't cry. Sh. If you're not quiet, the old nudnik will get you. You see how he fixed himself up like a young flirt. (*Recognizes* REYZL.) Oh, righteous God! Reyzele! (*Hides under the baby carriage.*)

REYZL. Isn't that beautiful?

FIRST SMITH BROTHER. Yes, wonderful, brilliant. (*Looks at her.*)

REYZL. But you're not even looking at it.

FIRST SMITH BROTHER. My Reyzele. When in 1847 my beloved younger brother and I established our firm for manufacturing cough drops, I felt as happy and young as I do now by your side. (*Coughs.*)

REYZL. Try this.

FIRST SMITH BROTHER. What is it?

REYZL. Cough drops. Close your eyes. That's it.

FIRST SMITH BROTHER. For the first time since 1847, these cough drops taste different to me somehow. What a pity my beloved brother can't enjoy the taste.

REYZL. All America knows how much you love your brother.

FIRST SMITH BROTHER. But there are certain people in the world whom I love even more than my brother.

REYZL. Is that so? Who can it be?

FIRST SMITH BROTHER. It is you, Reyzele. May I have the honor and the hope to call you Mrs. Smith Brothers Cough Drops?

REYZL. Oh! (MOYSHE *shakes the rolling chair.*)

HUNGERPROUD. Say no, Reyzele, no. You don't want it.

REYZL. This is so unexpected. But you are so sympathetic. What girl could refuse you?

FIRST SMITH BROTHER. I am so happy and so young. You'll see. I'm going straight to buy you a ring.

REYZL. An expensive one with big diamonds this big, like tears.

HUNGERPROUD. A mother's tears.

FIRST SMITH BROTHER. I'll be right back. (REYZL *sings a song.*)

MOYSHE. (*Weeps.*) I can't bear it any longer. I have to listen to another man speaking to you about love, and he's such a fool besides. I don't know what's pouring out of me more: sweat or tears.

REYZL. And you believe that it's so sweet for me? Rather than be an old man's darling, I'd sooner have . . . I'd sooner . . . you know what I'd sooner.

MOYSHE. I know. Someone from Shepetovke.

HUNGERPROUD. *Oy, vey iz mir.*

REYZL. But whose fault is it that everything got turned upside down? Whose fault is it, I ask you? My own father's.

MOYSHE. Don't talk like that. If your father heard your words, he would commit suicide from heartache. Gedalye Bitterzon would call it the last stage of Americanization. (*We hear* SMITH *coughing.*)

REYZL. I hear my darling bridegroom, still young since 1847. Drive me to him, and be happy.

MOYSHE. How can I be happy?

REYZL. I'm going to show you how. Ah, Mr. Smith, I've been waiting for you. (SMITH *sits in the rolling chair.* REYZL *puts one arm around him. The other she gives to* MOYSHE. *All three exit.* HUNGERPROUD *comes out of his hiding place.*)

HUNGERPROUD. That is my daughter. My Reyzele, daughter of a Jewish worker, Jewish millionaire, and union man. Feh! Feh! True: the last stage of Americanization. (*Runs toward the sea.*)

YOUNG PEOPLE. (*Gathering to watch.*)

Where's he going?

He's thrown himself into the water.

Somebody's drowning himself.

Lifeguard!

Where's the lifeguard?

(*Guard disappears into the sea.*)

He's swimming.

Who is he?

The millionaire Hungerproud.

(*Lifeguard, who is* FLAMES, *reappears carrying* HUNGERPROUD.)

Is he alive?

FLAMES. Are you alive, Mr. Hungerproud?

HUNGERPROUD. I don't know.

FLAMES. He's dead.

HUNGERPROUD. You're the one that dragged me out of the ocean? Here's a quarter for you.

FLAMES. If a person can't swim—

HUNGERPROUD. Yankl! Brother! Don't you want to take my hand?

FLAMES. Mr. Hungerproud . . . Khatskl, Khatskl. No good. (*Starts to leave.*)

HUNGERPROUD. No, this time I won't let go, Yankele. You are a brother to me. A true good friend. Come, let's talk things over a little, and have a bite. This is a good restaurant. Twenty dollars for a breakfast, fifty dollars a supper with music, with cigars and with waiters.

FLAMES. Kosher?

HUNGERPROUD. Who cares about kosher—not kosher—on Broadway? (HUNGERPROUD *takes along the baby carriage with* NESTLÉ, *and he and* FLAMES *enter the restaurant and sit down at a table. The* CONDUCTOR *gives them a menu.*) Waiter, give me one cantaloupe and one watermelon.

CONDUCTOR. Some soup?

HUNGERPROUD. Actually I'm not hungry. Give me julienne soup and vegetable soup and Boston beans.

CONDUCTOR. (*Writing*) Some fish?

HUNGERPROUD. I'm not hungry. Give me halibut and a broiled lobster and something from the entrees—I'm not hungry—some lamb chops, Long Island duckling, a sirloin steak, and boiled ham.

CONDUCTOR. (*Writing.*) Some vegetables?

HUNGERPROUD. I'm not hungry. French fried potatoes, asparagus, spinach, lettuce and tomatoes, spaghetti, and bananas with ice cream. (*Remembers.*) And two soft-boiled eggs. I'm not hungry.

CONDUCTOR. (*Writing.*) And for you, sir?

FLAMES. (*Studies the menu.*) I'm as hungry as a wolf. Give me—

CONDUCTOR. Some cantaloupe?

FLAMES. No.

CONDUCTOR. Some soup?

FLAMES. No.

CONDUCTOR. Some fish?

FLAMES. No. I'm dying of hunger.

CONDUCTOR. Nice boiled ham?

FLAMES. No. Give me something—I'm dying of hunger. Give me a cheese sandwich.

CONDUCTOR. Cheese sandwich. (*Off.*)

HUNGERPROUD. How did you come to be a lifeguard?

FLAMES. Do you remember when we met in the subway, I didn't have a penny?

HUNGERPROUD. I soon came to realize that.

FLAMES. I asked that when you made a million, you should give me a commission, and you gave me your word.

HUNGERPROUD. With us a word is no word. Business.

FLAMES. That's right. You didn't pay me any commission, and a man has to eat. So off I went to work in the button factory on Canal Street.

HUNGERPROUD. (*Joyfully.*) In my place—by the window, where you can see the subway entrance.

FLAMES. I'm working at buttons, and suddenly the management gives the order to work on Yom Kippur.

HUNGERPROUD. What do you mean, work on Yom Kippur? Those are Jewish workers there, old union brothers.

FLAMES. They promised to pay well, double wages, and you know yourself—

HUNGERPROUD. In my factory, Yom Kippur—ay ay! Well, a man must eat, after all.

FLAMES. A man must fast. No, sir. I left the factory and became a lifeguard.

HUNGERPROUD. Fine! Is it a good living?

FLAMES. Sometimes, if you're lucky, a millionaire drowns himself, you drag him out and get a cheese sandwich.

HUNGERPROUD. In other words even a millionaire has his uses on occasion?

FLAMES. Yes, so long as he's in deep water.

HUNGERPROUD. As a millionaire I'm useful underwater, and as a worker I'm useful underground. All that's left is fire. What the hell! (*Sunset.*)

FLAMES. Do you remember in the Bronx how your wife said to me that I'd be without a shirt someday?

HUNGERPROUD. And here you are, not wearing a shirt. But don't talk about Sara. If anyone finds out I have a wife, they'll lynch me on the spot. Where is she?

FLAMES. I thought you divorced her.

HUNGERPROUD. What do you mean divorced? She's my wife, after all.

FLAMES. But you're married to Murad, aren't you?

HUNGERPROUD. So what?

FLAMES. Where are you, in Turkey?

HUNGERPROUD. No, on Broadway.

FLAMES. Where is Sara now?

HUNGERPROUD. I have no idea.

FLAMES. Maybe in the Disappeared Wives column? (*Takes out Yiddish newspaper.*)

HUNGERPROUD. (*Joyfully.*) A Yiddish paper! My God! With editorials . . . Sh! Hide the paper, because here comes that— (CONDUCTOR *brings all the food.* FLAMES *eats with appetite.*) What's this? I didn't order this. Take it away.

CONDUCTOR. That is your order, Sir.

HUNGERPROUD. I can't eat this. Garbage. I'll order something else. Send me the cook.

CONDUCTOR. All right, sir. (*Off.*)

HUNGERPROUD. Believe it or not, Yankl, since I've been a millionaire, food doesn't taste good to me.

FLAMES. Why not?

HUNGERPROUD. It doesn't feel right in my mouth. Do you remember the Bronx? Her soup. Her stuffed derma. Her jellied calves' feet. And the fish with roe—ah, the roe, and the stewed prunes. Ah, Yankl, the stewed prunes.

FLAMES. But you can order whatever you want, after all—even prunes.

HUNGERPROUD. You can only eat stewed prunes with a clean spirit. And my spirit is soiled—forever. I am a sinner, the greatest sinner in the world.

FLAMES. Every millionaire has to be a sinner. How could it be otherwise?

HUNGERPROUD. Yes, but not like me.

FLAMES. You mean because you sold Yom Kippur?

HUNGERPROUD. Yom Kippur, my eye. Although it is a pity about Yom Kippur. Why did I have to sell such a sweet holiday? I did something even worse. I organized labor, then I organized world capital, and then I sold the entire international, working masses to the united world capital for a solid million. So, was there ever such a sinner in the world?

FLAMES. You certainly could have taken off ten percent, or five percent, commission for me.

HUNGERPROUD. Why did you save me from the water? My life has become dark and empty. All night this murderer baby Nestlé yells. All day I have nothing to eat, and from everywhere, even out of the ground, memories creep out like shadows and follow me around. The rebbe, the bashful bridegroom, Reyzele, Yosele. He whistles . . . whistles . . . They're pushing me into the crazy house—into the last stage of Americanization. (*Enter* CONDUCTOR *with* SARA *dressed as a cook.*)

CONDUCTOR. Here is the cook, sir.

SARA. You want to see me?

HUNGERPROUD. (*Doesn't recognize her.*) Listen, can you make me some stuffed fish, Jewish style, you know—

SARA. Gefilte fish, you mean?

HUNGERPROUD. Yes, gefilte fish with roe.

SARA. With roe? This is Khatskl. (MURAD *enters. It gets dark.*)

HUNGERPROUD. My wife!

MURAD. Oh God! You're alive? You're healthy? Honeybunch! (*Kisses him.*)

SARA. Who is this woman? Where did you get the child?

MURAD. What does she want?

HUNGERPROUD. Nothing. She wants to cook. (*Enter the* ADVERTISE-MENT CHARACTERS.)

SARA. She wants to cook? I've been his wife for twenty-two years. Who are you, Miss Purim Player?

VOICES. His wife.

Bigamy.

Betrayer.

Lynch him.

Lynch him here on the spot.

Hang the swindler.

(PLUTO *throws a rope around* HUNGERPROUD*'s neck.* NESTLÉ *cries.*)

HUNGERPROUD. Kind Pluto, let me go home to the Bronx, to the park. Darling Aunt Jemima, dear Wrigleys, I will always chew you. Mr. Arrow, I

made you rich, after all. I've worked for you for twenty-five years. I'll work another twenty-five years, and more . . . Don't strangle me. Let me live. My son,
help your father. They're tying a rope around my neck. My son . . . Children,
help me.

PLUTO. I'll show you Bronx Park.

Curtain

୶ℯ

Epilogue

*Back in the subway. The train has arrived at Bronx Park, 180th Street. In the car we
still see the Jewish housewife with the crying baby and* HUNGERPROUD, *who sleeps in
his corner with a Yiddish paper in his hand. The* CONDUCTOR *stands near him and
shakes him.*

CONDUCTOR. Bronx Park! Bronx Park! Get out. You've got to get out.

HUNGERPROUD. (*Asleep.*) Don't strangle me. Let me live. (*Comes to.*) What
is it?

CONDUCTOR. Last stop. Schildkraut Theatre.

HUNGERPROUD. Schildkraut Theater? What do I need that for? Why did-
n't you wake me up at Prospect Avenue? Now I have to pay another nickel.

CONDUCTOR. All right, sit down. (*The baby cries.*)

WOMAN WITH BABY. Sh, sh! Sweetie-pie. Little one. Sh!

HUNGERPROUD. Some sweetie-pie. Ruined my whole honeymoon. And
how about the closed shop?

WOMAN WITH BABY. What closed shop?

HUNGERPROUD. Yes, your sweetie-pie, what's she doing mixed up in
union business?

WOMAN WITH BABY. What have you got against the child, you anti-
Semite? (*Exits angrily.*)

HUNGERPROUD. Sure I'm an anti-Semite, a bigamist, and also a millionaire into the bargain. (*Notices that his hair is wet.*) It must have rained. (*Enter
MOYSHE, SMAROZHANSKI, YOSELE, and REYZL.*)

SMAROZHANSKI. Is this the right train?

MOYSHE. The right one, the right one.

HUNGERPROUD. What's going on here today? Am I still dreaming?

REYZL. Papa, how did you get here?

HUNGERPROUD. I fell asleep and went past my stop. You think it's the first time that happened to me? What a dream I had—it should only fall on their heads. Millions . . . millions . . . And at the end, I nearly had to pay another nickel. But what are you doing here?

REYZL. We went for a walk in the park and got caught in a rainstorm.

YOSELE. There was lightning and thunder.

SMAROZHANSKI. A fine rain. Good for the Jews.

MOYSHE. Now we're going home.

HUNGERPROUD. But why a walk in the park all of a sudden?

YOSELE. Flowers. (REYZL *makes signals to* YOSELE.)

HUNGERPROUD. Flowers? Why flowers? What's the matter?

REYZL. Today makes twenty-five years you've worked at the shop. So we thought— (*Hands him flowers.*)

YOSELE. And from me too. (*Gives him flowers.*)

HUNGERPROUD. (*Very moved.*) For my twenty-five years of labor, my children have given me flowers. (YOSELE *whistles.*) Stop whistling, you shoeshiner.

SMAROZHANSKI. I said we should send you a telegram to the shop.

HUNGERPROUD. No telegrams. I don't want any telegrams.

MOYSHE. I congratulate you. Here an article about your jubilee has been printed in the newspaper. Seven lines.

REYZL. He wrote it. Himself.

HUNGERPROUD. Seven lines, and all about me? Oh, my God. But tell me, children, how did you know that today was my universary?

YOSELE. Mama said.

HUNGERPROUD. Mama. Mama. (*Turns around, looks at Murad's picture, and spits. The train starts. They practically fall.*)

CONDUCTOR. (*We hear his voice.*) Next stop 177th Street. 177th Street next stop.

Curtain

Appendixes
Yiddish Plays in English Translation

Scene from *Messiah in America*
(Meshiakh in Amerike)
(1919)

ISAAC MOISHE NADIR

᳇᳇᳇

Nadir dramatized *Messiah in America* from his own story by the same name, which was printed in the New York weekly *Haynt (Today)* in 1919. This scene comes from the first act. Most of the rest of the action spins chaotically among the freaks in a Coney Island freak show. It culminates in a boxing match between two competing Messiahs: the one who appears in this scene and a young motorcycle tough.

I left several Yiddish words in the text for the sake of the sound of broken, green-horn English. *Nu* simply means "Well." *Peyes* are earlocks, and a gesture easily makes them clear to an audience. *Shabbes* means Sabbath, as is clear from the dialogue. When Menakhem-Yosef imagines a poster that will yell *gevald* (literally: "violence"), a director might substitute "Help!" or even "Fire!" since the word was a common exclamation of distress. It carries, however, a sound that is somehow simultaneously both dramatic and humorous. Note that pious Jewish men wear a hat of some kind at all times. Belief in the evil eye (and spitting) is superstition, not religion. Besides translating and pruning the scene, I also made several larger changes, such as arranging speeches to be delivered simultaneously.

The scene was part of the revue *Vagabond Stars* (composer Raphael Crystal and lyricist Alan Poul). Fyvush Finkel created the role of the Messiah at the Berkshire Theatre Festival in 1978. At the Jewish Repertory Theatre in 1982, Herbert Rubens played the Messiah, Steve Sterner and Steve Yudson played the producers, and Susan Victor played the secretary.

Nadir is a pen name. *Na dir* is an expression meaning "Here, take this," as when spoonfeeding a child or—more in Nadir's spirit—when delivering a sock to the jaw. The characteristic tone of his writing was a sock to the jaw—though with humor— aimed mostly at enemies of Communism (until 1939, when he left the Party).

Nadir's real name was Isaac Reiss (1885–1943). When he was about fourteen, his father brought the family over from Galicia, and Nadir spent his early years in a Lower East Side sweatshop. He became a journalist, writing such cutting reviews that he was banned from many theaters and had to disguise himself to sneak in. He wrote many sketches and plays, though generally for reading rather than for production. The clever puppet theater Modikot (Zuni Mod and Yosl Kotler) performed some of his material, as did Maurice Schwartz. At various periods Nadir also owned his own cafe theater and a hotel with a summer theater.

(from Act I)

Shabby theatrical office, Broadway area, 1920s. MENAKHEM-YOSEF *is a producer;* JACK *is his assistant.*

JACK. I've got it!

MENAKHEM-YOSEF. What?

JACK. A spitter.

MENAKHEM-YOSEF. A spitter. What do you mean, a spitter?

JACK. A novelty. I know this kid who can spit further than anyone in the world. His record is nineteen feet.

MENAKHEM-YOSEF. Nineteen feet is no novelty. It seems to me that somebody has already spit further. He's already been outspat.

JACK. What are you talking about, Mr. Menakhem-Yosef? Nobody has spit nineteen feet yet, except for the Philadelphia spitter, and he's dead.

MENAKHEM-YOSEF. See that? It's the nation's best men that die the youngest. How much will he take?

JACK. The spitter? Four hundred fifty a show. But I think he's good value.

MENAKHEM-YOSEF. Certainly he's good value, who's talking value? But that's too high for me. I can't be expected to work for the sake of ideals alone. I can't bring on the Messiah single-handed.

JACK. What did you just say? Messiah. Messiah? Quiet. Why not bring on the Messiah? How is the Messiah any worse than a spitter?

MENAKHEM-YOSEF. Are you just talking, or do you mean business?

JACK. I mean business. You understand, it's like this. In America we have so many and so many Jews. We have plenty of Jews in New York alone. Am I right, or not?

MENAKHEM-YOSEF. Right.

JACK. So good, figure it this way. Every Jew is waiting for the Messiah to come. And every Jew that's waiting for the Messiah to come can afford a ticket for, let's say, a dollar seventy-five. Am I right, or not?

MENAKHEM-YOSEF. Right.

JACK. So let's figure it this way. Two thousand people a night, at a dollar seventy-five each, makes three thousand five hundred dollars a night. Am I right, or not?

MENAKHEM-YOSEF. Right.

JACK. So figure it this way. (*Writing.*) Seven shows a week, plus two matinees, Saturday and Sunday, makes nine shows a week, at thirty-five hundred a show, comes to—

MENAKHEM-YOSEF. Wait a minute till I lock the door. (*Does so.*) All in all, I like it. It's a deal. But where do we get a Messiah?

JACK. Wait a minute, we'll get to that. Meanwhile, figure it this way. Besides the thirty-five hundred dollars a show, we also offer private redemptions. No, better yet, we set up a redemption corporation: First Messiah Redemption Corporation. Five dollars a share, and for five shares you're redeemed.

MENAKHEM-YOSEF. (*Forgets himself for a minute.*) Redeemed from what?

JACK. How the hell should I know? What difference does it make? Jews want to be redeemed. So good, we'll redeem them. The main thing is that we should do ourselves a little good. What do you say, Mr. Menakhem-Yosef?

MENAKHEM-YOSEF. Inspiration. And best of all, it's democratic. No poor people, no rich people—whoever gives five dollars will be redeemed. Only the poor get a little less redeemed, because they have to do it in installments.

JACK. A kind of redemption third class: fifty cents a day.

MENAKHEM-YOSEF. The more I think this over, Jack, the better I like it. I like it even better than the spitter. That is to say, the spitter isn't bad either, don't get me wrong; but he's asking too much money. After we make some money off the Messiah, then we can get hold of the spitter too. The whole question now is: where do we find a Messiah?

JACK. I've been wondering that too. Where do we find a Messiah? Quiet. I've got it. I've got a greenhorn uncle, just two weeks over from Galicia. He's still wearing his pious fur hat and his *peyes.* So then, how do we talk him into—quiet. Why don't I just call him up? (*Telephones.*) Hello, Jackson four—oh—three—one. Yes. Hello, Uncle Simkhe. Uncle Simkhe, it's Jack. Yes, Yankl, Yankl. Listen, Uncle, I've got a little work for you. Come right over. Take the streetcar, get off at Forty-third Street, and we're very close. But come right now, we'll wait for you. What? Yes, of course, what did

you think: you ride free in America? Don't dawdle, Uncle. Good-bye. (*Hangs up.*)
He'll fly right over, like a little bird. Wait till you get a look at him. If he isn't the
genuine Messiah, then I don't know. The main thing is, we can get him cheap, because he's going around looking for work, and besides he's sickly, so he can't take
too hard a job and can't stand on his feet too long.

MENAKHEM-YOSEF. We ought to begin thinking about a poster, something that
will really yell *gevald.* With a portrait of the Messiah, and with testimonials from rabbis, and priests, and with all the extras. And we'd better start on the press release.
(*Yells into the next room.*) Flossie! (*Secretary wiggles in carrying dictation pad; peroxide blonde,
heavy makeup, tight skirt, chewing gum.*) Sit next to me, Flossie, right here. I'm going to
dictate to you.

FLOSSIE. OK, dictate. But only with the mouth, not the hands.

JACK. (*Phone rings. He answers. He continues speaking while* MENAKHEM-YOSEF *dictates, so the two speak simultaneously.*) Who is speaking? What? The office furniture store?
No, Menakhem-Yosef is out. What? Yes, out. For how long? For a year. Good-bye.
(*Another phone rings.*) What? Who is speaking? The man from the electric company?
No, he isn't here. Mr. Menakhem-Yosef is away. Where? Argentina. Good-bye. (*Figuring on paper.*) So then. Thirty-five hundred dollars a show, nine shows a week, comes
to—minus rent—and—mm—eight eight five- six hundred forty-four, take away
nineteen, leaves eighteen thousand and six-eighths, minus thirty-one and a sixth,
makes nine hundred twenty-one times eight hundred eleven—carry the seven, minus
sixteen—comes to—

MENAKHEM-YOSEF. (*Dictating while* JACK *is talking on the phone and calculating, so
the two speak simultaneously.*) "Messiah in America, caps, exclamation point. The firm of
Menakhem-Yosef and Company, comma, has brought over the Messiah, underlined,
especially to redeem the Jewish people, comma, from exile, for all classes and sections, colon, at five dollars a share. Exclamation point. The messianic moment, dash,
is the greatest, underlined, moment in our history, semicolon." Have you already written "our history"? Cross it out, Flossie darling. Write "diaspora: di-as-po-ra." But
without spelling mistakes; you always write "diaspora" with spelling mistakes.

FLOSSIE. Is that all, Mr. Menakhem-Yosef?

JACK. (*The flirtation between* MENAKHEM-YOSEF *and* FLOSSIE *and* JACK*'s figuring
are both interrupted by knock at the door.* FLOSSIE *exits.*) That must be my uncle. We'd
better put on our hats and look pious. He's still a greenhorn, my uncle, and a fanatic,
and if he sees us with naked heads, he might not want to have anything to do with
us. (*MESSIAH enters.*) *Sholem aleykhem,* Uncle. (*Shakes Uncle's hand.*) Sit down. This is my
boss, Mr. Menakhem-Yosef. (*MESSIAH is elderly, countrified, very simple and slow. Old-
fashioned pious clothes, big beard like a broom, earlocks. Enters and sits, moving slowly and
smoking a pipe.*)

MENAKHEM-YOSEF. *Sholem aleykhem.* (*Shakes* MESSIAH*'s hand, looks him over, winks* *to* JACK *approvingly.*)

MESSIAH. So? *Nu?*

MENAKHEM-YOSEF. It's this way, Reb Uncle—what is your name?

MESSIAH. My name? My name is Simkhe.

JACK. This Mr. Menakhem-Yosef is a very big man. Has a heart of gold.

MESSIAH. *Nu.*

MENAKHEM-YOSEF. Have you ever been in a theater, Reb—uh, Reb Simkhe?

MESSIAH. Once, in Lemberg. So?

JACK. So nothing. Herr Menakhem-Yosef was just asking.

MESSIAH. Just like that?

MENAKHEM-YOSEF. And how did you like it, the theater?

MESSIAH: Do I know? Like it? My daughter left me off in the corridor. I looked in and saw it was dark in there, so I didn't want to go in. Why should I sit in the dark? When it got light, I went in. Do I know? It was nothing. Ten groschen for an apple, fifteen groschen for a little bottle soda water. Then they turn the lights out again, I go back out in the corridor and wait around some more. What is there for me to do in the dark? Then I go back in again. Again ten groschen an apple, fifteen groschen a little bottle soda water. Do I know? It's nothing, plain nothing.

JACK. That's OK, Uncle, we'll make an American out of you, and you'll earn some money too. We're going to give you an easy job.

MESSIAH. *Shabbes* I wouldn't, God forbid, have to work?

JACK. What are you talking about? Work on Sabbath? What are we, God forbid, not Jews?

MESSIAH. How should I know? In America, they say, not even the stones are kosher.

JACK. Don't you believe it, Uncle. In America there are many, many pious Jews, who pray, and make all the blessings, and wash at each meal, and go to the baths on Friday, and even believe in the Messiah.

MENAKHEM-YOSEF. It's this way. You'll get from us say, thirty-five dollars a week right from the start.

MESSIAH. (*To* JACK.) He's giving me thirty-five dollars a week? For what?

MENAKHEM-YOSEF. No reason. Just like that. Because I like your beard. You have an extremely handsome beard.

MESSIAH. (*Proudly.*) If God gives a Jew a handsome beard, no evil eye— (*Spits superstitiously three times.*)

JACK. That is just what I say. A Jew with a beard like that, no evil eye— (*Imitates spitting.*) And in America!

MENAKHEM-YOSEF. So . . . Ah . . . Why shouldn't you, let's say . . . In a manner of speaking, that is . . . You do believe that there is a Messiah in the universe?

MESSIAH. What then? And if I didn't believe, God forbid?

JACK. That is just what I say. And since we all believe in the Messiah, and since he is bound to come, why shouldn't he come a little sooner?

MENAKHEM-YOSEF. And if he is going to come, why shouldn't he come direct to our firm? We handle the biggest acts. Last year we had Jack Dempsey and Kid McCoy. Two years ago we had a man that chewed nails.

MESSIAH. Nails?

JACK. Nails, Uncle dear, but such nails! Used to chew them up.

MENAKHEM-YOSEF. And the woman with three feet, who handled her?

JACK. We did. We did them all.

MENAKHEM-YOSEF. So it's this way. Here is a paper, and you sign. (*Scribbles on a paper and gives it to* MESSIAH *to sign.*)

JACK. Sign, Uncle. Luck like this comes once in a hundred years. Don't forget, thirty-five dollars a week for a greenhorn.

MENAKHEM-YOSEF. Later, if business goes well, we'll give you forty-five.

JACK. And maybe even fifty.

MENAKHEM-YOSEF. It's a lot of money, but I'm doing it for the sake of your nephew Jack, and because . . . because I like your beard. That's a handsome beard you've got there.

MESSIAH. Thank God, in my family we all have handsome beards. Only none of us can make a living.

JACK. Now you've got a living too, Uncle. Just be healthy and sign the paper.

MESSIAH. In Yiddish?

MENAKHEM-YOSEF. In Yiddish, certainly in Yiddish.

MESSIAH. (*Signs at last.*) I made a blot. Should I cross it out?

MENAKHEM-YOSEF. No, no, leave it, leave it. It'll dry.

JACK. Mazl tov, Uncle. In a lucky hour.

MESSIAH. But what am I supposed to do?

MENAKHEM-YOSEF. Do? Act pious, holy, like a great rebbe, you get me? The main thing is, see, the beard and the *peyes.* You wouldn't mess around with the beard and the *peyes,* God forbid?

MESSIAH. What are you talking about? (*Grabs beard and peyes protectively.*) God forbid. So it's really for my beard and *peyes* that you're paying me thirty-five dollars a week?

JACK. What did you think, Uncle. In America, thank God, people know the value of a pious Jew.

Scene from *Yankl the Blacksmith* (*Yankl Der Shmid*)

(1906)

DAVID PINSKI

❧

(from Act III, Scene 1)

From the first scene of the play, when Yankl has sent a marriage proposal to a woman superior to him intellectually and socially, it is clear that the play is about his struggle to become a better person. Specifically, he has resolved to stop the womanizing for which he is notorious. The success of his marriage is explicitly the measure of his personal achievement of virtue. His wife Tamara understands and supports that. The two love each other and are happy.

But when a passionate, unhappy woman named Rivke comes to live with them as a boarder, both husband and wife are too proud to admit the danger. Tamara speaks to Yankl by indirection, fencing, trying to manipulate and deny. In this scene, while Tamara is busy with her new baby, Rivke tries to seduce Yankl. (In the end, Yankl's determination to hold on to his hard-won virtuous self, as well as his love for Tamara and Tamara's own good sense, defeat Rivke's efforts to break up their marriage. Rivke is left to the lonely misery of her own unsatisfactory marriage.

The stars Ester Rokhl Kaminska, David Kessler, and Sigmund Mogulesko all played in productions of *Yankl the Blacksmith*. Most recently, the 1997–98 season brought New York a Folksbiene production called *The Blacksmith's Folly*, with Hy Wolfe and Rachel Botchan as the couple; Ibi Kaufman and Richard Carlow as Rivke and her husband; and Mina Bern, Zypora Spaisman, I. W. Firestone, and Norman Kruger in other roles. There have also been productions in German, Russian, and Hebrew.

In addition, there is a 1938 film version, converted by Pinske himself, in collaboration with Osip Dymov and Ben-Zvi Baratoff, into a musical comedy vehicle for the popular cantor Moyshe Oysher. The film's title is *Der Zingendiker Shmid (The Singing Blacksmith)*.

For so short a selection, not many notes are necessary. Rivke (RIV-ke) in English is Rebecca; Yankl (YAN-kl) in English is a nickname for Jacob. Lilith is a folklore figure, a female demon and, in some accounts, Adam's first wife. Although Yiddish folk songs about blacksmiths exist, most of the singing and dancing in this scene is not specifically Jewish but instead Russian. I cut and shaped this scene so that it could stand alone.

Blacksmith's shed next to the blacksmith's own house. From inside the house we hear music; they are celebrating the circumcision of the blacksmith's newborn son. YANKL *the blacksmith is heating irons at the fiery forge. He is drunk.* RIVKE *watches him. She is a married woman, separated from her husband and boarding with* YANKL *and his wife. The music and all the dancing are in the Russian peasant style.*

YANKL. Where's the wagoner? Go tell him I'm not working today. No, I'll go. You go back to the party.

RIVKE. You want to get rid of me. Even in your own house, you never look at me.

YANKL. If only . . . !

RIVKE. No? You do glance in my direction once in a while? And here I never knew.

YANKL. No. Yes. I want to get rid of you. You shouldn't be living in any Jewish house. Lilith. Move out, move back to town, the sooner the better. And now go back to the party. Go.

RIVKE. What is this, all of a sudden? Why drive me away?

YANKL. I'm still not altogether cured.

RIVKE. Poor Yankl. Not altogether cured? And here I didn't even know you were sick. Was it serious?

YANKL. You understand perfectly.

RIVKE. A woman's not supposed to understand.

YANKL. I thought when I married Tamara, I thought it was gone, that I was a clean man starting a new life. But it was a lie. My old ways are still boiling inside me. If I could only bleed them out of my body. The old Yankl is still crouched inside me, the old dog, who wants women.

RIVKE. No. And I would have sworn on the holy Torah that you only wanted your wife.

YANKL. I didn't know, myself. Dirty, wild, animal. I've seen you a few times, you know, when you were a little bit . . . not quite . . . not altogether dressed, like your feet bare, or your naked arm, or—

RIVKE. Living in the same house, it happens sometimes. And this last week, with the baby, I had to be around Tamara so much, day and night.

YANKL. And I've had so much to drink.

RIVKE. A circumcision, after all. The first son.

YANKL. Not just that. I wanted to get drunk. You understand me, I wanted it. The wild animal in me: I wanted to drown him.

RIVKE. My, it's warm. So close to the fire. (*Unbuttons top buttons of her blouse.*)

WAGONER. (*Enters.*) Where's my axle? I've got to get going.

YANKL. I'm not working today.

WAGONER. What, they take your hands off for the day? Big deal, a circumcision.

YANKL. Yes. A circumcision, a son. And besides I'm here alone. I haven't got my apprentice here.

WAGONER. What am I supposed to do, stay in this village overnight?

RIVKE. You know what? I'll be your apprentice.

YANKL. He'll help me. (*To* WAGONER.) You'll hold the tongs for me.

WAGONER. Who's going to watch my load of apples?

RIVKE. What do you care? I can do it as well as he can. (*She lifts the big hammer easily.*)

YANKL. He'll hold the tongs.

RIVKE. No, I'll take the hammer. I'll hammer. You think I don't have the strength? (*She rolls up her sleeves, spits on her hands, takes up the hammer, and starts hammering on the anvil.*) See? One, and two, and again.

WAGONER. Those kids are at my apples again. Hurry up! (*He rushes off shouting.*) Get away from there!

RIVKE. (YANKL *picks up a bottle of schnapps and drinks deeply.*) Hey, hey, now you're drinking too much. (*He takes irons from the fire with the tongs and lays them on the anvil. She hammers.*) H-ah! H-ah! (*She sings in rhythm with the blows.*)

YANKL. You'll burn your hand.

RIVKE. No danger.

YANKL. Better roll your sleeves down. (RIVKE *hammers and sings.*) Schnapps in my head, a devil in my heart .

RIVKE. And Lilith by your side.

YANKL. That is the plain truth.

RIVKE. (*Hammering.*) H-ah! H-ah! (YANKL, *holding the tongs with his right hand, takes the bottle in his other hand and drinks.*) Don't drink. Don't drink.

YANKL. (*He drinks again, puts down the bottle, and points to a spot on his mouth.*) I want a kiss right here on the spot where the bottle touched me.

RIVKE. You've already got somebody to kiss you.

YANKL. Yes, and she's pretty good, too. (RIVKE *hammers and sings.*) Quit playing around. Hurry up. Exactly right here, a big kiss.

RIVKE. Watch out, you'll get it with the hammer. (*He grabs for her, but she pushes him away.*) Besides, the door to the street is wide open.

YANKL. (*He takes up a position with the tongs again.*) You'll kiss me yet.

RIVKE. We'll see. (*With his free hand, he drinks again. She hammers and sings.*)

GIRLS. (*Giggling at the door.*) Look. Come and look. Rivke's working at the forge. With a hammer. How do you like the new blacksmith? Look how she lifts the hammer.

YANKL. (*He goes toward them, unsteady on his feet but very cheerful.*) Hey! Girls!

GIRL. Look, he's drunk, he really is.

YANKL. Yes, I'm drunk. I am drunk. I want a kiss. I want a girl to kiss me. Come here, girls. (RIVKE *hammers and sings.*)

GIRL. I'll go get your wife. She'll give you a kiss.

YANKL. Not a wife. You. Come here. (*They run away, giggling.*) Girls! Ah, enough work. I don't want to work. No more work. I just want to get drunk and . . . and . . . yes, but now I'm happy. Now I want to dance. Hey hey hey hey! (*He dances a Russian dance.*)

RIVKE. Well, if you're not going to work, there's nothing for me to do here. (*She rolls down her sleeves and buttons up her blouse and goes toward the door.*)

YANKL. Rivke!

RIVKE. What?

YANKL. Nothing.

RIVKE. That's all?

YANKL. I'll tell you some other time.

RIVKE. If I feel like listening.

YANKL. You will, you will. (*She starts out.*) Rivke!

RIVKE. Go in the house and sleep it off.

YANKL. (*He grabs her hand.*) Come on, dance with me.

RIVKE. (*Sarcastically.*) That's all I'm dying to do: dance with you.

YANKL. Come on, dance with me.

RIVKE. Don't squeeze my hand like that. You'll break it.

YANKL. Come on, dance with me.

(*He dances. She stands in front of him, arms akimbo, shaking her shoulders and bosom, Russian fashion, to the music. He dances around her. She dances toward the door, dances out, and escapes, laughing.*)

Yiddish Plays Available in English Translation

꙳

Ansky, S. *The Dybbuk*. Translated by Golda Werman. In *The Dybbuk and Other Writings,* edited by David G. Roskies, 1–50. New York: Schocken Books, Library of Yiddish Classics, 1992.

———. *A Dybbuk and Other Tales of the Supernatural*. Translated by Joachim Neugroschel. Adapted by Tony Kushner, 1–107. New York: Theatre Communications Group, Inc., 1998.

Asch, Sholom. *God of Vengeance*. Translated by Joachim Neugroschel. *Der Pakntreger,* 23 (Winter, 1996): 11–42.

———. *Night*. Translated by Jack Robbins. In *Fifty One-Act Plays,* edited by C. M. Martin, 769–81. London: 1934.

———. *Sabbatai Zevi*. Translated by F. Whyte and G. R. Noyes. Philadelphia: Jewish Publication Society of America, 1930.

———. *With the Current*. Translated by Jack Robbins. New York: 1933.

Block, Etta, trans. *One-Act Plays from the Yiddish*. Cincinnatti: Steward Kidd Co., 1923. Contents: Peretz, *Champagne;* Halpern, *Mother and Son;* Hirschbein, *The Stranger, The Snowstorm,* and *When the Dew Falleth;* Arnstein, *The Eternal Song.*

———. *One-Act Plays from the Yiddish, 2nd Series*. New York: Block Publishing Co., 1929. Contents: Bimko, *"Liars!";* Hirschbein, *Bebele* and *Lone Worlds;* Reisen, *Brothers;* Peretz, *After the Funeral, Early Morning,* and *Sisters.*

Goldberg, Isaac, ed. and trans. *Six Plays of the Yiddish Theater*. Boston: J. W. Luce and Co., 1916. Contents (one-act plays): Pinski, *Abigail* and *Forgotten Souls;* Rabinovitsh (Sholom Aleichem), *She Must Marry a Doctor;* Asch, *The Sinner* and *Winter;* Hirschbein, *In the Dark.*

———. *Six Plays of the Yiddish Theater, 2nd Series*. Boston: J. W. Luce and Co., 1918. Contents (one-act plays): Pinski, *Little Heroes* and *The Stranger;* Hirschbein, *On the Threshold;* Kobrin, *The Black Sheep* and *The Secret of Life;* Z. Libin, *Poetry and Prose.*

Gordin, Jacob. *The Kreutzer Sonata*. Adapted by Langdon Mitchell. New York: H. G. Fiske, 1907.

Landis, Joseph C., ed. and trans. *The Great Jewish Plays.* New York: Avon Books, 1972. Contents: Anski, *The Dybbuk;* Asch, *God of Vengeance;* Hirschbein, *Green Fields;* Pinski, *King David and His Wives;* Leivick, *The Golem.*

Lifson, David S., ed. and trans. *Epic and Folk Plays of the Yiddish Theatre.* Rutherford, N.J.: Fairleigh Dickinson Univ. Press, 1975. Contents: Hirschbein, *Forsaken Nook* (Lifton suggests alternative titles, including *Far-Away Corner);* Leivick, *Hirsh Lekert;* Kobrin, *Yankl Boyle;* Aksenfeld-Reznik, *Recruits;* Sloves, *Haman's Downfall* (trans. by Max Rosenfeld).

Peretz, Isaac Leyb. *Night in the Old Marketplace.* Translated by Hillel Halkin. *Prooftexts* 12, no. 1 (Jan. 1992): 1–70.

Pinski, David. *King David and His Wives.* Translated by Isaac Goldberg. New York: B. W. Huebsch, Inc., 1923.

———. *Plays.* Translated by Isaac Goldberg. New York: Samuel French, 1920. Contents (one-act plays): *Cripples, A Dollar, Forgotten Souls.*

———. *Laid Off.* Translated by Anna K. Pinski. In *One-Act Plays for Stage and Study, 7th Series.* New York: Samuel French, 1932.

———. *Ten plays.* Translated by Isaac Goldberg. New York: B. W. Huebsch, 1920. Contents (one-act plays): *The Beautiful Nun; Cripples; Diplomacy; A Dollar; The Inventor and the King's Daughter; Little Heroes; The Phonograph; Poland–1919; The Stranger.*

———. *Three Plays.* Translated by Isaac Goldberg. New York: B. W. Huebsch, 1918. Contents: *Isaac Sheftl; The Last Jew; The Dumb Messiah.*

———. *The Treasure.* Translated by Ludwig Lewisohn. New York: B. W. Huebsch, 1915.

Sandrow, Nahma. *Kuni-Leml.* Adaptation, not translation, based on Avrom Goldfadn's *The Two Kuni-Lemls.* Music by Raphael Crystal, Lyrics by Richard Engquist. New York, Samuel French, Inc., 1986.

Sholem Aleichem (Sholem Rabinowitz). *Hard to Be a Jew.* Translated by Melech Grafstein. In *Melech Grafstein's Sholom Aleichem Panorama,* 235–66. Ontario: The Jewish Observer, 1948. This volume also includes two other Aleichem plays, *Heaven,* 226–29; and *She Must Marry a Doctor,* 230–34.

———. *The Jackpot* (also known as *The 200,00* or *The Big Win).* Translated by Kobi Weitzner and Barnett Zumoff. New York: Workmen's Circle Education Dept., 1989.

White, Bessie F., trans. *Nine One-Act Plays from the Yiddish.* Boston, J. W. Luce and Co., 1932. Contents: Berkowitz, *Landslayt (Folks from Home);* Daixel, *After Midnight;* Gordin, *Captain Dreyfus;* Levin, *The Doctor's First Operation;* Libin, *Colleagues;* Peretz, *The Sewing of the Wedding Gown* (also known as *The Seamstresses);* Pinski, *Sorrows;* Sholom Aleichem (also known as *The High School);* the first two scenes of Leivick, *The Golem.*

~❀~

Translations of Yiddish plays, made for specific productions and never published, can be tracked down in various places. The catalogue *Plays of Jewish Interest* edited by Ed Cohen for the National Foundation for Jewish Culture contains some plays based on Yiddish theater. Also the Jewish Repertory Theatre in New York City has presented several such productions. For example, Nathan Gross translated and adapted Jacob Gordin's *Mirele Efros; or, The Jewish Queen Lear* as a musical entitled *Pearls.* Composer Raphael Crystal, lyricist Alan Poul, and I translated and adapted a number of Yiddish play scenes and vaudeville sketches as a revue entitled *Vagabond Stars.*

The archives of the YIVO Institute for Jewish Research are a goldmine. YIVO has the collections of Jacob Ben-Ami, Jacob Jacobs, Jacob Mestel, Solomon Perlmutter, Maurice Schwartz, Zvee Scooler, and other theatrical figures. Many of these collections contain playscripts, and some of the plays, or pieces of plays, are in translation. These range wildly in quality of play, in quality of translation, and in actual physical condition. Most are actual typed playscripts, but some are handwritten—or scrawled. Buried in various folders and boxes are Goldfadn's *Shulamis,* Sholom Aleichem's *Wandering Stars,* and many others.

God, Man, and Devil: Yiddish Plays in Translation was composed in 10.5/14 Columbus in QuarkXPress 4.0 on a Macintosh by Kachergis Book Design; printed by sheet-fed offset on 50-pound, acid-free Glatfelter by Cushing-Malloy, Inc.; Smyth-sewn and bound over binder's boards in Arrestox B-grade cloth by John Dekker & Sons; and perfect bound with paper covers printed in 3 colors by Cushing-Malloy, Inc.; designed by Kachergis Book Design of Pittsboro, North Carolina; published by Syracuse University Press, Syracuse, New York 13244-5160.